Edinburgh College

LR04033

WITHDRAWN

BRITAIN

IN THE

TWENTIETH
CENTURY

A Documentary Reader

KT-471-822

VOLUME I

1900–1939

EDITED BY
LAWRENCE BUTLER AND
HARRIET JONES

INSTITUTE OF
CONTEMPORARY BRITISH
HISTORY

Heinemann

Heinemann Educational
a division of Heinemann Publishers (Oxford) Ltd
Halley Court, Jordan Hill, Oxford OX2 8EJ

OXFORD LONDON EDINBURGH MADRID
ATHENS BOLOGNA PARIS MELBOURNE
SYDNEY AUCKLAND SINGAPORE TOKYO
IBADAN NAIROBI HARARE GABORONE
PORTSMOUTH NH (USA)

© Lawrence Butler and Harriet Jones at The Institute of Contemporary British History

ISBN 0 435 31924 8

Also available in hardback ISBN 0 435 31922 1

First published 1994

94 95 96 97 98
10 9 8 7 6 5 4 3 2 1

British Library Cataloguing in Publication Data is available from the British Library
on request

Designed by Jim Turner

Cover design by Aricot-Vert Design

Front cover: *Flask Walk, Hampstead* by Charles Ginner. Tate Gallery, London

Printed in England by Clays Ltd, St Ives plc

Other titles in the series include:

Britain in the Twentieth Century Vol. II, 1939–1970	ISBN 0 435 31925 6 (softback)
	ISBN 0 435 31923 X (hardback)
	ISBN 0 435 31927 2 (3 Pack)
Modern European History 1871–1975	ISBN 0 435 31928 0 (softback)
	ISBN 0 435 31929 9 (hardback)
	ISBN 0 435 31930 2 (3 Pack)

All rights reserved. No part of this publication may be reproduced or transmitted in any
form or by any means, electronic or mechanical, including photocopy, recording, or any
information storage and retrieval system, without permission in writing from the
publisher or under licence from the Copyright Licensing Agency Limited. Further details
of such licenses (for reprographic reproduction) may be obtained from the Copyright
Licensing Agency Limited, 90 Tottenham Court Road, London W1P 9HE.

Contents

Acknowledgements

Grateful acknowledgement is made to the following sources for permission to reproduce material in this book.

DOCUMENTS IN CHAPTER 1

1.1: B.R. Mitchell, *British Historical Statistics*, Cambridge University Press, 1988. **1.5**: Crown copyright, by permission of the Controller of HMSO. **1.9**: B. Seebohm Rowntree, *Poverty: A Study of Town Life*, 1903, by permission of Macmillan Ltd. **1.12**: *Punch*. **1.17**: F. Thompson, *Lark Rise to Candleford*, 1939, by permission of Oxford University Press. **1.20**: W.H. Beveridge, *Unemployment: A Problem of Industry*, 1909, by permission of the Longman Group UK Ltd. **1.24**: *Punch*.

DOCUMENTS IN CHAPTER 2

2.2: Opinions of the Law Lords, in the custody of the House of Lords Record Office, by permission of the Clerk of the Records. **2.3**: By permission of The British Library. **2.6**: Geoffrey Ford, private collection / University of Bristol Arts Faculty Photographic Unit. **2.8**: Conservative Political Centre / The Bodleian Library, Oxford. **2.12**: Crown copyright, by permission of the Controller of HMSO. **2.16**: E. Sylvia Pankhurst, *The Suffragette Movement*, 1931, by permission of the Longman Group UK Ltd. **2.19**: The Bodleian Library, Oxford, John Johnson Collection. **2.20**: Fawcett Library, Mary Evans Picture Library. **2.23**: D. Butler and G. Butler (eds), *British Political Facts*, 1986, by permission of Macmillan Ltd, © David Butler 1963, 1968, 1969, 1975, 1980, 1986. **2.30**: Crown copyright, by permission of the Controller of HMSO.

DOCUMENTS IN CHAPTER 3

3.3: *Punch*. **3.4**: J. Amery, *The Life of Joseph Chamberlain, Vol. IV*, 1951, by permission of Macmillan Ltd. **3.6**: Crown copyright, by permission of the Controller of HMSO. **3.9**: D. Lloyd George, *War Memoirs, Vol. I*, Odhams Press, 1938, letter in the custody of the House of Lords Record Office, reproduced by permission of the Clerk of the Records.

3.13: National Maritime Museum, Greenwich. **3.14**: Crown copyright, by permission of the Controller of HMSO.

DOCUMENTS IN CHAPTER 4

4.1: Crown copyright, by permission of the Controller of HMSO. **4.2**: J. Turner (ed.), *Britain and the First World War*, Unwin Hyman, 1988. **4.3**: Crown copyright, by permission of the Controller of HMSO. **4.5**: P. Williamson (ed.), *The Modernization of Conservative Politics: The Diaries and Letters of William Bridgeman*, The Historians' Press, 1988 / Trustees of the Bridgeman Family Papers. **4.6**: Cameron Hazlehurst, *Politicians at War, July 1914 to May 1915*, London, Cape, 1971. **4.7**: G. Hardach, *The First World War 1914-1918*, Penguin, 1987. **4.8**: J. Turner (ed.), *Britain and the First World War*, Unwin Hyman, 1988. **4.9**: E. David (ed.), *Inside Asquith's Cabinet: From the Diaries of Charles Hobhouse*, John Murray (Publishers) Ltd, 1977. **4.10**: Lord Selborne / The Bodleian Library, Oxford. **4.11**: Crown copyright, by permission of the Controller of HMSO. **4.13**: D. Lloyd George, *War Memoirs, Vol. I*, Odhams Press, 1938, letter in the custody of the House of Lords Record Office, reproduced by permission of the Clerk of the Records. **4.14**: Viscount Samuel, *Memoirs*, The Cresset Press, 1945, by permission of the Trustees of the Samuel Estate. **4.16** and **4.17**: Imperial War Museum, London. **4.18**: G.C. Peden, *British Economic and Social Policy: Lloyd George to Margaret Thatcher*, Philip Allan, 1991; J. Turner (ed.), *Britain and the First World War*, Unwin Hyman, 1988; and H. Pelling, *A History of British Trade Unionism*, Penguin, 1976. **4.20**: P. Williamson (ed.), *The Modernization of Conservative Politics: The Diaries and Letters of William Bridgeman*, The Historians' Press, 1988 / Trustees of the Bridgeman Family Papers. **4.21**, **4.22** and **4.24**: Crown copyright, by permission of the Controller of HMSO. **4.25**: J. Turner (ed.), *Britain and the First World War*, Unwin Hyman, 1988. **4.27**: Lord Selborne / The Bodleian Library, Oxford. **4.29**: J. Ramsden (ed.), *Real Old Tory Politics: The Political Diaries of Robert Sanders*, Lord Bayford, The

Historians' Press, 1984. **4.30**: Geoffrey Ford, private collection / University of Bristol Arts Faculty Photographic Library. **4.31**: University of Bristol, National Liberal Club collection. **4.32**: F.W.S. Craig, *British General Election Manifestos*, The Macmillan Press Ltd, 1975. **4.34**: J. Turner, *British Politics and the Great War*, Yale University Press, 1992.

DOCUMENTS IN CHAPTER 5

5.1: *Punch*. **5.3**: Imperial War Museum, London. **5.4**: M. Hankey, *The Supreme Command*, Allen & Unwin, 1961. **5.5**: A.J. Stockwell, 'The war and the British Empire', in J. Turner (ed.), *Britain and the First World War*, Unwin Hyman, 1988. **5.8**: Imperial War Museum, London. **5.9**: L. Macdonald, *1914–1918: Voices and Images of the Great War*, Michael Joseph, 1988 / Penguin, 1991, © Lyn Macdonald 1988, by permission of Michael Joseph Ltd. **5.10**: H. Kinder and W. Hilgemann, *The Penguin Atlas of World History, Vol. II*, trans. E.A. Menze, maps by H. and R. Bukor, Penguin, 1978, © Deutscher Taschenbuch Verlag 1966, trans. © Penguin Books Ltd 1978. **5.11** and **5.13**: Imperial War Museum, London. **5.14**: Excerpt from *Testament of Youth* by Vera Brittain, 1933, by permission of Paul Berry, her literary executor, and Victor Gollancz Publishers. **5.16-5.18**: Crown copyright, by permission of the Controller of HMSO. **5.20**: Express Newspapers plc / Centre for the Study of Cartoons and Caricature, University of Kent at Canterbury. **5.21**: J.M. Keynes, *The Economic Consequences of the Peace*, Macmillan Ltd, 1919, © The Royal Economic Society, 1982. Taken from *The Collected Writings of John Maynard Keynes Vol. II*, Macmillan Press Ltd.

DOCUMENTS IN CHAPTER 6

6.1: Crown copyright, by permission of the Controller of HMSO. **6.5**: C.H. Feinstein, *National Income, Expenditure and Output of the UK, 1855-1965*, Cambridge University Press, 1972. **6.7**: *The Textile Manufacturers Yearbook*, Manchester. **6.8**: Crown copyright, by permission of the Controller of HMSO. **6.11**: © Joseph Rowntree Charitable Trust. **6.14**: J.M. Keynes, *The Economic Consequences of Mr. Churchill*, 1925, by permission of Macmillan Ltd, © The Royal Economic Society, 1982. Taken from *The Collected Works of John Maynard Keynes Vol. IX*, Macmillan Press Ltd. **6.16**: *Punch*. **6.18**: Crown copyright, by permission of theController of HMSO. **6.19**: K. Middlemas (ed.), *Thomas Jones: Whitehall Diary, Vol.1*, 1969, by permission of Oxford University Press. **6.22**: Lord Citrine, *Men and Work*, Hutchinson, 1964 / by permission of Lord Citrine of Wembley. **6.23**:

© D. Low, *Evening Standard* / Centre for the Study of Cartoons and Caricature, University of Kent at Canterbury / Solo Syndication & Literary Agency Ltd.

DOCUMENTS IN CHAPTER 7

7.1: J.M. Keynes, *The Economic Consequences of the Peace*, Macmillan Ltd, 1919, © The Royal Economic Society, 1982. Taken from *The Collected Writings of John Maynard Keynes Vol. II*, Macmillan Press Ltd. **7.4**: By permission of The British Library. **7.7**: J. Barnes and D. Nicholson (eds), *The Leo Amery Diaries*, Hutchinson, 1980 / The Rt Hon. Lord Amery. **7.8**: Conservative Political Centre / The Bodleian Library, Oxford. **7.9**: P. Williamson (ed.), *The Modernization of Conservative Politics: The Diaries and Letters of William Bridgeman*, The Historian's Press, 1988 / Trustees of the Bridgeman Family Papers. **7.10**: National Museum of Labour History. **7.11**: J. Barnes and D. Nicholson (eds), *The Leo Amery Diaries*, Hutchinson, 1980. **7.13**: M. Cole (ed.), *Beatrice Webb's Diaries*, 1956, by permission of the Longman Group UK Ltd. **7.14**: K. Middlemas (ed.), *Thomas Jones: Whitehall Diary, Vol. I*, 1969, by permission of Oxford University Press. **7.17**: J. Paton, *Left Turn!*, Secker & Warburg, 1936. **7.19**: By permission of The British Library. **7.21**: Express Newspapers plc / Centre for the Study of Cartoons and Caricature, University of Kent at Canterbury. **7.23**: D. Butler and G. Butler (eds), *British Political Facts*, 1986, by permission of Macmillan Ltd, © David Butler 1963, 1968, 1969, 1975, 1980, 1986. **7.25**: *The Spectator*. **7.27**: © D. Low, *Evening Standard* / Centre for the Study of Cartoons and Caricature, University of Kent at Canterbury / Solo Syndication & Literary Agency Ltd. **7.28**: S. Ball (ed.), *Parliament and Politics in the Age of Baldwin and MacDonald: The Headlam Diaries*, The Historians' Press, 1992 / Captain J. Headlam. **7.29** (Conservative poster) and **7.30**: Conservative Political Centre / The Bodleian Library, Oxford. **7.29** (Labour poster): Geoffrey Ford, private collection / University of Bristol Arts Faculty Photographic Unit.

DOCUMENTS IN CHAPTER 8

8.1 (cartoon): © D. Low, *Evening Standard* / Centre for the Study of Cartoons and Caricature, University of Kent at Canterbury / Solo Syndication & Literary Agency Ltd. **8.1** (poster): National Museum of Labour History. **8.2**: Crown copyright, by permission of the Controller of HMSO. **8.3**: G.C. Peden, *British Economic and Social Policy: Lloyd George to Margaret Thatcher*, Philip Allan, 1991. **8.4-8.5**: Crown copyright, by permission of the Controller of HMSO. **8.8**: Transcripts of

Crown copyright records in Oriental and India Office Collections of the British Library appear by permission of the Controller of HMSO. **8.9**: Crown copyright, by permission of the Controller of HMSO. **8.10**: Express Newspapers plc / Centre for the Study of Cartoons and Caricature, University of Kent at Canterbury. **8.13**: By permission of The British Library. **8.14**: Crown copyright, by permission of the Controller of HMSO. **8.15**: M. Gilbert, *Winston S. Churchill, Vol. IV: 1916-1922*, Heinemann, 1975, by permission of Curtis Brown Ltd, London, on behalf of the Estate of Sir Winston S. Churchill, copyright © the Estate of Sir Winston S. Churchill. **8.16**: G. Hardach, *The First World War*, Penguin, 1987. **8.17**: Crown copyright, by permission of the Controller of HMSO.

DOCUMENTS IN CHAPTER 9

9.3: C.L. Mowat, *Britain between the Wars*, Methuen & Co., 1955. **9.4**: B.R. Mitchell, *British Historical Statistics*, Cambridge University Press, 1988. **9.5**: S. Glynn and J. Oxborrow, *Interwar Britain: A Social and Economic History*, Allen & Unwin, 1976. **9.6**: E. Wilkinson, *The Town That Was Murdered*, Gollancz, 1939. **9.7**: A. Thorpe, *Britain in the 1930s*, Blackwell, 1992. **9.8**: Express Newspapers plc / Centre for the Study of Cartoons and Caricature, University of Kent at Canterbury. **9.9**: S. Constantine, *Unemployment in Britain between the Wars*, Longman, 1980. **9.10**:G. Orwell, *The Road to Wigan Pier*, 1937 / The Estate of the late Sonia Brownell Orwell and Martin Secker & Warburg. **9.12**: S. Constantine, *Unemployment in Britain between the Wars*, Longman, 1980. **9.13**: © D. Low, *Evening Standard* / Centre for the Study of Cartoons and Caricature, University of Kent at Canterbury / Solo Syndication & Literary Agency Ltd. **9.18**: B.R. Mitchell, *British Historical Statistics*, Cambridge University Press, 1988. **9.19**: J.B. Priestley, *English Journey*, William Heinemann Ltd, 1934. **9.22**: B.R. Mitchell, *British Historical Statistics*, Cambridge University Press, 1988. **9.23** and **9.25**: Crown copyright, by permission of the Controller of HMSO. **9.26**: J.M. Keynes, 'How to avoid a slump. 1', *The Times*, 1937, by permission of Macmillan Ltd, © The Royal Economic Society, 1982. Taken from *The Collected Writings of John Maynard Keynes Vol. XXI*, Macmillan Press Ltd.

DOCUMENTS IN CHAPTER 10

10.1: P. Williamson (ed.), *The Modernization of Conservative Politics: The Diaries and Letters of William Bridgeman*, The Historians' Press, 1988 / Trustees of the Bridgeman Family Papers. **10.2-10.4**: Crown copyright, by permission of the Controller of HMSO.

10.8: R.R.James (ed.), *Memoirs of a Conservative*, Weidenfeld & Nicolson, 1969. **10.8**: (Conservative poster): Conservative Political Centre / The Bodleian Library, Oxford. **10.8** (Labour poster): By permission of The British Library. **10.9**: F.W.S. Craig, *British General Election Manifestos*, The Macmillan Press Ltd, 1975. **10.10**: N. and J. Mackenzie (eds), *The Diary of Beatrice Webb, Vol. IV*, Virago, 1985. **10.12**: F.W.S. Craig, *British General Election Manifestos*, The Macmillan Press Ltd, 1975. **10.13**: H. Macmillan, *The Middle Way*, 1938, by permission of Macmillan London Ltd. **10.19**: Viscount Samuel, *Memoirs*, The Cresset Press, 1945, by permission of the Trustees of the Samuel Estate. **10.20**: J. Stevenson and C. Cook, *The Slump: Society and Politics during the Depression*, Quartet, 1979. **10.21**: Wal Hannington, *Unemployed Struggles*, Lawrence & Wishart, 1936. **10.22**: O. Mosley, *The Greater Britain*, 1932 / The Hon. Lady Mosley. **10.24**: Institute of Contemporary British History / Institute of Historical Research,University of London.

DOCUMENTS IN CHAPTER 11

11.1: S. Roskill, *Hankey: Man of Secrets, Vol. II*, Collins, 1954 / Trustees of the Roskill Estate. **11.2-11.5**: *Documents on British Foreign Policy*, by permission of the Controller of HMSO. **11.6**: Duff Cooper, *Old Men Forget: The Autobiography of Duff Cooper (Viscount Norwich)*, Rupert Hart-Davis, 1954. **11.7**: Crown copyright, by permission of the Controller of HMSO. **11.9**: © D. Low, *Evening Standard* / Centre for the Study of Cartoons and Caricature, University of Kent at Canterbury / Solo Syndication & Literary Agency Ltd. **11.10**: Duff Cooper, *Old Men Forget: The Autobiography of Duff Cooper (Viscount Norwich)*, Rupert Hart-Davis, 1954. **11.11**: Crown copyright, by permission of the Controller of HMSO. **11.13**: *Punch*. **11.14**: D.N. Dilks (ed.), *The Diaries of Sir Alexander Cadogan*, Cassell, 1971. **11.15** and **11.18**: *Documents on British Foreign Policy*, by permission of the Controller of HMSO. **11.20**: D.N. Dilks (ed.), *The Diaries of Sir Alexander Cadogan*, Cassell, 1971. **11.21**: *Documents on British Foreign Policy*, by permission of the Controller of HMSO. **11.24**: © D. Low, *Evening Standard* / Centre for the Study of Cartoons and Caricature, University of Kent at Canterbury / Solo Syndication & Literary Agency Ltd. **11.25**: *Documents on British Foreign Policy*, by permission of the Controller of HMSO.

Every effort has been made to contact copyright holders. Any omissions or errors will be rectified in subsequent printings if notice is given to the publisher.

Preface

THE Institute of Contemporary British History was founded in 1986 to promote the study of contemporary British history in schools and universities and to disseminate fresh scholarly research into Britain's recent past. We are an educational charity which survives on research grants, sales of publications and corporate sponsorship; we receive no public sector grants. The documentary reader project has been made possible through a major grant from the Leverhulme Trust, and the volume editors would particularly like to thank that organisation for its generous sponsorship. We would also like to thank Blackwell Scientific Publications Ltd and MITAC (UK) Ltd for donating computer software and equipment without which our work would have been far more tedious.

We have also depended upon the goodwill and support of a number of individuals and institutions, without which a project of this magnitude would not have been possible. The invaluable encouragement and advice of both A-level examiners and teachers, in particular Alan Midgley, W.O. Simpson, Michael Wells, R. Peacock, Anthony Seldon and Wayne Birks, has been of great help to us. Dr Sarah Street, at the Conservative Party Archives, has helped us to locate much unpublished graphic material, as has Philip Dunn, at the National Museum of Labour History. Jane Day, at the University of Kent Cartoon Archive, has helped us with many inquiries. We would also like to thank Dr Alice Prochaska, the Director of Special Collections at the British Library, and the staff at the Fawcett Library. Anne Crawford, at the Public Record Office, has also given us a great deal of useful advice. The staff of the Photograph and Art Departments at the Imperial War Museum have kindly allowed us to reproduce items from their collection. David Hodge at the photographic archive of the National Maritime Museum helped us to locate material relating to naval history. The staff of the Mary Evans Picture Library have also been most generous with their advice. We are particularly indebted to Geoffrey Ford, the librarian at the University of Bristol, who has very generously allowed us to use a number of general election posters from his private collection.

We have attempted to keep abreast of new historiographical debates, and we owe a debt of thanks to a number of academic specialists, including Dr Stephen Ashton, Dr Stuart Ball, John Barnes, Mark Bryant, Dr Kathleen Burk, Dr David Butler, Dr Richard Cockett, Dr Chris Cook, Denis Gifford, Professor Peter Hennessy, Dr Lewis Johnman, Professor Keith Middlemas, Dr John Ramsden, Frank Trentmann, Professor John Turner and Dr Philip Williamson.

Finally, we would like to thank our colleagues here at the Institute for their unflagging support: Dr Peter Catterall, Dr Brian Brivati, Virginia Preston, Matthew Elliot and Kate Huddie. Special thanks should go to Anthony Gorst, whose participation in the project in its early stages has helped to ensure its success.

Introduction

THE teaching of history has changed considerably in the past decade, as the focus has shifted away from the use of traditional textbooks and towards the use of primary sources. This book is intended to meet that need by providing a single comprehensive source of documents on British history between 1900 and 1939. Unlike other document collections, we have included a wide range of types of document, in keeping with the broadening definition of historical evidence. In doing so, our aim is to encourage the reader to become more familiar with primary sources and to become more imaginative about the use of evidence in history.

Although the book follows a conventional chronological framework, individual chapters address specific themes: social and economic policy, political developments or Commonwealth and foreign policy. Given the constraints of space, we have tried to include the most well-known items. But bearing in mind the tremendous variety and volume of material available, we have also tried to include documents which would not otherwise be available in print. Indeed, many of the sources collected here are published for the first time. In some instances, rather than sacrifice the treatment of such important but less familiar subjects, we have given relatively less attention to very familiar topics, which are well represented in other documents collections. In our criteria for selection, in short, we have attempted to strike a reasonable balance between comprehensiveness and variety.

Documentary evidence is the raw material of the historian, whose interpretations of the past are constructed from a careful sifting of many documents of varying kinds: official government records, parliamentary debates, political speeches and election addresses, journalistic accounts and commentaries, diaries and memoirs, private papers and letters, oral testimony and statistics. Increasingly, historians are coming to recognise the value of non-written evidence: political cartoons, party propaganda such as election posters, photographs, advertisements and miscellaneous ephemera.

The teaching of history today is coming increasingly to emphasize the use of primary source material, and students are encouraged to develop their own analytical skills through direct examination of historical documents. When approaching a new piece of evidence, three questions should always be borne in mind. Who wrote or created the document, and for what purpose? When was it written or produced? For what audience was it created? It follows, therefore, that no piece of evidence should ever be accepted at face value, and in this sense documents cannot be trusted to 'speak for themselves'.

Different types of evidence can pose their own special problems, and we will try here to give some examples of possible dangers of which students need to be aware. For example, official documents from the Public Record Office (PRO) have to be understood in terms of their function in the policy-making process. Policy formulation by government usually involves protracted attempts to reconcile competing interests. Discussion papers circulated in this process, generally written by civil servants, may reflect a particular stance based on economic, political or diplomatic concerns. The balance between such factors may vary; economic considerations may be outweighed, for example, by political expediency.

Equally, when considering extracts from parliamentary debates, the reader ought to be aware of the function and significance of such exchanges. Politicians asking questions, supplying answers or making statements are not necessarily simply aiming to convey factual information. Instead they may be trying to score party political points, discredit their opponents or disguise embarrassing policy difficulties or reversals. In document 2.7, the Liberal Prime Minister Henry Campbell-Bannerman proposes a motion confirming the constitutional predominance of the House of Commons. This was not simply an attempt to clarify constitutional tradition, or to propose a policy for reform; it was intended as a warning to the Conservative Party, which dominated the House of Lords, and which was using that advantage in an attempt to disrupt the work of the Liberal government. This is a good example of the importance of considering the context in which such a statement is delivered.

When using extracts from the press, the reader needs to consider questions such as the editorial allegiance of the newspaper or journal, normally determined by the political views of its proprietor. While this may be clear enough when considering editorial commentary, straightforward press reporting of events may not always be as objective as it is intended to appear. Such reports may implicitly be coloured by the political bias of the reporter or editor. For example, document 10.16, a *Daily Herald* report on the outcome of the 1934 London County Council elections, is predictably jubilant at Labour's victory, and magnifies the implications of what was in some-ways more of a symbolic than a genuine achievement for a bruised Labour Party. Here, the fact that the *Daily Herald* was effectively the only national mouthpiece of the Labour Party in those years must be remembered. A less obvious consideration is the way in which press coverage is commonly used as evidence. A regular pitfall among students of history is to assume that the press reflects public opinion, whereas in fact it may be attempting to shape it. When Neville Chamberlain returned from the Munich Conference in 1938, the British press was almost uniformly enthusiastic at his supposed achievement in preserving the peace with Germany, exemplified in document 11.17, a report in *The Times* on 1 October. Traditionally, historians have been tempted to interpret such coverage as evidence of widespread public support for the policy of appeasement. Recent research, however, has demonstrated the extent to which Chamberlain consciously sought to manipulate press approval of his foreign policy.

The personal accounts of participants – diaries, memoirs and oral testimony – while valuable, cannot be expected to be wholly objective. A diary entry, for example, may be simply the immediate response to a day's events, written from a very personal perspective, not necessarily with full access to the facts. Thus, a diary is not always a fair representation of the opinion of the author, whose views may well moderate as she or he gains more perspective on an issue. On the other hand, diary entries may be written up days or weeks after the events described, or even revised many years later, and it may be difficult to establish when that is the case. Some diarists consciously write for subsequent publication, a factor which may lead them to be selective in their version of events in a way which would not apply to a diary not originally intended for publication.

The problem of assessing memoirs or oral testimony is very different. Here recollections are affected by the passage of time, the application of hindsight, the need to justify one's own record and possible lapses of memory, commonly leading to the conflation of events. This means that such sources should not be relied upon exclusively, although they can reveal important background influences which may help to explain the position adopted by an individual, and give some indication of the context in which events unfolded. It is important to bear in mind, however, that individual recollections of the same event can vary enormously. Document 10.24, for example, gives three very different accounts of the 1936 demonstration which has come to be known as the 'battle of Cable Street'.

Private papers and correspondence can give glimpses into the true motives or opinions of individuals, which are often unclear from official records. In document 8.19, Foreign Secretary Austen Chamberlain felt free to reveal to Lord Crewe his understanding of the background to the Locarno pact, including his speculation on the state of public opinion within Britain regarding the highly sensitive question of diplomatic guarantees in Europe. Of course, letters are written to a known and specific individual. The same author may disclose quite different views to other acquaintances.

We have included a good deal of statistical information, presented in the form of graphic charts, which convey important trends and patterns in a more accessible way than raw statistical data. The problem with using statistical evidence is first to find reliable and consistent sources, then to establish why the statistics were collected in the first place and to understand the purposes for which they may have been used. Because the weight of such evidence may appear on the surface to be irrefutable, statistical data can be particularly misleading, and are often employed to lend credence to otherwise questionable assertions. For example, in the debate over Britain's economic competitiveness before 1914, statistical data were used to bolster both sides of the argument. As the charts provided as document 1.1 make clear, while the proportion of UK world exports did decrease after 1870, the total volume of external trade continued to grow. What this reveals about the overall character of the British economy, however, continues to be debated by economic historians today.

The themes which we have explored above apply equally to visual forms of evidence. The same questions of authorship, intention, date of origin and audience should be used in the interpretation of such documents. Political propaganda, of course, has an obvious audience in the electorate, and its intention is fairly clear. Cartoons can be used to put forward the editorial view of the publication in which they appear in a similar fashion to press reports, and a single dramatic image can often perform that task more powerfully than several column inches of reasoned argument. The problems of interpreting the press as reflecting public opinion are present when analysing the work of the noted political cartoonist David Low. In his cartoon reproduced as document 11.24, for example, is he expressing the popular attitude towards appeasement by 1939, or is he attempting to influence it?

One final point, of which we ourselves are well aware, is that while we have attempted to include a fair and broad selection of documents, our choices have inevitably been affected by our interests and experiences. Nevertheless, we believe that this collection will provide a useful new source of primary material for students of twentieth-century British history.

CHAPTER ONE

Economic Power in a Competitive World: Economy, Efficiency and Social Welfare, 1900–1914

WHILE the Edwardian era was one of prosperity and progress, it was also marked by anxiety and debate over economic and social policy. By the turn of the century the growth of industrialisation throughout the world had encouraged a climate of fierce competition between nations for limited markets and resources. An obsession of the Edwardian period was the quest for economic efficiency to meet this new spirit of international competition. While historians today still question the extent to which the nineteenth century was a period of laissez-faire, the belief that market forces were the most efficient and least corrupt way to distribute economic resources had been a central tenet of Victorian economic orthodoxy. Internationally, this attitude had been reflected by the belief that free trade, the free exchange of goods between countries, contributed to international peace and stability. Domestically, it had been thought that the encouragement of individual enterprise through free markets and minimal state intervention was the most likely way to ensure economic prosperity. But competition from abroad, and poverty and unemployment at home, were met with numerous calls for new, interventionist approaches. The question of whether free trade and domestic laissez-faire were still viable policies was a principle focus of political argument between 1900 and 1914.

Economic Competition and Tariff Reform

British economic policy at the turn of the century was still based on free trade, the maintenance of the gold standard and fiscal stringency. Supporters of this approach could point to the generally buoyant volume of UK trade and continued economic growth. Critics, however, argued that British economic power was declining relative to the country's competitors. Other nations, particularly Germany and the United States, were increasing their share of world manufacturing output under the mantle of high tariff barriers.

The statistics depicted in the following charts demonstrate both sides of the Edwardian arguments over British economic performance. The UK share of world exports was in decline, and imports from the USA and Germany were rising faster than exports to those countries. However, the growth of British exports was in real terms continuing to expand, and economic activity remained buoyant.

1.1   **UK trade statistics, 1870–1914 (derived from B.R. Mitchell, *British Historical Statistics* Cambridge, Cambridge University Press, 1988, pp. 509, 519, 524).**

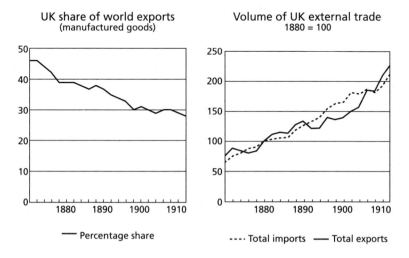

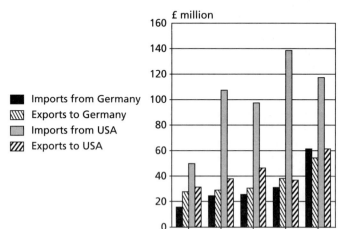

At the turn of the century there was increasing speculation in Britain about the prospect of economic decline, although opinion was by no means united. The following two examples are typical of the commentary which was circulating in these years.

1.2   Anonymous, 'The economic decay of Great Britain', *Contemporary Review*, May 1901 (vol. LXXIX, pp. 609–10).

■ It is perhaps the grandest, and at the same time the saddest, spectacle in the world to watch the decay of a mighty empire. This spectacle is at present afforded by Great Britain with the whole world as spectators.

… The lust of gain has become the mainspring and the guiding principle in the life of individuals and in the policy of nations, because wealth is power and power is wealth … The rapid increase of mankind, caused by the advent of steam power in manufacture and in transport by land and sea, has created an alarming pressure of over-population and of real and prospective pauperism in the countries of Europe. European nations feel instinctively that, with the opening of the new world beyond the sea, not only their ancient preponderance but even their very existence is threatened. They have entered upon a national struggle for life. Their desire for self-preservation and for continued prosperity has created those pronounced tendencies towards national aggressiveness and social consolidation … These and many other symptoms all point towards the danger of impending national, if not racial, wars, wars on the most pressing economic grounds, wars for existence rather than for expansion or for national vanity, wars of hitherto undreamed-of magnitude and of undreamed-of consequences.

The richer an empire is the more it is exposed to the danger of attack with the object of spoliation. … Consequently our power of defence must be strong enough to overawe our prospective enemies if we wish to avoid war. If we are weak, or if we are only believed to be weak by possible enemies, we shall certainly be involved in wars, wars in which we have little or nothing to gain, and all to lose. ■

1.3   Fred A. McKenzie, *The American Invaders: Their Plans, Tactics and Progress*, 1901 (London, Howard Wilford Bell, pp. 59–61).

■ In the domestic life we have got to this: the average man rises in the morning from his New England sheets, he shaves with 'Williams' soap and a Yankee safety razor, pulls on his Boston boots over his socks from North Carolina, fastens his Connecticut braces, slips his Waltham or Waterbury watch in his pocket, and sits down to breakfast. There he congratulates his wife on the way her Illinois straight-front corset sets off her Massachusetts blouse, and he tackles his breakfast, where he eats bread made from prairie flour (possibly doctored at the special establishments on the lakes), tinned oysters from Baltimore, and a little Kansas City bacon, while his wife plays with a slice of Chicago ox-tongue. The children are given 'Quaker' oats. At the same time he reads his morning paper printed by American machines, on American paper with American ink, and, possibly edited by a smart journalist from New York City.

He rushes out, catches the electric tram (New York) to Shepherd's Bush, where he gets in a Yankee elevator to take him on to the American-fitted electric railway to the City.

At his office, of course, everything is American. He sits on a Nebraskan swivel chair, before a Michigan roll-top desk, writes his letters on a Syracuse typewriter, signing them with a New York fountain pen, and drying them with a blotting-sheet from New England. The letter copies are put away in files manufactured in Grand Rapids.

At lunch time he hastily swallows some cold roast beef that comes from the Mid-West cow, and flavours it with Pittsburg pickles, followed by a few Delaware tinned peaches, and then soothes his mind with a couple of Virginia cigarettes.

To follow his course all day would be wearisome. But when evening comes he seeks relaxation at the latest American musical comedy, drinks a cocktail or some Californian wine, and finishes up with a couple of 'little liver pills' 'made in America'. ■

Fears that British exports were entering a period of terminal decline produced a ground swell of support for fiscal reform to protect British trade and industry. When it was decided to defray the costs of the Boer War by introducing a small duty on wheat and flour in the 1902 Budget, the fiscal reformers hoped that this indicated a permanent change of attitude. In the following year, when the Treasury made it clear that the duty was regarded as a temporary remedy for balancing the budget, the Cabinet divided. Joseph Chamberlain, the Colonial Secretary, proposed a new economic policy for the country which involved a preferential tariff system. This, he argued, would help industry, protect employment and strengthen the Empire. He introduced his policy in a speech to his constituency in Birmingham in May 1903.

1.4   **Joseph Chamberlain, speech at Birmingham, 15 May 1903 (in Charles W. Boyd, ed., *Mr. Chamberlain's Speeches, Vol. II*, London, Constable, 1903, pp. 131–9).**

■ ... In my opinion, the germs of a Federal Union that will make the British Empire powerful and influential for good beyond the dreams of any one now living are in the soil; but it is a tender and delicate plant, and requires careful handling ... it depends upon what we do now whether this great idea is to find fruition, or whether we must for ever dismiss it from our consideration and accept our fate as one of the dying empires of the world ...

You want an empire. Do you think it better to cultivate the trade with your own people, or to let that go in order that you may keep the trade of those who are your competitors and rivals? I say it is a new position. I say the people of this Empire have got to consider it. I do not want to hasten their decision. They have two alternatives before them. They may maintain, if they like, in all its severity, the interpretation ... which has been placed upon the doctrines of Free Trade by a small remnant of Little Englanders of the Manchester School, who now profess to be the sole repositories of the doctrines of Mr. Cobden and Mr. Bright. They may maintain that policy in all its severity, although it is repudiated by every other nation, and by all your own colonies. In that case, they will be absolutely precluded, either from giving any kind of preference or favour to any of their colonies abroad, or even from protecting their colonies abroad when they offer to favour us. That is the first alternative. The second alternative is that we should insist that we will not be bound by any purely technical definition of Free Trade; that while we seek as our chief object free interchange of trade and commerce between ourselves and all the nations of the world, we will nevertheless recover our freedom, [and] resume the power of negotiation and, if necessary, retaliation, whenever our own interests or our relations between our colonies and ourselves are threatened by other people ... ■

The weakness of Chamberlain's imperial preference plan was that it had to target those imports which both the Dominion countries and rival nations produced. This implied tariffs on food: wheat, for example, which was imported in large quantities from both Canada and the United States. Opponents of his policy retained the initiative because tariff reform was popularly seen as a tax on the stomach. This indeed was the Treasury view, as illustrated in a memorandum to the Cabinet later that summer.

1.5   Treasury memorandum on tariff reform, 25 August 1903 (PRO CAB 37/66/55).

■ ... Regard being had to the possible risks and dangers attending prefer-ential treatment, it may perhaps be well to bear in mind some remarkable words spoken by Mr. Lowe some forty years ago, lest a prophetic character is given to them. 'In the time of the American revolution,' he said, 'the Colonies separated from England because she insisted on taxing them. What I apprehend as likely to happen now is that England will separate from her Colonies because they insist on taxing her.' And to accord Colonies pref-erential treatment *is* taxing her. No one now-a-days is likely to take such a gloomy view of possible results; but it cannot be denied that a severe strain upon the present feeling in favour of the Colonies might be produced ... .

In short, State interference in Tariff matters, in however mild and unob-trusive a form, must tend to make commodities dearer. If you make com-modities dearer, whether they are food-stuffs, or apparel, or less necessaries of life, you make wages less effective: the sovereign, which will lose part of its purchasing power, won't go so far as it does now. A reduction in the value of wages means either that the wage-earner has less to spend and thus is obliged to curtail his wants, or else that there must be a rise in wages.

It is uncertain, therefore, whether the wage-earner will lose or not. It is certain that the manufacturer will suffer in both cases; for, either the demand for his goods will fall off, or the cost of his production will be enhanced. ■

Between the two extreme positions on trade of Chamberlain and the Treasury was a third view, adopted by the Prime Minister, Arthur Balfour. He argued that, in the short term, protection could be used to negotiate more favourable trade arrangements in the future. A summary of his response to Chamberlain was published as a pamphlet, and became the official policy of the Conservative and Unionist Parties.

1.6   **Arthur James Balfour,** *Notes on Insular Free Trade,* **September 1903 (reproduced in Arthur James Balfour,** *Fiscal Reform Speeches,* **London, Longmans, Green, 1906, pp. 94–5).**

■ The source of all the difficulty being protective tariffs imposed by fiscally independent communities, it is plain that we can secure no concession in the direction of a freer exchange except by negotiation, and that our negotiators can but appeal to self-interest, or, in the case of our colonies, to self-interest and sentiment combined.

Now, on the Free Trade theory self-interest should have prevented these tariffs being originally imposed. But it did not; and if argument failed before powerful vested interests were created, it is hardly likely to be effective now.

The only alternative is to do to foreign nations what they always do to each other, and, instead of appealing to economic theories in which they wholly disbelieve, to use fiscal inducements which they thoroughly understand. We, and we alone, among the nations are unable to employ this means of persuasion, not because in our hands it need be ineffectual, but because in obedience to 'principle' we have deliberately thrown it away …

This seems to me, and has always seemed to me, extraordinarily foolish. It is certainly quite inconsistent with rational Free Trade. There is one, and only one, standard by which we can measure the Free Trade merits of any policy, and that is the degree to which it promotes Free Trade …

I hold myself to be in harmony with the true spirit of Free Trade when I plead for freedom to negotiate that freedom of exchange may be increased … The first and most essential object of our national efforts should be to get rid of the bonds in which we have gratuitously entangled ourselves. ■

While Balfour's views on trade became the official policy of the Conservative and Unionist Coalition from 1903, its members remained divided into these three camps. The Liberal and Labour parties remained opposed to fiscal reform, and the fear of higher food prices under a system of tariffs was the main reason for the Liberal election victory in 1906.

1.7   Liberal Party free trade propaganda for the 1906 general election (Liberal Party, *Pamphlets and Leaflets for 1905*, London, Liberal Publications Department, 1906).

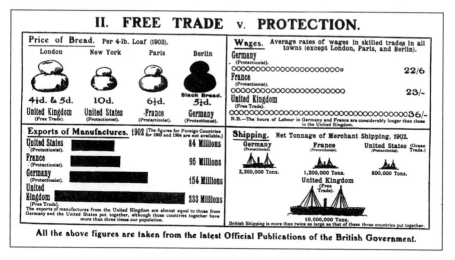

Urban Poverty and 'National Efficiency'

At the turn of the century public attention was focusing increasingly on the problems associated with widespread poverty, and the uneven distribution of wealth. Social statistics gathered for the first time from the end of the nineteenth century suggested that more than 30 per cent of working-class Londoners were living in conditions of poverty and deprivation.

Popular novels brought urban poverty to the attention of the general public. The American writer Jack London disguised himself as an unemployed workman and wrote a sensational exposé of the London slums, which was published in 1903.

1.8   Jack London, *People of the Abyss*, 1903 (London, Ibister, pp. 198–9).

■ Here, then, we have the construction of the Abyss and the shambles. Throughout the whole industrial fabric a constant elimination is going on. The inefficient are weeded out and flung downward. Various things constitute inefficiency. The engineer who is irregular or irresponsible will sink down until he finds his place, say as a casual labourer, an occupation irregular in its very nature and in which there is little or no responsibility. Those who are slow and clumsy, who suffer from weakness of body or mind, or who lack nervous, mental, and physical stamina, must sink down, sometimes rapidly, sometimes step by step, to the bottom. Accident, by disabling an efficient worker, will make him inefficient, and down he must go. And the worker who becomes aged, with failing energy and numbing brain, must begin the frightful descent which knows no stopping-place short of the bottom and death.

In this last instance, the statistics of London tell a terrible tale. The population of London is one-seventh of the total population of the United Kingdom, and in London, year in and year out, one adult in every four dies on public charity, either in the workhouse, the hospital, or the asylum. When the fact that the well-to-do do not end thus is taken into consideration, it becomes manifest that it is the fate of at least one in every three adult workers to die on public charity. ■

Life in London was notorious for its hardship; more surprising was the conclusion arrived at by the social investigator B. Seebohm Rowntree in his extensive social survey of the working-class population in York, where his family owned the chocolate and sweet manufacturing firm of the same name. Rowntree concluded that the level of poverty in York was roughly equivalent to that in London. He calculated in detail the absolute minimum income necessary to sustain a family there, based upon a 'subsistence diet' for various age groups.

1.9   **B. Seebohm Rowntree,** *Poverty: A Study of Town Life,* **1903 (London, Macmillan, pp. 101, 133-5).**

■   CHILDREN, Ages 8-16

	Breakfast	Dinner	Supper
Sunday	Bread, 6 oz. Margarine, ½ oz. Tea, ½ pt.	Boiled bacon, 3 oz. Bread, 3 oz. Potatoes, 8 oz.	Bread, 6 oz. Margarine, ½ oz. Cocoa, ½ pt.
Monday	Bread, 3 oz. New milk, ½ pt. Porridge, ¼ pt. Sugar, ½ oz.	Potatoes & milk, 16 oz. Bread, 2 oz. Cheese, 1½ oz.	Bread, 6 oz. Vegetable broth, ¼ pt. Cheese, 1½ oz.
Tuesday	do.	Vegetable broth, ½ pt. Bread, 3 oz. Cheese, 1½ oz. Dumpling, 6 oz.	Plain cake, 6 oz. Milk, ¼ pt.
Wednesday	do.	Boiled bacon, 3 oz. Bread, 3 oz. Potatoes, 8 oz.	Plain cake, 6 oz. Milk, ¼ pt.
Thursday	do.	Cocoa, ¼ pt. Bread, 6 oz. Cheese, 2 oz.	Bread, 6 oz. Broth, ¼ pt. Cheese, 1½ oz.

	Breakfast	Dinner	Supper
Friday	do.	Boiled bacon, 3 oz. Bread, 3 oz. Potatoes, 8 oz.	Plain cake, 6 oz. Cocoa, ¼ pt.
Saturday	do.	Suet pudding, 12 oz.	Bread, 6 oz. Milk, ¼ pt.

(In addition to the above, lunch in the form of bread, 2 oz.; butter, ¼ oz; cake, 2 oz.; or biscuits, 2 oz. is allowed on week-days only.)

[The] wages paid for unskilled labour in York are insufficient to provide food, shelter, and clothing adequate to maintain a family of moderate size in a state of bare physical efficiency. It will be remembered that the above estimates of necessary minimum expenditure are based upon the assumption that the diet is even less generous than that allowed to able-bodied paupers in the York Workhouse, and that no allowance is made for any expenditure other than that absolutely required for the maintenance of mere physical efficiency.

And let us clearly understand what 'merely physical efficiency' means. A family living upon the scale allowed for in this estimate must never spend a penny on railway fare or omnibus. They must never purchase a halfpenny newspaper or spend a penny to buy a ticket for a popular concert. They must write no letters to absent children, for they cannot afford to pay the postage. They must never contribute anything to their church or chapel, or give any help to a neighbour which costs them money. They cannot save, nor can they join sick club or Trade Union, because they cannot pay the necessary subscriptions. The children must have no pocket money for dolls, marbles, or sweets. The father must smoke no tobacco, and must drink no beer. The mother must never buy any pretty clothes for herself or for her children, the character of the family wardrobe as for the family diet being governed by the regulation, 'Nothing must be bought but that which is absolutely necessary for the maintenance of physical health, and what is bought must be of the plainest and most economical description.' Should a child fall ill, it must be attended by the parish doctor; should it die, it must be buried by the parish. Finally, the wage-earner must never be absent from his work for a single day.

If any of these conditions are broken, the extra expenditure involved is met, and can only be met, by limiting the diet; or, in other words, by sacrificing physical efficiency.

That few York labourers receiving 20s. or 21s. per week submit to these iron conditions in order to maintain physical efficiency is obvious. And even were they to submit, physical efficiency would be unattainable for those who had three or more children dependent upon them. It cannot therefore be too clearly understood, nor too emphatically repeated, that whenever a worker having three children dependent on him, and receiving not more than 21s.8d. per week, indulges in any expenditure beyond that required for the barest physical needs, he can do so only at the cost of his own physical efficiency, or of that of some members of his family. ∎

Concern over extreme levels of poverty was not motivated solely by altruism, or even by the political repercussions of the extension of the franchise to working-class men. Contemporary debate also considered the effects of poverty on the efficient functioning of the state in an increasingly competitive world.

Concern for the health of the poor on grounds of 'national efficiency' was reinforced when it transpired that large numbers of recruits examined during the Boer War were found to be physically unfit to serve. The Interdepartmental Committee on Physical Deterioration, which was subsequently directed to report on the incidence of physical deterioration among the poorer classes, while concluding that evidence of 'racial degeneration' had been exaggerated, made a wide variety of recommendations to improve the 'eugenic health' of the working classes. The national implications of an unfit population thus led to a political marriage between champions of the Empire and of social reform. 'National Efficiency' became a preoccupation of the Edwardian era.

1.10   *Report of the Interdepartmental Committee on Physical Deterioration, 1904 (Cd 2175, PP XXXII, 1904, pp. 84–5).*

∎ (1) *Anthropometric Survey*

With a view to the collection of definite data bearing upon the physical condition of the population, the Committee think that a permanent Anthropometric Survey should be organised as speedily as possible ... this Survey should have for its object the periodic taking of measurements of children and young persons in schools and factories ...

(2) *Register of Sickness*

It appears to the Committee in the highest degree desirable that a Register of Sickness, not confined to infectious diseases, should be established and maintained ...

(3) *Advisory Council*

The Committee are emphatic in recommending the creation of an Advisory Council, representing the Departments of State, within whose province questions touching the physical well-being of the people fall, with the addition of members nominated by the medical corporations and others, whose duty it should be not only to receive and apply the information derived from the Anthropometric Survey and the Register of Sickness, but also to advise the Government on all legislative and administrative points concerning public health in respect of which State interference might be expedient ...

(4) *Overcrowding*

The Committee believe that the time has come for dealing drastically with this problem. They advocate an experimental effort by the Local Authority in certain of the worst districts, in the direction of fixing a standard and notifying that after a given date no crowding in excess of such standard would be permitted. It is believed that, if the thing were carried through without hesitation or sentimentality, means would be found, through the ordinary channels of supply and demand, or within the sphere of municipal activity, for housing all but the irreclaimably bad.

(5) *Labour Colonies and Public Nurseries*

It may be necessary, in order to complete the work of clearing overcrowded slums, for the State, acting in conjunction with the Local Authority, to take charge of the lives of those who, from whatever cause, are incapable of independent existence up to the standard of decency which it imposes. In the last resort, this might take the form of labour colonies on the lines of the Salvation Army Colony at Hadleigh, with powers, however, of compulsory detention. The children of persons so treated might be lodged temporarily in public nurseries or boarded out. With a view to the enforcement of parental responsibility, the object would be to make the parent a debtor to society on account of the child, with the liability, in default of his providing the cost of a suitable maintenance, of being placed in a labour establishment under State supervision until the debt is worked off … ■

The Trend towards Interventionism

Just as fear over the economy led to calls for the abandonment of free trade, concern over social problems led to the gradual extension of state activity in an increasing number of previously unregulated sectors. Education and immigration are examples of the type of issue in which the state became more actively involved in these years.

Balfour's administration introduced one landmark piece of social legislation, the Education Act of 1902 which swept away the old school boards, and made local government the legal provider of elementary, secondary and technical education. The Act was the first to ensure a national standard of educational provision for all children.

1.11   **The Education Act 1902 (*Public General Acts*, 1902, ch. 42).**

■ 2.(1)   The local education authority shall consider the educational needs of their area and take such steps as seem to them desirable, after con-

WITHDRAWN College

sultation with the Board of Education, to supply or aid the supply of education other than elementary, and to promote the general co-ordination of all forms of education ...

4.(1) ...no pupil shall, on the ground of religious belief, be excluded from or placed in an inferior position in any school, college or hostel provided by the council, and no catechism or formulary distinctive of any particular religious denomination shall be taught in any school, college or hostel so provided ...

5. The local education authority shall, throughout their area, have the powers and duties of a school board and school attendance committee ..., and shall also be responsible for and have the control of all secular instruction in public elementary schools not provided by them; and school boards and school attendance committees shall be abolished ...

7.(1) The local education authority shall maintain and keep efficient all public elementary schools within their area ...; in the case of a school not provided by them, only so long as the following conditions and provisions are complied with:

(a) The managers of the school shall carry out any directions of the local education authority as to the secular instruction to be given in the school, including any directions with respect to the number and educational qualifications of the teachers ...

(c) The consent of the local education authority shall be required to the appointment of teachers, but that consent shall not be withheld except on educational grounds; and the consent of the authority shall also be required to the dismissal of a teacher, unless the dismissal be on grounds connected with the giving of religious instruction in the school;

(d) The managers of the school shall provide the school house free of any charge ... to the local education authority for use as a public elementary school, and shall, out of funds provided by them, keep the school house in good repair ... Provided that such damage as the local authority consider to be due to fair wear and tear in the use of any room in the school house for the purpose of a public elementary school shall be made good by the local education authority ...

7.(6) Religious instruction given in a public elementary school not provided by the local education authority shall ... be under the control of the managers ...

(7) The managers of a school maintained but not provided by the local education authority shall ... (subject to the powers of the local education authority under this section) have the exclusive power of appointing and dismissing teachers ....

22.(3) The power to supply, or aid the supply of, education, other than elementary, includes a power to train teachers ... ■

While the 1902 Education Act went a long way towards alleviating the worst problems in the education system, its provisions for the maintenance of religious schools caused a bitter dispute with the Nonconformists, who had previously hoped that the near-monopoly of Church of England schools in many rural areas would come to an end due to lack of money. Passive resistance to the Act continued throughout the Edwardian period by those opposed to the support of religious education by the taxpayer. The following cartoon from Punch shows Mr Punch seeking a better education for Britain's children, while the religious denominations are too busy fighting each other to help.

1.12   **Cartoon by E. Linley Sanbourne, 'The child and its champions',** *Punch,* **4 March 1908.**

THE CHILD AND ITS CHAMPIONS.

Mr. Punch. "GENTLEMEN, THESE CHILDREN WANT A BETTER EDUCATION. CAN'T YOU HELP THEM?"

Anglican, Nonconformist, Roman Catholic. "DON'T INTERRUPT US. WE'RE BUSY FIGHTING!"

Government policy on immigration was traditionally non-interventionist; by the turn of the century there were many different immigrant communities in Britain, although by far the largest, totalling over 600,000 people in 1900, was still the Irish. The fate of immigrants to Britain varied enormously, from the riches of plutocrats such as the German Sir Ernest Cassel to the political success of the Parsee nationalist, Dadhabai Naoroji, who was returned as the Liberal MP for Central Finsbury in 1892. But the focus of public attention was on the Jewish slums of the East End. Pressure to introduce immigration controls culminated in the appointment of a Royal Commission on Alien Immigration in 1902. It concluded that immigration into Britain was accelerating, and recommended that action should be taken to prevent the entry of 'undesirable aliens', a term which was only vaguely defined. Mounting public pressure culminated in the introduction of legislation to restrict immigration in 1904. In the debate, the reasoned arguments of those in favour of continuing to allow unrestricted immigration gave way to this popular clamour. The Aliens Act 1905 was a further reflection of the general drift away from the laissez-faire policies which had characterised the preceeding generation.

1.13   G.M. Trevelyan, speech at the second reading of the Aliens Bill, 25 April 1904 (*Hansard*, 4th ser., 133: 1075–82).

■ I am aware that my task is not an easy one in view of the anti-Jewish feeling which exists in some parts of the country, but I hope that this House may be made to feel that a good deal of outside public opinion has placed far too high an estimate upon the social and economic effects of alien immigration at the present time. This Bill appears to have many of the characteristics of panic legislation. In many directions the evils complained of have been exaggerated ... It may be pardonable in a working man, after seeing a few streets filling up with aliens and whose purview is limited to the East End boroughs, to believe that the state of things he sees is happening all over the country, but it is unpardonable in those who are acquainted with the statistics which any of the Government Departments can supply ...

I believe that a great part of this agitation is directed ... by those who are really forcing public opinion against those who cannot be called destitute as well as against those who are mean and poverty-stricken. All the evidence brought forward goes to prove that the great mass of these aliens do in the long run become good enough citizens, that they are fairly sober and industrious ... The evidence goes to prove that they love education, and that their children are active and clever in the schools ... The most that this Bill can effect is the exclusion of a few hundred people. Those people are largely, as is almost universally admitted, refugees from persecution, either direct or indirect ... I think we ought to have a far deeper necessity if we are going just at this time to enter into legislation which may exclude the Hebrew from asylum here. I have no particular belief in Providential return for national calamity or personal well-doing, but I cannot help thinking that at this very time while Eastern Europe is in some cases hounding to death and in many cases [proceeding] to exile these people, that we should keep open the shelter which only a small portion of them are glad to take. We shall not as a nation be the losers by it. We cannot doubt that those who in future have the teaching of the Jewish population will inculcate patriotism to this country, where for a half a century they have found complete civic freedom as they have not been able to do in most parts of the world ... Among many people already – not many in this House, but many people outside of it – there is a frankly anti-Semitic movement, and I deplore it ... It may be that it is not intended, but the action of many members of this House has been calculated to excite the feeling which we know to exist in part of our population, and with the case of the persecution of Dreyfus reverberating through the West of Europe there is no use saying that there is no danger of this kind in our own country. I think it is a fortunate thing that we have been peculiarly free from any anti-Semitic movement and we have not lost by it ... ■

1.14 The Aliens Act 1905 (*Public General Acts*, 1905, ch. 13).

1.(1) An immigrant shall not be landed in the United Kingdom from an immigrant ship except at a port at which there is an immigration officer appointed under this Act, and shall not be landed at any such port without the leave of that officer given after an inspection of the immigrants made by him on the ship ... and the immigration officer shall withhold leave in the case of any immigrant who appears to him to be an undesirable immigrant within the meaning of this section ...

(3) For the purposes of this section an immigrant shall be considered an undesirable immigrant –

- (*a*) if he cannot show that he has in his possession or is in a position to obtain the means of decently supporting himself and his dependants (if any); or

- (*b*) if he is a lunatic or an idiot, or owing to any disease or infirmity appears likely to become a charge upon the rates or otherwise a detriment to the public; or

- (*c*) if he has been sentenced in a foreign country with which there is an extradition treaty for a crime, not being an offence of a political character ... but, in the case of an immigrant who proves that he is seeking admission to this country solely to avoid prosecution or punishment on religious or political grounds or for an offence of a political character, or persecution, involving danger of imprisonment or danger to life or limb, on account of religious belief, leave to land shall not be refused on the ground merely of want of means, or the probability of his becoming a charge on the rates ...

8.(2). The expression 'immigrant ship' in this Act means a ship which brings to the United Kingdom more than twenty alien steerage passengers, who are to be landed in the United Kingdom, whether at the same or different ports, or such number of those passengers as may be for the time being fixed by order of the Secretary of State, either generally or as regards any special ships or ports. ■

After the Liberal election victory in 1906, the Aliens Act was administered very loosely, and in practice the loopholes in the new legislation meant that it was still relatively easy to circumvent. Continued pressure from the anti-alien lobby in the years before the outbreak of the First World War was boosted, however, by popular hysteria over criminal alien activity. This culminated with the siege of Sydney Street in January 1911, when the police trapped a gang of immigrant anarchists who had been responsible for a violent robbery in Houndsditch several weeks previously.

1.15   Anti-immigration satire, 1911 (*Punch*, 11 January, p. 28).

■   *A Home from Home*

The Anarchist who dwells abroad is not a happy man;
Unfeeling Governments refuse protection to his clan;
I simply shudder when I think how hard his lot would be
If England gave no welcome to the foreign refugee!

When other nations cease to view with nonchalant *aplomb*
His automatic pistol and his effervescing bomb,
When, harassed by a cruel foe, he has to take to flight,
It's 'Oh to be in England!' (with a ton of dynamite!)

When Hamburg grows too sensitive at loss of life and limb;
When Paris firmly intimates she has no use for him;
When even Barcelona gets a little bit too hot,
Who is it shakes him by the hand? It's England, is it not?

Though other countries turn him out and pulverise his dens,
We couldn't be so impolite to foreign citizens!
Our port authorities don't pry about and make a fuss,
But straightway take him to their hearts and hail him one of us!

I know some nervous Londoners display a deal of fear
And shake their heads and talk about the Coronation Year;
How can they be so foolish as to think they'll be attacked?
They're safe as any p'liceman while we have our Aliens' Act!

O England, to yourself be true; remember you are free!
You *can't* belie the name you've got for hospitality.
The British Burglar cannot be too mercilessly curbed;
But leave the Alien Criminal – *he* mustn't be disturbed! ■

Destitution and the New Liberalism

The culmination of this ground-breaking period in the adoption of new interventionist social strategies took place between 1908 and 1911, the age of 'New Liberalism'. Primarily through the efforts of two young ministers, David Lloyd George and Winston Churchill, the Radical wing of the Liberal Party pushed through a series of social reforms at this time, culminating in the National Insurance Act of 1911. Political debate centred on how to pay for these new measures; this was first revealed in the passage of the Old Age Pensions Bill in 1908.

Increasing longevity and the adoption of state pensions in many other countries had put the plight of the aged poor on the political agenda by the turn of the century. No party opposed the introduction of pensions in the 1906 election campaign, and the Liberal government introduced legislation two years later. The Old Age Pensions Act 1908 represented a compromise between those who demanded universal pensions without stigma, and those who believed that such benefits would undermine individual incentive and thrift. It provided for non-contributory pensions for every person at the age of 70 with an annual income below £31, with a few exceptions.

1.16   **The Old Age Pensions Act 1908 (*Public General Acts*, 1908, ch. 40).**

■ 1. (4) The receipt of an old age pension under this Act shall not deprive the pensioner of any franchise, right, or privilege or subject him to any disability.

2. The statutory conditions for the receipt of an old age pension by any person are –

(1) The person must have attained the age of seventy.

(2) The person must satisfy the pension authorities that for at least twenty years up to the date of the receipt of any sum on account of a pension he has been a British subject …

(3) The person must satisfy the pension authorities that his yearly means as calculated under this Act do not exceed thirty-one pounds ten shillings.

3. (1) A person shall be disqualified for receiving or continuing to receive an old age pension under this Act …

(*a*) While he is in receipt of any poor relief (other than relief excepted under this provision), and, until the thirty-first day of December nineteen hundred and ten unless Parliament otherwise determines, if he has at any time since the first day of January nineteen hundred and eight received, or hereafter receives, any such relief …

(*b*) If, before he becomes entitled to a pension, he has habitually failed to work according to his ability, opportunity, and need, for the maintenance or benefit of himself and those legally dependent upon him …

(*c*) While he is detained in any asylum within the meaning of the Lunacy Act, 1890 …

(2) Where a person has been before the passing of this Act, or is after the passing of this Act, convicted of any offence, and ordered to be imprisoned without the option of a fine or to suffer any greater punishment, he shall be disqualified … while he is detained in prison … and for a further period of ten years after the date on which he is released from prison. ■

The introduction of pensions proved immensely popular with the general public. In her classic description of village life in this period, the writer Flora Thompson gave a sentimental account of the difference those few shillings made in the lives of millions of elderly people.

1.17   Flora Thompson, *Lark Rise to Candleford*, 1939 (Oxford, Oxford University Press, p. 95).

■ The Poor Law authorities allowed old people past work a small weekly sum as outdoor relief; but it was not sufficient to live upon, and, unless they had more than usually prosperous children to help support them, there came a time when the home had to be broken up. When, twenty years later, the Old Age Pensions began, life was transformed for such aged cottagers. They were suddenly rich. Independent for life! At first when they went to the post office to draw it, tears of gratitude would run down the cheeks of some, and they would say as they picked up their money, 'God bless that Lord George! (for they could not believe one so powerful and munificent could be a plain 'Mr') and God bless you, miss!' and there were flowers from their gardens and apples from their trees for the girl who merely handed them the money. ■

The question of how to treat destitution came to a head in the debate over the future of the Poor Law. Public concern during the depression of 1904–5 had led the Balfour administration to appoint a Royal Commission on the Poor Laws and Relief of Distress. In 1909 it issued two reports which broadly reflected two competing strategies towards this question. The majority of the commissioners, influenced heavily by the thinking of its members from the orthodox Charity Organisation Society, were in favour of retaining the fabric of the Poor Law, although they did recommend a number of reforms: the transfer of administration from the Poor Law 'unions' created in 1834 to the county and county borough councils; the provision of more specialised treatment for the old, children and the able-bodied; the decasualisation of labour; the extension of the school-leaving age to 15; the introduction of labour exchanges and unemployment and invalidity insurance; and the implementation of public works during periods of heavy unemployment.

1.18   *Report of the Royal Commission on the Poor Laws and Relief of Distress,* 1909
(Cd 4499, PP XXXVII, 1909, pp. 596–644).

■ 4. The principles dominating the spirit of the existing English Poor Law,
so far as they determine the definition of those qualified for relief, seem to
us both sound and humane. They contain a positive and a negative element;
to relieve those who are qualified for public relief, and to discourage those
who do not legitimately come within this category from becoming a public
burden. The conditions under which relief is given ought to be prescribed,
not by the applicant, but by the authority that relieves the applicant. We do
not recommend any alteration of the law which would extend the
qualification for relief to individuals not now entitled to it, or which would
bring within the operation of assistance from public funds classes not now
legally within its operation ...

12. There was a scheme brought to our notice known as the 'Breaking up of
the Poor Law'. Its ideas appear to be the foundation of the alternative
proposals recommended by certain of our colleagues who dissent from our
Report. Under this scheme the whole existing machinery of Poor Law
administration would disappear with the abolition of the Guardians, and
the work previously performed by them would be broken up into sections
and transferred to existing Committees of County and County Borough
Councils.

13. ... The question at issue is, whether the work of maintaining those
members of the community who have lost their economic independence
can be safely entrusted to authorities whose primary duty is something
quite distinct – such as that of Education or Sanitation – or whether it is
essential that there should be an authority devoting itself entirely to the
work. We consider that the many and subtle problems associated with
Public Assistance, especially when it is a family rather than an individual
that requires rehabilitation, cannot be solved by the simple process of
sending off each unit to a separate authority for maintenance and
treatment. What is needed is a disinterested authority practised in looking at
all sides of a question, and able to call in skilled assistance ...

71. We have now completed the description of the new machinery we
propose to set up in place of the Boards of Guardians and their officers, and
we turn to the principles which we hope this new organisation will keep
before it in its exercise of its powers. These principles may be thus
epitomised:

(1) That the treatment of the poor who apply for Public Assistance should
be adapted to the needs of the individual, and, if institutional, should be
governed by classification.

(2) That the public administration established for the assistance of the
poor should work in co-operation with the local and private charities of
the district.

(3) That the system of Public Assistance thus established should include processes of help which would be preventive, curative, and restorative.

(4) That every effort should be made to foster the instincts of independence and self-maintenance amongst those assisted ...

173. ... Our investigations prove the existence in our midst of a class whose condition and environment are a discredit, and a peril to the whole community. Each and every section of society has a common duty to perform in combating this evil and contracting its area, a duty which can only be performed by united and untiring effort to convert useless and costly inefficients into self-sustaining and respectable members of the community. No country, however rich, can permanently hold its own in the race of international competition, if hampered by an increasing load of this dead weight; or can successfully perform the role of sovereignty beyond the seas, if a portion of its own folk at home are sinking below the civilization and aspirations of its subject races abroad. ∎

Taken together, the proposals in the majority report of the Royal Commission represented a considerable reform of the Poor Law system. It was nevertheless not as radical as the solution called for in the minority report, signed by four members of the commission, but influenced by one in particular, the Fabian socialist Beatrice Webb.

1.19   *Minority Report of the Royal Commission on the Poor Laws and the Relief of Distress, 1909 (Cd 4499, PP XXXVII, 1909, pp. 1218-23).*

∎ SUMMARY OF CONCLUSIONS AND RECOMMENDATIONS ...

1. That the General Mixed Workhouses of England, Wales and Ireland, and the Poorhouses of Scotland, whether urban or rural, new or old, large or small, sumptuous or squalid, all exhibit the same inherent defects, of which the chief are promiscuity and unspecialised management ...

6. That the abolition of Outdoor Relief to the non-able-bodied is, in our judgement, wholly impracticable, and, even if it were possible, it would be contrary to the public interest. There are, and, in our opinion, there always will be, a large number of persons to whom public assistance must be given, who can, with most advantage to the community, continue to live at home ...

13. That it is, however, not merely that 'many-headedness' of the existing tribunal that is the cause of the failure of the Outdoor Relief administration of to-day. We ascribe that failure quite as much to the fact that the duty is entrusted to a Destitution Authority, served by subordinates who are essentially Destitution Officers. To entrust, to one and the same authority, the care of the infants and the aged, the children and the able-bodied adults, the sick and the healthy, maids and widows, is inevitably to concentrate attention, not on the different methods of curative or reformatory treatment

that they severally require, but on their one common attribute of destitution, and the one common remedy of 'relief', indiscriminate and unconditional ...

34. That the task of dealing with Unemployment is altogether beyond the capacity of Authorities having jurisdiction over particular areas; and can be undertaken successfully only by a Department of the National Government.

35. That the experience of the Poor Law in dealing with destitute able-bodied men and their dependants ... [proves] that every attempt to deal only with this or that section of the Able-bodied and Unemployed class is liable to be rendered nugatory by the neglect to deal simultaneously with the other sections of men in distress ... from want of employment. That accordingly, in our judgement, no successful dealing with the problem is possible unless provision is simultaneously made in ways suited to their several needs and deserts for all the various sections of the Unemployed by one and the same Authority.

36. That the duty of so organising the National Labour Market as to prevent or to minimise Unemployment should be placed upon a Minister responsible to Parliament, who might be designated the Minister for Labour.   ■

Both of the Poor Law reports had stressed the problem of unemployment and casual labour, which was by this time widely recognised as a problem of inefficiency in the labour market. While traditional attitudes tended to view unemployment as a sign of individual failure, views of unemployment as a general failure of social organisation were becoming more widespread. In 1909 the social administrator William Beveridge (who would later become a household name when he published his well-known report proposing a comprehensive welfare state in 1942) published an influential study on unemployment, which stressed the problem of poor organisation and labour-market inefficiency.

1.20   **W.H. Beveridge,** *Unemployment: A Problem of Industry,* **1909 (London, Longmans, Green, pp. 193–229).**

■ Unemployment is a question not of the scale of industry but of its organisation, not of the volume of the demand for labour but of its changes and fluctuations. The changes are of several types; trades decay or are revolutionised by new machines. Through these changes particular parts of the labour supply get displaced. Unemployment arises through their difficulty in getting re-absorbed ... To meet these fluctuations – cyclical, seasonal and casual – there are required reserves of labour power. Unemployment arises as the idleness of these reserves between the epochs when they are called into action. The solution of the problem of unemployment must consist, therefore, partly in smoothing industrial transitions, partly in diminishing the extent of the reserves required for fluctuations or their intervals of idleness, partly, when this plan can go no further, in seeing that the men of the reserve are properly maintained both in action and out of it ...

... the deliberate organisation of the labour market ... is the first step in the permanent solution of the problem of unemployment.

The organisation of the labour market means simply that there shall be known centres or offices or Exchanges to which employers shall send or go when they want workpeople, to which workpeople shall go when they want employment ... When all over the United Kingdom and for every trade in it there is a connected system of Labour Exchanges so that no man thinks of applying anywhere else either for workpeople or employment and would not get either if he did, then the labour market for the United Kingdom may be said to be completely organised ...

Insurance against unemployment ... stands in the closest relation to the organisation of the labour market, and forms the second line of attack on the problem of unemployment ... The Labour Exchange is required to reduce to a minimum the intervals between successive jobs. Insurance is required to tide over the intervals that will still remain ... No plan other than insurance – whether purely self-supporting or with assistance from other sources – is really adequate. ■

The National Insurance Act of 1911, which crowned this period of New Liberalism, was divided into two parts, covering health and unemployment insurance respectively. The unemployment insurance scheme was relatively uncontroversial, limited to a few trades and actuarially sound. Health insurance, however, provoked some heated debate. It was to be compulsory for all manual workers and voluntary for anyone earning less than £160 a year. The Act set the pattern for insurance financing for the rest of the century: employees' contributions were supplemented by contributions from employers and central government. The debate over the scheme was centred on both financing and the broader question of the proper relationship between the individual and the state.

Lloyd George's reputation as a great social reformer was made as a result of the battle to get the Insurance Bill through Parliament. Extracts from his explanation to the House, as well as from the Conservative Lord Cecil and the left-wing Labour MP George Lansbury, are given overleaf.

1.21   David Lloyd George, speech on the second reading of the National Insurance Bill, 6 December 1911 (*Hansard*, 5th ser., 32: 1454, 1469).

■ Even if we have made mistakes ... there is nothing ... that could not be amended by legislation. After all, that is what has happened in every country where a measure of this kind has been brought into operation. Take the one great example we have got of an insurance scheme in Europe – Germany. They brought in a small Bill compared with the present state of things there ... after twenty-five years' experience, they brought in a gigantic Bill, in many respects altering it and recasting it. Have I ever claimed this Bill is going to be so perfect that there will be no defects in its machinery, and that there is nothing to be altered in it?

... I believe that this Bill is setting up a scheme which will be woven into the social fabric of this country, and will be regarded by the working men with gratitude as something which has given them a guarantee with regard to their daily lives. It is a Bill which the employers will accept as something which improves the efficiency of labour and gives stability to the existing order. ■

1.22   Lord Robert Cecil, speech on the second reading of the National Insurance Bill, 6 December 1911 (*Hansard*, 5th ser., 32: 1474–7).

■ The Chancellor of the Exchequer says that the principle of this Bill is that it is a contributory Bill. To my mind it contains three main principles. In the first place, it is a Bill for State-aided insurance. In the second place, it is a Bill for contributory insurance. In the third place, it is a Bill depending upon compulsory contribution. So far as the principle of State-aided insurance is concerned, I support the Bill most thoroughly ... So, too, so far as the principle of contributory insurance is concerned ... it is important that those who are going to benefit by this scheme, and also have a very large proportion of the political power in this country, should realise that there is no secret fund on which you can draw for any of these benefits, but that sooner or later they must pay for whatever they get. Therefore I have always been in favour of a contributory element.

I do not myself see why a contributory scheme involves a compulsory scheme. It is quite true that if you do not have a compulsory scheme you must, no doubt, abandon the principle of a contribution from the employer. I admit it. Personally, however, I see no advantage in the contribution from the employer ...

I am convinced that the compulsory element in this Bill is bound to destroy the friendly societies of this country. I observed the characteristic gibe of the right hon. Gentlemen when someone spoke of the tenacity with which the friendly societies hung on to their existence ... To my mind it is very right, very natural, and very proper that the friendly societies should recognise the immense work they have done in this country, be proud of it, and resent any interference with it ...

The backbone of the agitation against this Bill is that the people bitterly resent in this country being made to apply their own money for benefits in a way they do not approve. It is defended by the German example; but that example is wholly irrelevant. The whole history of Germany is the history of the control of the individual by the State ...

I have a fanatical belief in individual freedom. I believe it is a vital thing for this country, and I believe it is the cornerstone upon which our prosperity and our existence are built, and, for my part, I believe that the civic qualities of self-control, self-reliance, and self-respect depend upon individual liberty and the freedom and independence of the people of this country ... ■

1.23   George Lansbury, speech on the second reading of the National Insurance Bill, 6 December 1911 (*Hansard*, 5th ser., 32: 1488–91).

■ ... large masses of people are not able to supply the necessaries of life. Instead of Parliament voting to take away money from them it ought either to be voting to give them money or, what is very much better, it ought to pass some measure of reform which will enable these men and women to earn living wages. After all, you cannot get away from these absolute facts of the life of the ordinary working classes of this country. You may pass this Bill to-night and you may put it into operation, but I am perfectly certain that when you attempt to collect the money you will have just as big a revolt as our forefathers had when they last levied a poll tax in this country. The people who will be revolting will not be countesses and duchesses and the people you have made fun of in regard to the servant agitation, but it will be these poor people who are robbed and exploited. Then Parliament comes forward and says, 'Your physical condition leads on to sickness, only allows you to bring up your children physically inefficient, and tumbles them out into the world to get their living without real physical stamina. Because of the conditions which bring that about we are going to tax you so that we can deal with them in some kind of way afterwards.' A more topsy-turvy method of dealing with social reform was never dreamt of ...

I do not understand men who have three or four square meals a day thinking that a man can keep his family in a state of physical efficiency on 7s. a week, and to tell him that it is some great boon you are offering him, to tell him you are offering him something that is going to bring fruit to his parched lips, is really absurd ...

I believe this Bill fails absolutely to grapple with the cause. I believe it does not touch any root cause at all, either in sickness or unemployment. So far as sickness is concerned it arises because people are not paid proper wages; because they are not allowed to earn wages at all. I believe unemployment is caused by, and is inherent in, the social system of which we are part. It cannot be got rid of until you have got rid of the profit system ... I believe, further, that this House, instead of having sat down to consider the problem from the point of view of prevention, has allowed itself merely to be chloroformed into this idea of insurance. Someone said, 'There is more self-respect in paying something.' What rubbish all that is! ... Does one's independence suffer because he pays nothing out of his pocket for education? Is his moral fibre injured? ... And when I heard the Chancellor of the Exchequer preaching these homilies about working men getting something for nothing it struck me that working people do not get some-thing for nothing, because they themselves produce everything that is worth having. I am going into the Lobby quite cheerfully against this Bill ... ■

Punch's cartoonist has 'author' Lloyd George receiving an ovation for 'the first performance of his great 'Insurance Drama'.

1.24   **Cartoon by Leonard Ravenhill, 'Bringing down the House', *Punch*, 17 May 1911.**

BRINGING DOWN THE HOUSE.

Mr. Lloyd George (*responding to calls of "Author!" after the first performance of his great Insurance Drama*). "NEVER KNEW THE HALOES COME SO THICK BEFORE. PIT AND GALLERY I'M USED TO, BUT NOW THE STALLS AND DRESS-CIRCLE HAVE BROKEN OUT!"

CHAPTER TWO

The Road to Democracy: Inequality, Confrontation and Conflict, 1900–1914

BETWEEN 1900 and 1914 Britain experienced a series of social and political crises, which were only contained by the outbreak of war in Europe; these were turbulent years in the transition towards electoral democracy. While the question of efficiency, discussed in Chapter 1, led to the adoption of a wide range of social reforms, this was by no means a straightforward process. The question of how to finance these measures led to a confrontation between the Liberal government and the House of Lords in the years 1909 to 1911, culminating in major constitutional reform. For many other groups, the pace of change in the political system was too slow. Some disillusioned reformers turned to direct political action: militant suffragettes, organised labour and organisations on both sides of the Irish question. The dilemma for the government was finding a peaceful formula to accommodate these demands.

The Conservative Party had dominated British politics since the Second Home Rule Bill of 1886 split the Liberals. From that time the Conservatives had co-operated with the Liberal Unionists, led by Joseph Chamberlain, forming a government together in 1895. The two parties were to merge formally in 1912 to form the Unionist Party. From 1922, when the Irish Free State was founded, the party once again became commonly known as the Conservative Party.

In 1900 the country's attention was focused on the Boer War. The Conservative and Unionist government, led by Lord Salisbury, took advantage of the jingoistic mood to call a general election at the end of the year. An obvious attempt to capitalise on the patriotism generated by the war, the 'Khaki election', as it was dubbed, was much criticised at the time for violating the principle of fair play in politics.

The Birth of the Labour Party

In spite of their powerful position in the Commons, the Conservative and Unionist Parties entered into a period of steady popular decline over the course of this Parliament. Lord Salisbury was an old, ill leader who oversaw measures of reform, such as the Education Act 1902, without any enthusiasm. After his resignation in that year, his successor, Arthur Balfour, was saddled with the open split over tariff reform. His administration passed several important measures of social reform, including the Education Act 1902, the Irish Land Purchase Act 1903, the Licensing Act 1904 and the Unemployed Workmen Act 1905. But it was not enough to still the growing clamour for clear national leadership which resulted in defeat for the party in 1906. Both a cause and a reflection of this dissatisfaction with the pace of social reform was the growing strength of explicitly working-class political organisation in these years.

On 27 February 1900 a conference took place in London at the Memorial Hall in Farringdon Street. Convened to discuss the problems of organising increased labour representation in Parliament, the desirability for which had been expressed in a resolution passed at the Trades Union Congress the previous year, it was the first conference to bring together the very different strands represented by trade unionism, militant socialism and the more moderate reformist socialism represented by the Fabians, and is remembered as marking the birth of the modern Labour Party. The conference decided to form an independent Labour group in the Commons, whereas previously there had been several disparate groupings of pro-labour MPs. This new parliamentary Labour group would be represented in the country by a Labour Representation Committee.

2.1   Labour Representation Committee, *Report of the Conference on Labour Representation*, 27 February 1900 (London, LRC, p. 12).

■ The Conference on Labour Representation convened by the Parliamentary Committee of the Trades Union Congress, acting upon instructions given by the last Trades Union Congress at Plymouth, was opened in the Memorial Hall, London, on Tuesday, February 27th. Invitations to send delegates were issued to the Trade Unions and Co-operative Societies of the United Kingdom, the Independent Labour Party, the Social Democratic Federation, and the Fabian Society. The invitations were accepted by all the various organisations, with the exception of the Co-operative Union, who, in the absence of any mandate from their last annual conference, were unable to pledge their organisations. Preliminary meetings were held by selected representatives of the various organisations ...

This Committee agreed upon the agenda, which after alterations by the Parliamentary Committee, was issued as follows:

AGENDA

1. OBJECT OF CONFERENCE.

A resolution in favour of working-class opinion being represented in the House of Commons by men sympathetic with the aims and demands of the Labour movement.

2. LABOUR MEMBERS IN THE HOUSE OF COMMONS.

A resolution in favour of establishing a distinct Labour Group in Parliament, who should have their own Whips and agree upon their policy, which must embrace a readiness to co-operate with any party which, for the time being, may be engaged in promoting legislation in the direct interest of labour, and be equally ready to associate themselves with any party in opposing measures having an opposite tendency.

3. CONSTITUTION OF COMMITTEE.

The Executive Committee shall consist of twelve representatives from Trade Unions, ten from the Co-operative Societies, providing they are represented as a body at the Conference, two from the Fabian Society, two from the Independent Labour Party, and two from the Social Democratic Federation. Such members shall be elected by their respective organisations.

4. DUTY OF COMMITTEE AT ELECTIONS.

In the case of elections, the Executive Committee appointed for this purpose should collect information respecting candidates pledged to support the policy of the Labour Group, and recommend the United Labour Party to support them.

5. DUTY OF COMMITTEE.

This Committee should keep in touch with Trade Unions and other organisations, local and national, which are running Labour candidates.

6. FINANCIAL RESPONSIBILITY.

The Committee shall administer the funds which may be received on behalf of the organisation, and each body shall be required to pay 10s. per annum for every 1,000 members, or fraction thereof; also, that it shall be responsible for the expenses of its own candidates.

7. REPORTING TO THE CONGRESS, ETC.

It should also report annually to the Trades Union Congress and the annual meetings of the national societies represented on the Committee, and take any steps deemed advisable to elicit opinion from the members of the organisations to which the Committee is ultimately responsible ...

There were altogether 129 delegates present, representing 568,177 organised workers. ■

At first, the Labour Representation Committee made little impact, and its prospects were not thought to be promising. Most of the trade unions remained suspicious of the socialists and content to improve working conditions through independent action. But that option became more difficult as a result of the Taff Vale decision in 1901. When a group of employees of the Taff Vale Railway Company went on strike in 1900, the employers had taken action against the Amalgamated Society of Railway Servants, holding it financially responsible for the damages incurred during the action. The decision to find in favour of the plaintiff was eventually upheld by the House of Lords in 1901.

2.2   *Taff Vale Railway* v. *Amalgamated Society of Railway Servants,* **1901 (House of Lords Record Office, Opinions of the Law Lords.)**

■ July 22. **Lord Macnaghten** ... Parliament has legalised trade unions, whether registered or not; if registered, they enjoy certain advantages. The respondent society is a registered trade union. Subject to such control as an annual general meeting can exercise, the government of the society is in the hands of its executive committee, a small body with vast powers, including an unlimited power of disposition over the funds of the union, except so far as it may be interfered with by the annual general meeting, or restricted by the operation of the society's rules, of which, in case of doubt, the executive committee is the sole authorized interpreter ...

Has the Legislature authorized the creation of numerous bodies of men capable of owning great wealth and of acting by agents with absolutely no responsibility for the wrongs they may do to other persons by the use of that wealth and the employment of those agents? In my opinion, Parliament has done nothing of the kind. I cannot find anything in the Acts of 1871 and 1876, or either of them, from beginning to end, to warrant or suggest such a notion ...

Then, if trade unions are not above the law, the only remaining question, as it seems to me, is one of form. How are these bodies to be sued? I have no doubt whatever that a trade union, whether registered or unregistered, may be sued in a representative action if the persons selected as defendants be persons who, from their position, may be taken fairly to represent the body.

The further question remains: May a registered trade union be sued in and by its registered name? For my part, I cannot see any difficulty in the way of such a suit. It is quite true that a registered trade union is not a corporation, but it has a registered name and a registered office. The registered name is nothing more than a collective name for all the members. The registered office is the place where it carries on business ... I can see nothing contrary to principle, or contrary to the provisions of the Trade Union Acts, in holding that a trade union may be sued by its registered name.

I am, therefore, of opinion that the appeal should be allowed and the judgement of Farwell J. restored with costs, here and below ... ■

The ability of employers to sue trade unions for damages threatened the financial future of the labour movement. It was in this context that an increasing number of unions became converted to the idea of organised parliamentary action, and affiliated to the Labour Representation Committee. By 1903 the LRC had therefore become a serious new political force. By-election results had already demonstrated that Labour candidates could split the Liberal vote. From 1903, therefore, the LRC and the Liberals co-operated to ensure that this rivalry would not inadvertently lead to a further Conservative and Unionist victory at the next general election, which looked imminent from the time that the government divided over fiscal policy. In August 1903 a secret agreement was signed by LRC Secretary Ramsay MacDonald and the Liberal Chief Whip Herbert Gladstone, an arrangement in the interests of both parties. In the following document, Gladstone's secretary sets out some of the advantages and disadvantages of a Lib–Lab pact.

2.3   Memorandum by Jesse Herbert for Herbert Gladstone, 6 March 1903 (BL Add. MS. 46025).

■ ... I received an intimation from Mr. George Cadbury that the 'Labour people' were desirous of a friendly arrangement with the Liberal party, by which they might be left free to fight, at the next General Election, in a score or more constituencies, without the rivalry of Liberal candidates. I therefore let Mr. MacDonald, the secretary of the Labour Representation Committee know, by means of a mutual friend, that I would meet him if he wished me to do so. He invited me to meet him on neutral ground and privately, to avoid the comments of those members of his party who are ill-disposed towards the Liberal party ...

They asked for no alliance, but an exhibition of friendliness which will permit of good fellowship. They were unwilling to discuss their political principles or objects, and did not ask the Liberal party to approve them, or any of them. They thought it would be advantageous to the Labour party, and not less so to the Liberal party, if there were no rivalry of candidates ...

A determination of the course to be followed by the Liberal party is urgently needed, for to do nothing is to seem to reject the overtures of the LRC, who may be irretrievably committed to courses during delay which they would avoid if they anticipated future friendly relations.

I am keenly conscious that the matter is not so simple and clear that it may be determined in the off-hand manner in which it is dealt with by many Liberals as well as Labour men. The official recognition of a separate group unpledged to support of the Liberal party, a group which will harass every Government and whose representatives in Parliament will probably decline the Liberal whip, is not lightly to be given. It would be the recognition of a vital change in the organization of parties. But would it be other than the official recognition of a fact, indisputable, and clear to every individual politician? ...

The LRC can directly influence the votes of nearly a million men. They will have a fighting fund of £100,000. (This is the most significant new fact in the situation. Labour candidates have had hitherto to beg for financial help, and have fought with paltry and wholly insufficient funds). Their members are mainly men who have hitherto voted with the Liberal party. Should they be advised to vote against Liberal candidates, and (as they probably would) should they act as advised, the Liberal party would suffer defeat not only in those constituencies where LRC candidates fought, but also in almost every borough, and in many of the Divisions of Lancashire and Yorkshire. This would be the inevitable result of unfriendly action towards the LRC candidates. They would be defeated, but so also should we be defeated ... ■

In the years before the general election of 1906, the Liberal Party and the Labour Representation Committee worked closely together, both inside the House and in the country at large. While this angered many rank-and-file socialist members of the LRC, the formula worked well in practice. The LRC went into the election campaign with a moderate manifesto not dissimilar to that of the Liberals.

2.4   *Manifesto of the Labour Representation Committee,* **1906 (in F.W.S. Craig, ed, *British General Election Manifestos, 1900-1974,* London, Macmillan, 1975, pp. 9–10).**

■ To the Electors –

This election is to decide whether or not Labour is to be fairly represented in Parliament.

The House of Commons is supposed to be the people's House, and yet the people are not there.

Landlords, employers, lawyers, brewers, and financiers are there in force. Why not Labour?

The Trade Unions ask the same liberty as capital enjoys. They are refused.

The aged poor are neglected.

The slums remain; overcrowding continues, whilst the land goes to waste.

Shopkeepers and traders are overburdened with rates and taxation, whilst the increasing land values, which should relieve the rate-payers, go to people who have not earned them.

Wars are fought to make the rich richer, and underfed school children are still neglected.

Chinese labour is defended because it enriches the mine owners.

The unemployed ask for work, the Government gave them a worthless Act. And now, when you are beginning to understand the causes of your poverty, the red herring of Protection is drawn across your path.

Protection, as experience shows, is no remedy for poverty and unemployment. It serves to keep you from dealing with the land, housing, old age, and other social problems!

You have it in your power to see that Parliament carries out your wishes. The Labour Representation Executive appeals to you in the name of a million Trade Unionists to forget all the political differences which have kept you apart in the past ... ■

While the Liberal Party won a large overall majority in the 1906 election, the combination of solid trade union funding and co-operation with the Liberals resulted in a strong showing for the Labour Representation Committee as well. When the new parliamentary session began, the group of twenty-nine sat together on the opposition benches, and elected their own officers and whips. In addition, they decided to adopt a new title, 'the Labour Party'.

The Liberal Landslide of 1906

By the end of 1905 Balfour's position as Prime Minister was growing untenable. Given the controversy raging in his party over fiscal reform, it seemed surprising that he had not dissolved Parliament the previous year. But the Conservative/Unionist Coalition could not hope to outface a united Liberal Party unless they could themselves present a united policy on tariffs.

Fiscal reform and tariffs were not Balfour's only problem as Prime Minister in 1905. 'Chinese slavery', the use of indentured Chinese labour in the Transvaal to work the Rand gold-mines, had been condoned by the government. The opposition parties used the issue to undermine Conservative and Unionist efforts to portray themselves as a reforming party. The following pamphlet, for example, was written by a Labour MP upon his return from an investigative trip to the Transvaal.

2.5   **Thomas Burt MP,** *A Visit to the Transvaal; Labour: White, Black and Yellow,* **1905 (Newcastle, Co-operative Printing Society, pp. 60–1, 68–9).**

■ ... I was introduced to Mr. Gim Ah Chun, who came out to the Transvaal with the earliest Chinese arrivals, and who had been six months in the Comet Mine acting as interpreter ... Mr. Chun roundly asserts that the coolies were brought to the Transvaal under the most cruel false pretences ... Scarcely any of them were aware, he says, that they had to work underground, nor had they any conception of the exceedingly small purchasing power of money in the Transvaal ... 'Some coolies who came in October refused to go underground, alleging that they had been promised in Hong Kong that they would be employed as police. They were brought before the Resident magistrate at Boksburg, and were fined 20/-, or sent to prison for seven days with hard labour ...

I have a profound, an ineradicable objection to the importation and deportation of human beings in droves, and of shackling them by all sorts of galling restrictions and disabilities.

That the advent of the Chinamen will quicken the development of the mines, that it will give speedier and larger dividends to hungry share-holders, that it will make a few additional millionaires, and that it will benefit many poorer and most estimable people, does not at all reconcile me to the methods by which this has been accomplished. Whether the goldfields of the Transvaal shall be exhausted in fifty or in twice fifty years is not of vital moment to England, or to the British Empire. But it is of vital and enduring consequence that our best traditions should be handed for-ward to future generations untarnished; that we should continue to be a free country in which the worth and dignity of honest labour shall always be recognised and maintained. ∎

Pinning his political fortunes on divisions within the Liberal Party over Home Rule in Ireland, Balfour resigned his position as Prime Minister on 4 December 1905 without dissolving Parliament. The Liberal leader, Henry Campbell-Bannerman, formed a minority government on the following day. Balfour had miscalculated; while he believed that a minority Liberal government would fall to pieces before an election could be called, in fact the general election of January 1906 returned a landslide majority for the Liberal Party, and confirmed the decline of the Conservatives and Unionists. By far the most important election issue was fiscal reform; and the Liberals were returned with a mandate based on free trade and social reform. The Conservative and Unionist benches were reduced to a small rump of 157 MPs; Balfour himself, along with many of his senior colleagues, lost his seat.

2.6   **Conservative and Unionist Party and Liberal Party, 1906 general election posters (Geoffrey Ford, private collection).**

The Challenge to Democracy

In spite of a popular mandate for reform, the Liberal government under the premiership of Henry Campbell-Bannerman was hampered by the huge Conservative and Unionist majority in the House of Lords. The leadership of Balfour (soon returned to the Commons in a by-election) and, in the upper chamber, of the respected former Foreign Secretary Lord Lansdowne, deliberately used this advantage to obstruct the passage of legislation. This challenge to the democratic process finally culminated in the reform of the House of Lords in 1911, which set limits to its powers of veto over the House of Commons.

Campbell-Bannerman stayed on as Prime Minister until April 1908. But although some legislation, notably the Trades Dispute Act 1906 which reversed the effects of the Taff Vale decision, was allowed to pass, the Lords' veto plagued his administration. In the summer of 1907 the government responded by making clear its intention of introducing legislation to curb the Lords' obstruction should the present situation continue.

2.7   **Henry Campbell-Bannerman on constitutional reform intentions, 24 June 1907 (*Hansard*, 4th ser., 176: 909–24).**

■ THE PRIME MINISTER AND FIRST LORD OF THE TREASURY (Sir H. CAMPBELL-BANNERMAN, Stirling Burghs): I rise to move, 'That, in order to give effect to the will of the people as expressed by their elected representatives, it is necessary that the power of the other House to alter or reject Bills passed by this House should be so restricted by law as to secure that within the limits of a single Parliament the final decision of the Commons shall prevail' ... The passing of a Resolution by this House, even if it be tacitly accepted by the other House, does not have the effect of law, and it is laid down in this Motion that its objects are to be secured 'by law' ... Before I sit down I shall submit to the House the broad lines of the plan which at a later period will, according to our intention, have statutory form given to it; and the Government will exercise their own discretion as to when that Bill will be introduced. In the meantime we desire to test the opinion of the House, and to make sure before any further step is taken that we have the House of Commons behind us ...

My Motion affirms the predominance of the House of Commons as the representative House of Parliament, and I submit that in spirit and in fact that is a strictly true constitutional proposition ...

But let us be quite clear as to what we mean by predominance, and especially what we mean by the ultimate prevalence of the House of Commons ... We do not mean a supremacy that comes into play after one or two or more appeals to the country, before which a determined resistance of the other House will give way. That is not what we mean by the supremacy of the House of Commons. That arrangement does not in the least fulfil the requirements of the Constitution ...

It is proposed that, if a Bill is sent up to the other House, and in the result the two Houses find agreement impossible, a Conference shall be held between Members appointed in equal numbers by the two Houses ... Its proceedings will be private and its object will be to enable each Party to negotiate and to seek for a common measure of agreement ... Supposing, then, the Conference to be unproductive. The Bill – either the same Bill, with or without modifications, or a similar Bill with the same object – might at the discretion of the Government be reintroduced after a substantial interval; and by a substantial interval I have in my mind a minimum of perhaps, six months, unless in cases of great urgency. This Bill would be passed through its various stages in the House of Commons ... The Bill would then be sent up again, so that the other House would have a second and ample opportunity of considering it. If there was still a difference between the two Houses, a Conference might again be summoned. Supposing this time an arrangement again failed, this second Bill would be re-introduced and passed swiftly through all its stages in this House in the form last agreed to, and sent to the other House with an intimation that unless passed in that form it would be passed over their heads. Yet again there would be a Conference, and a further effort to agree ...

... we consider that the undoubted danger that the House of Commons, with the increased power which we claim for it, might for some years of its life have its genuine representative character impaired, can be best guarded against by a more frequent reference to the electorate ... we believe that the reduction of the period of Parliamentary existence to five years will add vigour, freshness, and life to our Parliamentary system. ■

The People's Budget

Campbell-Bannerman resigned in April 1908 through ill health. Leadership of the Liberal Party passed to Herbert Henry Asquith, who stood well to the right of his predecessor. In order to contain the Radical wing of the Liberal Party, Asquith shrewdly appointed David Lloyd George Chancellor of the Exchequer. Lloyd George was put in charge of the nation's purse at a particularly important juncture. The estimates, already badly upset by the naval Dreadnought programme, had been eroded further by the passage of the Old Age Pensions Act. The new Chancellor was faced with the prospect of finding an extra £15 million in revenue, a large amount at the time. This he decided to do by raising a number of new taxes, in an attempt to revitalise the administration, worn down by two years' confrontation with the House of Lords. It was in the subsequent fight over the passage of 'the People's Budget' that the peers forced the issue of constitutional reform to the forefront of the political agenda.

The reaction to Lloyd George's 1909 'People's Budget' was immediate and furious, made ugly in particular by the headlines in Alfred Harmsworth's Daily Mail. *Within a few weeks opposition to the Budget had gathered momentum; the Budget Protest League was founded by Walter Long, a prominent non-interventionist Conservative and Unionist MP, in the middle of June.*

2.8   **Budget Protest League poster, 1909 (Conservative Party Archives).**

2.9   Editorial commentary on the Budget, *Daily Mail,* **30 April 1909.**

■ *Plundering the middle class*

The Budget which Mr Lloyd George yesterday laid before the House of Commons is admirably calculated to harry every class of business man. It would indeed be difficult to exaggerate the mischief which its proposals may accomplish … It is true that here and there were some good points in his budget. The heavy tax on high-powered motor-cars is not unjust. But the tax which he proposes to levy on low-powered cars will prove extremely oppressive. The tax of 3d. per gallon on petrol is recklessly excessive, and though motor-omnibuses are apparently only going to pay half that amount, it may be enough to drive them off the streets. Mr Lloyd George does not seem to have thoroughly thought out the consequences of this new tax, and thus he has imposed a greater burden than he perhaps intended. The rebate of income tax for children, in the case of small incomes, is a good point, and another is the grant for agricultural development.

But when this has been said, we have to admit that the Budget resembles the production of wild Socialists, not of a Cabinet of sober and thoughtful business men. The middle class, and the income tax paying class in particular, are singled out for special and cruel attack. For them this Budget is 'the limit'. They are plundered and shorn in every possible way. Yet they have not even the consolation that their property is being adequately guarded. While these enormous burdens are being imposed, the Navy programme provides for only four Dreadnoughts, and the vote for British new construction and armaments in the present year is less than the German. They are being called upon to pay, pay, pay for the old-age pensions from which they derive no benefit.

Sixteen and a half millions have to be raised in a time, as the Budget memorandum admits, of acute depression and commercial distress. Mr Lloyd George began by promising fairly to distribute this load among the various sections of the community. He has carried out his promise by taxing capital and business in the most onerous manner. The Sinking Fund, that last resource for grave national emergencies, has been reduced by three millions. Mr Lloyd George boasted that he would not borrow for the Navy, forgetting that the effect of this raid is financially equivalent to the floating of a loan of one hundred million at 3 per cent. The income tax on what are ironically called 'unearned' incomes, is raised to 1s.2d. There is a super-tax on incomes over £5,000 of 6d. in each pound by which they exceed £3,000. The death duties on moderate estates are raised; the legacy duties are increased. The savings of the professional man and business man are held up to ransom in the hour of death and sorrow. There is a huge and most mischievous addition to the stamp duties. The settlement tax is doubled. There is a tax of 20 per cent. on the 'unearned increment' of land to be ascertained by fantastic methods.

The net result of this Budget is that Capital is taxed more heavily in Great Britain than in any other civilised country of the world. The new fertiliser, taxation, is to be applied with a vengeance … Tax is piled on tax till no one will know where he stands. The effect of the new stamp duties, as our city editor points out, will be withering. They will drive away financial business from London to Paris, Amsterdam and New York. The great 'free money' market of the world, of which Free Traders boasted, has the axe laid at the root of its prosperity. The consequences of the other direct taxes and duties will be to lower the scale of living for the middle class, to discourage saving, to penalise thrift, and to injure industry. It is the greatest possible mistake to suppose that such taxes will affect only those at whom they are directly aimed. If the 'rich' are impoverished the poor will be impoverished too, and unemployment and distress will be increased …

The Budget, in fact, is the bankruptcy of Free Trade. It lays every burden on the British subject. It leaves foreign goods free to compete with his products, while hampering him in every possible way. It mortgages his resources up to the hilt. It plunders the middle class. It destroys all confidence in the future and that sense of security without which business cannot flourish. ■

After a few months' silence, Lloyd George launched on a national tour to promote the Budget, beginning with a blistering attack on the Opposition at Limehouse in East London on 30 July. Despite the heat of the evening and a demonstration by suffragettes both inside and outside the hall, it was the best-remembered speech of his life.

2.10   **David Lloyd George, speech at Limehouse, 30 July 1909 (reported in**
The Times, 31 July 1909).

■ A few months ago a meeting was held not far from this hall, in the heart
of the City of London, demanding that the Government should launch out
and run into enormous expenditure on the Navy. That meeting ended up
with a resolution promising that those who passed that resolution would
give financial support to the Government in their undertaking ... What has
happened since to alter their tone? Simply that we have sent in the bill.
(Laughter and Cheers.) ... Somebody has got to pay, and these gentlemen
say, 'Perfectly true; somebody has got to pay, but we would rather that
somebody were somebody else.' (Laughter.) We started building; we wanted
money to pay for the building; so we sent the hat round. (Laughter.) We
sent it round amongst the workmen (hear, hear), and the miners of
Derbyshire (loud cheers) and Yorkshire, the weavers of High Peak (cheers),
and the Scotchmen of Dumfries (cheers), who, like all their countrymen,
know the value of money. (Laughter.) They all brought in their coppers.
We went round Belgravia, but there has been such a howl ever since that it
has completely deafened us.

But they say 'It is not so much the Dreadnoughts we object to, it is the
pensions.' (Hear, hear.) If they object to pensions, why did they promise
them? (Cheers.) They won the elections on the strength of their promises. It
is true they never carried them out. (Laughter.) Deception is always a pretty
contemptible vice, but to deceive the poor is the meanest of all crimes.
(Cheers.) But they say, 'When we promised pensions we meant pensions at
the expense of the people for whom they were provided. We simply meant
to bring in a Bill to compel workmen to contribute to their own pensions.'
(Laughter.) If that is what they meant, why did they not say so? (Cheers.)
The Budget, as your chairman has already so well reminded you, is
introduced not merely for the purpose of raising barren taxes, but taxes that
are fertile taxes, taxes that will bring forth fruit – the security of the country
which is paramount in the minds of all. The provision for the aged and
deserving poor – it was time it was done. (Cheers.) ... There are many in
the country blessed by Providence with great wealth, and if there are
amongst them men who grudge out of their riches a fair contribution
towards the less fortunate of their fellow countrymen they are shabby rich
men. (Cheers.) ....

But there are some of them who say that the taxes themselves are unjust,
unfair, unequal, oppressive – notably so the land taxes. (Laughter.) ... Let us
examine them, because it is perfectly clear that the one part of the Budget
that attracts all this hostility and animosity is that part which deals with the
taxation of land ...

Not far from here not so many years ago, between the Lea and the Thames,
you had hundreds of acres of land which was not very useful even for
agricultural purposes. In the main it was a sodden marsh. The commerce

and the trade of London increased under free trade (loud cheers), the tonnage of your shipping went up by hundreds of thousands of tons and by millions, labour was attracted from all parts of the country to help with all this trade and business done here. What happened? There was no housing accommodation. This part of London became overcrowded and the population overflowed. That was the opportunity of the owners of the marsh. All that land became valuable building land, and land which used to be rented at £2 or £3 an acre has been selling within the last few years at £2000 an acre, £3000 an acre, £6000 an acre, £8000 an acre. Who created that increment? (Cheers.) Who created that golden swamp? (More cheers.) Was it the landlord? (Cries of 'No'.) Was it his energy? Was it his brains (laughter and cheers), his forethought? It was purely the combined efforts of all the people engaged in the trade and commerce of that part of London … On the walls of Mr. Balfour's meeting last Friday were the words, 'We protest against fraud and folly.' (Laughter.) So do I. (Great cheering.) … In the future those landlords will have to contribute to the taxation of the country on the basis of the real value (more cheers) only one-halfpenny in the pound! And that is what all the howling is about …

The other day, at the great Tory meeting held at the Cannon-street Hotel, they had blazoned on the walls, 'We protest against the Budget in the name of democracy – (loud laughter) – liberty, and justice.' Where does the democracy come in in this landed system? Where is the justice in all these transactions? We claim that the tax we impose on land is fair, just and moderate. (Cheers.) … All I can say is this – the ownership of land is not merely an enjoyment, it is a stewardship. (Cheers.) … No country, however rich, can permanently afford to have quartered upon its revenue a class which declines to do the duty which it was called upon to perform. (Hear, hear.) …

… I am one of the children of the people. (Loud and prolonged cheering, and a voice, 'Bravo David: stand by the people and they will stand by you.') I was brought up amongst them. I know their trials; and God forbid that I should add one grain of trouble to the anxiety which they bear with such patience and fortitude. (Cheers.) When the Prime Minister did me the honour of inviting me to take charge of the National Exchequer (A voice, 'He knew what he was about', and laughter) at a time of great difficulty, I made up my mind, in framing the Budget which was in front of me, that at any rate no cupboard should be bared (loud cheers), no lot would be harder to bear. (Cheers.) By that test, I challenge them to judge the Budget. (Loud and long-continued cheers, during which the right hon. gentleman resumed his seat.) Afterwards the audience rose and sang, 'For he's a jolly good fellow'.

A resolution was carried in favour of the Budget. ■

During the summer of 1909 the question was whether the House of Lords would dare to reject the Budget, and Lloyd George's tactics in his July speech at Limehouse seemed calculated to dare the Lords to do so. By the autumn, the pressure on Lord Lansdowne for rejection had grown too hard to resist. While there were Conservative and Unionist peers who counselled caution, it was the wilder heads who ultimately prevailed, and at the beginning of November the decision was taken to reject the People's Budget.

On 2 December 1909 Asquith responded to the Lords' rejection of the Budget in the House of Commons. In announcing his decision to call a new election, he made clear the government's intention of confronting and challenging the action of the House of Lords.

2.11   H.H. Asquith on the Lords' rejection of the Budget, 2 December 1909 (*Hansard*, 5th ser., 13: 546–58).

■ The PRIME MINISTER (Mr. Asquith) moved, 'That the action of the House of Lords in refusing to pass into law the financial provision made by this House for the Service of the year is a breach of the Constitution and a usurpation of the rights of the Commons'.

We are met here this afternoon under circumstances which are unexampled in the history of the British Parliament ... When a short time ago the Finance Bill received its third reading, and as it left this House, it represented, I believe, in a greater degree than can be said of any measure of our time, the matured, the well-sifted, the deliberate work of an overwhelming majority of the representatives of the people, upon a matter which, by the custom of generations, and by the course of a practically unbroken authority, is the province of this House and of this House alone. In the course of a week, or little more than a week, the whole of this fabric has been thrown to the ground ...

I come to the course – the only course – which, in the circumstances, is open to the Government, without either breaking the law or sacrificing constitutional principle, to pursue. That course is to advise, as we have advised the Crown, to dissolve this Parliament at the earliest possible moment ...

The truth is that all this talk about the duty or the right of the House of Lords to refer measures to the people is, in the light of our practical and actual experience, the hollowest outcry of political cant ... The sum and substance of the matter is that the House of Lords rejected the Finance Bill last Tuesday, not because they love the people, but because they hate the Budget ... The real question which emerges from the political struggles in this country for the last 30 years is not whether you will have a single or a double chamber system of government, but whether when the Tory Party is in power the House of Commons shall be omnipotent, and whether when the Liberal Party is in power the House of Lords shall be omnipotent ...

The House of Lords have deliberately chosen their ground. They have elected to set at nought in regard to finance the unwritten and time-honoured conventions of our Constitution. In so doing, whether they foresaw it or not, they have opened out a wider and a more far-reaching issue. We have not provoked the challenge, but we welcome it ... ■

The constitutional crisis

The general election which followed the 1909 Budget crisis, in January 1910, made Asquith's already problematic position even more difficult. While the Liberal Party's fortunes had certainly improved from its pre-Budget slump in popularity, the party emerged with a reduced majority, dependent upon the support of the Irish Nationalists. But now there was a popular mandate for reform of the House of Lords. And the Nationalists were united, along with the Labour Party, on the issues of Home Rule and the introduction of a scheme to limit the power of the Lords along the lines of the 1907 Campbell-Bannerman formula. So Conservative and Unionist opposition to reform of the upper chamber was further entrenched by the prospect of Home Rule in Ireland.

The introduction of the Parliament Bill in 1910 to reform the House of Lords was not a straightforward process. The Cabinet was split between the Radicals, who wanted to proceed with a 'veto bill', and those who wanted a veto to be incorporated in a more general reform of the Lords.

The Cabinet decided to introduce three resolutions on reform in the Commons – on money bills, all other bills and the reduction of the life of a single Parliament from seven to five years. Once this had been accomplished in mid-April 1910, the Parliament Bill was introduced. On 27 April the Budget was finally passed without substantial amendment. On 6 May, however, King Edward VII died suddenly. His successor, George V, was anxious to settle the Lords' dispute through negotiation; but the conference convened at his request, which met over a five-month period from June, failed to arrive at any settlement. The sticking point now was Irish Home Rule, to which the Unionists were passionately opposed. Thus, a second general election took place in December 1910; when this returned a similar result as that of January, the Liberals had won a clear mandate to proceed with the Parliament Bill, with the threat of a creation of enough new peers to force its passage, should opposition continue.

By the middle of May 1911, the Bill had passed through the Commons. But in the House of Lords a final effort to obstruct reform gained force in June. The 'die-hard' movement of peers who were determined to insist on the Lords' amendments to the Bill gained force throughout the summer, despite the efforts of the 'hedgers', led by Lord Lansdowne, to avoid what would surely be a disastrous show-down. By the time that the final debate took place in the Lords, the outcome was uncertain, and the atmosphere one of high drama.

2.12   House of Lords debate on the Parliament Bill, 9 August 1911 (*Hansard*, 5th ser. [Lords], 9: 887–900).

■ THE MARQUESS OF LANSDOWNE: ... it seems to me obvious that this House is no longer in a position to offer effectual resistance to the policy of His Majesty's Government, and in these circumstances some of us, myself amongst the number, are convinced that further insistence on our Amendments would be not only unprofitable, but detrimental to the public interest. Those who so think hold that it will be wiser to abstain from further intervention in these discussions, that we should assume no responsibility for the Bill, and that we should part with it making it clear that whenever the opportunity presents itself to us we shall spare no effort to redress the balance of the Constitution ...

We know, or at least I know, that we have no means of preventing this Bill from finding a place on the Statute Book ... I doubt whether your Lordships would achieve much or add greatly to the credit and reputation of this House if you were to resort to unparliamentary methods such as often repeated adjournments and various technical modes of opposing the accomplishment of the policy of His Majesty's Government, I am convinced that such attempts would be unsuccessful and would probably be much misunderstood in the country ...

THE EARL OF HALSBURY: ... It seems to me that upon a question of principle, if I believed a thing to be wrong, I ought to do my best to prevent it. The temptation given to us is that we must allow the Bill to pass, and then, forsooth! agitate, until we get the country to take our view. Thus we are told that we shall be satisfied that we have saved this House from degradation. Have we? Is it saving this House from degradation when that which is admitted to be so degrading to it is yielded to as a threat?

I myself certainly will not yield to the threat. Let the Government take the responsibility of introducing 400 or 500 Peers – I care not how many – in the circumstances that my noble friend has pointed out and then let him shield himself by saying 'And you forced them to do it'. I never heard such an extraordinary argument in my life. It is as if a highwayman came and said, 'Give me your watch or I cut your throat', and if you did not give him your watch that you are the author of your own throat being cut ... nothing in the world will induce me not to vote against a Bill which I believe to be wrong and immoral and a scandalous example of legislation. ■

After an emotional two-day debate, the House of Lords narrowly voted to allow the Parliament Bill to pass, by seventeen votes. The Parliament Act 1911 was an important milestone in constitutional history. It removed the Lords' right of veto, but retained its right to amend and delay legislation passed in the House of Commons. While the Parliament Act was intended to be followed up with a more complete reform of the second chamber, other events soon pushed the issue to the periphery of political debate.

2.13   **The Parliament Act 1911** (*Public General Acts*, 1911, ch. 13).

■ ... Whereas it is expedient that provision should be made for regulating the relations between the two Houses of Parliament:

And whereas it is intended to substitute for the House of Lords as it at present exists a Second Chamber constituted on a popular instead of hereditary basis, but such substitution cannot be immediately brought into operation:

And whereas provision will require hereafter to be made by Parliament in a measure effecting such substitution for limiting and defining the powers of the new Second Chamber, but it is expedient to make such provision as in this Act appears for restricting the existing powers of the House of Lords:

Be it therefore enacted ...

1. (1) If a Money Bill, having been passed by the House of Commons, and sent up to the House of Lords at least one month before the end of the session, is not passed by the House of Lords without amendment within one month after it is so sent up to that House, the Bill shall, unless the House of Commons direct to the contrary, be presented to His Majesty and become an Act of Parliament on the Royal Assent being signified, notwithstanding that the House of Lords have not consented to the Bill ...

2. (1) If any Public Bill (other than a Money Bill or a Bill containing any provision to extend the maximum duration of Parliament beyond five years) is passed by the House of Commons in three successive sessions (whether of the same Parliament or not), and, having been sent up to the House of Lords at least one month before the end of the session, is rejected by the House of Lords in each of those sessions, that Bill shall, on its rejection for the third time by the House of Lords, unless the House of Commons direct to the contrary, be presented to His Majesty and become an Act of Parliament on the Royal Assent being signified thereto, notwithstanding that the House of Lords have not yet consented to the Bill: Provided that this provision shall not take effect unless two years have elapsed between the date of the second reading in the first of those sessions of the Bill in the House of Commons and the date on which it passes the House of Commons in the third of those sessions ...

7. Five years shall be substituted for seven years as the time fixed for the maximum duration of Parliament under the Septennial Act, 1715 ... ■

The Campaign for Women's Suffrage

The constitutional question came to a head in the summer of 1911, coinciding with the Agadir crisis, and a wave of industrial strife. But this was not the earliest sign of serious domestic unrest; women's suffrage campaigners were the first to employ militant tactics in this period. The first sign that organised pressure for women's suffrage was reviving took place in 1897, when the National Union of Women's Suffrage Societies (NUWSS) was founded to unite seventeen suffrage organisations from various parts of the country. Led by Millicent Garrett Fawcett, the sole aim of the politically neutral NUWSS was to achieve the franchise for women on the same terms as those granted to men. It was NUWSS policy to sponsor Private Members' Bills on the suffrage question in the House of Commons. Increasing frustration with the apparent fruitlessness of this course soon led, however, to the founding of the Women's Social and Political Union (WSPU) in Manchester in 1903.

In 1905 the WSPU leaders, Mrs Emmeline Pankhurst and her daughters Christabel and Sylvia, broke with the NUWSS to begin a militant campaign of civil disobedience. In the weeks leading to the 1906 general election, the WSPU began a policy of disruption which soon gained notoriety in the press.

2.14 Report of suffragette protest, *Manchester Guardian*, 16 October 1905.

■ Arising out of the scenes towards the close of the Liberal meeting held on Friday night in the Free-trade Hall, Miss Christabel Pankhurst, of Manchester, and Miss Annie Kenney, the latter an Oldham lady, appeared as defendants at the Manchester police court, on Saturday, charged with assaulting the police, and also with causing an obstruction in South Street … Mr Bell prosecuted on behalf of the police; the two ladies were not defended. Mr Bell said … if the evidence was to be believed, the defendants' behaviour was such as one was accustomed to attribute to women from the slums. It was regrettable that such a charge should be brought against persons who ought, at least, to be able to control themselves. The police, in bringing the case forward, disclaimed any prejudice or bias; they did not seek the infliction of any heavy penalty; all they asked was, if the magistrates considered the charges proved, to take measures which would prevent a recurrence of such scenes.

Inspector Mather said he was on duty on Friday night, and at 8.50 visited the Free-trade Hall where the Liberal meeting was in progress. Police assistance was called for during the meeting, and he was present when these ladies were ejected. They were taken into an ante-room. Superintendent Watson asked them to behave as ladies should, and not create a further disturbance. They were then at liberty to leave. Miss Pankhurst, however, turned and spat in the Superintendent's face, repeating the same conduct by spitting in the witnesses' face, and also striking him in the mouth …

Addressing the Bench Miss Pankhurst said: I have no intention to deny the main facts which have been put forward. The charge I do not deny; but what I plead in defence is that my conduct was justified owing to the treatment I received at the hands of Sir Edward Grey and other persons in the Free-trade Hall. I want to explain as clearly as I can that at the time I committed the assault that is complained of I was not aware that the individuals assaulted were police officers. I thought they were Liberals … I am only sorry that one of them was not Sir Edward Grey himself …

The magistrates then retired to consider their decision. Whilst they were out a white flag, said to have been exhibited in the Free-trade Hall, and bearing the legend 'Votes for Women' in large letters, was produced, and the ladies hung it on the dock rail. It was, however, removed before the magistrates returned and announced their decision, which was that for assaulting the police Miss Pankhurst must pay a fine of 10s.6d. and costs, or seven days, and for causing an obstruction in South Street each of the defendants must pay a fine of 5s. or 3 days.

Miss Pankhurst: I shall pay no fine.

Miss Kenney: Hear, hear.

The Clerk: Have you any goods which may be distrained upon?

Both ladies answered in the negative. They were taken below. A little later they were taken in a cab to Strangeways Gaol. ■

The WSPU were soon christened 'suffragettes', a term used to distinguish them from the less militant 'suffragists' of the NUWSS. Initial ridicule of the revived women's rights movement soon gave way to irritation and serious concern, as the suffrage organi- sations became well financed, and as the militant tactics of the WSPU escalated in intensity. From 1909, angered by the failure of the Liberal government to act, the WSPU began to endorse the destruction of property, and the defiance of the treatment of women prisoners through a series of hunger strikes. The WSPU explained its decision in its own newspaper, Votes for Women.

2.15   Editorial commentary, *Votes for Women*, 24 September 1909.

■ Questions have been raised regarding the new development of militant tactics in this Union. For three years our battle for the vote was fought without resort to physical violence on the part of women, in spite of immense provocation. This can no longer be said. Women have thrown stones to the destruction of property and the risk of injury to persons … Is this right? Is it wrong? …

It must be remembered that this war of freedom was begun when women had deliberately arrived at the conclusion that after forty unavailing years, the uses of argument and persuasion were at an end … Their first militant move was to question members of the Government at public meetings – at question time. These representatives of Liberalism, taking advantage of their superior position, and ignoring the justice of women's claim, met this move by having the women flung out with violence … They thereupon carried the militant action one stage further – they protested during the speeches of Cabinet Ministers. The Government … met the new protest by excluding women from public meetings … They then conceived and carried out the policy of holding protest meetings, and of attempting to force an entrance to those public meetings where a member of the Government was discussing questions vitally important to them, calling upon sympathisers in the crowd to back them up in their endeavour. Again, choosing to ignore the seriousness of the position, the Government thought to finally crush the agitation by means of a cleverly devised police method. Women were kidnapped the moment they appeared on the scenes, and shut up in the police-court, without being charged, until all the proceedings of the meeting were over, when they were quietly turned out ...

Women, in direct opposition to their instinct, tradition, and normal character, have thus been forced into a revolution in defence of their rights and liberties, and for this the Government is responsible, not the women. Women, even more than men, hate war. Women, even more than men, love peace. But there is one thing better even than peace. It is honour. And there is one thing worse than war. It is the ignoble bondage of subjection ...

This is a revolution. This is a war. But it is a revolution forced upon us. It is a war which we are called upon to wage in the name of liberty and justice. Let the heart of every woman in the movement be the heart of a hero and a warrior, then shall we fight unflinchingly to the very end, and shall forget the strain and the stress in the joy of the battle, which is bound to end in victory for the right. ■

The Liberal government was thrown off guard by the suffrage movement. Asquith himself was opposed, and it became increasingly difficult for his administration to convey an image of democratic reform when faced with the constant protest from suffrage campaigners. In the autumn of 1909 the Home Secretary ordered the forcible feeding of hunger strikers. Sylvia Pankhurst vividly recalled the violence with which the protesters were treated in her memoirs of the women's suffrage movement.

2.16   E. Sylvia Pankhurst, *The Suffragette Movement: An Intimate Account of Persons and Ideals*, 1931 (London, Longmans, pp. 318–19, 331).

■ Only when an action at law, against the Home Secretary and the governor and doctor of Birmingham prison, was commenced on behalf of Mary Leigh, could direct testimony be obtained from the prisoners. It now transpired that Mrs. Leigh had been handcuffed for upwards of thirty hours, the hands fastened behind during the day and in front with the palms outward at night. Only when the wrists had become intensely painful and swollen were the irons removed. On the fourth day of her fast, the doctor had told her that she must either abandon the hunger strike or be fed by force. She protested that forcible feeding was an operation, and as such could not be performed without a sane patient's consent; but she was seized by the wardresses and the doctor administered food by the nasal tube. This was done twice daily, from September 22nd to October 30th ...

'Jane Wharton' [Constance Lytton, the sister of Lord Lytton, in disguise] was forcibly stripped and clothed in prison dress, and put in a punishment cell. She had not been medically examined on entering the prison, and on the fourth day of her hunger strike she was forcibly fed, without examination. She alleged that Dr. Price, the senior medical officer, struck her contemptuously on the cheek, and left her in a state of collapse. At the second forcible feeding she vomited over his clothes. He was angry: 'if you do that again I shall feed you twice!' At the third feeding she vomited continuously, but he pressed the tube down more firmly, and poured in more food. This produced an attack of shivering so serious as to alarm him. He ordered the wardresses to lay her on the bed board, and called to his junior, who was passing, to test her heart. The junior, in jovial mood, listened through his stethoscope for a brief instant, and exclaimed: 'Oh, ripping! Splendid heart! You can go on with her!' ■

The suffragettes agreed to a period of truce in 1910, as rumours spread that the government would be willing to support an all-party 'Conciliation' Bill to introduce suffrage reform, provided it was done in a peaceful atmosphere. Although it passed its second reading in the Commons in July 1910, members voted in favour of committing the Bill to the whole House rather than to a standing committee; and Asquith, beleaguered by the constitutional crisis, declined to give it further time in that session. When it became clear that the Bill would not be considered again in the near future, the WSPU called off the truce.

In spite of the increasing violence surrounding suffragette activities, the WSPU was persuaded to return to a state of truce after the second election of 1910, in hopes of reviving the Conciliation Bill. But when the government proposed to introduce a general Government Franchise Bill, providing for full manhood suffrage instead, the women's suffrage societies divided in their attitude. The WSPU relaunched its campaign of civil disobedience in November 1911. It remained suspicious of Asquith's intentions; the Prime Minister made no secret of his continued opposition to votes for women.

2.17 **The National League for Opposing Woman Suffrage,** *Deputation to Mr. Asquith on Woman's Suffrage,* **December 1912 (London, NLOWS, pp. 10–13).**

■ Mr Asquith: I am very pleased to have the opportunity of meeting you this morning, and I may say without flattery, that after a long and somewhat chequered experience of deputations of various kinds I do not think I have ever heard a case, strong in itself, presented with more sound sense and with less superfluous rhetoric. (Cheers.) As you know, I occupy a somewhat peculiar position in regard to this question. On the one hand, as an individual, I am in entire agreement with you that the grant of the Parliamentary franchise to women in this country would be a political mistake of a very disastrous kind … I hold that opinion and I have held it ever since I entered political life, and I have never seen anything in the arguments and other manifestations – (laughter) – which we have seen, which has induced me in the least degree to alter it. So far we are in complete harmony with one another. On the other hand, I am, as you know, for the time being the head of the Government in which a majority of my colleagues – a considerable majority of my colleagues ... are of a different opinion; and the Government in those circumstances has announced a policy which is the result of the combined deliberations, and by which it is the duty of all their members, and myself not least, to abide loyally. That is the position so far as I am personally concerned.

I do think – I say this quite frankly – that it is time for those who hold strong views upon this subject ... [to] take off their coats, those, at any rate, who belong to my own sex, and that the ladies should lend the co-operation which they can in whatever panoply they think best adapted for effective militant operations of a constitutional kind; and I entertain a very strong hope that if that was done, and the case was clearly and cogently presented to the public opinion of the country, it would be found that some of the jubilations which are now already being heard from the supporters of the movement, were premature, and that public opinion would declare that it is not fair to make this gigantic experiment, for which there is no parrellel [*sic*] in the history of any other country in Europe ... ■

While suffragette tactics made the headlines, the more moderate NUWSS was also changing its strategy in the years preceding the First World War. While always anxious to pursue a 'constitutional' road to reform, the NUWSS enjoyed the benefits of increased membership that the glare of publicity on the suffrage issue brought. By 1913 membership of the NUWSS had grown to include some 500 constituent societies and 50,000 members. Moreover, the combined effect of the failure of the Liberal government to take positive action on the issue, and the formal adoption of women's suffrage reform as Labour Party policy in 1912, persuaded the NUWSS to change tactics. In that year, it set up an Election Fighting Fund to support Labour candidates in constituencies where anti-suffrage Liberals were standing.

2.18   NUWSS, Election Fighting Fund minutes, 8 November 1912 (Fawcett Library 2/NWS/A/4/1).

■ Friday November 8th 1912   10.30 am

Treasurer's Report

The Hon. Treasurer reported that of the £5,348-7s-9 raised at the Albert Hall Meeting, £1,342-1s-6 was ear-marked for the Fighting Fund, while there was a transferable fund of about £700, to be used for NU or EFF work at the discretion of Mrs Fawcett or the Executive Committee ...

Hon. Secretary's Report

Miss Marshall reported an interview ... from which she gathered that the FF policy was causing considerable alarm in the Liberal Party ...

The Hon. Secretary reported on the interview which she and Miss Courtney had had with the officials of the Labour Party at the House of Commons ... They advised the NU to get as many pledges as possible from individual members of the Labour Party to vote against the Third Reading of the Reform Bill if women were not included, and to publish the number ...

They further said that it was no longer necessary to maintain secrecy with regard to money grants made by the FF in support of Labour candidates ...

Report of Organisation Sub-committee

Mr. Holmes having told officers that his expenses for organisation in Crewe would amount to £250 pa, the organisation committee recommended that the grant of £100 be increased to £125 for two years. Agreed on condition that the candidate was Mr Holmes or another equally good ... ■

By 1912 the women's suffrage lobby wielded considerable political power. It retained public notoriety through the escalating violence of the WSPU, and was financially strong enough to put large sums of money behind candidates in favour of the cause and to counter anti-suffrage propaganda with effective propaganda of its own.

2.19 National League for Opposing Women's Suffrage poster, 'A suffragette's home', *c.*1912 (Bodleian Library, John Johnson Collection).

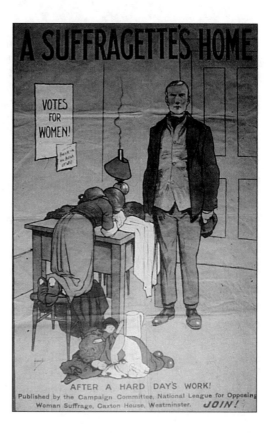

AFTER A HARD DAY'S WORK!
Published by the Campaign Committee, National League for Opposing Woman Suffrage, Caxton House, Westminster. *JOIN!*

2.20   Women's Freedom League propaganda, 'Suffragettes at home no. 3: Mrs How Martyn makes jam', *c.*1912 (Fawcett Library, photographic collection).

In March 1913 the government introduced the Prisoners' Temporary Discharge for Ill-Health Bill, which would soon be known popularly as the 'Cat and Mouse Act'. Its purpose was to enable the Home Secretary to avoid the extreme of forcibly feeding hunger strikers in prison, by temporarily releasing and then rearresting prisoners, meanwhile suspending the duration of the sentence until the return to prison. But by the summer of 1914 there were signs that the government's position was weakening. Suffrage reform would clearly have been a priority on the agenda of the next Parliament. When the war intervened in August, the Home Secretary responsible for the Cat and Mouse Act, Reginald McKenna, released all political prisoners in a general amnesty. With this, the militant suffragette movement was ended. Both the WSPU and the NUWSS suspended their activities, although a number of smaller women's suffrage societies continued to lobby for reform.

Industrial Militancy

In addition to the threat posed by the suffrage movement, Britain experienced a new wave of industrial unrest beginning in 1910. National stoppages on the railways in 1911 and in the mining industry in 1912, brought home to the general public the extent of the power of organised labour. These years of growth in the trade union movement reflected a dissatisfaction among many workers over the apparent decline in real wages in recent years on the one hand, and frustration over the failure of conventional political and legal processes to redress their grievances on the other.

The high hopes for the Parliamentary Labour Party which had followed the general election of 1906 had been eroded by the failure of the party to achieve substantial reform, and the first election of 1910 reduced its representation. Moreover, the financial stability of the Labour Party was threatened by the House of Lords decision in Osborne v. The Amalgamated Society of Railway Servants *in 1910.*

2.21   Report on the Osborne judgement, *Reynold's Newspaper,* **26 December 1909.**

LABOUR MPS' WAGES

Lords Decide that Compulsory Levies are Illegal

VITAL JUDGEMENT

Trade Union Leaders Declare that the Law must be Altered

Compulsory levies on members of trade unions for the purpose of paying the expenses of Labour members of Parliament are illegal. This is the broad effect of the revolutionary decision which has been given by the House of Lords, the highest judicial tribunal in the land ...

The action out of which the appeal arose was brought by Mr Osborne, an official of the Walthamstow branch of the ASRS, who objected to the funds of the Society being applied in promoting the election of members of Parliament, paying their election expenses, and providing for their main-tenance. It was not till 1906 that the rules of the ASRS were amended for the purpose of ordering a levy of one shilling a member yearly to provide for the representation of railwaymen in Parliament, with the condition that all candidates should sign and accept the constitution of the Labour Party and subject to their whip ...

The House of Lords decision, which was forecasted in Reynold's last week, strikes a heavy blow against direct labour representation. It will not, how-ever, affect the coming elections in any way, as the Labour Party had taken precautions against the possibility of the judgement going against them. The ASRS had fully anticipated the issue, and after the Court of Appeal had decided against them they, while carrying the case to the final court, set up a committee for the purpose of collecting voluntary funds for Parliamentary purposes. Other trades unions followed suit, or are expected shortly to do so, and the Labour Party has ample funds in hand or in sight for the payment of election expenses and salaries for some years to come. ■

Legislative reversal of the Osborne judgement did not come until 1913. In the short term, however, the decision resulted in the institution of the payment of Members of Parliament in August 1911, an important step in the democratisation of parliamentary representation.

2.22 David Lloyd George, speech proposing the payment of Members of Parliament, 10 August 1911 (*Hansard*, 5th ser., 29: 1365–93).

■ I rise to move the important motion that stands in my name:

'That, in the opinion of this House, provision should be made for the payment of a salary at the rate of four hundred pounds a year to every Member of this House, excluding any Member who is for the time being in receipt of a salary as an officer of the House, or as a Minister, or as an officer of His Majesty's Household' ...

In the old days we had practically only two classes here. We had the great county families and the legal profession, and we had odds and ends coming in; but, in the main, representation was confined to these two great classes. Since then you have brought in one class after another – the great middle class, the labouring population, and factory representation. I think everybody will agree that this process of broadening has raised the average of the House ...

What is the demand embodied in this Resolution? It is practically a demand from a democracy, which still is under the impression, and, I think, sound impression, that it is labouring under a good many ills that Parliament alone can remedy ... Instead of confining, as it were, those who were able to remedy their evils and cure them to a small class, they say, 'We want an unlimited choice in picking out the men who will suit us best'...

After the Osborne Judgment we are left face to face with this proposition. We must either be restricted to a limited choice, which we have got at the present moment, or find some method whereby men of limited means, who have a capacity as well as a desire for public service, should be able to come to this House ... There is a large and growing class whose presence in this House, in my judgment, is highly desirable, men of wide culture, of high intelligence, and of earnest purpose, whose services in this House would be invaluable in the interests of the community as a whole, who I think would lift the level of discussion, and who would contribute to it in every respect, but whose limited means prevent their taking up a political career ...

When we offer £400 a year as payment of Members of Parliament it is not a recognition of the magnitude of the service, it is not a remuneration, it is not a recompense, it is not even a salary. It is just an allowance, and I think the minimum allowance, to enable men to come here, men who would render incalculable service to the State, and whom it is an incalculable loss to the State not to have here, but who cannot be here because their means do not allow it. ■

In spite of the introduction of payment for MPs, the labour movement grew increasingly frustrated with the parliamentary road to reform. Industrial militancy increased rapidly from the summer of 1910.

2.23 Industrial militancy in the UK, 1900–10 (derived from David Butler and Gareth Butler, eds, *British Political Facts, 1900–1985,* Macmillan, 6th edn, 1986, p. 372).

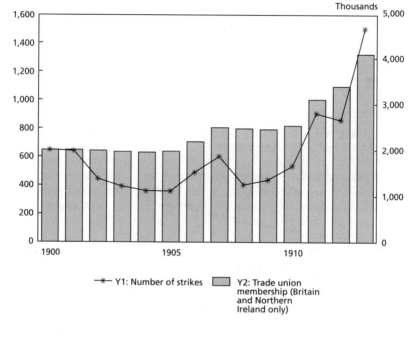

- ─✳─ Y1: Number of strikes
- ▢ Y2: Trade union membership (Britain and Northern Ireland only)

In November 1910, rejecting the new rates of pay recommended by a conciliation board, the miners of the Cambrian Combine in South Wales embarked on a ten-month strike which led to the intervention of troops to control rioting. Press coverage of these events was generally sensational.

2.24 Report of rioting in Tonypandy, *Daily Mail,* 10 November 1910.

■ *TONYPANDY* – Wednesday night.

The effect of the presence of the cavalry in this town – the scene of five hours' continuous rioting and looting last night – has been to restore comparative peace and order to the Rhondda Valley. There is still, however, the danger of a renewed outbreak of violence.

Tonight the streets are being patrolled by a squadron of the 18th (Queen Mary's Own) Hussars with their carbines, and bodies of the London police are marching slowly up and down through dense masses of strikers, who, up to eight o'clock, were quite orderly.

The looted shops, and those which have escaped damage, have been barricaded with wooden shutters and corrugated iron, and the whole of the main street is fortified against any further attack …

Tonypandy this morning presented the appearance of a town that had been bombarded by guns. Stone walls had been overthrown, and the roadway leading to the Glamorgan pit gates was bespattered with blood. There were bloodstains on the walls in the town and even inside the looted shops. ...

All day long the streets of Tonypandy have sounded with the tramp of soldiers and police. In addition to the Glamorgan constabulary and the reinforcements from Bristol, there are now about 300 men belonging to the Metropolitan Police either patrolling the valley or guarding the pits. ■

At Tonypandy the British worker's movement flirted for the first time with the more militant tactics of syndicalism, brought from France and the United States principally by Tom Mann, of the Amalgamated Engineers. Mann's organising ability, and his advocacy of the amalgamation of workers into larger, more powerful unions, soon proved effective. From mid-1911 a still more serious series of strikes, including the first general railway strike, was met again with the widespread use of troops. A new generation of more militant union activists rose to positions of influence during this period.

Tom Mann and members of the Plebs League of former students of Ruskin College set up the Unofficial Reform Committee of the South Wales Miners' Federation in 1912. The Miners' Next Step, a pamphlet issued under the committee's auspices, is regarded as the manifesto for syndicalist action in Britain at this time. Supporters of this militant policy did win backing in the South Wales Miners' Federation in this period, taking up key posts in that organisation before 1914. But while the policy of amalgamation won some converts before the war, notably achieving the merger of several of the railwaymen's unions to form the National Union of Railwaymen in 1913, on the whole, the trade union movement remained opposed to the idea of a general strike for political purposes.

2.25   **The Unofficial Reform Committee,** *The Miners' Next Step: Being a Suggested Scheme for the Reorganisation of the Federation,* **1912 (Tonypandy, Robert Davies & Co., pp. 19–30).**

■ ... [T]he working class, if it is to fight effectually, must be an army, not a mob. It must be classified, regimented and brigaded, along the lines indicated by the product. Thus, all miners ... delve in the earth to produce the minerals, ores, gems, salt, stone, &c., which form the basis of raw material for all other industries. Similarly the Railwaymen, Dockers, Seamen, Carters, etc., form the transport industry. Therefore, before an organised and self-disciplined working class can achieve its emancipation, it must coalesce on these lines ...

The old policy of identity of interest between employers and ourselves [must] be abolished, and a policy of open hostility installed ...

... our objective [will] be, to build up an organisation, that will ultimately take over the mining industry, and carry it on in the interest of the workers...

This can only be obtained gradually and in one way. We cannot get rid of employers and slave-driving in the mining industry, until all other industries have organized for, and progressed towards, the same objective. Their rate of progress conditions ours, all we can do is to set an example and the pace ...

Our objective begins to take shape before your eyes. Every industry thoroughly organized, in the first place, to fight, to gain control of, and then to administer, that industry. The co-ordination of all industries on a Central Production Board, who, with a statistical department to ascertain the needs of the people, will issue its demands on the different departments of industry, leaving to the men themselves to determine under what conditions and how, the work should be done. This would mean real democracy in real life, making for real manhood and womanhood. Any other form of democracy is a delusion and a snare ... ■

Ireland and the Third Home Rule Bill

The question of Home Rule for Ireland posed further problems for the government from 1912. This new phase in the struggle of the Irish Nationalists began with the general elections of January and December 1910, in both of which the government's majority depended upon the support of the Irish Nationalist MPs. In return for support for constitutional reform, the Nationalists counted on a new Home Rule Bill, which could no longer be vetoed in the House of Lords. The Liberal government believed that Home Rule could provide a middle way for the future of Ireland, between outright independence and continued union in the United Kingdom. But the problem, as always, was the opposition of the Protestant Unionists in Ulster; they remained bitterly opposed to any move towards separation, and in this they were supported by the 'Unionist' (Conservative) Party.

In 1903 the Conservative and Unionist government had passed the 1903 Land Purchase Act, which, while an important reform that went some way towards quelling the grievances of the landless poor in the South of Ireland, failed to stem the Nationalist demand for Home Rule. In the following extract, John Redmond, the moderate Irish Nationalist leader, reiterates the demand.

2.26   **John Redmond, speech delivered at Mansion House, Dublin, 4 September 1907 (in John Redmond, *Some Arguments for Home Rule*, Dublin, Sealy, Bryers & Walker, 1908, p. 15).**

■ Recent events have made it essential that Ireland and the capital of Ireland should once more reiterate, and declare in perfectly unmistakable language, the National demand. That the government of every purely Irish affair shall be controlled by the public opinion of Ireland, and by that alone.

We demand this self-government as a right. For us the Act of Union has no binding, moral or legal force. We regard it as our fathers regarded it before us, as a great criminal act of usurpation, carried by violence and by fraud; and we say that no lapse of time, and no mitigation of its details, can ever make it binding upon our honour or our conscience. Resistance to the Act of Union will always remain for us so long as that Act lasts, a sacred duty, and the method of resistance will remain for us merely a question of expediency. There are men to-day – perfectly honourable and honest – for whose convictions I have the utmost respect, who think that the method we ought to adopt is force of arms. Such resistance, I say here, as I have said more than once on the floor of the House of Commons, would be absolutely justifiable if it were possible. But it is not under present circumstances possible, and, I thank God, there are other means at our hands. The demand for National Self-government is, therefore, founded by us, first of all, upon right, and we declare that no ameliorative reforms, no number of Land Acts, or Labourers Acts, or Education Acts, no redress of financial grievances, no material improvement or industrial development, can ever satisfy Ireland until Irish laws are made and administered upon Irish soil by Irishmen. ■

Signs of serious confrontation were evident from the moment that the Liberals introduced the third Home Rule Bill in April 1912. At a gathering of Conservative and Unionist supporters at Blenheim Palace in July, the party leader, Andrew Bonar Law, began what would be a highly inflammatory and dangerous campaign of opposition to government policy.

2.27   Bonar Law, speech at Blenheim Palace, 28 July 1912 (reported in *The Times*, 29 July 1912).

■ ... The Chief Liberal Whip has told us ... that the Home Rule Bill will be carried through the House of Commons before Christmas ... we do not acknowledge their right to carry such a revolution by such means. We do not recognize that any such action is the constitutional government of a free people. We regard them as a revolutionary committee which has seized by fraud upon despotic power. (Cheers.) In our opposition to them we shall not be guided by the considerations, we shall not be restrained by the bonds, which would influence us in an ordinary political struggle. We shall use any means (loud cheers), whatever means seem to us likely to be most effective. That is all we shall think about. We shall use any means to deprive them of the power which they have usurped and to compel them to face the people whom they have deceived. Even if the Home Rule Bill passes through the House of Commons, what then? I said in the House of Commons, and I repeat here, that there are things stronger than Parliamentary majorities ...

Does any one imagine that British troops will be used to shoot down men who demand no privilege which is not enjoyed by you and me and no privilege which any one of us would ever surrender? The thing is unthinkable. Nations, and great nations, have, indeed, taken up arms to prevent their subjects from seceding, but no nation will ever take up arms to compel loyal subjects to leave their community. (Cheers.) I do not believe for a moment that any Government would ever dare to make the attempt, but I am sure of this – that, if the attempt were made, the Government would not succeed in carrying Home Rule. They would succeed only in lighting fires of civil war which would shatter the Empire to its foundations. On this subject I shall say one word, and one word more only. While I had still in the party a position of less responsibility than that which I have now I said that in my opinion if an attempt were made without the clearly expressed will of the people of this country, and as part of a corrupt Parliamentary bargain, to deprive these men of their birthright, they would be justified in resisting by all means in their power, including force. (Cheers.) I said so then, and I say now, with a full sense of the responsibility which attaches to my position, that if the attempt be made under present conditions I can imagine no length of resistance to which Ulster will go in which I shall not be ready to support them and in which they will not be supported by the overwhelming majority of the British people. (The audience rose from their seats and cheered this declaration for some minutes.) ◼

It soon became clear that Bonar Law's threats against the Irish Home Rule Bill were no game of bluff. Sir Edward Carson, the Ulster Loyalist leader, proceeded to obtain some 250,000 signatories in Ulster to a covenant which pledged to use all necessary means to resist the imposition of Home Rule. Over the next two years his army of resistance, the Ulster Volunteers, became a highly organised force, armed with weapons smuggled from Germany. The Nationalists formed their own volunteer force to counter the Ulster action.

2.28 Ulster solemn league and covenant, 19 September 1912 (reported in *The Times*, 20 September 1912).

◼ Being convinced in our consciences that home rule would be disastrous to the material well-being of Ulster as well as the whole of Ireland, subversive of our civil and religious freedom, destructive of our citizenship, and perilous to the unity of the empire, we, whose names are underwritten, men of Ulster, loyal subjects of His Gracious Majesty King George V, humbly relying on the God whom our fathers in days of stress and trial confidently trusted, do hereby pledge ourselves in solemn covenant throughout this our time of threatened calamity to stand by one another in defending for ourselves and our children our cherished position of equal citizenship in the United Kingdom, and in using all means which may be necessary to defeat the present conspiracy to set up a home rule parliament in Ireland. And in the event of such a parliament being forced upon us we further solemnly and mutually pledge ourselves to refuse to recognise its authority. In sure confidence that God will defend the right we hereto subscribe our names. And further, we individually declare that we have not already signed this covenant. God save the King. ■

Between 1912 and 1913 the Government of Ireland Bill was rejected twice by the House of Lords. Its final passage was scheduled for 1914, and as both sides made their preparations to meet that eventuality, the Cabinet faced the prospect of using its armed forces to enforce Home Rule. In an address at Bradford in March 1914, Winston Churchill left no doubt that the government was prepared to face the consequences of armed revolt over Home Rule.

2.29 Winston Churchill, speech at Bradford, 15 March 1914 (reported in the *Daily Telegraph*, 16 March 1914).

■ ... It is enough for Liberals to remember that these Ulstermen are anxious and unhappy, and alarmed and resentful; that in Ireland we seek to allay old hatreds and not to kindle new ones; that we seek to unite and not to divide ... Therefore I have always hoped, and always urged, that a fair and full offer should be made to Northeast Ulster, in all friendship and goodwill ...

That offer has been made. (Cheers.) It was made last Monday by the Prime Minister. (Cheers.) ... God forbid that I should ever stand in the path of conciliation. But it seems to me, and I hope it will seem to you, that in principle – I do not speak of details – this is the last offer which his Majesty's Government can make, or ought to make. (Loud and prolonged cheers.) Consider what that offer is! Any Ulster county, upon the request of a fifth of the electors, can, by simply voting, stand out for six years of the whole operation of the Home Rule Bill, and remain exactly as they are. That is to say, that two General Elections in this country must take place before any county exercising this option would be compelled to change the system of government under which it has hitherto been administered....Before the offer was made the Unionist Party demanded exclusion or a General Election. We have now given them both. (Laughter and cheers.) Unless they had exclusion or a General Election they said there would be civil war. They have got both, and they still tell us there is going to be civil war ...

Mr Bonar Law is really in some respects a public danger. He believes – apparently he measures others by what he finds in himself – that these threats of force are the only means by which settlement can be achieved. He quite sincerely thinks, if I may judge from his speeches, that he has only to continue to make them to terrorise the Government and wreck the Home Rule Bill, and force his way into the councils of the sovereign.

That is a disastrous and fatal delusion. Those who think that these events can be adjusted by the use of threats of violence against the Government do not know the British democracy, they do not know England, they do not know Asquith. (Cheers.) ....

From the language which is employed, it would almost seem that we are face to face with a disposition on the part of some sections of the propertied classes to subvert the system of Parliamentary Government, and to challenge the civil and the constitutional foundations of society. Against such a mood, were it ever to manifest itself in action, there is no lawful measure from which a Government can shrink, and there is no lawful measure from which this Government will shrink.

Bloodshed, no doubt, is lamentable ... But there are worse things than bloodshed, even on an extensive scale. ■

The government's new firmness on Home Rule was complicated by growing doubts over the reliability of the armed forces and police in enforcing Home Rule in Ulster. The 'Curragh mutiny' in March underscored such fears.

The Government's final offer on Home Rule was rejected by Redmond and the Irish Nationalists at the end of June 1914 in an atmosphere of tension. Further attempts at reconciliation, under the sponsorship of the King, failed in July. Military advice to the Cabinet at this time was grim.

2.30 **Army memorandum to the Cabinet on the military situation in Ireland, 4 July 1914 (PRO CAB 37/120/81).**

■   **SECRET**

A MEMORANDUM BY THE MILITARY MEMBERS OF THE ARMY COUNCIL ON THE MILITARY SITUATION IN IRELAND.

1. At the present time two opposing forces, with approximately a total strength of 200,000 men, are being systematically and deliberately raised, trained equipped and organized on a military basis in Ireland.

2. In view of this fact we, as the responsible military advisers to His Majesty's Government, deem it to be our duty to point out that if, unfortunately, these two large forces should come into conflict, a situation may arise which may require the whole of our available forces at home to deal with.

3. As we have not been informed what policy the Government proposes to adopt in the event of such a conflict, it is not possible for us to estimate the number of troops which might be required to restore order. No plan of operations of this nature has been prepared or even considered by the War Office, and no plan can, in the circumstances, be prepared.

4. We think it likely, however, that it might be necessary to employ the whole of our Expeditionary Force to restore order, and this would probably involve general mobilization, placing Special Reserve troops in the ports, and assembling the Local and Central Forces now composed of Territorial troops.

5. So far as numbers alone are concerned there might be no great difficulty in finding garrisons for the ports or in providing a Central Force, but a factor which cannot be overlooked is that as the Territorial Force cannot be used to maintain order in Great Britain, we should probably be unable to use the whole of our six divisions in Ireland.

6. A still more important factor is that if the whole of our Expeditionary Force were used in Ireland and to maintain order in Great Britain we should be quite incapable of meeting our obligations abroad, and in this connection India and Egypt must be specially borne in mind. It seems to us at least possible that unrest in India and in Egypt may follow the commencement of such operations, whilst certain countries in Europe may take this opportunity of creating trouble … ■

At the end of the month, when a foiled nationalist gun-running incident resulted in the death of three civilians after soldiers opened fire, it seemed that Ireland, not events on the Continent, posed the greatest threat to the fabric of the British state. But the sudden outbreak of war in Europe interrupted, and the threat of civil war over home rule receded.

CHAPTER THREE

The Road to Crisis: Britain and the Origins of the First World War, 1900–1914

BRITAIN's dominance of world affairs in the nineteenth century had been based on its geography, colonial possessions and early Industrial Revolution. Because of the shelter from continental turmoil provided by the English Channel there had been no need for a large standing army, and it had been possible for several centuries to concentrate on the development of a large and commanding navy. That natural barrier also enabled the British to concentrate on the development of an empire and international trade while their rivals on the Continent fought among themselves. As the world's first industrial nation, Britain was therefore uniquely placed to take advantage of the commercial opportunities offered by its command of the seas and territorial possessions abroad. By the middle of the nineteenth century, the British dominance of the world economy was unprecedented. But that superpower status was the product of a set of singular circumstances, and the subsequent 'decline' of British power was inevitable as other nations industrialised.

Nevertheless, the British have experienced the twentieth century from the perspective of a declining world power. As we have seen in Chapter 1, there was already widespread anxiety in 1900 over economic competition from abroad. In foreign affairs, the position was equally acute. The commitments involved in protecting the Empire left the navy hopelessly overstretched. While British military power was still impressive, it was not possible to compete against the expanding naval power of Japan, Germany, France and the United States simultaneously. Thus the 'splendid isolation' which Britain had enjoyed, when the 'two-power standard' of maintaining a navy stronger than that of the next two powers combined had been a realistic proposition, gave way increasingly to a system of *ententes* and agreements before the First World War. This new system was intended to avoid military confrontation. In spite of the efforts of the Foreign Office, however, Britain failed to reach an understanding with Germany, or to clarify its new obligations to France and Russia. Inexorably, Britain was drawn into a web of entanglements which culminated in the onset of the First World War in the summer of 1914.

The Impact of the Boer War

The difficulties encountered during the Boer War of 1899–1902 came as a shock to the British and led to a series of major reforms. Although since 1815 the British had controlled the Cape Colony in southern Africa, two independent republics, the Transvaal and the Orange Free State, had been established by the Boers, the descendants of Dutch settlers in the region. British administrators had not interfered with these developments, but political tension increased rapidly after gold was discovered in the Transvaal in 1886, and British settlers flocked there. The British from this time were increasingly concerned for the safety of their position in the region, as German influence and investment in the Transvaal increased, and British immigrants or *uitlanders* were disenfranchised and restive. The disastrous Jameson raid which began in December 1895, supported by Cecil Rhodes, the premier of the Cape Colony, failed in its aim of overthrowing the government of the Transvaal, and the subsequent build-up of British forces in southern Africa exacerbated Anglo-Boer tension. But when the Boers declared war on Britain in October 1899, the British confidently saw this as an opportunity of confirming their position. But by the time that the Peace of Vereeniging brought hostilities to an end in 1902, it had taken nearly three years and half a million British soldiers to defeat the Boers. There was a universal feeling that the nation had failed to pass an important test of its strength and 'efficiency'.

The initial success of the Boers came as a profound shock to the British. In the so-called 'black week' of 10–15 December 1899 the Boers inflicted a series of defeats on the ill-organised British army. The account of these events written by the author Arthur Conan Doyle conveys something of the effect which this had on public opinion at home.

3.1   **Arthur Conan Doyle, *The Great Boer War: A Two Years' Record, 1899–1901*, 1901 (London, Smith, Elder, 2nd edn, pp. 195–7).**

■ The week which extended from December 10th to December 17th, 1899, was the blackest one known during our generation, and the most disastrous for British arms during the century. We had in the short space of seven days lost, beyond all extenuation or excuse, three separate actions. No single defeat was of vital importance in itself, but the cumulative effect, occurring as they did to each of the main British forces in South Africa, was very great. The total loss amounted to about 3,000 men and twelve guns, while the indirect effects in the way of loss of prestige to ourselves and increased confidence and more numerous recruits to our enemy were incalculable.

It is singular to glance at the extracts from the European press at that time and to observe the delight and foolish exaltation with which our reverses were received ... Never again, I trust, on any pretext will a British guinea be spent or a British soldier or sailor shed his blood for such allies. The political lesson of this war has been that we should make ourselves strong within the empire, and let all outside it, save only our kinsmen of America, go their own way and meet their own fate without let or hindrance from us ... Such was the wave of feeling over the country that it was impossible to hold a peace meeting anywhere without a certainty of riot. ■

The British succeeded in defeating the Boer army in 1900. But in the two years of guerrilla warfare which followed, the ruthlessness of the new military leadership in breaking the remaining Boer resistance drew widespread condemnation, both at home and abroad. Conditions in the 'concentration camps' were brought to wider public attention by Emily Hobhouse, who visited South Africa as a representative of the South African Women and Children Distress Fund in 1901.

3.2   **Emily Hobhouse, *Report of a Visit to the Camps of Women and Children in the Cape and Orange River Colonies*, 1901 (London, Friars Printing Association, pp. 3–6).**

■   THE BLOEMFONTEIN CAMP

January 26th

The exile camp here is a good two miles from the town, dumped down on the southern slope of a Kopje, right out on to the bare brown veldt, not a vestige of a tree in any direction, nor shade of any description ... There are nearly 2,000 people in this one camp...and over 900 children ...

I call this camp a system of wholesale cruelty. It can never be wiped out of the memories of the people ... To keep these camps going is murder to the children ...

January 31st

I was at the camp to-day, and just in one little corner this is the sort of thing I found. The nurse, underfed and overworked, just sinking on to her bed, hardly able to hold herself up, after coping with some thirty typhoid and other patients, with only the untrained help of two Boer girls – cooking as well as nursing to do herself.

Next I was called to see a woman panting in the heat, just sickening for her confinement ... Next tent, a six months' baby gasping its life out on its mother's knee. Next, a child recovering from measles, sent back from hospital before it could walk, stretched on the ground, white and wan ... Next a girl of twenty-one lay dying on a stretcher. The father, a big, gentle Boer, kneeling beside her; while, next tent, his wife was watching a child of six, also dying, and one of about five drooping. Already this couple had lost three children in the hospital, and so would not let these go, though I begged hard to take them out of the hot tent. 'We must watch these our-selves,' he said ... Then a man came up and said ... 'come and see my child, sick for nearly three months'. It was a dear little chap of four, and nothing left of him but his great brown eyes and white teeth, from which the lips were drawn back, too thin to close. His body was emaciated ... I can't describe what it is to see these children lying about in a state of collapse. It's just exactly like faded flowers thrown away. And one has to stand and look on at such misery, and be able to do almost nothing.

April 22

Here I am again in Bloemfontein. I arrived yesterday … The camp work grows so vast and so rapidly that I feel it is almost impossible to cope with it. Here there are now 4,000 or double the number I left six weeks ago … If only the camps had remained the size they were even six weeks ago, I saw some chance of getting them well in hand, organizing and dealing with the distress. But this sudden influx of hundreds and thousands has upset everything, and reduced us all to a state bordering on despair. ■

Politically, the split in the Liberal Party between the pro- and anti-Boers weakened its position in the first years of the century. The anti-Boer Liberal 'imperialists' were led by the former Prime Minister, Lord Rosebery. The pro-Boers were led by former party leader Lewis Harcourt, while the current leader, Henry Campbell-Bannerman, attempted to steer a middle course between the two. In this cartoon from Punch, *the bemused old Liberal Party ponders her destination.*

3.3   **Cartoon by John Tenniel, 'So perplexing', *Punch*, 1 August 1900.**

"SO PERPLEXING!"

Old Liberal Party. "OH, DEARY ME! WHICH PLATFORM SHALL I TAKE?"

International criticism of Britain's South African policy, particularly in Germany and France, made strong links within the Empire seem imperative to safeguard its international position. Joseph Chamberlain, as we have seen in Chapter 1, began campaigning for a system of imperial tariff preferences – a single imperial market – in 1903. At the Colonial Conference of 1902, Chamberlain made an impassioned plea to the Dominions for greater financial contributions towards the cost of imperial defence, borne overwhelmingly by Britain.

3.4   Joseph Chamberlain, speech to the Colonial Conference, 1 July 1902 (in Julian Amery, *The Life of Joseph Chamberlain. Vol. Four: 1901–1903*, London, Macmillan, 1951, pp. 420–1).

■ … Our paramount object is to strengthen the bonds which unite us, and there are only three principal avenues by which we can approach this object. They are: through our political relations in the first place; secondly, by some kind of commercial union; in the third place, by considering the questions which arise out of Imperial defence … I may be considered, perhaps, to be a dreamer, or too enthusiastic, but I do not hesitate to say that, in my opinion, the political federation of the Empire is within the limits of possibility. I recognise, as fully as anyone can do, the difficulties which would attend such a great change in our constitutional system … But … it is my opinion that, as time goes on, there will be a continually growing sense of the common interests which unite us, and also perhaps, which is equally important, of the common dangers which threaten us … I would venture to refer to an expression in an eloquent speech of my right honourable friend, the Premier of the Dominion of Canada … 'If you want our aid call us to your Councils.' Gentlemen, we do want your aid. We do require your assistance in the administration of the vast Empire which is yours as well as ours. The weary Titan staggers under the too vast orb of its fate. We have borne the burden for many years. We think it is time that our children should assist us to support it, and whenever you make the request to us, be very sure that we shall hasten gladly to call you to our councils. If you are prepared at any time to take any share, any proportionate share, in the burdens of the empire, we are prepared to meet you with any proposal for giving to you a corresponding voice in the policy of the Empire … ■

A further far-reaching effect of the Boer War on Britain was the reorganisation of the government's defence bureaucracy. This was initiated in response to the early disasters of the military campaign, as well as to the growing realisation that the whole question of defence policy was in need of review, given the rapidly changing international environment of the time. Under Arthur Balfour's leadership, the inept Cabinet Defence Committee was reconstituted in 1902 as the Committee of Imperial Defence (CID), and now included permanent professional advisers as well as government ministers. In 1904 the War Office (Reconstitution) Committee, chaired by Lord Esher, urged that the CID should be given a permanent staff. The subsequent incorporation of a permanent secretariat led by Sir George Clarke was a constitutional innovation. For the first time, a committee of the Cabinet was given a modern civil service apparatus. Lord Esher's reasoning for this reform is set out here.

3.5   *Report of the War Office (Reconstitution) Committee,* 1904 (Cd 1932, PP VIII, 1904, pp. 3–4).

■ **1.** We have been directed to make recommendations for the reconstitution of the War Office. Our task, as we understand it, is specially difficult from the fact that for many years this Department of State has been administered from the point of view of peace. It is necessary to make a complete breach with the past, and to endeavour to reconstitute the War Office with a single eye to the effective training and preparation of the Military Forces of the Crown for war. Thus improvements of the existing machinery cannot alone suffice to remedy the grave evils which the recent war has disclosed. Those evils must, in great part, be traced to a deeper source than defects in the administration of the War Office. The evidence taken by the Royal Commission proves that the Cabinet had in 1899 no adequate means of obtaining reasoned opinions on which to base a war policy. We are strongly impressed by the gravity of the danger thus incurred, which would, in circumstances easily imagined, lead to national disaster. At the outset of our inquiry, therefore, we are driven to the conclusion that no measure of War Office reform will avail, unless it is associated with provision for obtaining and collating for the use of the Cabinet all the information and the expert advice required for the shaping of national policy in war, and for determining the necessary preparations in peace. Such information and advice must necessarily embrace not only the sphere of the War Office, but those of the Admiralty and of other offices of State.

2. The Defence Committee of the Cabinet, as now reconstituted, is intended to fulfil this imperative requirement; but we are convinced that further development is essential. A committee which contains no permanent nucleus, and which is composed of political and professional members, each preoccupied with administrative duties widely differing, cannot, in our opinion, deal adequately with the complex questions of Imperial defence. Valuable as is the work which this Committee has accomplished, the fact remains that there is no one charged with the duty of making a continuous study of these questions, of exercising due foresight in regard to the changing conditions produced by external developments, and of drawing from the several departments of State, and arranging in convenient form for the use of the Cabinet, such information as may at any moment be required. Failing the provision of such an equipment, we are convinced that the Government cannot be in a position to arrive at sound conclusions in regard either to the needs of war or to the preparations required in peace. We believe that the result has been, and must be, misdirected effort, involving risk on the one hand and waste on the other. The object should be to secure for the British Empire, with the least possible derangement of existing machinery, the immense advantages which the General Staff has conferred upon Germany ...

7. The existing Defence Committee has, under the auspices of the present Prime Minister, proved capable of useful work. There have been, however, in the past, and there will be in the future, Prime Ministers to whom the great questions of Imperial defence do not appeal. The Committee is necessarily a changing body. It is not safe to trust matters affecting national security to the chance of a favourable combination of personal character-istics. We are, therefore, convinced that the addition of a permanent nucleus to the Defence Committee is essential as the only valid guarantee (1) that vitally important work with which no one is now charged shall be continuously and consistently carried on, and (2) that the Prime Minister shall have at his disposal all the information needed for the due fulfilment of his weighty responsibilities. And, further, we can conceive no other means of focusing questions of national defence under existing conditions without involving constitutional changes which would be undesirable if not impracticable ... ∎

The End of Splendid Isolation

So long as British military and economic power could outmatch any combination of the country's rivals, there had been no need to become enmeshed in a system of diplomatic alliances. But this period of 'splendid isolation' was coming to an end by 1900, as growing awareness of relative decline forced strategists to consider a series of local *ententes*, increasingly necessary to ensure national security and to keep defence spending within reasonable limits. International criticism of the British role in the Boer War, as well as a series of imperial conflicts around the globe, led to the conclusion of a series of agreements with rival powers.

In 1900 and 1901 the British signed two treaties with the United States, which conceded to the Americans the right to build and fortify a canal across Panama, linking their Atlantic and Pacific navies. In effect, Britain had accepted US naval dominance in the Americas, and subseqently withdrew nearly all its forces from that arena; henceforward the British were bound to court US friendship, as the only realistic way to ensure the protection of Canada and British holdings in that hemisphere. Agreement in other regions, however, would not prove so straightforward.

The Far East closely followed the Americas as a prime focus for British strategists. Russia's coercion of China in 1901, which resulted in its virtual control of Manchuria, seemed to portend the partition of China – a new imperial scramble which the British could ill afford. In order to contend with the allied Franco-Russian forces there, it became increasingly logical to come to an understanding with Japan. In 1901 the First Lord of the Admiralty, Lord Selborne, argued the case for an Anglo-Japanese treaty, a view shared by the Treasury. An agreement with Japan was signed in 1902. In 1905, the agreement was renewed and extended.

3.6   Lord Selborne, 'The balance of naval power in the Far East', 4 September 1901 (PRO CAB 37/58/87).

■ It is true that victory in European waters would scarcely be dimmed by even serious disasters in the Far East, but its value, though not obliterated, would be impaired to a dangerous degree if British naval power in the Far East were crushed out of existence.

We could afford to lose a certain number of merchantmen, or even to see a weaker squadron of battleships blockaded for a time in Hong Kong; but we could not afford to see our Chinese trade disappear, or to see Hong Kong and Singapore fall, particularly not at a moment when a military struggle with Russia might be in progress on the confines of India ...

The effect of [having to reinforce the China Station] would be twofold. It would leave us with little or nothing more than a bare equality of strength in the Channel and Mediterranean, and a bare equality at the heart of the Empire is a dangerous risk. It would strain our naval system greatly and would add to our expenditure on the manning of the Navy ... The case would bear a different aspect were we assured the alliance of Japan.

Great Britain and Japan together would next year be able to show eleven battleships against the French and Russian nine, as well as a preponderance of cruisers.

Great Britain would be under no necessity of adding to the number of battleships on the China Station, and at last would be in a position to contemplate the possibility of shortly establishing a small margin of superiority in reserve at home; the number of our cruisers could be reduced on that station, and increased on other stations where badly required; our Far Eastern trade and possessions would be secure. ■

The effects of the Anglo-Japanese agreement were far-reaching. The very real possibility of conflict between Japan and Russia made it vital that their respective allies, Britain and France, come to an understanding lest they become drawn into a confrontation neither desired. An Anglo-French entente *did indeed follow rapidly upon the outbreak of the Russo-Japanese War in February 1904. The agreement, consisting of two conventions, a declaration on Morocco and a series of articles, largely settled the outstanding differences over colonial issues. At the heart of the* entente *lay a settlement of Anglo-French rivalry in North Africa: in return for the abandonment of French claims on Egypt, Britain agreed to support the French claims in Morocco. This latter agreement, however, was made in secret, and would prove to be a major cause for worry in the coming years.*

3.7   **Despatch to His Majesty's Ambassador at Paris forwarding agreements between Great Britain and France, 8 April 1904 (Cd 1952, PP CX, 1904, pp. 9-11).**

■

ARTICLE I

His Britannic Majesty's Government declare that they have no intention of altering the political status of Egypt.

The Government of the French Republic, for their part, declare that they will not obstruct the action of Great Britain in that country by asking that a limit of time be fixed for the British occupation ...

ARTICLE II

The Government of the French Republic declare that they have no intention of altering the political status of Morocco.

His Britannic Majesty's Government, for their part, recognize that it appertains to France, more particularly as a Power whose dominions are coterminous for a great distance with those of Morocco, to preserve order in that country, and to provide assistance for the purpose of all administrative, economic, financial, and military reforms which it may require ...

ARTICLE VI

In order to insure the free passage of the Suez Canal, His Britannic Majesty's Government declare that they adhere to the stipulations of the Treaty of the 29th October, 1888, and that they agree to their being put in force ...

ARTICLE VII

In order to secure the free passage of the Straits of Gibraltar, the two Governments agree not to permit the erection of any fortifications or strategic works on that portion of the coast of Morocco comprised between, but not including, Melilla and the heights which command the right bank of the River Sebou ...

ARTICLE IX

The two Governments agree to afford to one another their diplomatic support, in order to obtain the execution of the clauses of the present Declaration regarding Egypt and Morocco ... ■

Britain's commitment to support the French position in Morocco contributed to the deterioration of Anglo-German relations after 1904. German intervention in Morocco was taken by the British as a determined effort to ruin the new Anglo-French entente. The French, vulnerable to German bullying now that their traditional ally, Russia, was weakened as a result of the war with Japan, looked increasingly to the British entente to bolster their own diplomatic position.

In addition the new Liberal Foreign Secretary, Sir Edward Grey, was more concerned with European affairs than his predecessor, Lord Lansdowne, had been. For Grey, the diplomacy of the alliances was the best means of containing German restlessness on the Continent. Grey was thus disposed to support the French side in the conference held at Algeciras in January 1906, between Germany and France, to reach a settlement in the Moroccan dispute. Fearing that a vulnerable France would move closer to Germany, Grey, although unwilling to enter into a formal alliance, did agree to joint Anglo-French military discussions, which began early in 1906. Although it was made clear that this did not represent a commitment to come to the aid of France in the event of an attack by a third party, his failure to inform the Cabinet of this development until 1911, and the uncertainty surrounding the degree of commitment implied by the talks, were widely criticised when they were made known. The contrasting opinions of Lord Grey and Lloyd George give some idea of the tensions within the Cabinet in these years.

3.8   **Lord Grey, *Twenty-Five Years, 1892–1916, Vol. I*, 1925 (London, Hodder and Stoughton, pp. 83–99).**

■ My object ... was to make the Germans understand that the situation was serious, and let the French feel that we were sympathetic, while carefully avoiding anything that might raise expectations in their minds which this country might not fulfil. To do this it was necessary to avoid bluff in the one case and promises in the other.

Campbell-Bannerman was apprehensive lest the military conversations should create an obligation or at least an 'honourable understanding'. ... But the honourable understanding between myself and M. Cambon was very clear, and it was that nothing that passed between French and British military authorities was to entail or imply any obligation whatever on either Government ...

There has been much criticism of the line we took. It has been urged that we ought to have given France a definite promise of support, if not in 1906, at any rate at some time before the war came; that we ought to contend that even the non-committal preparation that we did make was improper and impolitic ...

The Algeciras Conference crisis passed; the fact of the military conversations was not at that time made known to the Cabinet generally, but must subsequently have become known to those Ministers who attended the Committee of Imperial Defence. Nothing more respecting it appears in my papers till 1911 ...

The Agadir affair ... brought the military conversations into prominence. They must have been familiar to several members of the Cabinet in discussion at the Committee of Imperial Defence, and in 1912 the fact of their taking place became known to other members of the Cabinet... The only difficulty arose from the thing having gone on so long without the Cabinet generally being informed. Ministers who now heard of these military conversations for the first time suspected that there was something to conceal ... There was a demand that the fact of the military conversations being non-committal should be put into writing ...

The letter, as approved by the Cabinet, was signed and given by me to Cambon, and I received one in similar terms from him in exchange. From that time onwards every Minister knew how we stood ... ■

3.9   **David Lloyd George, *War Memoirs of David Lloyd George, Vol. I*, 1938 (London, Odhams Press, pp. 28–30).**

■ There was a reticence and a secrecy which practically ruled out three-fourths of the Cabinet from the chance of making any genuine contribution to the momentous questions then fermenting on the continent of Europe, which ultimately ended in an explosion that almost shattered the civilisation of the world. During the whole of those eight years, when I was a member of the Cabinet, I can recall no ... review of the European situation being given to us ... There was in the Cabinet an air of 'hush hush' about every allusion to our relations with France, Russia and Germany. Direct questions were always answered with civility, but were not encouraged. We were made to feel that, in these matters, we were reaching our hands towards the mysteries, and that we were too young in the priesthood to presume to enter into the sanctuary reserved for the elect. So we confined our inquisitiveness and our counsel to the more mundane affairs in which we had taken part in Opposition during the whole of our political careers ...

There is no more conspicuous example of this kind of suppression of vital information than the way in which the military arrangements we entered into with France were kept from the Cabinet for six years ... When in 1912 ... Sir Edward Grey communicated these negotiations and arrangements to the Cabinet the majority of its Members were aghast. Hostility scarcely represents the strength of the sentiment which the revelation aroused: it was more akin to consternation ... a number of Cabinet Ministers were not reconciled to the action taken by the Foreign Office, the War Office and the Admiralty, and these commitments undoubtedly added a good deal to the suspicions which made the task of Sir Edward Grey in securing unanimity in 1914 very much more difficult. ■

At Algeciras the British were careful to back French claims for the special position in Morocco which had been agreed under the terms of the 1904 Anglo-French convention. Foreign Secretary Grey's suspicions of Germany's diplomatic objectives were confirmed by its behaviour over the Moroccan question; and the Act of Algeciras (7 April 1906), concluded between the Germans and the French, which confirmed a dominant French position in a still nominally independent Morocco, was a victory for the entente. The following memorandum by Grey illustrates the tangled concerns of the British at this time.

3.10   **Sir Edward Grey, memorandum on Franco-German tension in Morocco, 20 February 1906 (in G.P. Gooch and Harold Temperley, eds, *British Documents on the Origins of the War, 1898–1914. Vol. III: The Testing of the Entente, 1904–1906*, London, HMSO, 1928, pp. 266–7).**

■ ... If there is war between France and Germany it will be very difficult for us to keep out of it. The *Entente* and still more the constant and emphatic demonstrations of affection (official, naval, political, commercial, Municipal and in the Press), have created in France a belief that we should support her in war. The last report from our naval attache at Toulon said that all the French officers took this for granted ... If this expectation is disappointed the French will never forgive us.

There would also I think be a general feeling in every country that we had behaved meanly and left France in the lurch. The United States would despise us, Russia would not think it worth while to make a friendly arrangement with us about Asia, Japan would prepare to re-insure herself elsewhere, we should be left without a friend and without the power of making a friend and Germany would take some pleasure, after what has passed, in exploiting the whole situation to our disadvantage, very likely by stirring up trouble through the Sultan of Turkey in Egypt ...

On the other hand the prospect of a European War and of our being involved in it is horrible.

I have also a further point in view. The door is being kept open by us for a *rapprochement* with Russia; there is at least a prospect that when Russia is re-established we shall find ourselves on good terms with her. An *entente* between Russia, France and ourselves would be absolutely secure. If it is necessary to check Germany it could then be done. The present is the most unfavourable moment for attempting to check her. Is it not a grave mistake, if there must be a quarrel with Germany for France or ourselves, to let Germany choose the moment which best suits her.

There is a possibility that war may come before these suggestions of mine can be developed in diplomacy. If so it will only be because Germany has made up her mind that she wants war and intends to have it anyhow, which I do not believe is the case. But I think we ought in our own minds to face the question now, whether we can keep out of war, if war breaks out between France and Germany. The more I review the situation the more it appears to me that we cannot, without losing our good name and our friends and wrecking our policy and position in the world. ■

Grey's primary objective in Europe at this time was to secure an agreement with Russia, in order to complete an alliance system aimed at deterring German aggression in Europe. After protracted negotiations, an Anglo-Russian convention was signed on 31 August 1907. In theory, it resolved the outstanding colonial disputes between the two countries and paved the way for broader diplomatic cooperation.

3.11   Foreign Office, memorandum respecting the Anglo-Russian convention, 29 January 1908 (in G.P. Gooch and Harold Temperley, eds, *British Documents on the Origins of the War, 1898–1914. Vol. IV. The Anglo-Russian Rapprochement, 1903–1907*, London, HMSO, 1929, pp. 613–16).

■   PERSIA

... The creation of a Russian and British sphere of influence is in reality only a self-denying Ordinance, by which each Government pledge themselves not to seek for concessions in the other's sphere. Other Powers are at liberty, as formerly, to seek concessions all over Persia, and British trade will be carried on in the Russian and neutral zones on the same terms as hitherto and as the trade of other foreign countries, the sole restriction on British enterprise being that British concessions cannot be sought in the Russian zone ...

AFGHANISTAN

We have now for the first time obtained from Russia, in writing and in the form of a definite Treaty engagement, assurances on the following three points, which had hitherto been only verbal and, as the Russian Government stated, not binding indefinitely upon them:–

1. That the Russian Government consider Afghanistan as outside the sphere of Russian influence.

2. That all their political relations with Afghanistan shall be conducted through the intermediary of His Majesty's Government.

3. That they will not send any Agents into Afghanistan ...

THIBET

... The position is that, in return for agreeing to embody the assurances of the late Government in a formal document, we have obtained similar assurances from Russia; and that in addition, we actually get formal Russian consent to the maintenance of a preferential position for Great Britain in Thibet over all other foreign countries in regard to frontier and commercial matters ...

With regard to the Anglo-Russian Convention as a whole, it may be generally stated that it has successfully removed causes of friction between Great Britain and Russia in Asia, and has enabled the two Powers to co-operate usefully together in Persia in maintaining a peaceful policy which it would quite recently have been difficult to secure had no such Convention existed. The removal of all causes of discord in Asia will no doubt contribute to more harmonious relations between the two powers in Europe. ■

Anglo-German Tension: Cold War or *Détente*?

Between 1900 and 1907 British foreign policy had undergone a remarkably rapid transformation. In response to the international challenges posed by the increasing strength of rival powers across the globe, agreements had been reached with the United States, Japan, France and Russia. The diplomatic 'appeasement' of these powers had been achieved, moreover, without significant opposition at home. The one nation with which this approach did not work was Germany. Although similar attempts were made by the British to reach an understanding with the Kaiser, relations between Britain and Germany became a 'cold war', expressed primarily through an expensive naval arms race.

The threat posed by Germany's sudden growth into a first-rank military and economic power was, as discussed in Chapter 1, well understood in Britain by the turn of the century. But opinion at home was divided in its approach towards Germany. While many believed in fostering good relations with this young and powerful neighbour, it was only sensible to redirect defence policy to take account of the new threat in the North Sea.

The challenge posed by the rise of German naval power was widely understood. In 1903, for example, the Anglo-Irish writer and champion of Irish nationalism Erskine Childers published The Riddle of the Sands, *an early spy novel which warned of British vulnerability to the growing German command of the North Sea and the Baltic.*

3.12   **Erskine Childers, *The Riddle of the Sands*, 1903 (London, Penguin edn, 1978, pp. 119–21).**

■ We're a maritime nation – we've grown by the sea and live by it; if we lose command of it we starve. We're unique in that way, just as our huge empire, only linked by the sea, is unique. And yet, read Brassey, Dilke, and those 'Naval Annuals', and see what mountains of apathy and conceit have had to be tackled. It's not the people's fault. We've been safe so long, and grown so rich, that we've forgotten what we owe it to. But there's no excuse for those blockheads of statesmen, as they call themselves, who are paid to see things as they are …

'We're improving, aren't we?'

'Oh, of course, we are! But it's a constant uphill fight; and we aren't ready.' … This is only a sample of many similar conversations that we afterwards held, always culminating in the burning question of Germany … He used to listen rapt while I described her marvellous awakening in the last generation, under the strength and wisdom of her rulers; her intense patriotic ardour; her seething industrial activity, and, most potent of all, the forces that are moulding modern Europe, her dream of a colonial empire, entailing her transformation from a land-power to a sea-power. Impregnably based on vast territorial resources which we cannot molest, the dim instincts of her people, not merely directed but anticipated by the genius of her ruling house, our great trade rivals of the present, our great naval rival of the future, she grows, and strengthens, and waits, an ever more formidable factor in the future of our delicate network of empire, sensitive as gossamer to external shocks, and radiating from an island whose commerce is its life, and which depends even for its daily ration of bread on the free passage of the seas.

'And we aren't ready for her,' Davies would say; 'we don't look her way. We have no naval base in the North Sea, and no North Sea Fleet. Our best battleships are too deep in draught for North Sea work. And, to crown all, we were asses enough to give her Heligoland, which commands her North Sea coast. And supposing she collars Holland; isn't there some talk of that?'

That would lead me to describe the swollen ambitions of the Pan-Germanic party, and its ceaseless intrigues to promote the absorption of Austia, Switzerland, and – a direct and flagrant menace to ourselves – of Holland.

'I don't blame them,' said Davies, who, for all his patriotism, had not a particle of racial spleen in his composition. 'I don't blame them; their Rhine ceases to be German just when it begins to be most valuable. The mouth is Dutch, and would give them magnificent ports just opposite British shores. *We* can't talk about conquest and grabbing. We've collared a fine share of the world, and they've every right to be jealous. Let them hate us, and say so; it'll teach us to buck up; and that's what really matters.' ∎

Under the direction of the First Sea Lord between 1904 and 1910, Sir John Fisher, British naval policy was thoroughly overhauled and reorganised, largely in response to the rapid expansion of the German fleet. The agreements reached with the United States, Japan and France in the first decade of the century enabled Fisher to concentrate naval power in home waters, and to focus on speed and efficiency. On 10 February 1906 HMS Dreadnought *was launched at Portsmouth. A new class of battleship – larger, faster and better armoured than anything built previously – the* Dreadnought *rendered all existing battleships obsolete.*

3.13   HMS *Dreadnought* **in 1906 (National Maritime Museum, London).**

Because the Dreadnought *made existing battleships obsolete, its launch signalled the beginning of a naval arms race with Germany. As discussed in Chapter 1, the new Liberal government was under intense pressure to find money to finance social reform at home. Many influential Liberals called for an understanding with Germany to avoid the need for an expensive naval building programme. Thus, partly for fiscal reasons and partly as a signal to the forthcoming international arms limitations talks at The Hague, the government proceeded with the construction of only two Dreadnought-class battleships in the 1906–7 estimates. The Hague Conference (15 June to 18 October 1907) achieved little headway. There proved to be little enthusiasm for disarmament on the Continent at this time, in spite of hopes within Liberal circles.*

The continued German naval build-up was greeted in Britain with increasing dismay from 1907. At the Foreign Office, many officials were pressing home the message that German intentions were ultimately hostile and must be confronted. Eyre Crow, senior clerk in the Western Department, was particularly forceful on this issue.

3.14   Eyre Crow, memorandum on British relations with France and Germany, 1 January 1907 (PRO FO 371/257).

■ ... If, merely by way of analogy and illustration, a comparison not intended to be either literally exact or disrespectful be permitted, the action of Germany towards this country since 1890 might be likened not inappropriately to that of a professional blackmailer, whose extortions are wrung from his victims by the threat of some vague and dreadful consequences in case of a refusal. To give way to the blackmailer's menaces enriches him, but it has long been proved by uniform experience that, although this may secure for the victim temporary peace, it is certain to lead to renewed molestation and higher demands after ever-shortening periods of amicable forbearance. The blackmailer's trade is generally ruined by the first resolute stand made against his exactions and the determination rather to face all risks of a possibly disagreeable situation than to continue in the path of endless concessions. But, failing such determination, it is more than probable that the relations between the two parties will grow steadily worse.

Either Germany is definitely aiming at a general political hegemony and maritime ascendency, threatening the independence of her neighbours and ultimately the existence of England;·

Or Germany, free from any such clear-cut ambition, and thinking for the present merely of using her legitimate position and influence as one of the leading Powers in the council of nations, is seeking to promote her foreign commerce, spread the benefits of German culture, extend the scope of her national energies, and create fresh German interests all over the world wherever and whenever a peaceful opportunity offers, leaving it to an uncertain future to decide whether the occurrence of great changes in the world may not some day assign to Germany a larger share of direct political action over regions not now a part of her dominions, without that violation of the established rights of other countries which would be involved in any such action under existing political conditions.

In either case Germany would clearly be wise to build as powerful a navy as she can afford ...

It is clear that the second scheme (of semi-independent evolution, not entirely unaided by statecraft) may at any stage merge into the first, or conscious-design scheme....and against such danger, whether actual or contingent, the same general line of conduct seems prescribed ...

So long as England remains faithful to the general principle of the preservation of the balance of power, her interests would not be served by Germany being reduced to the rank of a weak Power, as this might easily lead to a Franco-Russian predominance equally, if not more, formidable to the British Empire. There are no existing German rights, territorial or other, which this country could wish to see diminished. Therefore, so long as Germany's action does not overstep the line of legitimate protection of existing rights she can always count upon the sympathy and good-will, and even the moral support, of England. ■

Germanophobes in the Foreign Office such as Eyre Crow backed Admiralty demands for an expanded naval building programme. But this was an issue subject to heated Cabinet debate in this period. When Asquith became Prime Minister in April 1908 the position of the naval 'economists' – those who wanted to cut spending – was strengthened. Lloyd George and Churchill became strong advocates of an Anglo-German naval agreement to obviate the need for an arms race, and Grey's foreign policy came under increasing pressure.

**3.15   Winston Churchill, speech to miners at Swansea, 15 August 1908
(reported in *The Times*, 17 August 1908).**

■ ... I think it is greatly to be deprecated that persons should try to spread the belief in this country that war between Great Britain and Germany is inevitable. It is all nonsense. (Cheers.) In the first place, the alarmists have no ground whatever for their panic or fear. This country is an island and no government which is in power in this country in the near future, or likely to be in power, will depart in any degree from the naval policy which shall secure us effectively from outside invasion. (Cheers.) All parties are pledged to those necessary measures of naval defence which secure our peaceful development in this island, which frees us from the curse of continental militarism and which can never be a menace to any other great Power in the world. I say, in the second place, there is no collision of primary interests – big imperial interests – between Great Britain and Germany in any quarter of the globe. Why, they are among our very best customers and, if anything were to happen to them, I don't know what we should do in this country for a market. (Cheers.) While there is no danger of a collision of material interests, there is no result which could be expected from any struggle between the two countries except a destruction of a most idiotic and appalling character (Cheers.) ... I have come here this afternoon to ask you to join with me in saying that far and wide throughout the masses of the British dominions there is no feeling of ill-will towards Germany. (Cheers.) ... ■

In spite of Foreign Office scepticism, Grey proceeded to make two approaches to the Germans, but his efforts were rebuffed. Lloyd George too, despite his persistent attempts in 1908, made no headway towards agreement in principle on a naval accord. By the end of 1908 Anglo-German relations had deteriorated considerably. It was against this background that a full-blown naval scare developed in Britain over the following months. The Cabinet eventually agreed to the building of eight Dreadnoughts, four to be started immediately, and four later if necessary.

3.16   **The Anglo-German naval race, 1906–14 (derived from** *Fleets (Great Britain and Foreign Countries)***, Return 113, PP LIV, 1914).**

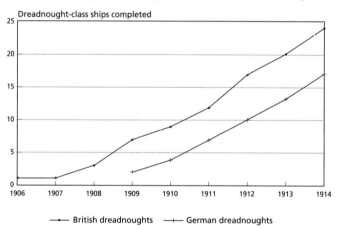

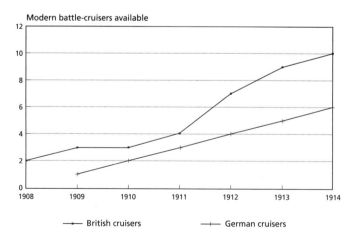

Cabinet tensions over Germany erupted again in July 1911, when Germany sent the gunboat Panther *to the port of Agadir as a blunt warning to the French, whose involvement in Morocco had become increasingly cavalier. Anglo-French relations had cooled considerably by 1911, and Grey believed the German action to be aimed deliberately at breaking up the* entente *and forcing the French to come to an agreement with Berlin. The Agadir crisis resulted in a shift in the balance of power in the Cabinet, as it convinced both Churchill and Lloyd George that German bellicosity must be met with force. The latter delivered an intransigent warning that Britain would risk war to safeguard its interests.*

3.17   David Lloyd George, speech at the Mansion House, 21 July 1911 (reported in *The Times*, 22 July 1911).

■ ... I believe it is essential in the highest interests, not merely of this country, but of the world, that Britain should at all hazards maintain her place and her prestige amongst the Great Powers of the world. (Cheers.) Her potent influence has many a time been in the past, and may yet be in the future, invaluable to the cause of human liberty. It has more than once in the past redeemed Continental nations, who are sometimes too apt to forget that service, from overwhelming disaster and even from national extinction. I would make great sacrifices to preserve peace. I conceive that nothing would justify a disturbance of international good will except questions of the gravest national moment. But if a situation were to be forced upon us in which peace could only be preserved by the surrender of the great and beneficent position Britain has won by centuries of heroism and achievement, by allowing Britain to be treated where her interests were vitally affected as if she were of no account in the Cabinet of nations, then I say emphatically that peace at that price would be a humiliation intolerable for a great country like ours to endure. (Cheers.) National honour is no party question. (Cheers.) The security of our great international trade is no party question; the peace of the world is much more likely to be secured if all nations realize fairly what the conditions of peace must be. And it is because I have the conviction that nations are beginning to understand each other better, to appreciate each other's points of view more thoroughly, to be more ready to discuss calmly and dispassionately their differences, that I feel assured that nothing will happen between now and next year which will render it difficult for the Chancellor of the Exchequer in this place to respond to the toast proposed by you, my Lord Mayor, of the continued prosperity of the public purse. (Cheers.) ■

The continued German naval build-up led the British to enter naval co-operation talks with the French in 1912. The resulting agreement enabled the British to move ships from the Mediterranean to the North Sea, and allowed the French to leave the Channel to the British navy, concentrating their forces in the Mediterranean. At the insistence of the Cabinet, the exchange of letters between Grey and the French Ambassador, Paul Cambon, in November 1912 made it clear that Britain did not consider itself committed to a military alliance with France. But although the entente *was still not a formal alliance, naval co-operation went a stage further in committing Britain to help the French in the event of a war with Germany.*

3.18   Sir Edward Grey, letter to Paul Cambon on Anglo-French naval co-operation, 22 November 1912 (PRO FO 371/1368).

■ My dear Ambassador,

From time to time in recent years the French and British naval and military experts have consulted together. It has always been understood that such consultation does not restrict the freedom of either Government to decide at any future time whether or not to assist the other by armed force. We have agreed that consultation between experts is not, and ought not to be regarded as, an engagement that commits either Government to action in a contingency that has not arisen and may never arise. The disposition, for instance, of the French and British fleets respectively at the present moment is not based upon an engagement to co-operate in war.

You have, however, pointed out that, if either Government had grave reason to expect an unprovoked attack by a third Power, it might become essential to know whether it could in that event depend upon the armed assistance of the other.

I agree that, if either Government had grave reason to expect an uproviked attack by a third Power, or something that threatened the general peace, it should immediately discuss with the other, whether both Governments should act together to prevent aggression and to preserve peace, and if so what measures they would be prepared to take in common. If these measures involved action, the plans of the General Staffs would at once be taken into consideration, and the Governments would then decide what effect should be given to them.

Yours, &c.

E. Grey. ■

The Advent of War

The collapse of the alliance system in Europe came suddenly and unexpectedly in the summer of 1914. Paradoxically, there had been a marked improvement in Anglo-German relations in the years following the Agadir crisis of 1911. As the charts above (document 3.21) indicate, Britain was clearly winning the naval arms race by 1912. Moreover, Britain and Germany had co-operated successfully to help resolve two successive crises in the Balkans in 1912 and 1913, were negotiating over the future of the Portuguese colonies in 1913, and concluded a treaty over the Baghdad railway in 1914. But in spite of such signs of co-operation, the basic ingredients of conflict between Britain and Germany had not changed.

Until the assassination of Archduke Franz Ferdinand in June 1914, the European situation seemed calmer than it had done for many years. The following letter, written by Sir Arthur Nicolson, Permanent Under-Secretary of State for Foreign Affairs at the Foreign Office, to Sir Edward Goschen, Britain's Ambassador to Berlin, shows that the immediate threat of civil war over Ireland was of far more concern than Europe in the spring of 1914.

3.19   **Sir Arthur Nicolson, letter to Sir Edward Goschen, 18 May 1914 (in G.P. Gooch and Harold Temperley, eds, *British Documents on the Origins of the War, 1898–1914, Vol. X: Part II: The Last Years of Peace*, London, HMSO, 1938, pp. 745–6).**

■ My dear Goschen:–

I did not write my letter to you last week as I thought you would be away in Brunswick. Moreover, I really had very little to say, for as you know matters are pretty calm ... Buchanan's French colleague is starting a hare that Russia is becoming a little uneasy as to Germany's attitude, and even goes so far as to say that the Russian Minister of War considers that war is almost inevitable within the next year. I do not myself believe that there is anything at all in this. There is no question at present existing which would necessarily lead to any strained relations between Russia and Germany, and I am quite sure that neither Sovereign has the slightest intention or desire to break the peace. The French Ambassador at Petersburg is well known as an alarmist and disseminates some exaggerated reports ...

You will see from the print that there is very little of interest taking place at this moment in Europe, and were it not for the troubles in Mexico we should be in comparative calm here.

I am afraid that the health of the Austrian Emperor is causing a good deal of uneasiness in his immediate entourage. It is naturally not very satisfactory that a man of his age should have been an invalid during six or seven weeks without any marked improvement. I do not myself think that there will immediately be a great change on the accession of his successor, although there is no doubt that the advent of Franz Ferdinand will cause a good deal of disquietude ...

We are entering into a phase of great anxiety and crisis in this country ... I must say that I do not see much hope of a peaceful solution, though everybody is crying out that it is absolutely necessary that one should be found. Next week will be an important one. I do not know for how long it will be possible for Ulster to passively maintain the severe strain which has been put upon her ...

Yours ever,

A. Nicolson ■

When the Austro-Hungarian Archduke Franz Ferdinand and his wife were assassinated in Sarajevo in June 1914, Grey initially believed that the crisis could be resolved through diplomacy. But as news filtered through of the harsh terms of Austria-Hungary's proposed ultimatum to Serbia, Foreign Office officials began to suspect that Germany, instead of restraining its ally, was encouraging a confrontation. Over the following week, Grey, although increasingly sceptical in private, frantically attempted to persuade the Germans to rein in their allies in Vienna.

3.20   Sir Edward Grey, telegram to Sir Edward Goschen, 27 July 1914 (in G.P. Gooch and Harold Temperley, eds, *British Documents on the Origins of the War, 1898–1914, Vol. XI: The Outbreak of War*, London, HMSO, 1926, p. 124).

■ German Ambassador has informed me that German Government accept in principle mediation between Austria and Russia by the four Powers, reserving, of course, their right as an ally to help Austria if attacked. He has also been instructed to request me to use influence in St. Petersburg to localise the war and to keep up the peace of Europe.

I have replied that the Servian reply went further than could have been expected to meet the Austrian demands. German Minister for Foreign Affairs has himself said that there were some things in the Austrian note that Servia could hardly be expected to accept. I assumed that Servian reply could not have gone as far as it did unless Russia had exercised conciliatory influence at Belgrade, and it was really at Vienna that moderating influence was now required. If Austria put the Servian reply aside as being worth nothing and marched into Servia, it meant that she was determined to crush Servia at all costs, being reckless of the consequences that might be involved. Servian reply should at least be treated as a basis for discussion and pause. I said German Government should urge this at Vienna.

I recalled what German Government had said as to the gravity of the situation if the war could not be localised, and observed that if Germany assisted Austria against Russia it would be because, without any reference to the merits of the dispute, Germany could not afford to see Austria crushed. Just so other issues might be raised that would supersede the dispute between Austria and Servia, and would bring other Powers in, and the war would be the biggest ever known; but as long as Germany would work to keep the peace I would keep closely in touch. I repeated that after the Servian reply it was at Vienna that some moderation must be urged. ■

Grey was severely hampered by the ambivalence of Britain's entente diplomacy. The Cabinet was still divided over the extent of Britain's obligations to France and Russia, and it seemed doubtful that public opinion and the Dominions would back British involvement in a war fought over the Balkans. Thus, while the strongest deterrent to Germany would have been an assurance that Britain would support Russia and France in the event of a German attack, he had no permission from the Cabinet to play that trump card. Even the word of caution which he spoke to the German Ambassador, Count Lichnowsky, went beyond what he was technically authorised to say.

3.21 **Sir Edward Grey, telegram to Sir Edward Goschen, 29 July 1914 (in G.P. Gooch and Harold Temperley, eds, *British Documents on the Origins of the War, 1898–1914. Vol. XI: The Outbreak of War*, London, HMSO, 1926, p. 182).**

■ After speaking to the German Ambassador this afternoon about the European situation, I said that I wished to say to him, in a quite private and friendly way, something that was on my mind. The situation was very grave. While it was restricted to the issues at present actually involved we had no thought of interfering in it. But if Germany became involved in it, and then France, the issue might be so great that it would involve all European interests; and I did not wish him to be misled by the friendly tone of our conversation – which I hoped would continue – into thinking that we should stand aside.

He said that he quite understood this, but he asked whether I meant that we should, under certain circumstances, intervene?

I replied that I did not wish to say that, or to use anything that was like a threat or an attempt to apply pressure by saying that if things became worse, we should intervene. There would be no question of our intervening if Germany was not involved, or even if France was not involved. But we knew very well that if the issue did become such that we thought British interests required us to intervene, we must intervene at once, and the decision would have to be very rapid, just as the decisions of other Powers had to be ... ■

The Cabinet's position only became clear when it was too late. The decisive shift in favour of intervention came on 2 August, when Germany had already declared war on Russia and had begun mobilising under the terms of the Schlieffen plan, which entailed attacking France through neutral Belgium. This violation of the long-standing treaty guaranteeing Belgian neutrality persuaded most of the wavering ministers that Britain must become involved. Of particular concern was the moral obligation to France, whose northern coast was unprotected as a result of the naval agreements with Britain concluded in 1912. On the following day, Grey addressed the House of Commons, and Britain's entry into the Great War became inevitable.

3.22 **Sir Edward Grey, speech to the House of Commons, 3 August 1914 (*Hansard*, 5th ser., 65: 1809–27).**

■ Last week, I stated that we were working for peace not only for this country, but to preserve the peace of Europe. To-day events move so rapidly that it is exceedingly difficult to state with technical accuracy the actual state of affairs, but it is clear that the peace of Europe cannot be preserved. Russia and Germany, at any rate, have declared war upon each other ... In the present crisis, it has not been possible to secure the peace of Europe; because there has been little time, and there has been a disposition – at any rate in some quarters on which I will not dwell – to force things rapidly to an issue, at any rate, to the great risk of peace ...

I can say this with the most absolute confidence – no Government and no country has less desire to be involved in war over a dispute with Austria and Servia than the Government and the country of France. They are involved in it because of their obligation of honour under a definite alliance with Russia. Well, it is only fair to say to the House that that obligation of honour cannot apply in the same way to us. We are not parties to the Franco-Russian Alliance. We do not even know the terms of that alliance.

... For many years we have had a long-standing friendship with France ... But how far that friendship entails obligation ... let every man look into his own heart, and his own feelings, and construe the extent of the obligation for himself ... The French Fleet is now in the Mediterranean, and the Northern and Western coasts of France are absolutely undefended ... because of the feeling of confidence and friendship which has existed between the two countries. My own feeling is that if a foreign fleet engaged in a war which France had not sought, and in which she had not been the aggressor, came down the English Channel and bombarded and battered the undefended coasts of France, we could not stand aside and see this going on practically within sight of our eyes with our arms folded, looking on dispassionately, doing nothing! I believe that would be the feeling of this country ...

But I also want to look at the matter without sentiment, and from the point of view of British interests, and it is on that that I am going to base and justify what I am presently going to say to the House. If we say nothing at this moment, ... it may be that the French Fleet is withdrawn from the Mediterranean ...

Nobody can say that in the course of the next few weeks there is any particular trade route the keeping open of which may not be vital to this country. What will be our position then? We have not kept a fleet in the Mediterranean which is equal to dealing alone with a combination of other fleets in the Mediterranean. It would be the very moment when we could not detach more ships to the Mediterranean, and we might have exposed this country from our negative attitude at the present moment to the most appalling risk ...

And, Sir, there is the more serious consideration – becoming more serious every hour – there is the question of the neutrality of Belgium ... The Treaty [with Belgium] is an old Treaty ... It is one of those Treaties which are founded, not only on consideration for Belgium, which benefits under the Treaty, but in the interests of those who guarantee the neutrality of Belgium ...

If Belgium is compelled to submit to allow her neutrality to be violated, of course the situation is clear ... if it be the case that there has been anything in the nature of an ultimatum to Belgium, asking her to compromise or violate her neutrality, whatever may have been offered to her in return, her independence is gone if that holds. If her independence goes, the independence of Holland will follow. I ask the House from the point of view of British interests, to consider what may be at stake ...

The most awful responsibility is resting upon the Government in deciding what to advise the House of Commons to do.

I have put the vital facts before the House, and if, as seems not improbable, we are forced, and rapidly forced, to take our stand upon those issues, then I believe, when the country realizes what is at stake, what the real issues are, the magnitude of the impending dangers in the west of Europe, which I have endeavoured to describe to the House, we shall be supported throughout, not only by the House of Commons, but by the determination, the resolution, the courage, and the endurance of the whole country. ■

CHAPTER FOUR

A State Transformed?
Politics and the Impact of War,
1914–1918

THE First World War had profound effects on the British political system, replacing the traditional four-party system with one dominated by three parties. The Liberals, the governing party at the outbreak of war, emerged from it divided, taking second place to the Unionists, though they could hardly be written off after 1918. The Labour Party grew both in parliamentary strength and in geographical appeal, and, by 1918 had equipped itself with an efficient national organisation and a programme. The Unionists not only became the biggest party in the Commons in 1918, but also were increasingly identified as the party of 'business'. The Irish Nationalists, whose role before 1914 had been vital, ceased to exist at Westminster.

The war also ended with an important extension of the franchise, giving the vote to most working-class men and, for the first time, to some women. In 1918, therefore, Britain was closer to being a true 'democracy' than before the war. The sheer scale of the demands of total war was unprecedented. The strains on the social and economic fabric of the country had required major expansion in state intervention and government controls, affecting the everyday lives of millions of civilians. As government powers grew, representatives of both business and labour were brought into the process of government. As a result, attitudes towards the role of the state would never be quite the same as in 1914.

The War and the Liberal Government

The war at first gave H.H. Asquith's troubled and increasingly divided Liberal government a respite, as it produced a 'political truce' which stifled parliamentary opposition and saw the suspension of by-elections. Otherwise, there was little political change in the first six months of the war, as all political parties and public opinion rallied behind the government. Within the government, there were few protests at the decision to go to war, only two ministers, Burns and Morley, resigning in consequence.

The government's assumptions about the course of the war were very quickly shown to be false. The hope that Britain's military contribution would be limited to dispatching a small expeditionary force to France was already fading by the end of 1914, as trench warfare on the Western Front degenerated into a stalemate. Equally, confidence that the country could be allowed to function on a 'business-as-usual' basis slumped as the economic and social strains of war increased. The following official report on the early months of the war, prepared in October 1914, gave little indication of the enormous changes in the relationship between the state and the economy which the war would soon require.

4.1   Committee of Imperial Defence (Historical Section), 'Report on the opening of the war', 1 November 1914 (PRO CAB 17/102B).

■ ... It is needless here to enumerate all the articles of supply of which a shortage was in sight, or all the measures taken by the Government either to purchase supplies themselves or to assist the trade to discover supplies. Among the more important commodities was timber, and more particularly pit props (an indispensable requirement in coal mines), which are normally obtained mainly from Scandinavia and Russia. Great efforts were required to obtain the necessary supplies. There was also a shortage of many important chemicals, and an Advisory Committee of distinguished chemical experts was formed by the Board of Trade, under the Chairmanship of Lord Haldane, to consider and advise as to the best means of obtaining for the use of British industries sufficient supplies of chemical products, colours and dye-stuffs of kinds hitherto largely imported from the enemy countries. The activities of this Committee suggest that very important and permanent results may ensue in freeing British industry from the German monopoly in many chemical products ...

With a view to stimulating industry the Board of Trade early in the war started a campaign with the object of supplanting German trade both in English and foreign markets. Exhibitions of samples of German commodities were organised, manufacturers were put in touch with the retail traders, and series of special pamphlets were prepared and circulated to the trade ...

Simultaneously with this action by the Board of Trade the Admiralty and War Office were giving very large orders for war material, and the armament firms, finding their resources unequal to the emergency, found it necessary to pass on orders to firms whose business was normally of a peaceful character. All over industrial Great Britain firms were soon rapidly equipping themselves to provide warlike stores of every sort and description. Not only were these required to order of the British Government, but enormous orders were booked for allied nations, whose industries were seriously dislocated by the belligerent operations in their territory, or by the calling out of a great proportion of the population to the colours. A commission was set up before the end of August to purchase supplies and equipment for the allied countries.

Briefly, then, the policy of His Majesty's Government with regard to the internal economy of the country during the war was to ensure the safety of seaborne supplies; to secure an adequate quantity of all supplies normally obtained from sources rendered not available by the war, resorting even to Government purchase when necessary; to stimulate industry by supplying the needs of our allies, and by replacing our enemy's trade in all markets; by these and other means to provide as much employment as possible; and finally, and in the last resort, to give relief through distress committees &c. ... ■

Soon after the war began, it became necessary to abandon the traditional doctrine of 'Treasury control', which ensured that no government department spent without prior Treasury approval. Consequently, the service ministries were able to order unlimited war supplies, with the Treasury undertaking to find the necessary finance. This important change was also based on the assumption that the war would be short; but as fighting dragged on, it proved impossible to avoid major increases in taxation, intended in part to pay for the rocketing cost of the war.

4.2   **Government expenditure and revenue 1913–18 (derived from J. Turner, ed, *Britain and the First World War*, London, Unwin Hyman, 1988, p. 81).**

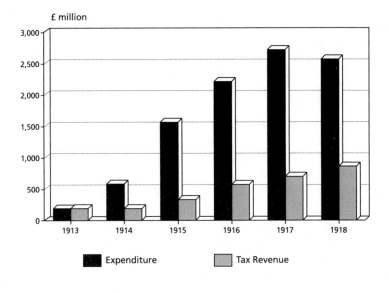

By the end of 1914 some members of the government, notably Winston Churchill, were becoming impatient with the stalemate in France and wanted to engage the enemy elsewhere, for example in the Middle East. The government seemed to be losing its hold on public confidence, while many Conservatives doubted Asquith's abilities, and became restless with the political truce. These problems came to a head in spring 1915, first when Lloyd George attacked his colleagues' existing strategy, and then when a major scandal erupted over the supply of ammunition to the army in France. Lloyd George's criticisms centred on the military wisdom of concentrating on the Western Front, and on the policy of 'business as usual'. As a result, Lloyd George concluded the 'Treasury agreements' with the trade unions to accelerate munitions production, thereby recognising labour's role in the war effort. This was another important step in the erosion of the 'business-as-usual' principle.

4.3 David Lloyd George, memorandum, 'Some further considerations on the conduct of the war', 22 February 1915 (PRO CAB 42/1/39).

■ … I am anxious to put before my colleagues a few considerations on the general situation. It must be acknowledged to be one of the utmost gravity, and one which, if it is not taken in hand at once firmly and boldly, may end in irretrievable disaster for the cause of the Allies and for the future of the British Empire. This may very well appear to some of my colleagues to be the language of morbid pessimism, but I hope, before they come to that conclusion, they will do me the honour of perusing the reasons set forth here which have led me to this conclusion.

The press and the country have up to the present treated the progress of the war as one of almost unbroken success. Their method is a simple one. Every trivial military incident which turns to our advantage is magnified and elaborated in headlines which occupy half a column and descriptions which take a page. On the other hand, grave misfortunes such as those which have befallen the armies of our Russian Allies in the course of the last few days are relegated to a few lines of type, whilst they are explained away in a column of leaded matter. I am afraid that many who have a more intimate acquaintance with the facts are pursuing the same mental process. They concentrate their gaze upon those incidents and aspects of the military situation which suit their hopes, whilst they deliberately shut their eyes to developments which might conduce to the awakening of their fears. The only pathway to ultimate success is paved by reality. Unless we look facts, however unpleasant, in the face, we shall never grapple with them …

… What next? Every effort must be made to increase the number of men whom we can put into the field and to shorten the period in which they could be put into the fighting lines. How is that to be done? If France could put 3,000,000 of men under arms and Germany 5,000,000, then the whole of the Allied countries ought to be able, on the basis of population, sooner or later to arm 20,000,000. That may be an impossibility, but it is an indication of the enormous reserves of men fit to bear arms that the Allies have to draw upon.

The problem resolves itself into one of:

(1) The training and equipping of these men in the shortest space of time;

(2) The maintaining of the status quo without any appreciable aggravation until the Allied countries are prepared to throw overwhelming forces into the battlefield.

How are these two objects to be attained? The first and the greatest difficulty is equipment. The number of men we could put in the field is seriously limited by the out-put of guns and rifles. In this respect we have a great advantage. We are at a disadvantage as compared with the Germans in one material respect, but we are at a great advantage in other respects. As to the disadvantage, the Germans and Austrians between them had, even at the commencement of the war, much larger supplies of war material and more extensive factories for the turning out of further supplies than the Allied countries possessed, and they have undoubtedly since made much better use of their manufacturing resources for the purpose of increasing that out-put. Germany is the best organised country in the world, and her organisation has told.

… I do not believe Great Britain has even yet done anything like what she could do in the matter of increasing her war equipment. Great things have been accomplished in the last few months, but I sincerely believe that we could double our effective energies if we organised our factories thoroughly. All the engineering works of the country ought to be turned on to the production of war material. The population ought to be prepared to suffer all sorts of deprivations and even hardships whilst this process is going on …

… My first suggestion, therefore, would be that full powers should be taken, if we do not already possess them, as I think we do, to mobilise the whole of our manufacturing strength for the purpose of turning out at the earliest possible moment war material … But legislation which would enable us to commandeer all the works in the United Kingdom and, if necessary, to deal with labour difficulties and shortcomings, would undoubtedly strengthen our hands. We might even take full powers to close public houses altogether in areas where armaments were being manufactured … ∎

Even more significant, politically, than Lloyd George's criticism was the storm surrounding the army's failure to breach the German lines, a failure the army attributed to the shortage of shells. It was a war correspondent, Major Charles Repington, who unveiled the extent of the problem.

4.4   Major Charles Repington on the 'shell scandal' 1915 (in C. Repington, *The First World War: 1914–1918: Personal Experiences of Lieut.-Col. C. à Court Repington, Vol. I*, London, Constable, 1920, pp. 34–7).

∎ The episode which aroused the greatest public interest, so far as I was concerned, during the first months of the war, was the share which I took in the revelation of the want of shells in the British Army. I had been able, during my frequent visits to France, to ascertain how lamentably short we were of high explosive shells for our field artillery in particular, and it was with this gun and this projectile, at this period of t ie war, that we prepared the way for the infantry assault. We were also short of heavy guns of all calibres, in which the enemy enormously outnumbered us, and of shells for those which we possessed; we were short of trench mortars, of maxims, of rifle and hand grenades, and, in fact, of almost all the necessary instruments and materials for trench warfare; and the trouble was that Lord K[itchener] did not comprehend the importance of artillery in the war, took no effective measures to increase our supplies of it, and concealed the truth of the situation from his colleagues in the Cabinet. There were no regular Press correspondents with our Army at this time.

… I suppose that General von Donop the M[aster] G[eneral of the] O[rdinance], did his best, but all that I can say is that all deliveries promised in France were late, and that our Army, on every occasion during the earlier battles of the war, was completely outmatched by the guns, shells, and maxims of the enemy. I believe that the War Office had given our contracts to men of straw who were unable to produce the goods, but I do not think that this absolved the M.G.O. I had watched the state of our ammunition in France with great anxiety and growing anger. Every time I went over I heard promises from the War Office, and found on my next visit that the promises had not been kept. Representation after representation had had no effect … Three times I endeavoured to see Lord K. on this subject, and three times I failed. It was useless to see any one else, and I found that my allusions to the subject in the *Times*, censored as everything inconvenient to the Government was censored during the war, were not enough to rouse the country to the facts. The Army in France knew the situation. Lord K. and the M.G.O.'s branch knew it. The public knew nothing, and it was not certain that the Cabinet was any wiser.

… I therefore determined to expose the truth to the public, no matter at what cost. I sent off to the *Times*, on May 12 [1915], without consulting any one, a telegram which became famous, and stated, among other things, 'that the want of an unlimited supply of high explosive shells was a fatal bar to our success'. These words were my own, and were not suggested by Sir John French. The original of my telegram contained much more than saw the light when it was published on May 14. General Macdonogh censored it, and cut out all allusion to the Rifle Brigade casualties, as well as all my remarks about the want of heavy guns, howitzers, trench mortars, maxims, and rifle grenades. I believe that Sir John French never saw the telegram, though he told me afterwards that he approved of it. Macdonogh consulted Brinsley Fitzgerald, who told him that he felt sure that Sir John would approve, and away the fateful telegram went, dreadfully bowdlerised, it is true, but still containing, in the one little phrase, enough high explosive to blow the strongest Government of modern times into the air. ■

The 'shell crisis' of 1915 provoked an outraged press response in Britain, coinciding with the resignation of the First Sea Lord, Admiral Sir John Fisher, in protest at the Dardanelles campaign, for which Churchill was heavily criticised. A revolt against the government by Conservative MPs, some of whom had been approached by disgruntled army officers, seemed possible, and many Liberal MPs were equally unhappy, especially those who had always opposed entry into the war. However, the Conservative leader, Bonar Law, realised the danger of appearing unpatriotic in wartime by challenging the government. William Bridgeman, a Conservative junior whip, described these frustrations in his diary.

4.5   William Bridgeman, diary, May 1915 (in P. Williamson, ed, *The Modernisation of Conservative Politics: The Diaries and Letters of William Bridgeman 1904–1935*, London, The Historians' Press, 1988, pp. 83–4).

■ All the time we have been going on abstaining from forcible criticism, when we might have been doing good by calling public attention to reveal points in which the action of the Govt. has done harm, & will do more, if they do not mend their ways. Such matters as

(1) The suppression of unfavourable views, and the secrecy as to the progress of recruiting etc. The nation does not want to be treated as a child, and will never wake up until the real situation is revealed, and until every man realises the gravity of the danger, and the fact that it requires a gigantic effort to end the War. The nation is sound & will respond to any clear call, but it must be clear.

(2) The interference of politicians in naval & military matters such as Winston's Antwerp expedition & the more recent Dardanelles adventure.

(3) The utter incompetence of those who are supposed to be dealing with aliens.

But our leaders seem to have allowed themselves to accept the position that 'the truce' involves abstention from all serious & sustained criticism, whereas it really never meant anything more than abstention from discussion of party controversies and questions in dispute unconnected with the War. ■

Asquith did not welcome the prospect of losing a vote of confidence on account of the poor progress of the war and facing a general election, theoretically due in 1916. He attempted a compromise, hoping to strengthen his government by calling in outside assistance. In May 1915 he invited Bonar Law and some of his Conservative colleagues to join the government. A.MacCallum Scott, a radical Liberal MP, recalled Asquith's explanation to his fellow Liberals.

4.6   A. MacCallum Scott, diary, 19 May 1915 (in Cameron Hazlehurst, *Politicians at War, July 1914 to May 1915*, London, Cape, 1971, pp. 275–6).

■ Asquith announced today that the Government was under reconstruction – personal and political. Pringle and Hogge and I put down an amendment to reduce the Whitsuntide adjournment from 3 weeks to 1 week. Afterwards we attended a scratch party meeting with Whittaker in the chair. Whittaker spoke very strongly against a coalition. Then Pringle announced an amendment and moved that the meeting support it. Holt supported. Leif Jones and Russell Rea and Murray MacDonald opposed. They all took the party line that the Prime Minister owed some explanation to his party – ought to take his party into his confidence. They wanted to have it out with him but they could not attack the coalition in the House – it had gone too far for that, and they strongly deprecated Pringle's motion as a vote of no confidence. Just then Asquith was fetched by Gulland who had heard how things were shaping. Asquith spoke with deep feeling – his voice husky and his face twitching. He looked old and worried. He flung himself on our mercy. Within a week a wholly new situation had been revealed to him. There had been unexpected disclosures which had taken them wholly by surprise. He could not reveal the truth to us yet without imperilling national safety.

But the situation was of the gravest kind. Coalition became inevitable. He had no desire to retain office – he would not do it without our confidence. He was ready to resign tonight. It was not pleasant to go into harness with men who were the bitter enemies of everything he held dearest in public life – still less to part even temporarily from old friends and colleagues. He asked for our confidence – he would not let us down. He appealed to us not to have any discussion in the House, at the present stage. It would be disastrous. He could but suggest, he feared he was saying too much, that the intervention of neutrals hung in the balance and it was only by their intervention that the war could be brought to a successful conclusion. The meeting gave him an over-powering ovation. ■

In the reconstruction of the government in 1915, Asquith, who remained Prime Minister, removed Churchill, ironically a loyal Liberal, but held responsible for the Dardanelles fiasco, from the Admiralty. Initially, the Asquith Coalition appeared not to be a disaster for the Liberals, who continued to control key posts in government. Especially important was the transfer of Lloyd George from the Treasury to the new Ministry of Munitions, where he oversaw huge increases in state intervention in the economy, which distanced him from many traditional Liberals. At the same time, he involved businessmen closely in the process of government. While establishing new government factories, he also gave incentives to private firms to increase production.

Accompanying the growth of state intervention in the economy in 1915 was a general increase in state controls, for example over alcohol consumption, factories, mines, prices, profits and rents, together with increases in taxation. Although the government set food production targets for farmers, it did not introduce food rationing until 1918. Particularly difficult for Liberals to accept was the abandonment of free trade with the levying of the 'McKenna duties' on luxury imports. Overall, the new approach seemed massively successful, achieving an enormous increase in arms production.

4.7   **British shell production, 1914–18 (derived from G. Hardach, *The First World War 1914–1918*, London, Penguin, 1987, p. 87).**

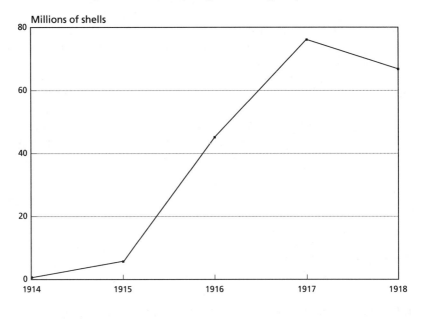

Tensions were present in the new Coalition government from the outset. During 1915 both anti-war Liberals and Conservatives who sought a more vigorous approach to the war had to be assuaged, over the Dardanelles campaign and over military conscription. More serious, however, was the fact that Lloyd George sided with the Conservatives in demanding the immediate introduction of conscription. This proved highly controversial, at odds with traditional Liberal principles and much closer to Conservative aims. Yet by mid-1915 voluntary enlistment had clearly become inadequate.

4.8   British military enlistment, 1914–15 (derived from J. Turner, ed., *Britain and the First World War*, London, Unwin Hyman, 1988, p. 101).

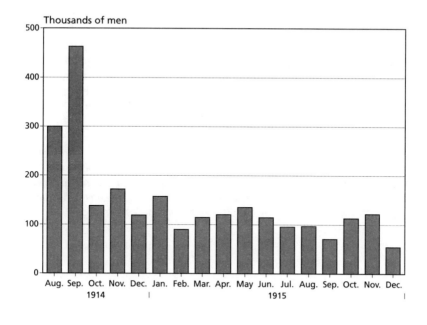

The political dimension to the developing debate on conscription was described by the Liberal Cabinet member Charles Hobhouse in late 1915.

4.9   Charles Hobhouse, diary, 14 October 1915 (in E. David ed., *Inside Asquith's Cabinet: From the Diaries of Charles Hobhouse*, London, Murray, 1977, p. 255).

■ Also this afternoon I saw W[alter] R[unciman]. He gave an interesting picture of Cabinet discord; Lansdowne, Curzon, Law, A. Chamberlain were for leaving the Cabinet if conscription were not proposed. Law chiefly because the Gallipoli peninsula was not abandoned and Chamberlain because of his position as reversionary leader. Curzon qualified his desire to resign by a declaration that in that event his criticism would be confined to any subject of actual disagreement. Balfour and Long would remain in whatever happened, to carry on the Govt. A.J.B. being against and Long for compulsory service. With them [evidently the resigners] would go Churchill who was pining to get abroad to the Dardanelles, and Ll.G. who saw no opening to a leadership, and was much afraid that he had muddled the Ministry of Munitions, for which he would be called to account, and thought he had better get out of harness while there was yet time to throw the blame on someone else. The P.M. was still a convinced voluntaryist, but equally determined on keeping the Govt. together and was trying to find a hypothetical formula of a Bill falling due 3 months hence! McKenna who was the P.M.s only confidant was determined to resign as was W.R. and these two thought Loulou [Lewis Harcourt] would also go, if conscription was carried in Cabinet. K[itchener] had been won over, and had told the Cabinet he wanted 35,000 men a week, whereas his departmental people had only asked for 30,000. Simon characteristically could only express his determination to stand by the P.M. Henderson had a violent altercation with Ll.G. and told him and the Cabinet squarely that Labour would resist conscription by every means, in and out of Parliament. ■

In December 1915 Asquith relented on conscription, but the government's Military Service Act of January 1916 failed to satisfy Lloyd George or his Conservative allies. Facing continued criticism, in May 1916 the government extended conscription to married men. By then, however, Asquith's reputation was already badly damaged, not only by conscription but also by the disastrous Dardanelles campaign.

Ireland

Against the background of discord and dissatisfaction in government circles, the Easter Rising by Irish nationalists in Dublin was especially unwelcome. The Third Home Rule Bill became law in September 1914, but its provisions were suspended for the duration of the war. This only postponed the problem, allowing nationalist and Unionist tensions to grow alarmingly. Although the majority of nationalists loyally supported the war effort, impatience grew, especially after the Coalition government was formed in May 1915. Home Rule had, arguably, only been conceded because the Liberals depended on the support of Irish Nationalist MPs. Now the Nationalists, outside the Coalition, no longer held the balance of power at Westminster. Home Rule might conceivably be delayed until after the next general election, at which the electorate might reject the idea entirely.

Extremist nationalism was also fostered by the insensitive treatment meted out to Ireland during the war. Despite demonstrations of loyalty in the South, London insisted on maintaining large numbers of troops there, implying that the Catholic population could not be trusted. The consequence was a steady drift in support towards the more extreme *Sinn Fein* elements, among whom Home Rule was rejected in favour of outright independence, and support grew for a symbolic show of strength. In the Dublin Easter Rising of April 1916, doomed by its small scale, key sites were seized and a republic proclaimed. After 450 people had died and 2,600 were wounded, the rebels surrendered, and martial law was imposed.

Although the Easter Rising of 1916 was quickly put down, the force used by Britain horrified Irish opinion, and constituted another challenge to Liberal values at home. Fifteen rebel leaders were executed, immediately becoming nationalist martyrs, and hundreds more were imprisoned, further inflaming public opinion. Yet in this climate, the government tried to reach a final settlement of the Irish problem. In discussions with the Ulster Unionists and the Irish Nationalists, Lloyd George, still Minister of Munitions, reached an agreement to partition Ireland, giving the South Home Rule. Whereas many Liberals regarded partition as a surrender to the Unionists, the Nationalists felt humiliated. Ultimately, opinion in the South would drift away from the more moderate Nationalists, such as Redmond, and towards the radical Sinn Fein party. The incident's significance within British politics, however, was that Lloyd George had not consulted his Unionist Cabinet colleagues prior to the agreement, and they reacted furiously against the Liberals and their own leaders. Lord Selborne later described the perplexed Unionist response.

4.10 **Lord Selborne, 'Memorandum on the crisis in Irish affairs which caused my resignation from the Cabinet, 30 June 1916 (Bodleian Library, MS Selborne 80, fol. 226).**

■ ... I do not believe that it crossed the mind of one single Unionist member of the Cabinet that the bringing into existence during the war of Home Rule in any shape or form could possibly form part of such a settlement. I understood, and I believe that my Unionist colleagues understood, that an effort was to be made to get the Ulster Unionists and the Nationalists of Ireland to agree to the exclusion of Ulster or of a part of Ulster from the operation of the Government of Ireland Act, and in addition to see whether there were any safeguards which would induce the Unionists of the South, Centre and West of Ireland to accept a government and parliament in Dublin for the rest of Ireland. If an agreement on these points could be reached an Act amending the Government of Ireland Act would be passed during the war, but it never entered our heads that anyone contemplated bringing in the Government of Ireland Act, amended or unamended, modified, into operation during the war. I say this confidently in respect of Lord Lansdowne, Lord Curzon, Lord Robert Cecil, Mr Austen Chamberlain and Mr Walter Long, as of myself. I believe it to be true also of Sir F.E. Smith, Mr Bonar Law, and Mr Arthur Balfour, but, as they subsequently adopted a somewhat unexpected attitude, I do not state it of them with the same confidence as· of the others ... Under these circumstances we all concurred in approving the Prime Minister's Commission to Mr Lloyd George. This was where we went wrong. Knowing Mr Asquith and Mr Lloyd George we ought to have insisted on joining some Unionist like Lord Robert Cecil or Mr Austen Chamberlain to Mr Lloyd George in the negotiations ... ■

The Decline of Asquith

Arguments over conscription, Ireland and military strategy weakened confidence in Asquith's government. In 1916 there were worrying indications that civilian morale was in decline. Strikes had occurred, especially in the engineering industry, as a result of rising food prices. Conscription and the 'dilution' of skilled labour were further sources of grievance. A poor harvest added to the economic problems which were becoming serious late in the year. In addition to the persistent labour shortages, Britain's financial reserves, essential for purchases of material from the United States, were nearly exhausted, and the Russian war effort seemed close to collapsing. A series of military setbacks culminating in the Somme disaster in summer 1916 compounded the government's apparently dismal record.

Within the government in late 1916 calls were made for a quick peace settlement, before Britain's political fabric suffered serious damage. These came in the form of a memorandum by the senior Conservative minister Lord Lansdowne, which was presented to the Cabinet that November.

4.11   Lord Lansdowne, memorandum, 13 November 1916 (PRO CAB 37/159/32).

■ ... I do not suppose for an instant that there is any weakening in the spirit of the people of this country, and I should hope, although I do not feel absolute confidence on the subject, that the same might be said of our Allies, but neither in their interests nor in ours can it be desirable that the War should be prolonged, unless it can be shown that we can bring it to an effective conclusion within a reasonable space of time.

What does the prolongation of the War mean?

Our own casualties already amount to over 1,100,000. We have had 15,000 officers killed, not including those who are missing. There is no reason to suppose that, as the force at the front in the different theatres of war increases, the casualties will increase at a slower rate. We are slowly but surely killing off the best of the male population of these islands. The figures representing the casualties of our Allies are not before me. The total must be appalling.

The financial burden which we have already accumulated is almost incalculable. We are adding to it at the rate of over 5,000,000l. per day. Generations will have to come and go before the country recovers from the loss which it has sustained in human beings, and from the financial ruin and the destruction of the means of production which are taking place.

All this it is no doubt our duty to bear, but only if it can be shown that the sacrifice will have its reward. If it is to be made in vain, if the additional year, or two years, or three years, find us still unable to dictate terms, the

War with its nameless horrors will have been needlessly prolonged, and the responsibility of those who needlessly prolong such a War is not less than that of those who needlessly provoke it … ■

The Asquith Coalition was in crisis. Although many of Asquith's colleagues rejected Lansdowne's pessimism, not all were convinced that the Prime Minister could deliver either effective leadership or victory. Eventually Lloyd George emerged as the dynamo of political change. Having succeeded Kitchener at the War Office earlier in the year, he quickly became impatient with Asquith. On 26 September 1916, seeking to stifle talk of an early peace, he seized the initiative by making an unauthorised statement to an American journalist that Britain must continue the war until Germany had been given a 'knock-out blow'.

4.12 David Lloyd George, 'knock-out blow' speech, 28 September 1916 (reported in *The Times*, 29 September 1916).

■ … None of the carnage and suffering which is to come can be worse than those of the Allied dead who stood the full shock of the Prussian war machine before it began to falter.

But in the British determination to carry the fight to a decisive finish there is something more than the natural demand for vengeance. The inhumanity and the pitilessness of the fighting that must come before a lasting peace is possible is not comparable with the cruelty that would be involved in stopping the war while there remains the possibility of civilization again being menaced from the same quarter. Peace now or at any time before the final and complete elimination of this menace is unthinkable. No man or no nation with the slightest understanding of the temper of the citizen Army of Britons, which took its terrible hammering without a whine or a grumble, will attempt to call a halt now … ■

Late in 1916 Lloyd George also began discussions with Bonar Law on restructuring the government. Law, fearing that his loyalty to Asquith might heighten the hostility of some Conservatives to his leadership of the party, joined forces with Lloyd George. Together, they demanded changes at the top, with Lloyd George heading a new War Cabinet, in which Asquith would remain Prime Minister. The circumstances were described in Lloyd George's subsequent ultimatum to Asquith.

4.13 David Lloyd George, letter to H.H. Asquith, 5 December 1916 (in D. Lloyd George, *War Memoirs*, Vol. I, London, Odhams, 1938, pp. 593–4).

■ … On Friday I made proposals which involved not merely your retention of the Premiership, but the supreme control of the War, whilst the executive functions, subject to that supreme control, were left to others. I thought you then received these suggestions favourably. In fact, you yourself proposed that I should be chairman of this Executive Committee, although, as you know, I never put forward that demand. On Saturday you wrote me a letter in which you completely went back on that proposition ...

I have striven my utmost to cure the obvious defects of the War Committee without overthrowing the Government. As you are aware, on several occasions during the last two years I have deemed it my duty to express profound dissatisfaction with the Government's method of conducting the War. Many a time, with the road to victory open in front of us, we have delayed and hesitated whilst the enemy were erecting barriers that finally checked the approach. There has been delay, hesitation, lack of forethought and vision. I have endeavoured repeatedly to warn the Government of the dangers, both verbally and in written memoranda and letters, which I crave your leave now to publish if my action is challenged; but I have either failed to secure decisions or I have secured them when it was too late to avert the evils. The latest illustration is our lamentable failure to give timely support to Roumania.

I have more than once asked to be released from my responsibility for a policy with which I was in thorough disagreement, but at your urgent personal request I remained in the Government. I realise that when the country is in peril of a great war, Ministers have not the same freedom to resign on disagreement. At the same time I have always felt – and felt deeply – that I was in a false position inasmuch as I could never defend in a whole-hearted manner the action of a Government of which I was a member. We have thrown away opportunity after opportunity, and I am convinced, after deep and anxious reflection, that it is my duty to leave the Government in order to inform the people of the real condition of affairs, and to give them an opportunity, before it is too late, to save their native land from a disaster which is inevitable if the present methods are longer persisted in. As all delay is fatal in war, I place my office without further parley at your disposal ... ■

With the government split between those Liberals still loyal to Asquith, and Lloyd George, Law and the bulk of the Conservative benches, Asquith attempted to force the issue by resigning. He soon discovered that he was not indispensable. Lloyd George, supported by the Conservatives, about half the Liberal MPs and Labour, formed a new coalition, which took power in December 1916, and remained in office for the rest of the war.

In his memoirs, Herbert Samuel, who resigned from his post as Home Secretary on Asquith's departure, provided an insight into the views of many of his fellow Liberals on the formation of the Lloyd George Coalition in 1916.

4.14   **Herbert Samuel, diary, 6 December 1916 (in Viscount Samuel, *Memoirs*, The Cresset Press, London, 1945, p. 122).**

■ In the morning I went to see Asquith at 10 Downing Street to tell him that there was no foundation for the statement which had appeared in *The Times*, *Daily News* and *Manchester Guardian* that I would be willing to separate myself from him and my Liberal colleagues and t ke office under Bonar

Law or Lloyd George. I said that in no circumstances would I serve under the latter and that if the former invited me to take office, I should like to consult him and others when the pros and cons would have to be considered. But I had heard no suggestion of anything of the kind from anyone and had discussed it with no one. I was at a loss to know how the paragraphs had originated. Asquith said that he would certainly not dissuade any of his colleagues from serving in a Coalition Govt. under a Unionist Prime Minister.

At 5.15 a conference was held at Downing St. of the Liberal members of the Cabinet. Henderson was also present. Asquith had been at the Palace where the King had made an attempt to reconcile differences. He had summoned Asquith, Bonar Law, Balfour, Lloyd George and Henderson to confer. The outcome was a suggestion that Law should form a Govt. and that Asquith should serve in it. He wanted our opinion on that. Henderson strongly supported it, but all the Liberals were definitely against it. In the first place, the Govt. would really be a Lloyd George Govt. and all the old difficulties would recur. It was much better that L.G. should be the ostensible as well as the real head of the Government, should have with him people who would trust him, and should show what he could do or not do. Secondly, if Asquith were absorbed as a unit in such a Govt. his influence would disappear. Outside it, his influence would remain. Under his leadership we should form a possible alternative Govt. which it was to the interest of the country to have. ∎

The Lloyd George Coalition

The new Coalition government under Lloyd George depended heavily on support from Bonar Law and the Conservatives. Most former Liberal ministers followed Asquith out of government, allowing Conservatives to occupy the major ministerial posts. Another feature of the new government was its inclusion of more Labour Party representatives, led by Arthur Henderson.

Lord Curzon recorded the discussions among Conservatives which preceded the formation of the 1916 Coalition.

4.15 **Lord Curzon, memorandum, 7 December 1916 (in Lord Beaverbrook,** *Politicians and the War***, London, Oldbourne, 1960, pp. 520–2).**

∎ On the evening of December 7, Lord Curzon, Lord Robert Cecil, Mr Chamberlain and Mr Walter Long, who had earlier in the afternoon been invited by Mr Bonar Law, on behalf of Mr Lloyd George, to join the Administration, had an interview with the latter at the War Office to discuss certain matters in connection with the proposed arrangements. Mr Bonar

Law was present during part of the interview.

The following were the main points which were touched upon in the conversation:

1. Convinced of the supreme necessity of setting up a stable Administration, the Unionist ex-Ministers inquired what support Mr Lloyd George might expect to receive from the Liberal Party and his late Liberal colleagues, in the House of Commons. Mr Lloyd George replied that, according to his present information, none of the Liberal members of Mr Asquith's Cabinet was prepared to join him, having, it was believed come to an understanding to the contrary; but that, in the event of his Administration becoming a settled fact, he was not without hopes of obtaining the services of one or more of their number.

As regards the Liberal MPs, he had received assurances of the support of 136, and believed that the numbers would grow. He anticipated a favourable reception of the new Government, when once formed, from the House of Commons.

2. In reply to a question whether, at a later date, if threatened with serious opposition, rendering the position of the Government difficult or untenable in the House, he would contemplate a dissolution of Parliament and a general election, he replied that in the last resort he would not shrink from such a step, and, indeed, had mentioned it to the King, from whom no opposition was likely to be encountered.

3. As regards the attitude of the Labour party, Mr Lloyd George stated that a meeting of the Labour MPs together with some representatives of the outside Labour organisation, had just been held, and had agreed to support his Government by as large a majority as accorded a similar support to Mr Asquith earlier in the war, the minority consisting in the main of professed Pacifists, and the majority containing the men – including Mr J.H. Thomas, MP (who had not supported the Coalition Government at its formation) – on whom he would most wish to rely … ∎

The Lloyd George Coalition faced an even more daunting range of problems in running the war economy than had Asquith's. Financially, the problem of purchasing essential supplies from the still neutral United States had become acute. The situation on the Western Front could not be allowed to persist much longer. The rationale behind forming the new government had been to return control of the war to civilians, to prevent the political and social breakdown which some, like Lansdowne, had predicted might follow repeated costly military blunders. Lloyd George's dilemma was that popular discontent resulted from the policies which he had defended during 1916, and which the generals, whom he had also supported, were keen to continue.

The Social Impact of War

The problems of 1916 continued into 1917, and military success remained elusive. Within Britain, the strains of war were increasingly being felt by the civilian population.

Food and raw materials became scarce as the war went on, and prices rose. In the factories and in service industries such as transport, male workers who had enlisted were increasingly replaced with female labour. By late 1918, 90 per cent of workers in munitions factories were female.

4.16   'The kitchen is the key to victory', poster *c.*1916 (Imperial War Museum, London, PST/4907)

4.17   Crane girls at work in a Nottingham shell factory, undated (Imperial War Museum, London, Q 30038).

The process of 'diluting' labour in industry with unskilled or female workers, the effects of conscription and suspicions that some industrialists were profiting from the war led to discontent, growing trade union membership and fresh waves of strikes.

4.18   **The civilian experience of total war (derived from G.C. Peden, *British Economic and Social Policy: Lloyd George to Margaret Thatcher*, Philip Allan, Oxford 2nd edn, 1991, p. 39; J. Turner, ed., *Britain and the First World War*, London, Unwin Hyman, 1988, p. 76; H. Pelling, *A History of British Trade Unionism*, London, Penguin, 1976, p. 294).**

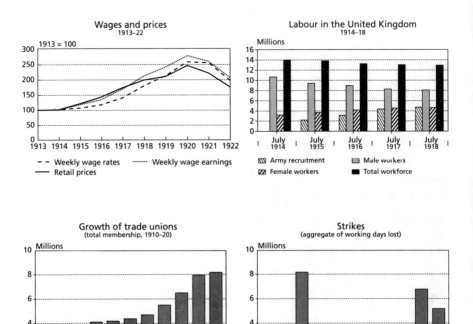

Government concern at civilian unrest, coloured by instability in Russia throughout 1917, prompted an investigation by a parliamentary commission into the causes of industrial disputes. The commission's findings, published in July 1917, illustrated the problems faced by those on the 'Home Front'.

4.19 **Commission of Enquiry into Industrial Unrest,** *Report,* **July 1917, (Cd 8696, PP XV, 1917–18, pp. 5–8).**

■ SUMMARY OF THE REPORTS BY THE RIGHT HON. G.N. BARNES, M.P. TO THE RIGHT HON. DAVID LLOYD GEORGE, M.P. (*Prime Minister*)

1. *Introductory*

The Commission of Enquiry into Industrial Unrest, which was appointed by you on the 12th June, has now completed its work. The Terms of Reference to the Commission were – 'To enquire into and report upon the causes of industrial unrest and to make recommendations to the Government at the earliest practicable date.' ...

5. A comparison of the reports shows that there is a strong feeling of patriotism on the part of employers and employed throughout the country and they are determined to help the State in its present crisis. Feelings of a revolutionary character are not entertained by the bulk of the men. On the contrary, the majority of the workmen are sensible of the national difficulties, especially in the period of trial and stress through which we are now passing.

6. Whilst the eight reports agree as to the main causes of industrial unrest, important differences appear in the emphasis laid by the various Commissions upon specific causes.

7. In order that the principal points of agreement and difference between the eight reports may be readily seen, I submit the following brief summary of the Commissioners' findings and recommendations:

(1) High food prices in relation to wages, and unequal distribution of food.

(2) Restriction of personal freedom and, in particular, the effects of the Munitions of War Acts. Workmen have been tied up to particular factories and have been unable to obtain wages in relation to their skill. In many cases the skilled man's wage is less than the wage of the unskilled. Too much centralisation in London is reported.

(3) Lack of confidence in the Government. – This is due to the surrender of Trade Union customs and the feeling that promises as regards their restoration will not be kept ...

(4) Delay in settlement of disputes. – In some instances 10 weeks have elapsed without a settlement, and after a strike has taken place, the matter has been put right within a few days.

(5) Operation of the Military Service Acts.

(6) Lack of housing in certain areas.

(7) Restrictions on liquor. – This is marked in some areas.

(8) Industrial fatigue.

(9)   Lack of proper organisation amongst the Unions.

(10) Lack of communal sense. – This is noticeable in South Wales, where there has been a break-away from faith in Parliamentary representation.

(11) Inconsiderate treatment of women, whose wages are sometimes as low as 13s.

(12) Delay in granting pensions to soldiers ...

(13) Raising of the limit of Income Tax Exemption.

(14) The Workmen's Compensation Act.– The maximum of £1 weekly is now inadequate.

Recommendations of the Commissioners:-

(1)   Food Prices. – There should be an immediate reduction in price, the increased price of food being borne to some extent by the Government, and a better system of distribution is required.

(2)   Industrial Councils, &c. – The principle of the Whitley Report should be adopted; each trade should have constitution.

(3)   Changes with a view to further increase of output should be made the subject of an authoritative statement by the Government.

(4)   Labour should take part in the affairs of the community as partners, rather than as servants.

(5)   The greatest publicity possible should be given to the abolition of Leaving Certificates ...

(8)   Announcements should be made of policy as regards housing ...

(10) Closer contact should be set up between employer and employed ...

(14) A higher taxation of wealth is urged by one Commissioner. ■

The delicacy of the wartime labour problem, from the government's point of view, was described by the Conservative MP William Bridgeman, then in the Ministry of Labour.

4.20   **William Bridgeman, diary, February 1918 (in P. Williamson, ed., *The Modernisation of Conservative Politics: The Diaries and Letters of William Bridgeman 1904-1935*, London, The Historians' Press, 1988, p. 125).**

■ ... The worst part of our business of the past year has been the perpetual friction over wages, war bonuses etc. which has been increased by several difficulties for which we are not responsible.

(1) The existence of other departments dealing with Labour, such as M. of Munitions, Shipyard Labour, War Office Contracts, National Service, who all

go their own way until some serious difficulty arises when we are called in at a point where matters have gone too far for remedy. We hardly ever have to bat on any but a spoilt wicket. The M. of Munitions are the worst offenders: and Winston's accession to office has made it worse. He signalised it by giving a 12½% rise of wages to time workers in such a way as to cause an all-round demand for increase which was not really wanted. The M. of Labour opposed his plan but he managed to stampede the War Cabinet, who did not find out their mistake until there was a real muddle, and then handed the whole mess over to us to try to clear up.

(2) Some time ago Ll. George made a great mistake by treating the Amalg. Soc. of Engineers as a privileged body among the Unions in giving them power to give exemptions from military service to their members. This caused a lot of trouble, and has made the A.S.E. very overweening in their demands ever since. They were too gently dealt with in the strike in May 1917, and have always been funked by the Govt. until Auckland Geddes as M. of Nat. Service began his comb-out of this year. The A.S.E. Executive are a poor lot, and seldom dare to stand up to the local agitation, and their constitution deprives them of a good deal of the power which is vested in the Executives of other Unions. ■

The Labour Party

The events of 1917 led to renewed government interest in the attitudes of organised labour, and of the Labour Party, to the war. When the war had broken out in 1914, the Parliamentary Labour Party had divided between a small pacifist wing, led by Ramsay MacDonald, and the majority of MPs, especially those sponsored by trade unions, who supported the war and chose Arthur Henderson to lead them. Following this split, there was confusion in the party, with some members hoping MacDonald would resume his chairmanship.

Late in August 1914, MacDonald wrote to Henderson, confirming his resignation as party chairman.

4.21   **Ramsay MacDonald, letter to Arthur Henderson, 24 August 1914 (PRO 30/69/1232).**

■ ... The Party must make up its mind what it is to do for the next month or two. Is it to throw itself out of action altogether and allow each individual to drift whither it seems good to him? Or is it to attempt to take up a distinctive position which will in due course be the rallying centre for those who will wish that this war should not have been fought in vain. If it is to do the latter, it must think things out from now onwards, and it must be prepared to co-operate with outside organisations with which it agrees in this respect. It has been suggested to me that it might be possible for the Party to pass some kind of resolution which I could accept and which would not, in view of the statements of my position which I have made, make it impossible for me to continue in the chair... I do not see how some of those who spoke at the last meeting of the Party could support a vote of confidence and a resolution that I should withdraw my resignation, more particularly as the resolution would have to be sent to the press. I should therefore imagine that the Party will really have to fill my position and let me become one of its rank and file. ■

Labour had been given token representation in Asquith's Coalition, but it was Lloyd George who extended this, bringing several Labour MPs into the government in December 1916. Its role in wartime government almost certainly helped to improve the Labour Party's general 'respectability'. Although divided over the war, the party continued to work as a single unit, not only on its National Executive Committee, but also at a local level. Above all, Labour kept up its interest in international issues, remaining part of the international socialist movement. In 1917 the government sent Henderson to Russia to sound out the new regime, and what he saw there reinforced his suspicion of 'Bolshevism'. Nevertheless, he decided to take part in a Russian-proposed conference at Stockholm of socialist groups from all the nations at war, to consider ways of persuading their respective governments to seek peace. Although Lloyd George initially favoured the proposed conference, Conservatives in the government blocked it. When Henderson overrode them, by urging the Labour Party to attend Stockholm, he was forced to resign from the War Cabinet. Eduard Bernstein, the prominent German revisionist socialist, later wrote to MacDonald expressing his disappointment at these developments.

4.22   Eduard Bernstein, letter to Ramsay MacDonald, 30 September 1917 (PRO 30/69/1161).

■ ... At present the hopes for an early and good peace are still very low. For the governments it is almost impossible to come to an agreement. Help must come from other sources, and who more called to provide it than the socialists? But they can only provide it if acting internationally on an agreed basis. There is at present going on ... an agitation for an international simultaneous general strike ... Seeing what humanity in both senses of the word suffers I am not so opposed to it as I would under other circumstances ... But from what I know of my country, I must in all honesty confess that there are the greatest odds against its feasibility ... [W]ith a most strongly organised military government at the helm ... the whole middle classes, the majority socialists, the big trade unions as opponents, they would have little chance of lasting any length of time ... There is no means of saving the labour of bringing about an understanding of the mass of the socialists in all the countries. Had the Stockholm conference come to pass, we would, I am sure, [have] achieved a good step in this direction. We must go on in the work of pressing public opinion in its favour. Governments must be made [to] understand that they risk worse things if they continue in blocking the conference ...

In writing this all I am driven by the conviction that the time has come where an exchange of views should take place between English and German Socialists ... I hoped to meet you and some of your comrades in Stockholm. Unfortunately, the short-sightedness of foolish politicians has willed it otherwise. Is there no means to meet on less suspicious ground?... I have followed as much as opportunities allowed your doings in your country and I believe it qualifies you to [*sic*] the role of a socialist ambassador, a call worth striving for at this time of disgrace and disruption. ■

Although it was defeated over the Stockholm Socialist conference in 1917, the Labour Party thereafter began to establish itself as an effective opposition. Freed from Cabinet responsibilities, its leaders could devote themselves to policy development, to organising the party for the future and to producing the party's 1918 constitution, written by Henderson and Sidney Webb.

4.23 **Labour Party,** *Constitution (adopted at the London Conference, February 26th 1918,* **1918 (London, Labour Party, p. 1).**

■ LABOUR PARTY CONSTITUTION OF 1918

1. Name

The Labour Party

2. Membership

The Labour Party shall consist of all its affiliated organisations, together with those men and women who are individual members of a Local Labour Party and who subscribe to the Constitution and Programme of the Party.

3. Party Objects

National

(*a*) To organise and maintain in Parliament and in the country a Political Labour Party, and to ensure the establishment of a Local Labour Party in every County Constituency and every Parliamentary Borough, with a suitable divisional organisation in the separate constituencies of Divided Boroughs;

(*b*) To co-operate with the Parliamentary Committee of the Trades Union Congress, or other Kindred Organisations, in joint political or other action in harmony with the party Constitution and Standing Orders;

(*c*) To give effect as far as may be practicable to the principles from time to time approved by the Party Conference;

(d) To secure for the producers by hand or by brain the full fruits of their industry, and the most equitable distribution thereof that may be possible, upon the basis of the common ownership of the means of production and the best obtainable system of popular administration and control of each industry or service;

(e) Generally to promote the Political, Social, and Economic Emancipation of the People, and more particularly of those who depend directly upon their own exertions by hand or by brain for the means of life. ■

Looking to the future

There had been no general election since 1910, and throughout the war the calling of an election remained a possibility. Despite the difficulties it experienced in Parliament, the government felt confident of public support. An election was discussed by Lloyd George and his closest colleagues as early as May 1917, as the year drew on, the incentive to go to the polls grew stronger. Not only was there a risk of further food shortages at the end of the year, but also little progress had been made on the military front, and after August 1917 the government was under increasing pressure to justify the enormous cost of the war. Moreover, Lloyd George needed a position of political strength if he were to take on the generals, and Asquith was beginning to emerge as a potential rallying-point for opposition to the government. These factors convinced the government that it must act to strengthen its appeal in advance of an election.

In August 1917 Lloyd George appointed the radical Liberal Christopher Addison as Minister for Reconstruction, and many reformers were recruited to official committees. In February 1917 Addison presented the Cabinet with a list of seven major areas which would have to be addressed urgently. These were: housing; road and railway repair; land purchase; government financial help to key industries; broader unemployment insurance coverage; improved health provision; and state-guaranteed credit to manufacturing industry. In his supporting memorandum, Addison tried to pre-empt arguments that reconstruction would have to be subordinated to post-war debt repayment.

4.24   Christopher Addison, memorandum, 'Reconstruction Finance',
10 February 1917 (PRO RECO 1/775).

■ ... Capital expenditure on every one of the subjects I have cited is as vital to efficient production as if it were invested in machinery or factory buildings. To say that the workman must be healthy and must have a house is simply to state two of the primary factors in the scheme of production which we all desire ...

The restoration of prosperity and public credit can only be secured if we ... incur expenditure essential for establishing ... the fullest means of national productivity. By all means let us pay off our debts if we can. But how can we until the conditions required for creating wealth and restoring credit are first of all restored even though the process involves a fresh drain upon our depleted credit? A discontented population and an ill-repaired machine offer ... an improvident means of debt-extinction.

... the restoration and development of our productive capacity to its fullest extent with the assistance of State credit and public services, wherever ... private means and enterprise are unavailing, should be accepted for what it is ... the condition precedent to extinguishing debt and restoring credit ... If support should not be given to this view, the difficulties awaiting us after peace will be too much for this or any Government. ... If I and my colleagues concerned can count upon financial support, plans can be matured which ought to tide us over some of our most dangerous problems; but ... in uncertainty as to whether these plans are to be given effect to, our task will become impossible.

It will be no defence to say that vital proposals were not enacted for want of money. Nobody will believe it. We shall be told that the money would have been forthcoming if ... required for the war, and we shall be pressed to accept all manner of wild proposals and to devise hastily extemporised expedients which will satisfy nobody. I hope that we shall not have to ... and spend money for reconstruction purposes in any atmosphere of panic engendered by violent agitation and well-founded discontent, but ... this is an alternative that cannot be disregarded if our plans are laid for a half-hearted scheme of Reconstruction based on the view that we cannot afford to prepare for peace. ■

The enthusiasm for post-war reconstruction produced, in practice, only limited achievements, including H.A.L. Fisher's Education Act 1918, which raised the school-leaving age to 14, and made provision for extended secondary and tertiary education. The majority of reconstruction plans, which remained incomplete, lacked a secure financial basis. In an effort to boost civilian morale, therefore, the government encouraged unfounded hopes of 'homes fit for heroes to live in' after the war.

Yet the financial realities were not promising. The war had had a serious effect on Britain's balance of payments, strengthening the arguments of those who sought a return to 'orthodox' government finance.

4.25   Britain's balance of payments, 1914–18 (derived from J. Turner, ed., *Britain and the First World War*, London, Unwin Hyman, 1988, p. 83).

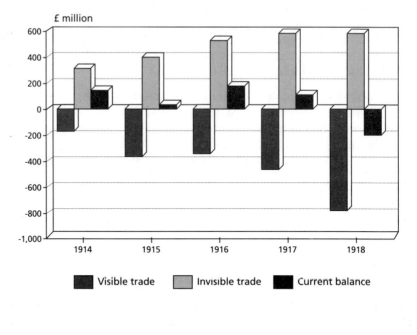

Lloyd George felt obliged to pre-empt any manoeuvring among political groups designed to achieve a quick peace, especially when in November 1917 Lord Lansdowne made public the calls for an early settlement he had already made privately late in 1916. In January 1918, speaking to trade unionists at Caxton Hall in London, Lloyd George described Britain's war aims as moderate and reasonable, in accord with those of the United States.

4.26   David Lloyd George, speech at Caxton Hall, 6 January 1918 (reported in *The Times*, 7 January 1918).

■ … When the Government invite organised labour in this country to assist them to maintain the might of their armies in the field, its representatives are entitled to ask that any misgivings and doubts which any of them may have about the purpose to which this precious strength is to be applied should be definitely cleared, and what is true of organised labour is equally true of all citizens in this country without regard to grade or avocation.

When men by the million are being called upon to suffer and die and vast populations are being subjected to the sufferings and privations of war on a scale unprecedented in the history of the world, they are entitled to know for what cause or causes they are making the sacrifice. It is only the clearest, greatest and justest of causes that can justify the continuance even for one day of this unspeakable agony of the nations. And we ought to be able to state clearly and definitely not only the principles for which we are fighting, but also their definite and concrete application to the war map of the world ...

We have arrived at the most critical hour in this terrible conflict, and before any Government takes the fateful decision as to the conditions under which it ought either to terminate or continue the struggle, it ought to be satisfied that the conscience of the nation is behind these conditions, for nothing else can sustain the effort which is necessary to achieve a righteous end to this war. I have therefore during the last few days taken special pains to ascertain the view and the attitude of representative men of all sections of thought and opinion in the country ...

I am glad to be able to say as a result of all these discussions that although the Government are alone responsible for the actual language I propose using, there is national agreement as to the character and purpose of our war aims and peace conditions, and in what I say to you to-day, and through you to the world, I can venture to claim that I am speaking not merely the mind of the Government but of the nation and of the Empire as a whole ...

... If, then, we are asked what we are fighting for, we reply, as we have often replied: We are fighting for a just and a lasting peace, and we believe that before permanent peace can be hoped for three conditions must be fulfilled.

First the sanctity of treaties must be re-established; secondly, a territorial settlement must be secured based on the right of self-determination or the consent of the governed; and, lastly, we must seek by the creation of some international organisation to limit the burden of armaments and diminish the probability of war.

In these conditions the British Empire would welcome peace; to secure those conditions its peoples are prepared to make even greater sacrifices than those they have yet endured ... ■

Of enormous significance for post-war politics was the decision in 1916, by all parties, to accept the Representation of the People Bill, which became law in 1918. This promised to double the size of the electorate, enfranchising all men over 21 years, and 8.4 million women over the age of 30, producing an electorate of more than 21 million and heralding the arrival of a more genuine democracy. It was decided to postpone an election until the enlarged electoral roll was complete, that is, until mid-1918 at the earliest. Perhaps most significant was the achievement of votes for at least some women. Lord Selborne provides some interesting insights into ministerial thinking on this important measure.

4.27   **Lord Selborne, letter to Lord Salisbury, 25 August 1916 (Bodleian Library, MS Selbourne 6, fols 174–6, quoted in J. Turner, *British Politics and the Great War: Coalition and Conflict 1915–1918*, London, Yale University Press, 1992, p. 120).**

■ … Personally I think it would be most unjust to women and dangerous to the State to enfranchise the adult fighting man and no women. Dangerous to the State because I firmly believe in the steadying influence of the women voters in essentials and in the long run. Unjust to women because I believe that the interests of labour women, and of the woman's view of certain social matters, would be ruthlessly sacrificed …

When I said I was prepared for a bold course I referred to the post-war or permanent franchise.

On theory I would always enlarge the franchise by stages. But I think that the history of the war has settled the question for us. In my judgement the way that the men of our race have behaved in this war has made adult manhood suffrage inevitable; we shall have to do in one stage what I should have preferred to do in several …

I do not believe that 23 million voters will act any differently to 15 or 12. I think that a labour government is not likely to do worse now with a huge electorate than a radical government was able to do with the present electorate. On the whole I should prefer the labour government now. Before the war I should have been more afraid of their attitude on imperial questions. I am not afraid of that now. Of course things will be done which I vehemently dislike, but those things were already being done before the war; and the war has confirmed the intense belief which I have had now for a good many years in the instincts and intentions of my fellow countrymen and women. ■

The Coalition government's problems were not over with the passage of the Representation of the People Act. A major German offensive in March 1918 forced the government to concentrate as many troops as possible on the Western Front, and this required the extension of conscription. Worse still, conscription had, for the first time, to be applied to Ireland, previously exempt, arousing deep hostility there. Unfortunately, this occurred at a sensitive point in the work of the 'Irish Convention', which had been discussing a compromise political settlement for Ireland. The convention disintegrated, and most of the Nationalist Party joined Sinn Fein. Attempting to maintain order, the government suggested linking conscription in Ireland to a promise of Home Rule. This provoked a major row when the Conservatives concluded that the Union was being betrayed.

The government's already difficult position was further complicated by the decision of Sir Frederick Maurice, formerly the Director of Military Operations, and so responsible for allocating military manpower, to make public his belief that the government had deliberately limited the supply of men to France, and that Lloyd George had lied to the Commons about the number of troops being sent to France. The resulting political controversy encouraged Asquith to come out openly against the government, for first time since 1916. Moreover, the Conservatives, instinctively pro-military and wary of Lloyd George, were inclined to believe Maurice. When the issue was debated in the House of Commons on 9 May 1918, the government survived the vote, being opposed only by 106 Liberal and Labour MPs and one Conservative.

The Maurice debate destroyed the Liberals' alleged 'unity'. In the December 1918 election, Liberals who had voted against the Coalition would be opposed by government-endorsed candidates. Fundamentally, the choice in the debate was between Lloyd George and Asquith. Although many Conservatives were hostile to the government over its Irish policy, their desire to keep Asquith out of office persuaded them to back Lloyd George.

4.28 **The Maurice debate, 9 May 1918 (*Hansard*, 5th ser., 105: 2347, 2355–6, 2359).**

■ Mr Asquith: I beg to move, 'That a Select Committee of this House be appointed to inquire into the allegations of incorrectness in certain Statements of Ministers of the Crown to this House, contained in a letter of Major-General Maurice, late Director of Military Operations, published in the Press on the 7th day of May.' ...

The PRIME MINISTER (Mr Lloyd George): The demand put forward in the Motion ... is absolutely without precedent, as far as I can see, in the history of this House. Statements made by Ministers in this House have been challenged times without number ... My right hon. Friend's statements during this War have been challenged seriously once or twice ... What is the present demand? A general, a distinguished general, who, for good or bad reasons, has ceased to hold an office which he has occupied for two years, challenged, after he has left office, statements made by two Ministers during the time he was in that office. During the time he was in such office he never challenged those statements, when he had not merely access to official information, but when he had access to the Ministers themselves.

General Maurice was in office for weeks after I delivered that speech in the House of Commons. He attended a meeting of the Cabinet, in the absence of the Chief of Staff, the very day after I delivered the speech. He never called attention to it; he never asked me to correct it ... He was there the following day, but he never called my attention to the fact that these statements were inaccurate ... I was under the impression, in fact, that he was a great friend of mine. We were constantly discussing these questions of figures, because, as the Director of Military Operations, he was the authority. Was it not his business to come to me – especially if he thought that this was so important that it justified a great general in breaking the King's Regulations and setting an example of indiscipline – was it not his business, first of all, to come to the Cabinet, or, at any rate, to come to the Minister whom he impugned, and say to him, 'You made a mistake in the House of Commons on a most important question of fact'? He might have put it quite nicely ... Never a word was said to me! Never a syllable until I saw it in the newspapers!

I say that I have been treated unfairly. I will say more than that. I thought that probably General Maurice had not talked to me about it, because he thought that it was his business to talk to his immediate Chief first of all – either to the Secretary of State for War or perhaps to the Chief of the Imperial General Staff. Perhaps he thought that it was not his business to talk to me. I therefore inquired; but until he left office, during the whole of the time that these questions were being discussed, he never made any representations to his Chief on the subject. And this on a question which is so important that you must set up a Select Committee to inquire into it! ...

The issue is a very clear one. I said that the fighting strength of the Army had increased. General Maurice says that it had diminished, as compared with the previous year. The figures that I gave were taken from the official records of the War Office, for which I sent before I made the statement. If they were incorrect, General Maurice was as responsible as anyone else. But they were not inaccurate. I have made inquiries since. I am not sure what he quite means. There is absolutely no doubt that there was a very considerable addition to the man-power of the Army in France at the beginning of 1918 as compared with the man-power at the beginning of 1917 ...

Before I sit down, there are two general considerations which I must urge. I should like to say something about the effect of such action as General Maurice's on the discipline of the Army. It was a flagrant breach of discipline. The right hon. Gentleman admitted it. I wish he had deprecated it. May I say, quite respectfully, that I think he ought to have done so? He has been responsible for the conduct of this War for two years. If this Motion be carried, he will again be responsible for the conduct of the War. Make no mistake! This is a Vote of Censure upon the Government. If this Motion were carried, we could not possibly continue in office, and the right hon. Gentleman, as the one who is responsible for the Motion, would have to be responsible for the Government ... ■

The result of the Maurice debate reminded Lloyd George that he could rely on Conservative support only for the duration of the war, emphasising the need for an early election. Both Lloyd George and the Conservatives wanted an effective electoral pact against the Labour Party. During the summer of 1918 the Lloyd George Liberals and the Conservatives began to plan their joint campaign.

The 'Coupon Election'

After some disagreement, the Liberal and Conservative party managers allocated seats between the two parties. Conservative candidates supporting the Coalition were returned without opposition. Liberals broadly sympathetic to the Coalition were also secure. Similarly unopposed were the majority of 'patriotic' Labour MPs. Candidates supported by the Coalition were given a 'coupon', that is, a letter of endorsement by Lloyd George and Bonar Law. This coupon gave the election its popular title. The Coalition's election manifesto comprised the bare minimum of social legislation acceptable to both parties.

In November 1918 Lloyd George wrote to Bonar Law outlining his views on a joint election campaign platform.

4.29   **David Lloyd George, letter to Bonar Law, 2 November 1918 (in John Ramsden, ed., *Real Old Tory Politics: The Political Diaries of Robert Sanders, Lord Bayford, 1910–1935*, London, The Historians' Press, 1984, pp. 114–15).**

■ ... If there is to be an Election I think it would be right that it should be a Coalition Election, that is to say, that the country should be definitely invited to return candidates who undertake to support the present Government not only to prosecute the War to its final end and negotiate the peace, but to deal with the problems of reconstruction which must immediately arise directly an armistice is signed ... I am convinced also that such an arrangement will be best for the Country. The problems with which we shall be faced immediately on the cessation of hostilities will be hardly less pressing and will require hardly less drastic action than those of the war itself. They cannot, in my opinion, be dealt with without disaster on party lines. It is vital that the national unity which has made possible victory in the war should be maintained until at least the main foundations of national and international reconstruction have been securely laid.

If an election on these lines is to take place I recognise that there must be a statement of policy of such a nature as will retain to the greatest extent possible the support of your followers and of mine ...

I do not think it necessary to discuss in detail how this programme is to be carried out. I said something on the subject at Manchester in September last, especially in regard to the imperative need of improving the physical conditions of the citizens of this country through better housing, better wages and better working conditions. I lay emphasis on this because the well-being of all the people is the foundation upon which alone can be built the prosperity, the security, and the greatness both of the United Kingdom and of the Empire. ■

The 1918 general election campaign began three days after the Armistice. It was marked by a wave of patriotic feeling, including calls for the Kaiser to be hanged, in which Lloyd George emerged as the man who had won the war. Polling was held on 14 December.

4.30   Labour Party poster, 1918 general election (Geoffrey Ford, private collection).

SUPPORT THE MEN & WOMEN WHO GAVE YOU VICTORY

VOTE LABOUR

4.31   Coalition 'coupon', 1918 (University of Bristol, National Liberal Club collection). ▼

Polling Day, Saturday, December 14, 1918.

The following is a copy of a letter received by Sir John Bethell :—

DOWNING STREET,
LONDON, S.W.1.

20th November, 1918.

Dear Sir John Bethell,

We have much pleasure in recognising you as the Coalition candidate for East Ham, North.

We have every hope that the electors will return you as their representative in Parliament to support the Government in the great task which lies before it.

Yours truly,

Central Liberal Coalition   339, High Street North,
     Committee Rooms.   Manor Park, E.12.

4.32   Manifesto of Mr Lloyd George and Mr Bonar Law, 1918, (F.W.S. Craig, *British General Election Manifestos 1900–1974*, London, Macmillan, 1975, pp. 28–30).

■ The Coalition Government, supported by the strenuous and united labours of the whole nation, has now accomplished the gravest portion of its task. Our enemies have been defeated in the field, their armies are broken, and their Governments are overturned. Thanks to the patient valour of the hosts of freedom, the knell of military autocracy has sounded forever in the Continent of Europe. Other tasks directly arising out of the war now await our nation, and can only be surmounted by the good sense, the patriotism, and the forbearance of our people. The unity of the nation which has been the great secret of our strength in war must not be relaxed if the many anxious problems which the war has bequeathed to us are to be handled with the insight, courage, and promptitude which the times demand.

... We appeal, then, to every section of the electorate, without distinction of party, to support the Coalition Government in the execution of a policy devised in the interests of no particular class or section, but, so far as our light serves us, for the furtherance of the general good ...

The care of the soldiers and sailors, officers and men, whose heroism has won for us this great deliverance, and who return to civilian life, is a primary obligation of patriotism, and the Government will endeavour to assist such members of the armed forces of the Crown as may desire to avail themselves of facilities for special industrial training and to return to civil life under conditions worthy of their services to the country. Plans have been prepared ... whereby it will be the duty of public authorities and, if necessary, of the State itself to acquire land on a simple and economical basis for men who have served in the war, either for cottages with gardens, allotments, or small holdings as the applicants may desire and be suited for, with grants provided to assist in training and initial equipment ...

The principal concern of every Government is and must be the condition of the great mass of the people who live by manual toil. The steadfast spirit of our workers, displayed on all the wide field of action opened out by the war – in the trenches, on the ocean, in the air, in field, mine, and factory – has left an imperishable mark on the heart and conscience of the nation. One of the first tasks of the Government will be to deal on broad and comprehensive lines with the housing of the people, which during the war has fallen so sadly into arrears, and upon which the well-being of the nation so largely depends. Larger opportunities for education, improved material conditions, and the prevention of degrading standards of employment ... are among the conditions of social harmony which we shall earnestly endeavour to promote ...

Until the country has returned to normal industrial conditions it would be premature to prescribe a fiscal policy intended for permanence. We must endeavour to reduce the war debt in such a manner as may inflict the least injury to industry and credit ... One of the lessons which has been most clearly taught us by the war is the danger to the nation of being dependent on other countries for vital supplies on which the life of the nation may depend. It is the intention therefore of the Government to preserve and maintain where necessary these key industries in the way which experience and examination may prove to be best adapted for the purpose. If production is to be maintained at the highest limit at home, security must be given against the unfair competition to which our industries may be subjected by the dumping of goods produced abroad and sold on our market below the actual cost of production ...

Active measures will be needed to secure employment for the workers of the country. Industry will rightly claim to be liberated at the earliest possible moment from Government control. By the development and control in the best interests of the State of the economical production of power and light, of the railways and the means of communication, by the improvement of the Consular Service, and by the establishment of regular machinery for consultation with representative trade and industrial organisations on matters affecting their interest and prosperity, output will be increased, new markets opened out, and great economies effected in industrial production.

It will be the duty of the new Government to remove all existing inequalities of the law as between men and women.

It has been recognised by all parties that reform is urgently required in the constitution of the House of Lords, and it will be one of the objects of the Government to create a Second Chamber which will be based upon direct contact with the people, and will therefore be representative enough adequately to perform its functions ...

It is a source of pride to be of this age, and to be members of this nation. In the whole course of the world's history no generation has been compelled to face sacrifices such as we have steadfastly endured, or perils such as we have victoriously confronted. Well and truly have rich and poor, castle and cottage, stood the ordeal of fire. Right earnestly do we trust that the united temper, the quiet fortitude, the high and resolute patriotism of our nation may be long preserved into the golden times of peace. ■

4.33   Labour Party, *Labour's Call to the People!*, 1918 (London, Labour Party, pp. 1–2).

■ The Labour Party has left the Coalition, and is appealing to the men and women of the country with a programme that is a challenge to reaction.

A PEACE OF RECONCILIATION

Victory has been achieved, and Labour claims no mean share in its achievement. Not only have the workers supplied the vast majority of our soldiers and sailors, and sustained the burden of war at home; the democratic diplomacy which found expression in the War Aims of Labour has been one of the most powerful factors in winning the war, and must be the most powerful factor in the rebuilding of the world. The Peace which Labour demands is a Peace of International Co-operation. It declares absolutely against secret diplomacy and any form of economic war, and demands, as an essential part of the Peace Treaty, an International Labour Charter incorporated in the very structure of a League of Free Peoples.

HANDS OFF DEMOCRACY!

Labour welcomes the extension of liberty and democracy in Europe. It has warned the Coalition that opposition towards the young democracies of the Continent, and especially that intervention on the side of European reaction, will be disastrous. Labour demands the immediate withdrawal of the Allied forces from Russia. In the interests of world-democracy it stands for the immediate restoration of the Workers International …

NO CONSCRIPTION

The returning soldier or sailor will find himself once more a worker. His cause is one with that of the workers at home. Civil and industrial liberties have been largely suspended during the war; and soldier and worker want their liberties back now. The Labour Party stands for the destruction of all war-time measures in restraint of civil or industrial liberty, the repeal of the Defence of the Realm Act, the complete abolition of Conscription, and the release of all political prisoners. It stands for free citizenship, a Free Parliament, for Free Speech, and against the domination of the Press by sinister political influences.

THE LAND FOR THE WORKERS

The Labour Party means to introduce large schemes of land reorganisation, and it is fully aware that this can only be done in the teeth of the most powerful vested interests. Land nationalisation is a vital necessity; the land is the people's and must be developed so as to afford a high standard of life to a growing rural population not by subsidies or tariffs, but by scientific methods, and the freeing of the soil from landlordism and reaction.

A MILLION GOOD HOMES

Labour demands a substantial and permanent improvement in the housing of the whole people. At least a million new houses must be built at once at the State's expense, and let at fair rents, and these houses must be fit for men and women to live in. Labour will press for a really comprehensive Public Health Act co-ordinating all health authorities, based on prevention rather than cure, and free from servile or inquisitorial features. It will also press for real public education, free and open to all, with maintenance scholarships without distinction of class, and for justice to the teachers, upon whom education finally depends.

[A LEVY ON CAPITAL]

Labour will resist every attempt to place burdens on the poor by indirect taxation. Labour is firm against tariffs and for Free Trade. The way to deal with unfair competition of imports made under sweated conditions is not by tariffs, but by international labour legislation, which will make sweating impossible. In paying the War Debt, Labour will place the burden on the broadest backs by a special tax on capital. Those who have made fortunes out of the war must pay for the war; and Labour will insist upon heavily graduated direct taxation with a raising of the exemption limit. That is what Labour means by the Conscription of Wealth.

[INDUSTRIAL DEMOCRACY]

In industry, Labour demands the immediate nationalisation and democratic control of vital public services, such as mines, railways, shipping, armaments, and electric power; the fullest recognition and utmost extension of trade unionism, both in private employment and in the public services. It works for an altogether higher status for Labour, which will mean also better pay and conditions. The national minimum is a first step, and with this must go the abolition of the menace of unemployment, the recognition of the universal right to work or maintenance, the legal limitation of hours of labour, and the drastic amendment of the Acts dealing with factory conditions, safety, and workmen's compensation.

THE REAL WOMEN'S PARTY

Labour has always stood for equal rights for both sexes, when other parties were ignoring or persecuting women. In politics, the Labour Party stands for complete adult suffrage, in industry for equal pay and the organisation of men and women workers in one trade union movement. To the woman worker and to the wife of the working man or the soldier, Labour can make a confident appeal. Better pay and pensions for the workman or soldier mean better conditions for his wife and family. There must be no sex party: the Labour Party *is* the Women's Party. Woman is the Chancellor of the Exchequer of the home. Labour stands with the Co-operative Movement in its insistence on reasonable food prices and fair distribution, and in its resistance to unfair taxation ...

... Even in an election as sinister as this, in which a large part of the nation's youth is arbitrarily disenfranchised by the Government, Labour confidently appeals to the country to support its programme of social justice and economic freedom. ∎

The Coupon Election: Results

The results of the 1918 coupon election were a triumph for the Coalition, although the distribution of seats in the Commons distorted the actual vote won by each party. The Liberals suffered a severe defeat, one from which, arguably, they never recovered. The Labour Party did well, but did not advance much on its performance in the 1910 election, bearing in mind the much increased working-class vote in 1918. *Sinn Fein* supplanted the Irish Nationalists but refused to attend Westminster, choosing instead to establish its own parliament in Dublin. Among the new intake of MPs, there were a large number of businessmen, an increased number of trade union officials, but no women.

4.34 General election results, 1918 (derived from J. Turner, *British Politics and the Great War: Coalition and Conflict 1915–1918*, London, Yale University Press, 1992, p. 403).

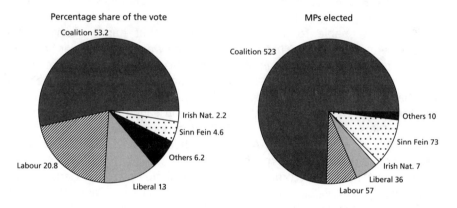

CHAPTER FIVE

War and Peace: Strategy, Diplomacy and War Aims, 1914–1920

THE First World War – always for those involved in it 'the Great War' – plunged Britain into nearly four and a half years of bitter conflict, which few could foresee in August 1914. Diplomatically bound to France and Russia, the country was unable to act as a free agent, but had to consider the requirements of its allies. Almost throughout the war, it was unclear how long Russia, creaking under the strain of the conflict, could carry on the fight. Britain was increasingly dependent on finance and materials from the United States, and had to tread cautiously to avoid offending American opinion – a difficult task given the US President's enthusiasm for an early peace. Even when the United States entered the war in 1917, as an 'associate', rather than as a formal ally, the prospect of American influence over a post-war peace settlement constrained British policy.

In August 1914, in accordance with the Schlieffen plan, the German army advanced through Belgium and came dangerously close to Paris. Although its progress was stopped at the Battle of the Marne (September 1914), it occupied much of Belgium and large areas of north-east France. A 'Western Front' of heavily fortified entrenchments was established, extending from the Belgian coast to the Swiss border, along which the armies of France, Britain and Belgium faced their German counterparts. Until 1918, with the major exception of the assault on Verdun in 1916, Germany's strategy in the west was essentially defensive, the major effort being devoted to tackling Britain's eastern ally, Russia. Abortive Allied attempts were made in 1915, 1916·and 1917 to break through the German lines in the west, at enormous human cost, ensuring that the horrific and bloody image of the trenches would haunt future generations. Meanwhile, Britain opened secondary theatres, for example against Turkey, intended to harry the enemy elsewhere, though again with only limited success.

Pre-war expectations that naval strength would be decisive were not borne out after 1914. The largest sea engagement of the war, the Battle of Jutland (1916), was indecisive, in that much of the German fleet was able to return to its bases. However, it remained there for the rest of the war, posing little threat to the Royal Navy. Much more serious was the German submarine war, which threatened to sever vital supply lines between Britain and the United States. Ironically, the unrestricted submarine warfare conducted by Germany was partly responsible for bringing the United States into the war on the side of the Allies, a development which tipped the scales definitely in the Allies' favour. Although Germany succeeded in knocking Russia out of the war in 1918, and launching a major offensive in the west in the spring of that year, the German army overreached itself against Allied armies which were being strengthened during 1918. In the autumn of 1918 an Allied counter-offensive forced Germany to accept an armistice and to seek a negotiated peace.

Strategy and survival

British strategy in the summer of 1914 was firmly grounded in the belief that the war would be short. A British Expeditionary Force, initially composed of four divisions, quickly joined the French and Belgian armies, helping to prevent further German advances.

The war became fertile ground for the development of propaganda techniques. The contradiction between images of German cultural supremacy and allegations, often spurious, of German atrocities against Belgian civilians provided a rich theme for British propaganda.

THE TRIUMPH OF "CULTURE."

5.1   **Cartoon by Bernard Partridge, 'The triumph of "culture"',** *Punch,* **1914.**

For Britain, the war's purpose was to defeat German militarism and prevent its revival, making impossible a second German bid for European dominance. In the summer of 1914, however, few observers in Britain could be confident about what this might entail. Inside the Foreign Office, the view gained ground that Germany was divided between 'moderates' and 'extremists', suggesting that a secure peace would require the extremists to be deposed and Germany's political structure to be fundamentally adjusted to remove 'Prussian' militaristic influences. The British Foreign Secretary, Sir Edward Grey, was at pains to convey these ideas to the United States government. On the day Britain entered the war, Grey met the US Ambassador in London, Walter H. Page, who subsequently recorded their conversation.

5.2   **Walter H. Page, description of meeting with Sir Edward Grey, 4 August 1914 (in B.J. Hendrick, *The Life and Letters of Walter H. Page, 1885–1918*. *Vol. I*, London, Heinemann, 1923, p. 315).**

■ [The meeting took place at three o'clock on Tuesday afternoon, August 4th … As Page came in, Sir Edward, a tall and worn and rather pallid figure, was standing against the mantelpiece; he greeted the Ambassador with a grave handshake and the two men sat down … Sir Edward at once referred to the German invasion of Belgium.]

'The neutrality of Belgium,' he said, and there was the touch of finality in his voice, 'is assured by treaty. Germany is a signatory power to that treaty. It is upon such solemn compacts as this that civilization rests. If we give them up, or permit them to be violated, what becomes of civilization? Ordered society differs from mere force only by such solemn agreements or compacts. But Germany has violated the neutrality of Belgium. That means bad faith. It means also the end of Belgium's independence. And it will not end with Belgium. Next will come Holland, and, after Holland, Denmark. This very morning the Swedish Minister informed me that Germany had made overtures to Sweden to come in on Germany's side. The whole plan is thus clear. This one great military power means to annex Belgium, Holland, and the Scandinavian states and to subjugate France … England would be forever contemptible,' Sir Edward said, 'if it should sit by and see this treaty violated. Its position would be gone if Germany were thus permitted to dominate Europe. I have therefore asked you to come to tell you that this morning we sent an ultimatum to Germany. We have told Germany that, if this assault on Belgium's neutrality is not reversed, England will declare war.'

'Do you expect Germany to accept it?' asked the Ambassador.

Sir Edward shook his head.

'No. Of course everybody knows that there will be war.'

There was a moment's pause and then the Foreign Secretary spoke again: 'Yet we must remember that there are two Germanies. There is the Germany of men like ourselves – of men like Lichnowsky and Jagow. Then there is the Germany of men of the war party. The war party has got the upper hand.'

At this point Sir Edward's eyes filled with tears.

'Thus the efforts of a lifetime go for nothing. I feel like a man who has wasted his life.' ■

The outbreak of war released a wave of patriotic feeling across Europe. By Christmas 1914 more than a million British men had volunteered for military service. Lord Kitchener, whose portrait was used in the most memorable recruiting poster of the war, realised, however, that even larger numbers of men, formed into 'new armies', would be required in the protracted war ahead. Initially, conscription was a sensitive political issue, its implementation being delayed until January 1916, by which time military reversals during the winter of 1915–16 had convinced the British government that more assistance to France was necessary.

5.3   **Alfred Leete, 'Britons join your country's army!', poster, 1914 (Imperial War Museum, London, PST, 2734).**

The unexpected stalemate on the Western Front exposed the absence of a clear strategy for conducting the war. Kitchener had hoped that the bulk of the fighting could be left to the French and Russians, enabling Britain to build up its armies, but this was unacceptable to the other Allies. It also soon became clear that the war was unlikely to be won at sea, despite the elaborate preparations before 1914, although naval losses, and particularly the vulnerability of British merchant ships to German submarines, might lose the war for Britain. While some influential figures, including Kitchener, were convinced that the Western Front was the decisive theatre, others, including Winston Churchill, hoped to engage the enemy in other areas. It was this hope, fuelled in part by concern about civilian responses to the lack of progress in the west, which encouraged plans to confront Turkey, a threat to Britain's strategic interests in Egypt. This produced the Dardanelles campaign, during which a naval bombardment of Turkish positions in March 1915 was followed by a disastrous attempt to land troops at Gallipoli, resulting in heavy casualties, ignominious withdrawal and the removal of Churchill from the Admiralty.

Maurice Hankey, Secretary of the Committee of Imperial Defence, had produced a memorandum in December 1914 setting out the military position and suggesting possible courses of action for the Allies.

5.4   **M. Hankey, 'Boxing Day memorandum', 1914, *The Supreme Command*, (in *M. Hankey, 1914–1918. Vol. I*, 1961, London, Allen & Unwin, pp. 244–50).**

■   THE 'BOXING DAY MEMORANDUM'

The remarkable deadlock which has occurred in the western theatre of war invites consideration of the question whether some other outlet can be found for the effective employment of the great forces of which we shall be able to dispose in a few months' time.

2. The experience of the offensive movements of the Allies in this theatre within the last few weeks seems to indicate that any advance must be both costly and slow ...

3. There is no reason to suppose that the enemy's successive positions can be captured merely by weight of numbers ...

5. If the deadlock on our side is complete it is no less complete as regards the enemy. He has had bitter and costly experience of the difficulty of attacking entrenched positions, and; whatever force he brings to bear, there is no reason to suppose that he can penetrate our lines ...

6. Such deadlocks are not a feature peculiar to the present war. They have been the commonplace of wars in all ages ...

7. Two methods have usually been employed for circumventing an *impasse* of this kind. Either a special material has been provided for overcoming it, or an attack has been delivered elsewhere, which has compelled the enemy so to weaken his forces that an advance becomes possible ...

9. Is it possible by the provision of special material to overcome the present

impasse? Can modern science do nothing more? Some of the following devices might possibly be useful:

(*a*) Numbers of large heavy rollers, themselves bullet proof, propelled from behind by motor engines, geared very low, the driving wheels fitted with 'caterpillar' driving gear to grip the ground, the driver's seat armoured, and with a Maxim gun fitted. The object of this device would be to roll down the barbed wire by sheer weight, to give some cover to men creeping up behind, and to support the advance with machine-gun fire.

(*b*) Bullet-proof shields or armour ... Lord Esher has informed me that an officer has recently invented a light form of armour that covers the vital organs, and the French are reported in the newspapers to be employing a shield in the Argonne.

(*c*) Smoke balls, to be massed in the trenches before an advance, and to be used if the wind is in a favourable quarter. They would be thrown by the troops towards the enemy's trenches to screen the advancing troops.

(*d*) Rockets throwing a rope with a grapnel attached, which are being used by the French to grip the barbed wire, which is then hauled in by the troops in the trench from which the rocket is thrown.

(*e*) Spring catapults, or special pumping apparatus to throw oil or petrol into the enemy's trenches ...

12. The above proposals may perhaps be deemed fantastic and absurd. This brings us, therefore, to the consideration of the second method of surmounting an *impasse,* viz. the possibility of a diversion elsewhere ...

17. If our main military effort against German territory is unattainable for the present, the principal weapon remaining is economic pressure, and this, in the writer's opinion, is the greatest asset we have in the war. Economic pressure, however, appears to be breaking down to a certain extent owing to the enormous trade with Holland and Denmark, and at the best is a weapon slow in operation. In the meantime there is every reason for using our sea-power and our growing military strength to attack Germany and her allies in other quarters ...

18. Germany can perhaps be struck most effectively and with the most lasting results on the peace of the world through her allies, and particularly through Turkey ...

21. ...Supposing Great Britain, France, and Russia, instead of merely inciting [the Balkan countries] ... to attack Turkey and Austria, were themselves to participate actively in the campaign, and to guarantee to each nation concerned that fair play should be rendered ...

22. If Bulgaria, guaranteed by the active participation of the three Great Powers, could be induced to co-operate, there ought to be no insuperable obstacle to the occupation of Constantinople, the Dardanelles, and

Bosphorus. This would be of great advantage to the Allies, restoring communication with the Black Sea, bringing down at once the price of wheat, and setting free the much-needed shipping locked up there.

23. It is presumed that in a few months' time we could, without endangering the position in France, devote three army corps ... to a campaign in Turkey, though sea transport might prove a difficulty. This force, in conjunction with Greece and Bulgaria, ought to be sufficient to capture Constantinople.

24. If Russia, contenting herself with holding the German forces on an entrenched line, could simultaneously combine with Serbia and Roumania in an advance into Hungary, the complete downfall of Austria-Hungary could simultaneously be secured.

25. Failing the above ambitious project, an attack in Syria would prove a severe blow to Turkey, particularly if combined with an advance from Basra to Baghdad by a reinforced army ...

32. It is not suggested that the above campaigns should all be undertaken simultaneously. It is, however, suggested that, if our advance into Flanders and Germany cannot be effected either by superiority of numbers or by a preparation of special material, it would be wise, without releasing our grip on the position in France, to set to work at once, and in concert with our Allies to choose a field, among those indicated above, for the employment of the surplus armies which will soon be available, and to make all preparations. Failing the invasion of Germany itself, which, in accordance with correct strategical principle, has hitherto been our aim, it is suggested that we should endeavour by the means proposed to get assets into our hands wherewith to supplement the tremendous asset of sea-power and its resultant economic pressure, wherewith to ensure favourable terms of peace when the enemy has had enough of the war. ■

During the war, Britain received enormous support, both military and economic, from its Empire. In all, some two and a half million men from the Empire, including Indians and Africans, fought for Britain. While Indian troops played a major role in the Middle East campaigns, Australian and New Zealand forces, the 'Anzacs', came to be especially associated with the fateful Gallipoli campaign of 1915.

5.5 Empire casualties, 1914–1918 (derived from A.J. Stockwell, 'The war and the British Empire', in J. Turner, ed., *Britain and the First World War*, London, Unwin Hyman, 1988, p. 37).

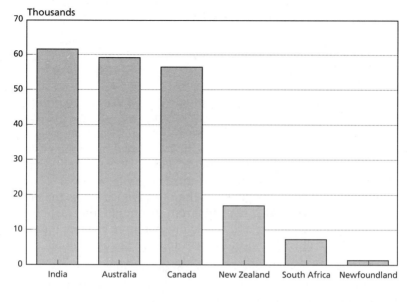

An important feature of the war was the scope it created for tension between politicians and the generals. Initially, the generals enjoyed great respect, and Kitchener seemed a natural choice when he was appointed War Secretary in August 1914. The lack of decisive military breakthroughs, however, combined with the appalling casualties that the British army sustained, gradually eroded the position of the military leaders. Partly to appease the French, who had been disturbed by the diversion of British efforts from the Western Front, attempts were made in spring 1915 to strike the Germans at Neuve Chapelle and at the Second Battle of Ypres, both of which were indecisive and produced heavy casualties. Sir John French was replaced as commander in France by Douglas Haig, and later in the year Sir William Robertson became Chief of the Imperial General Staff. The British army's position in France remained difficult, and, given the sheer scale of the French military contribution, for example at Verdun, British generals were reluctant to question French strategy openly. The joint British– French offensive on the Somme, beginning in June 1916, intended to conclude the war within the year, succeeded only in pushing back the Germans some five miles, at the cost of nearly half a million British casualties.

At the end of 1916 Lloyd George became Prime Minister, determined to curb the generals' power. Politically, it was necessary for him to limit British casualties, saving the country's reserves for a long struggle. However, he was unable to withstand pressure from Haig and Robertson for a fresh assault in 1917 (the 'Passchendaele' offensive), which proved as futile as the Somme had been. Lloyd George sought a unified command structure in the west, and in October 1917 he succeeded in creating the Supreme War Council, responsible for joint Allied strategic planning. After renewed manpower problems in February 1918, Lloyd George replaced Robertson with the more amenable Sir Henry Wilson, although he found Haig, who enjoyed backbench Tory

*support, more difficult to dislodge. After the Germans launched their major offensive in
March 1918, the Frenchman Marshal Foch was appointed Supreme Commander of the
Allies, paving the way for successful counter-offensives.*

*In his memoirs, Robertson captured some of the problems arising from the mutual
incomprehension of the political and military leaderships.*

5.6   **Sir William Robertson, *Soldiers and Statesmen 1914-1918, Vol. I*, 1926
(London, Cassell, pp. 184–9).**

■ Again, just as the lack of visible progress on the Western Front led to the
belief that some new form of strategy was needed, so the daily recurring list
of casualties repeatedly gave rise to the suggestion that something was
wrong with our tactics. For instance, in 1916 I had more than once to meet
the ministerial argument, put forward with great ingenuity, that to shoot
down the enemy from behind cover must surely be a less costly as well as a
more simple method of waging war than to advance across the open and so
get shot down oneself. It was apparently thought that defensive action
alone would bring victory, and would bring it more cheaply than would the
offensive policy of which most soldiers appeared to be so fond.

In reply to tiresome heresies such as these I would recall the demoralizing
effect upon troops which prolonged defensive tactics inevitably have; urge
that although the attacker might at first be the heavier loser, it was the
defender who would certainly lose most in the long run, once his physical
and moral powers began to break down; and that, as in the conduct of any
business, civil no less than military, without offensive action, without initiative, success could never, in point of fact, be achieved. But the Ministers
to whom I refer would shake their heads, condemn the so-called process of
'attrition' as being merely the unintelligent application of brute force, and
maintain that there must be some way of securing victory without engaging
in too much of that hard fighting which, unhappily, all wars involve –
especially when the combatants are counted, as in 1914–1918, by tens of
millions of men. The appalling losses suffered by the defending British
armies in France in March–April, 1918, and by the defending German
armies six months later, showed how fatuous these defensive notions were.

The longer concrete evidence of coming victory was delayed the harder it
became for the General Staff to keep the direction of the war on right lines.
Especially was this the case during 1917, and it was mainly caused by the
fact that certain members of the Government brooded too much over our
own difficulties and losses, and took too little credit for those that were
being suffered by the enemy. Mr. Lloyd George, in particular, would unfairly
belittle British military efforts as compared with German, and the attempt
on my part to put the other point of view, and to look at things through
German eyes, would be met with the reply that the same sort of thing had
been said many times before, and that we were still as far from winning the
war as ever. The daily communiqués issued by G.H.Q. on the Western Front
were frequently criticised in this sense, and as often as not the enemy's

account of the fighting would be accepted as the more correct version of the two. That the enemy would naturally so draft his communiqués as to present his own position in the most favourable light and ours in the worst was seldom realized

Another dilemma often encountered was how far I could rightfully go in trying to meet ministerial proposals which were militarily unsound, and which, if opposed, might impair those good relations with Ministers which it was essential to maintain. In peace-time differences of opinion may be allowed to slide without great harm being done, as it may be possible to adjust them at a more convenient season. In war, compromises are much more dangerous; errors and omissions can seldom be rectified (the enemy will see to that); and men's lives are at stake. In war, too, things do not proceed on the smooth and simple lines of peace, and I, at any rate, often found it very difficult to make a choice between acquiescing in a course of military action which seemed undesirable, and saying outright that I could be no party to it ... ■

Of increasing importance during the war was the need to clarify, for domestic and foreign consumption, what Britain was fighting for. It was thought essential to emphasise that Britain's aims were not aggressive. In January 1918, addressing the Trades Union Congress, Lloyd George attempted to explain his government's position in detail, anxious to pre-empt any declaration of peace terms by US President Wilson. Only three days later, Wilson unveiled his 'Fourteen Points' to the US Congress, a programme designed not only to eliminate 'Prussian militarism', but also to forestall Allied aggrandisement. It was on the basis of Wilson's scheme that Germany sought an armistice in November 1918.

5.7   David Lloyd George, speech on war aims, 5 January 1918 (reported in *The Times*, 7 January 1918).

■ ... We may begin by clearing away some misunderstanding and stating what we are not fighting for. We are not fighting a war of aggression against the German people. Their leaders have persuaded them that they are fighting a war of self-defence against a league of rival nations bent on the destruction of Germany. That is not so. The destruction or disruption of Germany or the German people has never been a war aim with us from the first day of this war to this date. Most reluctantly and, indeed, quite unprepared for the dreadful ordeal, we were forced to join in this war in self-defence, in defence of a violated public law of Europe and in vindi-cation of the most solemn treaty obligations on which the public system of Europe rested, and on which Germany had ruthlessly trampled in her invasion of Belgium. We had to join in the struggle or stand aside and see Europe go under and brute force triumphant over public life and international justice. It was only the realization of that dreadful alternative that forced the British people into the war. And from that original attitude they have never swerved. They have never aimed at the break-up of the

German peoples or the disintegration of their State or country. Germany has occupied a great position in the world.

Nor did we enter this war merely to alter or destroy the imperial constitution of Germany, much as we consider that military autocratic constitution a dangerous anachronism in the twentieth century. Our point of view is that the adoption of a really democratic constitution by Germany would be the most convincing evidence that in her the old spirit of military domination has indeed died in this way, and would make it much easier for us to conclude a broad democratic peace with her. But, after all, that is a question for the German people to decide ...

The days of the Treaty of Vienna are long past. We can no longer submit the future of European civilization to the arbitrary decisions of a few negotiators, striving to secure by chicanery or persuasion the interests of this or that dynasty or nation. The settlement of the new Europe must be based on such grounds of reason and justice as will give some promise of stability. Therefore it is that we feel that government with the consent of the governed must be the basis of any territorial settlement in this war. For that reason also, unless treaties be upheld, unless every nation is prepared, at whatever sacrifice, to honour the national signature it is obvious that no treaty of peace can be worth the paper on which it is written.

The first requirement, therefore, always put forward by the British Government and their allies has been the complete restoration, political, territorial, and economic, of the independence of Belgium and such reparation as can be made for the devastation of its towns and provinces. This is no demand for war indemnity such as was imposed on France by Germany in 1871. It is not an attempt to shift the cost of warlike operations from one belligerent to another which may or may not be defensible. It is no more and no less than an incident that before there can be any hope for stable peace, this great breach of the public law of Europe must be repudiated, and, so far as possible, repaired. Reparation means recognition. Unless international life is recognized by insistence on payment for injury done in defiance of its canons, it can never be a reality. Next comes the restoration of Servia, Montenegro and the occupied part of France, Italy, and Roumania. The complete withdrawal of the alien armies and the reparation for injustice done is a fundamental condition of permanent peace.

We mean to stand by the French Democracy to the death in the demand they make for reconsideration of the great wrong of 1871, when, without any regard to the wishes of the population, two French provinces were torn from the side of France and incorporated in the German Empire. This sore has poisoned the peace of Europe for half a century and until it is cured healthy conditions will not have been restored. There can be no better illustration of the folly and wickedness of using a transient military success to violate national life.

I will not attempt to deal with the question of the Russian territories now in German occupation. The Russian policy since the Revolution has passed so rapidly through so may phases that it is difficult to speak without some suspension of judgement as to what the situation will be when the final terms of European peace come to be discussed. Russia accepted the war with all its horrors because, true to her traditional guardianship of the weaker communities of her race, she stepped in to protect Servia from a plot against her independence. It is this honourable sacrifice which not merely brought Russia into the war but France as well. France, true to the conditions of her treaty with Russia, stood by her ally in a quarrel which was not her own. Her chivalrous respect for her treaty led to the wanton invasion of Belgium; and the treaty obligations of Great Britain to that little land brought us into the war.

The present rulers of Russia are now engaged, without any reference to the country whom Russia brought into the war, in separate negotiations, with their common enemy. I am indulging in no reproaches; I am merely stating facts with a view to making it clear why Britain cannot be held accountable for decisions taken in her absence and concerning which she has not been consulted or her aid invoked ... We shall be proud to fight to the end side by side with the new democracy of Russia, so will America and so will France and Italy, but if the present rulers of Russia take action which is independent of their allies, we have no means of intervening to arrest the catastrophe which is assuredly befalling their country. Russia can only be saved by her own people. We believe, however, that an independent Poland, comprising all those genuinely Polish elements who desire to form part of it, is an urgent necessity for the stability of Western Europe. ■

The Experience of War

For the majority of soldiers who fought in the First World War, the conflict was experienced in trenches. For four years the opposing sides faced one another along the Western Front, dug into elaborate systems of trenches, intended to provide some protection from machine-guns and shells. From time to time, attacks would be launched, involving waves of infantry attempting to advance, theoretically aided by heavy artillery fire. The Battle of the Somme (1916) and the Third Battle of Ypres ('Passchendaele', 1917) are among the best-remembered of these massively futile episodes, during which hundreds of thousands of soldiers faced the full panoply of modern industrialised warfare, including shrapnel, poison gas and shells. Trench warfare created a surreal way of life for the soldiers. As the surrounding landscape was denuded of features by heavy bombardment, the men huddled in their waterlogged, muddy trenches. The conditions made communication and transport difficult, but rats and lice flourished.

Much of the fighting on the Western Front took place under cover of darkness. The troops would often snatch their rest and the chance to read eagerly awaited letters from home, during the day.

5.8 Canadian troops at rest, February 1918 (Imperial War Museum, London, Q 2533).

Between the periods of intense activity, a soldier's life at the front was often characterised by boredom.

At the other extreme from the long periods of boredom at the front were the nightmarish conditions of battle. The following extract is taken from the recollections of a soldier who took part in the Battle of the Somme.

5.9 Corporal W.H. Shaw, 9th (S) Battalion, Royal Welch Fusiliers, recollections of the Somme (in Lyn Macdonald, *1914–1918: Voices and Images of the Great War*, London, Penguin, 1991, pp. 155–6).

■ We were moved up and we were herded into this field behind the reserve line, and when we looked back it appeared as if we were sitting on the lee of a hill, it would be like a big mound. Well, the next thing we knew, we were being given this cotton wool and told to put it in our ears. Well, there was no guns firing, but we had to do as we were told and put this cotton wool in our ears. The next thing is, this mound, what we thought was a mound, well camouflaged, is two big twelve-inch Naval guns, came out on a track, just the muzzle of the gun showing and manned by Royal Marines. Well, without any warning (and from where I was sitting, it couldn't have been thirty yards), these two guns blasted off. Well, we shot up in the air! We were lying in front of them and the blast from those twelve-inch guns! My God! It shook us!

Our artillery had been bombing that line for six days and nights, trying to smash the German barbed-wire entanglements. The result was we never got anywhere near the Germans. Never got anywhere near them. Our lads was mown down. They were just simply slaughtered. It was just one continuous go forward, come back, go forward, come back, losing men all the time and there we were, wondering when it was going to end. You couldn't do anything. You were either tied down by the shelling or the machine-guns and yet we kept at it, kept on going all along the line, making no impact on the Germans at all. We didn't get anywhere, we never moved from the line, hardly. The machine-guns were levelled and they were mowing the top of the trenches. You daren't put your finger up. The men were just falling back in the trenches.

Now there was a saying in the Royal Welch Fusiliers, 'Follow the flash.' Now, I don't know whether you've ever seen a Royal Welch Fusiliers officer, but there's a flash on the back of his collar. The officers were urging us on, saying, 'Come on, lads, follow the flash!' But you just couldn't. It was hopeless. And those young officers, going ahead, that flash flying in the breeze, they were picked off like flies. We tried to go over and it was just impossible. We were mown down, and that went on and if some of the Battalions did manage to break through, it was very rare and it was only on a small scale. If they did, the Germans would counter-attack, they'd fall back, and that's how it was, cat and mouse all the time. ■

5.10   Casualties during the First World War (derived from H. Kinder and W. Hilgemann, *The Penguin Atlas of World History Vol. II*, (London, Penguin, 1978), p. 126).

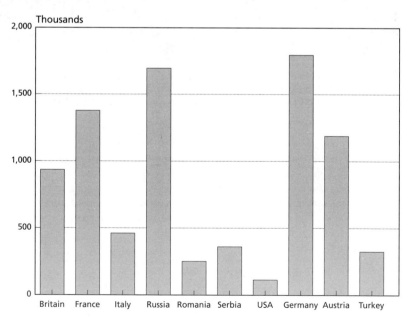

Along with the Somme, the name Passchendaele (a village in west Flanders) has come to symbolise the horrors and scale of the war. In an abortive attempt to break out of the Ypres salient and attack the Germans from the rear, the British and French armies launched a major offensive on 31 July 1917. After three months, about 300,000 Allied men had died. The offensive was accompanied by sustained shell bombardment, reducing the Passchendaele area to a sea of cratered mud in which many soldiers were to drown. The following aerial photographs give some impression of the impact of the bombardment.

5.11   Passchendaele before and after bombardment, 1917 (Imperial War Museum, London, Q 429 18A).

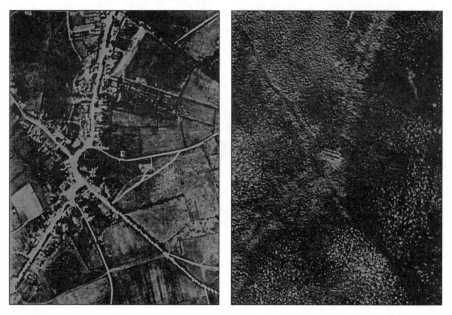

The unprecedented experience of modern warfare gave rise to some of the most powerful literature in the English language. The 'War Poets', including Siegfried Sassoon, Edmund Blunden and Isaac Rosenberg, served in the trenches and witnessed the fighting directly. Their poems, contrasting strikingly with traditional glorification of war, were graphic, hard-hitting and unsentimental, a collective protest at the futility of this mass slaughter. Wilfred Owen came to be regarded as one of the most talented of the War Poets. An infantry officer, he was decorated for bravery and was killed only a week before the Armistice, aged 25. In the following poem, Owen sought to dispel any lingering notions that war could be equated with chivalry and glory.

5.12   **Wilfred Owen, 'Dulce et decorum est', 1917 (in Edmund Blunden, ed., *The Poems of Wilfred Owen*, London, Chatto & Windus, 1933).**

■   Bent double, like old beggars under sacks,
Knock-kneed, coughing like hags, we cursed through sludge,
Till on the haunting flares we turned our backs
And towards our distant rest began to trudge.
Men marched asleep. Many had lost their boots
But limped on, blood-shod. All went lame; all blind;
Drunk with fatigue; deaf even to the hoots
Of gas-shells dropping softly behind.

Gas! Gas! Quick, boys! – An ecstasy of fumbling,
Fitting the clumsy helmets just in time:
But someone still was yelling out and stumbling,
And flound'ring like a man in fire or lime …
Dim, through the misty panes and thick green light,
As under a green sea, I saw him drowning.

In all my dreams, before my helpless sight,
He plunges at me, guttering, choking, drowning.

If in some smothering dreams you too could pace
Behind the wagon that we flung him in,
And watch the white eyes writhing in his face,
His hanging face, like a devil's sick of sin;
If you could hear, at every jolt, the blood
Come gargling from the froth-corrupted lungs,
Obscene as cancer, bitter as the cud
Of vile, incurable sores on innocent tongues, –
My friend, you would not tell with such high zest
To children ardent for some desperate glory,
The old Lie: Dulce et decorum est
Pro patria mori. ■

Although the First World War had major implications for the women who remained in Britain on the 'Home Front', many women experienced the fighting at close hand. Among these were the predominantly middle- and upper-class women who served in uniformed 'VADs' – Voluntary Aid Detachments – organised by the Red Cross and attached to the Territorial Army, often employed in nursing work.

5.13   Joyce Dennys, 'VAD are urgently needed', undated poster (Imperial War Museum, London, PST 3268).

In 1914 the 18-year-old Vera Brittain commenced her studies at Oxford University. After a year she left Oxford to become a VAD nurse, serving on the Western Front. Her experiences, and the loss of those dearest to her, inspired her to write the autobiographical Testament of Youth, *published in 1933 and quickly a bestseller. By articulating the wartime experiences of her generation, Vera Brittain provided an eloquent case for pacifism.*

5.14   Vera Brittain, *Testament of Youth*, 1933 (London, Virago, 1978 edn, pp. 410–1).

■ Only a short time ago, sitting in the elegant offices of the British Red Cross Society in Grosvenor Crescent, I read in the official *Report of the Joint War Committee of the British Red Cross Society and Order of St. John* the following words – a little pompous, perhaps, like the report itself, but doubtless written with the laudable intention of reassuring the anxious nursing profession:

'The V.A.D. members were not ... trained nurses; nor were they entrusted with trained nurses' work except on occasions when the emergency was so great that no other course was open.'

And there, in that secure, well-equipped room, the incongruous picture came back to me of myself standing alone in a newly created circle of hell during the 'emergency' of March 22nd, 1918, and gazing, half hypnotised, at the dishevelled beds, the stretchers on the floor, the scattered boots and piles of muddy khaki, the brown blankets turned back from smashed limbs bound to splints by filthy blood-stained bandages. Beneath each stinking wad of sodden wool and gauze an obscene horror waited for me – and all the equipment that I had for attacking it in this ex-medical ward was one pair of forceps standing in a potted-meat glass half full of methylated spirit ...

I had to bombard the half-frantic dispensary for nearly an hour before I could get my stores, and without them it was impossible even to begin on the dressings. When I returned I found to my relief that a Sister had been sent to help me. Though only recently out from England she was level-headed and competent, and together we started on the daily battle against time and death which was to continue, uninterrupted, for what seemed an eternity.

However long I may be destined to survive my friends who went down in the Flood, I shall never forget the crushing tension of those extreme days. ■

Wartime Diplomacy

The partnership with its allies placed limits on Britain's freedom of manoeuvre during the war. To maintain the alliance, Britain was obliged to make concessions, for example by participating in military offensives such as the Somme in order to placate the French. Similarly, although the war demonstrated the ties of loyalty within the British Empire, it also strained those relations. In Australia, Canada and South Africa there were significant minorities opposed to involvement in a conflict seen mainly as Britain's concern. The Empire's older members, such as Australia and Canada, while making a huge contribution to the war effort, were unwilling to do so unconditionally and expected recognition from London for their own interests. Responding to these sentiments, Lloyd George created an Imperial War Cabinet in 1916, comprising the five War Cabinet members and other British and Dominion ministers, including the South African statesman General Jan Smuts, who was made Defence Minister in the new Cabinet.

Under Dominion pressure, Britain agreed to discuss relations within the Empire after the war. In 1917, during the Imperial War Conference, the Canadian Prime Minister, Sir Robert Borden, described the changing relationship between Britain and the Dominions, anticipating the formal realignments which would occur in the inter-war years.

5.15   Sir Robert Borden, extract from minutes of proceedings of the Imperial War Conference, 16 April 1917 (in Department of External Affairs, *Documents on Canadian External Relations. Vol. I: 1909–1918,* Ottawa, Roger Duhamel, 1967, pp. 309-10).

■ This subject is one upon which I might speak at great length. Many proposals with regard to the subject have been discussed in the United Kingdom and in all the Dominions of the Empire for many years past in all possible phases. There can be no doubt as to its importance. The growth of the Dominions in wealth and population has been very remarkable during the past fifty years, and especially during the last twenty-five years. Their future growth we hope – and, more than that, we believe – will be even more marked. Foreign policy and foreign relations, with which is intimately connected the question of the common defence of the Empire, have been under the immediate control of the Government of the United Kingdom. It would appear from the views of constitutional writers that this condition during the later phases of the growth of the Oversea Dominions has proceeded on a theory of trusteeship which, whatever may be said of it in the past, is certain to prove not only entirely inadequate to the needs of the Empire but incompatible with the aspirations of the people of the Dominions in the future. I have spoken of the growth of the Dominions; it is by no means improbable that children now living will see their population surpass that of the United Kingdom. It is quite within the range of possibility that a single Dominion might grow to the extent which I have mentioned. Therefore it seems to me beyond question that the theory of trusteeship to which I have alluded cannot be continued indefinitely in the future.

In approaching the subject one is impressed especially with this consideration, that the greatest intellects of the Empire in the past have miscalculated the conditions that would develop in the Dominions, and have failed to foresee the relations of the Empire under the policy of developing full powers of self-government which was supposed to have the tendency of weakening, if not severing, the ties which unite the Dominions to the Mother Country. The policy of complete control in domestic affairs and complete autonomy in all local affairs, instead of weakening the ties which unite the Empire, has very greatly strengthened them. It was said by a statesman of the highest capacity after that policy had been embarked upon (that is, the policy of granting to the Dominions complete autonomy) that it was an absolute mistake, that it could only lead to the weakening and severance of relations, and that it would have been a wise policy to preserve in the United Kingdom control of the natural resources of the Dominions, and control over their fiscal policy; that this would have tended to unite the Empire, and regret was expressed that some such policy had not been maintained. All of us in the Dominions, and I think the people of the British Isles, realise now that any such policy would have had most unfortunate and, more than that, disastrous results. The policy which was supposed to weaken the Empire has really strengthened it, and I look forward to a development in the future along the line of an increasingly equal status between the Dominions and the Mother Country. It seems to me that the attainment of full citizenship, which involves a voice in foreign relations, will proceed along the line to which I have alluded. The nations of the Empire are really bound together by the tie of a common allegiance, by like institutions and ideals of democracy, and by like purposes. Such ties will bring the nations of the Empire together more closely upon the line which I have mentioned. I say this with a full understanding that it is unwise, having regard to the lessons of the past, for any of us to predict absolutely the developments of the future. But, nevertheless, the line of development which has been noticeable during the past twenty or twenty-five years seems to point unmistakably to that conclusion. Indeed, the action of the Dominions in this war has made the spirit of nationhood splendidly manifest. The fact that one million men in the Dominions have taken up arms for the defence of the Empire's existence and the maintenance of its future influence is so significant a lesson that one would be unwise not to have it constantly in mind. I believe that the Dominions fully realise the ideal of an Imperial Commonwealth of United Nations and one should not forget the importance of the crown as a tie between the Dominions and the Mother Country. ■

During the early years of the war, Britain was concerned not only to maintain good relations with its allies, but also, if possible, to find new allies.

One of the British government's major tasks in the early years of the war was to remain on friendly terms with the neutral United States, increasingly a vital source of the money and materials needed to fight the war. Relations were not made any easier by President Woodrow Wilson's efforts to secure peace negotiations. In January 1917 Wilson called for a 'peace without victories', but this was acceptable to neither side. In April 1917, following the resumption of unrestricted submarine warfare by Germany, together with a German offer to Mexico of an offensive alliance, the United States entered the war on the Allied side. Although this numerical strengthening of the Allied forces was ultimately to prove decisive, the US army was unable to contribute much to fighting on the Western Front until 1918.

The following extract is from the War Cabinet's discussion following talks in 1916 between the British Foreign Secretary Sir Edward Grey and President Wilson's special adviser, Colonel Edward House, who enjoyed good relations with Grey and was sympathetic to the Allied cause.

5.16   Cabinet War Committee, minutes, 21 March 1916 (PRO CAB 42/11/6).

■ ... SIR EDWARD GREY referred to conversations he had had with Colonel House, who had recently visited England, France, and Germany. A record of these conversations had already been circulated to the Cabinet Ministers who were also members of the War Committee. The general tenor of this record had been that, according to Colonel House, President Wilson, if desired by Great Britain and France, was prepared to propose a peace Conference, and, if the proposal was accepted by the parties to the war, to conduct it in a manner generally sympathetic to the Allies. Further, if the Central Powers refused to take part in the Conference, or to agree to terms reasonably favourable to the Allies, there was every prospect that the United States would intervene on the side of the Allies ...

It appeared to him that our attitude should depend very largely on the views of our naval and military prospects taken by the responsible naval and military advisers of the Government. If in the next six months, the Allies were likely to be able to dictate their own terms to Germany or to improve considerably their military position it was certain that we could get better terms then with or without the intervention of the United States than could be obtained now, and it would be better not to consider President Wilson's proposals. But if there was a prospect of a deadlock at the end of six months, when he gathered our financial and economic power to meet the demands of our allies would be less than at present; or if there was any prospect of the weakening of the relative position vis-a-vis the enemy of the Allies by (say) the defeat of one of the Allies (Russia for example) in either of these eventualities it might be worth while or even imperative to consult the French Government as to the expediency of making use of President Wilson's suggestion now. He presumed also that it would be considered if either France or Russia intimated that it could not continue to struggle ...

THE PRIME MINISTER considered that the proposal ought to be put aside for the present. Personally he doubted whether President Wilson's position was strong enough to enable him to carry through this policy.

SIR EDWARD GREY thought President Wilson would have the support of the whole nation of the United States in a proposal to end the war by a Conference if the Allies agreed to it.

MR. BALFOUR said that at present the proposal was not worth five minutes' thought. No doubt, if carried out, it would get the President of the United States out of political difficulties. If he could bring about peace his prestige in the United States would be greatly enhanced.

SIR EDWARD GREY said that, so far as his information went hitherto, the French would not wish to avail themselves of this offer.

MR. BALFOUR asked whether there was any dark spot in the situation except money and ships?

MR. LLOYD GEORGE added the Russian military situation. He would like to know the views of the military advisers as to whether the Russian army could withstand a German attack in the spring.

SIR WILLIAM ROBERTSON said that according to his information the Russians themselves wished to take the offensive.

LORD KITCHENER said that he always felt some hesitation in accepting

Russian estimations of their own strength, but he was satisfied that General Alexeieff felt confident of holding up the Germans on the Riga front.

MR. LLOYD GEORGE pointed out that the position of the Russian army in regard to munitions was not such as to justify hopes of a successful offensive ... ■

Of particular concern to both Britain and France was the capacity of their ally, Russia, to maintain its war effort. This concern was heightened by the two Russian Revolutions of 1917. Although the provisional government formed by Kerensky in February 1917 was committed to continuing the war, the October Revolution, which brought the Bolsheviks to power, prompted Allied fears that Russia might seek a separate peace with Germany, releasing German troops from the Eastern Front who could be deployed in the west. In fact, the Bolshevik government rapidly sought an armistice with Germany, leading to the Treaty of Brest-Litovsk of March 1918, and Russia's withdrawal from the war. In December 1917 Lord Milner of the War Cabinet, and Lord Robert Cecil, Under-Secretary of State at the Foreign Office, urged the Cabinet to pursue moderation in relations with Russia. Soon, however, some ministers, including Winston Churchill, were clamouring for armed intervention against the Bolshevik regime.

5.17   Lord Milner and Lord Robert Cecil, memorandum, 26 December 1917 (PRO CAB 23/4, WC 306, Appendix).

■ ... We should represent to the Bolsheviki that we have no desire to take part in any way in the internal politics of Russia, and that any idea that we favour a counter-revolution is a profound mistake. Such a policy might be attractive to the autocratic Governments of Germany and Austria, but not to the Western democracies or America. But we feel it necessary to keep in touch as far as we can with the Ukraine, the Cossacks, Finland, Siberia, the Caucasus, &c, because these various semi-autonomous provinces represent a very large proportion of the strength of Russia. In particular, we feel bound to befriend the Ukraine, since upon the Ukraine depends the feeding of the Roumanians, to whom we are bound by every obligation of honour.

As for the war, we should carefully refrain from any word or act condoning the treachery of the Russians in opening peace negotiations with our enemies. But we should continually repeat our readiness to accept the principles of self-determination, and, subject to that, of no annexation or indemnities. We should press on the Bolsheviki the importance of not being satisfied with empty phrases from the Germans, and point out that unless they get specific undertakings from them as to such questions as Poland, Bohemia, the Roumanian parts of Transylvania, not to speak of Alsace-Lorraine and the Trentino, they will get nothing. Meanwhile their powers of resistance are melting away, and they will soon be, if they are not now, at the mercy of the German Kaiser, who will then snap his fingers at all their fine phrases and impose on them any terms he pleases. They should be told that it is now probably too late to do anything to save the personnel of the army. But the material of the artillery can still be preserved, and at the very least it should not be transferred to our enemies to be used against the Western democracies. Most important of all, the Bolsheviki should prevent, if they can, the wheat districts of Russia, such as the Ukraine, falling into the control of or being made available for the Central Powers. This makes another reason why we are anxious to support and strengthen the Ukraine, and why we urge on the Bolsheviki that, so far from trying to coerce the Ukrainians, they should enter into close co-operation with them ... ∎

The Peace Settlement

As the war neared its end, discussions began on whether the Allies should carry on fighting until they achieved the best possible peace terms.

Within the Cabinet, one point of view was that Germany should receive a crushing military defeat, in order to teach it a lesson. An important consideration for the British government was the fact that the German Revolution of October and November 1918 had brought about the Kaiser's abdication, and seemed to have eradicated Prussian militarism by introducing a democratic republic. Another consideration, stressed by General Smuts, was that if Britain carried on the war, it might later be forced to accept peace on less advantageous terms, framed under United States influence, which could only increase the longer the war continued. The Americans had already threatened to withdraw altogether from the war if the Allies resisted the peace initiative.

5.18   War Cabinet minutes, 26 October 1918 (PRO CAB 23/14, 491B).

∎ ... the War Cabinet resumed the discussion commenced on the previous day on the question of whether the British representatives at the forthcoming Conference should base their attitude on the assumption that we desired immediate peace or to continue the War ...

The Prime Minister pointed out that there was an important school of thought, which at times made considerable appeal to him, who said that we ought to go on until Germany was smashed; that we ought to force our way on to German soil, and put Germany at our mercy; that we should actually dictate terms on German soil, very possibly such terms as we would now accept; but that the enemy should be shown that War cannot be made with impunity. He felt that this preliminary question ought to be cleared up in our own minds before the forthcoming Conference with our Allies.

Mr. Balfour said that he himself would not go on with the War if we could now get the terms which he thought ought to be got. Those terms would include the loss of territory in Schleswig-Holstein ... as well as territory to the West of Germany of the most valuable kind from an aggressive point of view, since it contained coalfields and ironfields, and on the East territory containing coalfields which had belonged to Germany since the time of Frederick the Great. By these terms the Eastern frontier of Germany would be within 70 miles of Berlin. By these terms Germany would lose her Colonies. If these conditions could be secured it would be ludicrous to say that Germany was not beaten. The fact that our Armies were across the Rhine and had perhaps sacked Frankfurt would not really mean greater defeat to Germany.

The Prime Minister said that industrial France had been devastated and Germany had escaped. At the first moment when we were in a position to put the lash on Germany's back she said, 'I give up.' The question arose whether we ought not to continue lashing her as she had lashed France.

Mr. Chamberlain said that vengeance was too expensive in these days.

The Prime Minister said it was not vengeance but justice ...

General Smuts said that he had placed his views on paper ... In this he had pointed out that peace made at the present time would be a British peace. We had now got into our hands everything of material importance that we required; our communications were secure, as was our supply of raw material. By fighting for twelve months more we should get nothing more ... In a continuance of the War, Europe would break up into a number of small nominally free nations. The only powerful unit on the Continent would be Germany. All Germany's rivals would disappear ... As Europe went down, so America would rise. In time the United States of America would dictate to the world in naval, military, diplomatic and financial matters. In that he saw no good ...

The War Cabinet agreed that:

The Prime Minister and Mr. Balfour should, in the forthcoming Conferences at Paris, base their attitude on the question of an armistice on the assumption that the British Government desires a good peace if that is now available. ■

Although in October 1918 Lloyd George appeared to take a belligerent stance on the treatment of Germany, by the time he reached Paris for the Peace Conference, with the 'coupon election' safely behind him, he appeared to be more conciliatory. In March 1919 he sketched out his ideas for the benefit of his colleagues in government. A dominant concern was the revolutionary atmosphere of post-war Europe, and the need to prevent the spread of Bolshevism from Russia. Furthermore, keen to achieve a lasting peace, Lloyd George believed that a settlement which was excessively harsh on Germany would not only undermine the stability of the new German Republic, but would also make a future war highly likely. Moreover, the fact that neither Britain nor the United States was willing to contemplate massive commitments in Europe meant that measures against Germany were themselves constrained.

5.19   David Lloyd George, 'Fontainebleu memorandum', 25 March 1919 (Cmd 1614, PP XIII, 1922, pp. 1–5).

■ When nations are exhausted by wars in which they have put forth all their strength and which leave them tired, bleeding and broken, it is not difficult to patch up a peace that may last until the generation which experienced the horrors of the war has passed away. Pictures of heroism and triumph only tempt those who know nothing of the sufferings and terrors of war. It is therefore comparatively easy to patch up a peace which will last for 30 years.

What is difficult, however, is to draw up a peace which will not provoke a fresh struggle when those who have had practical experience of what war means have passed away. History has proved that a peace, which has been hailed by a victorious nation as a triumph of diplomatic skill and statesmanship, even of moderation in the long run, has proved itself to be shortsighted and charged with danger to the victor ...

... You may strip Germany of her colonies, reduce her armaments to a mere police force and her navy to that of a fifth-rate power; all the same in the end if she feels that she has been unjustly treated in the peace of 1919 she will find means of exacting retribution from her conquerors. The impression, the deep impression, made upon the human heart by four years of unexampled slaughter will disappear with the hearts upon which it has been marked by the terrible sword of the great war. The maintenance of peace will then depend upon there being no causes of exasperation constantly stirring up the spirit of patriotism, of justice or of fair play. To achieve redress our terms may be severe, they may be stern and even ruthless, but at the same time they can be so just that the country on which they are imposed will feel in its heart that it has no right to complain. But injustice, arrogance, displayed in the hour of triumph, will never be forgotten or forgiven.

For these reasons I am, therefore, strongly averse to transferring more Germans from German rule to the rule of some other nation than can possibly be helped. I cannot conceive any greater cause of future war than that the German people, who have certainly proved themselves one of the most vigorous and powerful races in the world, should be surrounded by a number of small states, many of them consisting of people who have never previously set up a stable government for themselves, but each of them containing large masses of Germans clamouring for reunion with their native land ...

... The whole of Europe is filled with the spirit of revolution. There is a deep sense not only of discontent, but of anger and revolt, amongst the workmen against pre-war conditions. The whole existing order in its political, social and economic aspects is questioned by the masses of the population from one end of Europe to the other. In some countries, like Germany and Russia, the unrest takes the form of open rebellion; in others, like France,

Great Britain and Italy, it takes the shape of strikes and of general disinclination to settle down to work – symptoms which are just as much concerned with the desire for political and social change as with wage demands.

Much of this unrest is healthy. We shall never make a lasting peace by attempting to restore the conditions of 1914. But there is a danger that we may throw the masses of the population throughout Europe into the arms of the extremists whose only idea for regenerating mankind is to destroy utterly the whole existing fabric of society. . .

The greatest danger that I see in the present situation is that Germany may throw in her lot with Bolshevism and place her resources, her brains, her vast organising power at the disposal of the revolutionary fanatics whose dream it is to conquer the world for Bolshevism by force of arms. This danger is no mere chimera. The present Government in Germany is weak; it has no prestige; its authority is challenged; it lingers merely because there is no alternative but the spartacists, and Germany is not ready for spartacism, as yet ...

If Germany goes over to the spartacists it is inevitable that she should throw in her lot with the Russian Bolshevists. Once that happens all Eastern Europe will be swept into the orbit of the Bolshevik revolution and within a year we may witness the spectacle of nearly three hundred million people organised into a vast red army under German instructors and German generals equipped with German cannon and German machine guns and prepared for a renewal of the attack on Western Europe.

From every point of view, therefore, it seems to me that we ought to endeavour to draw up a peace settlement as if we were impartial arbiters, forgetful of the passions of the war. This settlement ought to have three ends in view. First of all it must do justice to the Allies by taking into account Germany's responsibility for the origin of the war and for the way in which it was fought. Secondly, it must be a settlement which a responsible German Government can sign in the belief that it can fulfil the obligations it incurs. Thirdly, it must be a settlement which will contain in itself no provocations for future wars, and which will constitute an alternative to Bolshevism, because it will commend itself to all reasonable opinion as a fair settlement of the European problem ... ■

Britain's position at the Peace Conference was constrained by domestic factors, especially by growing demands for financial retrenchment, which made rapid cuts in military spending essential. By the end of the war Britain was maintaining a total of three and a half million troops. By late 1920 this figure had been cut to 370,000. The government could not ignore demands from the soldiers themselves for quick demobilisation, especially when military discipline, in both Britain and France, was compromised by disturbances among disgruntled troops. The following cartoon, which appeared in 1919, depicts the Minister for Reconstruction and former Director of Recruiting, Brigadier-General Sir Auckland Geddes, receiving the soldiers' unambiguous demand.

5.20   Cartoon by Sidney 'George' Strube, 'Geddes the new orderly officer: "Any complaints?" ', *Daily Express*, 1919.

In the inter-war years, there was growing support, particularly in Britain, for the idea that the peace settlement had been unsatisfactory. One of the settlement's earliest critics was the young economist John Maynard Keynes, who represented the Treasury at the Paris Peace Conference. Keynes was so hostile to the draft peace treaty that he resigned in disgust. His views were set out in his influential The Economic Consequences of the Peace *(1919), in which he argued that the German economy could not meet the planned level of reparations payments established as a central part of the peace settlement.*

5.21   John Maynard Keynes, *The Economic Consequences of the Peace*, 1919 (London, Macmillan, pp. 211–13).

■ This chapter must be one of pessimism. The Treaty includes no provisions for the economic rehabilitation of Europe – nothing to make the defeated Central Empires into good neighbours, nothing to stabilise new States of Europe, nothing to reclaim Russia; nor does it promote in any way a compact of economic solidarity amongst the Allies themselves; no arrangement was reached at Paris for restoring the disordered finances of France and Italy, or to adjust the systems of the Old World and the New.

The Council of Four paid no attention to these issues, being preoccupied with others – Clemenceau to crush the economic life of his enemy, Lloyd George to do a deal and bring home something which would pass muster for a week, the President to do nothing that was not just and right. It is an

extraordinary fact that the fundamental economic problem of a Europe starving and disintegrating before their eyes, was the one question in which it was impossible to arouse the interest of the Four. Reparation was their main excursion into the economic field, and they settled it as a problem of theology, of politics, of electoral chicane, from every point of view except that of the economic future of the States whose destiny they were handling
...

The essential facts of the situation, as I see them, are expressed simply. Europe consists of the densest aggregation of population in the history of the world. This population is accustomed to a relatively high standard of life, in which, even now, some sections of it anticipate improvement rather than deterioration. In relation to other continents Europe is not self-sufficient; in particular it cannot feed itself. Internally the population is not evenly distributed, but much of it is crowded into a relatively small number of dense industrial centres. This population secured for itself a livelihood before the War, without much margin of surplus, by means of a delicate and immensely complicated organisation, of which the foundations were supported by coal, iron, transport, and an unbroken supply of imported food and raw materials from other continents. By the destruction of this organisation and the interruption of the stream of supplies, a part of this population is deprived of its means of livelihood. Emigration is not open to the redundant surplus. For it would take years to transport them overseas, even, which is not the case, if countries could be found which were ready to receive them. The danger confronting us, therefore, is the rapid depression of the standard of life of the European populations to a point which will mean actual starvation for some (a point already reached in Russia and approximately reached in Austria). Men will not always die quietly. For starvation, which brings to some lethargy and a helpless despair, drives other temperaments to the nervous instability of hysteria and to a mad despair. And these in their distress may overturn the remnants of organisation, and submerge civilisation itself in their attempts to satisfy desperately the overwhelming needs of the individual. This is the danger against which all our resources and courage and idealism must now co-operate. ■

CHAPTER SIX

Stagnation or Progress?:
The Economy and Social Policy,
1919–1929

THE 1920s were a decade of mixed economic performance and achievement for Britain. On the one hand, the First World War had exacerbated many of the country's economic problems and raised new concerns as well. As a result of four years of concentration on the defeat of Germany, Britain had lost its previously predominant foothold in many of its traditional markets. The expected boom in world trade after the war failed to materialise, and the sluggishness of the export trades led to the stagnation of staple industries such as coal, shipbuilding and textiles. The domestic repercussions of these problems were considerable: concentrated unemployment, industrial unrest and local government protest. On the other hand, new industries showed encouraging signs of growth by the end of the decade, and after 1925 there were signs of stability and recovery. In Stanley Baldwin's second administration of 1925–9, steady progress and the consolidation of social policy culminated in the passage of the Local Government Act of 1929. By the end of the decade, the country had experienced several years of prosperity and relative tranquillity. But the economic upheavals of recovery from the war, punctuated first by the return to the gold standard in 1925, and second by the General Strike in the following year, meant that the boom of the later 1920s was not as marked in Britain as it was, for example, in the United States.

From Boom to Bust, 1919–21

The strength of labour

The early post-war period was seen as an unprecedented opportunity to achieve progress in social reform. Various factors associated with the War – increased powers of the state, patriotism and social cohesion, popular awareness of poverty, sympathy for the plight of the returning soldier, and the political promises made by Lloyd George in the 1918 election – meant that the advocates of radical reform measures were in a stronger position than ever before.

Initially, post-war reformist hopes appear to have been justified. In Cabinet, the fears of Unionist ministers over rising expenditure were overcome by the political need to smooth the process of demobilisation. In the extract which follows, for example, it is apparent that Lloyd George was able to play on fears of revolution to win the support of his Unionist colleagues for a state-subsidised housing scheme, including Bonar Law, who at this time was serving as Lord Privy Seal, and Austen Chamberlain (son of Joseph), who had recently been appointed Chancellor of the Exchequer.

6.1 War Cabinet minutes, 3 March 1919 (PRO CAB 23/9/539).

■ Mr Bonar Law thought that they were all agreed that the scheme would have to be undertaken in the case of ex-Service men, but the cost to the State would be very great ...

The Prime Minister said that he thought we should regard this matter from a wider point of view ... In Europe we were now faced with very serious conditions. Russia had gone almost completely over to Bolshevism, and we had consoled ourselves with the thought that they were only a half-civilised race; but now even in Germany, whose people were without exception the best educated in Europe, prospects are very black. Bavaria was already in chaos, and the same fate might await Prussia. Spain seemed to be on the edge of upheaval. In a short time we might have three-quarters of Europe converted to Bolshevism. None would be left but France and Great Britain. He believed that Great Britain would hold out, but only if the people were given a sense of confidence – only if they were made to believe that things were being done for them. We had promised them reforms time and time again, but little had been done. We must give them the conviction this time that we meant it and we must give them that conviction quickly. We could not afford to wait until prices went down. If nothing were done the people themselves would break down prices ... Even if it cost £100,000,000 what was that compared with the stability of the State? ... So long as we could persuade the people that we were prepared to help them and to meet them in their aspirations, he believed that the sane and steady leaders amongst the workers would have an easy victory over the Bolsheviks among them.

The Chancellor of the Exchequer thought that they all agreed with the general attitude expressed by the Prime Minister ... but the whole of the situation had not been put forward. We would come to a time finally when we should have to pay, and heavy taxation would affect markets and prices. He regarded housing as the first problem to be faced. It was a very big one, but we ought to push on with it immediately, at whatever cost to the State. ■

In contrast to earlier periods of militancy, labour demands in the early post-war period were often focused on conditions and hours of employment rather than simply on higher wages. During the war itself, workers enjoyed the benefits of full employment and a rise in real wages, but the austere conditions of the wartime economy had reduced spending on consumer goods. Organised labour was undoubtedly in a strong position at the end of the war; and in the immediate post-war years this was reflected in the reduction of hours worked by approximately 13 per cent.

6.2   **The working-class standard of living, 1914–21 (derived from C.H. Feinstein, *National Income, Expenditure and Output of the United Kingdom, 1855–1965*, Cambridge, Cambridge University Press, 1972, table 65; and B.R. Mitchell, *British Historical Statistics*, Cambridge, Cambridge University Press, 1988, p. 739.**

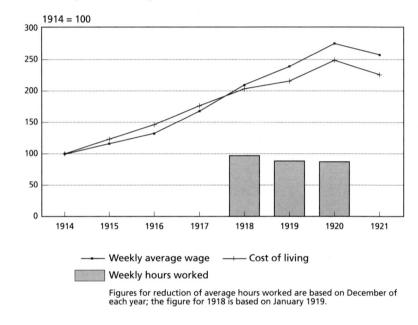

Figures for reduction of average hours worked are based on December of each year; the figure for 1918 is based on January 1919.

When the Miners' Federation threatened in 1919 to revive the triple alliance of miners, railway workers and dockers in support of its post-war programme, based on higher wages, shorter hours and nationalisation of the industry, the government persuaded it to co-operate with a Royal Commission composed of representatives from both the mine owners and the labour movement. While the Sankey Commission divided along predictable lines, its final report narrowly approved nationalisation.

6.3   **Report by the Honourable Mr Justice Sankey, *Coal Industry Commission Act 1919. Second Stage. Reports*, 20 June 1919 (Cmd. 210, PP XI, 1919, pp. 10–11).**

■ Coal mining is our national key industry upon which nearly all other industries depend. A cheap and adequate supply of coal is essential to the comfort of individuals and to the maintenance of the trade of the country. In this respect, and in the peculiar conditions of its working, the coal mining industry occupies a unique and exceptional place in our national life, and there is no other industry with which it can be compared …

The lack of capital in some mines and the lack of proper management in others prevent the development of coalfields and the extraction of coal to the best advantage for the benefit of the Nation.

There are in the United Kingdom about 3,000 pits owned by about 1,500 companies or individuals. Unification under State ownership makes it possible to apply the principles of standardization of materials and appliances and thereby to effect economies to an extent which is impossible under a system where there are so many individual owners.

It may be argued that the foregoing defects in the present system could be removed by changes in the direction of unification falling short of State ownership.

But a great change in outlook has come over the workers in the coalfields, and it is becoming increasingly difficult to carry on the industry on the old accustomed lines. The relationship between the masters and workers in most of the coalfields in the United Kingdom is, unfortunately, of such a character that it seems impossible to better it under the present system of ownership. Many of the workers think they are working for the capitalist and a strike becomes a contest between labour and capital. This is much less likely to apply with the State as owner, and there is fair reason to expect that the relationship between labour and the community will be an improvement upon the relationship between labour and capital in the coalfields. ■

For the labour movement, 1919 and 1920 were years of optimism. The experience of the war was thought permanently to have transformed the power of the working class. The mood of the time was captured by the moderate railworkers' leader J.H. Thomas. His idealism was shared widely in the early post-war period.

6.4   J.H. Thomas, *When Labour Rules*, 1920 (London, W. Collins, pp. 10–11).

■ There is nothing Utopian in my vision of the England of to-morrow; I am not one of those confident and optimistic people who imagine that once Labour comes into power all will be well with the world; nevertheless, I do foresee a far happier England than any historian has yet been in a position to describe …

It may safely be assumed, however, that whatever progress tomorrow may be able to look back upon it will find human nature still very much what it is to-day; there will still be jealousies and bickerings and disputes and discontent … but the discontent of tomorrow will differ fundamentally from the discontent of the past, inasmuch as it will not be based upon a sense of injustice and will not be received in a spirit of hostility.

Furthermore, the grounds for discontent will be considerably fewer. The holiday-maker will still have the weather to grumble about; the dyspeptic will continue to complain of his breakfast, and the farmer will still find a grievance in the state of his crops, but no man will have occasion to protest against the condition under which he is expected to live; no man will be able to state that someone else is living on his sweated labour, and no man will be able to proclaim that he lacks the opportunity to improve his lot if he wishes to do so.

There will be no profiteers, no unemployment, no slums, no hungry children. ■

Boom and speculation

The optimistic post-war mood of the trade union movement was initially shared by the business community. There was a realistic awareness of the extent to which pre-war trading patterns had been disrupted since 1914. But it was believed that domestic and world demand would expand enormously in the coming years. These expectations fuelled a speculative boom which lasted for over a year.

Pent-up demand led to an initial burst of consumer spending in Britain. Forecasts in the business press gave no reason to doubt that international trade would continue to boost prosperity at home. But as access to credit remained easy, and a process of speculative borrowing accelerated, price rises began to spiral out of control. The boom broke in the spring of 1920. In April a deflationary Budget and rising interest rates signalled the beginning of what would be one of the most serious economic slumps in twentieth-century British history.

6.5 Consumer expenditure, 1916–20 (derived from C.H. Feinstein, *National Income, Expenditure and Output of the United Kingdom, 1855–1965,* Cambridge, Cambridge University Press, 1972, pp. 65–69).

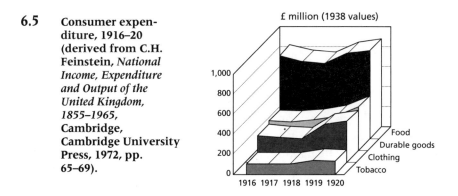

£ million (1938 values)

6.6 Editorial commentary, *British Export Gazette,* June 1919.

■ It is a very different world upon which re-awakening trade and commerce opens its eyes at the signing of the Peace Treaty with Germany from that to which it had been accustomed before our late enemies wantonly unleashed the dogs of war upon a score of peaceful populations in those first fateful days of August, 1914. Before the great cataclysm 75 p.c. of the world's trade had been carried by the British mercantile marine, and 55 p.c. of the manufactured goods shipped directly from their countries of origin had come from the workshops of the United Kingdom, the United States and Germany. As may be supposed, over four years of the most terrible and ruthless war ever waged in history have materially altered such proportions. British shipping, enormously reduced by shameless submarine warfare, by mines, and temporarily by requisitioning, is by no means in the position it was previously, and while German shipping has been swept from the ocean, other countries, notably Japan, the United States, Canada and Australia, are entering the lists as world trade carriers. Moreover, they are doing so with every prospect of offering successful competition in this direction not only to Great Britain, but to other countries which have hitherto taken an active part in ocean transport, notably France, Holland, Norway, Sweden, etc.

FACTORS MAKING FOR INCREASING TRADE.

The future trade of the world will need them all, for nothing is more certain than that after nearly five years of unparalleled devastation and destruction, and of compulsory business stagnation, not only is all possible effort being made to expedite the work of reconstruction, and the bringing of stocks up to necessary levels, but, in addition, there is every indication of commercial expansion in numberless directions ...

A HIGHER COMMERCIAL STANDARD FOR THE WORLD.

Further, there is every prospect that in all parts of the world a tendency will reveal itself towards a higher standard of living, entailing commercial requirements in much greater variety and larger volume than the period which came to an end with the outbreak of war ever knew. Indeed, such a tendency is already making itself felt in many markets, though for the time being its full expression is held in check by the needs of the world to make good the ravages of war ...

These are great changes, but, on the whole, they make for increased rather than reduced trade, for a great commercial forward stride rather than for any backward movement or mere marking time. The changes will be in trade venue as well as in trade volume. Countries that have held second rank industrially and commercially will advance to front rank – Japan and Canada are particular instances. Countries, already before the war in the front rank, will push still further ahead. The United States is the pre-eminent example, and there is no reason why Great Britain, with Government control nearing the end and labour troubles on the point of being adjusted, should not once again take her former high position and considerably swell the former volume of her overseas trade. As for Germany's commercial future, time only will show to what extent her arrogant Junkers, in thrusting war upon mankind, have robbed their country of what formerly seemed her probable commercial place in the sun.

6.7   'Manufacturers! ... the trade boom coming', advertisement, 1919 (in *The Textile Manufacturers' Yearbook*, Manchester, p. 74).

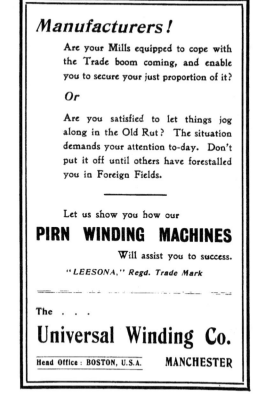

Treasury orthodoxy and retrenchment

The orthodox response of the government to the economic problems which followed was due largely to the prevailing views on economic policy set within the Treasury, which emerged in this period in a far more dominant position within Whitehall than had hitherto been the case. Concern had grown throughout the war that, as new ministries emerged and bureaucracy expanded, it would be necessary to tighten Treasury control over the rest of Whitehall.

The Treasury was reorganised and given increased powers in September 1919, and the role of the Permanent Secretary to the Treasury was redefined. By the spring of 1920 the Treasury's enhanced role in Whitehall ensured that its new head, Sir Warren Fisher, would come to exercise extraordinary influence on the machinery of government in the inter-war period. He was empowered to advise the Prime Minister on the appointment of senior officials in all departments; staffing and accounting methods were standardised according to Treasury guidelines; and from 1924 the Treasury was able to vet all policy proposals involving increased expenditure before submission to the Cabinet.

6.8   **Treasury minute on civil service reorganisation, 4 September 1919 (PRO T 199/50B).**

■   4 September 1919

The Chancellor of the Exchequer calls the attention of the Board to the fact that the Joint Permanent Secretaryships will shortly become vacant through the appointments of Sir Thomas Heath, K.C.B., K.C.V.O., F.R.S., to be Secretary and Controller of the National Debt Office and Sir John Bradbury, K.C.B., to be principal British Delegate on the Reparations Commission.

The Chancellor recommends that in place of the arrangements recently in operation under which the work of the Treasury has been organised under three or two Joint Permanent Secretaries the Permanent Secretariat should in future be constituted as follows:

1 Permanent Secretary

3 Controllers of Departments

The functions of the Permanent Secretary would include responsibility for the organisation of the Treasury, for the general supervision and coordination of the work of the Treasury as a whole, and for advising the Board.

He would act as Permanent Head of the Civil Service and advise the First Lord [the Prime Minister] in regard to Civil Service appointments and decorations ... ■

One hoped-for effect of the Treasury's greater role was the reduction of what was perceived as widespread profligacy in public expenditure. The best-known expression of the efforts at spending reductions in the 1920–2 period was the report of the Committee on National Expenditure, chaired by the businessman Sir Eric Geddes, which recommended large cuts in spending programmes in 1922.

6.9   **Committee on National Expenditure,** *First Interim Report,* **1922 (Cmd. 1581, PP IX, 1922, pp. 122–3, 136).**

■ As a result of our consideration, we are of the opinion:

[Board of Education]

(**1**) That of recent years the national expenditure on Education has far exceeded what the country can at present afford. The cost of Elementary and Secondary Education per pupil has increased unreasonably. The incidence of cost has been transferred increasingly from the local Ratepayer to the Taxpayer, and this has had the serious effect of decreasing the financial responsibility of those who actually spend the money. The Board of Education Vote has since 1918/19 grown from £19 millions to £50 millions.

(**2**) That children should not be taken into State-aided schools until they have reached the age of 6.

(3) That the cost of teaching must be brought down by the Local Authorities, and that the only way to effect this is to tell each Local Authority how much money it can have, and leave it to the Local Authority to reap thereafter the full benefit of any economies it may make. ...

(4) That the grants for Secondary Education are providing State-aided or free education to a class which can afford to pay an increased proportion or even the full cost of education, and that children whose mental capabilities do not justify this higher and much more costly education are receiving it ...

(5) That as regards Higher Education generally and Scholarships, the expenditure is in excess of the nation's ability to pay, and must be reduced.

(6) That the Estimates for the Board of Education for the year 1922/23 should be reduced from £50,600,000 to £34,500,000 ...

[Ministry of Health]

(1) That both in policy and where administrative possibilities existed, successful efforts to economise have recently been made. We have indicated a few directions in which we think that further economies might be made. The principal items of this Vote appertain to the Housing schemes, which is entailing a cost to the Taxpayer of £10,000,000 a year for the next 60 years, and we recommend a vigorous policy of sale of these houses in order to reduce that burden.

(2) That no financial incentive to economy is given to those who are entrusted with the administration of this vast property. Economies in administration and upkeep are entrusted to those who have no financial interest whatsoever in decreasing the loss on the undertaking they manage. ... ■

The 'Geddes axe' marked the end of the postwar climate of social reform. Indeed, already by 1921 the mood of optimism which had marked the labour movement immediately after the war had soured. The young economist William Orton reflected this changed mood in his history of recent industrial relations which appeared in 1921.

6.10   **William Aylott Orton,** *Labour in Transition: A Survey of British Industrial History since 1914*, **1921 (London, Philip Allan, pp. 257–8).**

■ Like the inflated currency of the war, the inflated hopes of the peace shrink and subside. The cost of living declines by 46 points of the official index in six months – a swifter movement than in any such period of the past seven years; and the wage-rates of 4 1/2 million workers suffer their first general reduction. So also the great reform projects of 1918 are left suspended in the region of aspiration. The national education scheme is indefinitely postponed ... The half-a-million houses that figured in the national reconstruction scheme dwindle to a bare 176,000 ... minimum wage legislation is perforce curtailed, while in at least one section of industry the hours of labour are extended ... Thus does the country settle down, late and painfully, on the edge of the financial crater, uncertain whether on the whole it is more likely to blow up again, or fall in, or by good luck remain comparatively stable; and those who were nethermost before find themselves nethermost again.

The worker, looking on with doubtful eyes and lighter pocket ... Short of financial revolution, the 'pre-war level' would seem the utmost limit of what can for many years be hoped for; and the miner, the engineer, the builder, the textile worker and many another may not unnaturally wonder in ruminant silence whether that is what it is all come to – whether the best the years can bring is the gradual and painful restoration of the status quo ante. ■

The human cost of the end of the boom in 1921, of falling prices and declining markets overseas, was the emergence of mass unemployment. This would be the issue to dominate British politics in the inter-war period, and one which left scars on the political agenda for many decades more. The level of unemployment in traditionally staple industries of the British economy from this time was quickly recognised to be without precedent, as the following investigation, undertaken by a group of economists and social scientists, illustrates.

6.11   J.J. Astor, B. Seebohm Rowntree, et al., *The Third Winter of Unemployment*, 1922 (London, P.S. King, pp. 3–9).

■ The years 1921 and 1922 are the worst in the records of unemployment in this country ... On the threshold of the third winter signs of improvement are few, and the strain of unemployment is not diminished ... At the end of August, 1922, in Great Britain and Northern Ireland, 1,427,311 persons, or 12 per cent. of the insured population, were recorded as unemployed. In addition 74,669 persons (0.6 per cent.) were working organised short time to qualify for intermittent benefit. These figures, serious as they are, do not fully represent the extent of the problem.

In the first place, not all the unemployed are recorded in the Employment Department Records ... In the second place, the general average conceals the intensity of the depression in the worst trades ... Even the figures for individual trades do not reveal the true intensity of the problem. Within any one industry some districts are much worse off than others.

Even these high figures must be added if we are to allow for the large amount of short time among workers in employment ... In other words, in industry proper, the insufficiency of employment is not the 11.9 of the insurance returns, but something between 20 and 22½ per cent ...

How has the country met this abnormal unemployment? ... The Unemployment Insurance scheme has served as the basis of relief ... But in meeting this emergency need the scheme has changed its character. Its actuarial basis had to be disregarded from the beginning, and special arrangements made to bring unemployed workers into benefit ... Altogether, it may be fairly said that the scheme has lost something of the character of insurance and taken on that of relief.

As relief the insurance scheme is not quite comprehensive. It does not cover all unemployed workers, and those whom it does cover it does not relieve all the time they are unemployed, nor proportionately to their needs. There has been, therefore, a great increase in Poor Law relief to unemployed workers and their dependants, costing according to the latest returns available, about £1,000,000 a month for the country as a whole. It has been necessary for Parliament to grant additional borrowing powers to the Poor Law Authorities. This large expenditure, however, is not distributed evenly over the country as a whole; it varies not only with the varying needs of different localities, but also with the varying policies of different Boards of Guardians ... ■

The Response to the Slump

Economic policy debates of the early 1920s conditioned by growing awareness of the long-term nature of the dislocation in many industries, centred on a variety of proposals for easing unemployment.

In 1923 Prime Minister Stanley Baldwin, speaking at the Conservative Party Conference at Plymouth, announced his intention to introduce tariff reform in order to protect British industry and secure jobs. The announcement led to a general election in December, which resulted in defeat for the Conservatives. The introduction of fiscal reform was thus set aside once more.

6.12   Stanley Baldwin, speech to the Conservative Party Conference at Plymouth, 25 October 1923 (reported in *The Times,* 26 October 1923).

■ ... My thoughts day and night for long past have been filled with the problem [of unemployment], not only as Prime Minister, but as a man who for years was an employer of labour, and who has lived amongst the working people. I know what unemployment means, and no man who knows that can think of much else in these days. And almost as bad as unemployment is that apprehension of unemployment in the minds of those at work, who see the men being paid off and wonder week by week when their turn will come. It takes the spirit out of a man. No Government, no statesman, can function, can remain in power, deserves to remain in power, unless the people are convinced that everything is being done that is possible to human foresight and human wisdom ...

I told you that we must consider seriously together tonight the new facts, new since the war, an increased population in a country already industrialised to the saturation point, and secondly, we are beginning to realise now, what was difficult to realise two years ago and what no one realised at the time of the Armistice, that it will be a long, long time before the economic reconstruction of Europe is complete ...

The chief industrial country is ours. The country with most open markets is ours, and we shall be shock-absorbers for the whole world ... And I would say, in passing, that, if there were a danger – I won't say that there is a danger – but when the danger is upon us of the dumping into this country of accumulated stocks from the Ruhr to the detriment of our own manufactures, I have no doubt that Parliament, whatever party may be in power, whatever pledges may have been given, will take steps to see that no trading of the kind is allowed.

Dealing with Mr Bonar Law's pledge given a year ago that there should be no fundamental change in the fiscal arrangements of the country, Mr Baldwin said:

That pledge binds me, and in this Parliament there will be no fundamental change ... [but] the unemployment problem was the crucial problem of our country. He regarded it as such. He could fight it. He was willing to fight it, but he could not fight it without weapons. He had come to the conclusion that if we went pottering along as we were we should have grave unemployment with us to the end of time, and he had come to the conclusion himself that the only way to fight the subject was by protecting the home market ... ∎

By the mid-1920s the British economy showed some signs of recovery, but it received a further blow as a result of the decision in 1925 to return sterling to the gold standard at the pre-war dollar parity. The decision, while supported in the City, reflected the Treasury view that fixed exchange rates would boost confidence in the pound and help revive exports. But, because of the overvaluation of sterling, the return to gold did not lead to the benefits anticipated by its supporters. This factor accounts for the relatively subdued performance of the British economy in the second half of the decade. The decision to return to the gold standard was announced by the then Chancellor, Winston Churchill, in his first Budget speech. A leading contemporary critic of the decision was the economist John Maynard Keynes.

6.13 Winston Churchill, Budget speech announcing the return to the gold standard, 28 April 1925 (*Hansard*, 5th ser., 183: 52–8).

∎ A return to an effective gold standard has long been the settled and declared policy of this country. Every Expert Conference since the War – Brussels, Genoa – every expert Committee in this country, has urged the principle of a return to the gold standard. No responsible authority has advocated any other policy. No British Government – and every party has held office – no political party, no previous holder of the Office of

Chancellor of the Exchequer has challenged, or so far as I am aware is now challenging, the principle of a reversion to the gold standard in international affairs at the earliest possible moment. It has always been taken as a matter of course that we should return to it, and the only questions open have been the difficult and the very delicate questions of how and when ...

This is the moment most favourable for action. Our exchange with the United States has for some time been stable, and is at the moment buoyant. We have no immediate heavy commitments across the Atlantic. We have entered a period on both sides of the Atlantic when political and economic stability seems to be more assured than it has been for some years. If this opportunity were missed, it might not soon recur, and the whole finance of the country would be overclouded for a considerable interval by an important factor of uncertainty. Now is the appointed time ...

These matters are very technical, and, of course, I have to be very guarded in every word that I use in regard to them. I have only one observation to make on the merits. In our policy of returning to the gold standard we do not move alone, Indeed, I think we could not have afforded to remain stationary while so many others moved. The two greatest manufacturing countries in the world on either side of us, the United States and Germany, are in different ways either on or related to an international gold exchange ... As far as the British Empire is concerned ... there will be complete unity of action ...

Thus over the wide area of the British Empire and over a very wide and important area of the world there has been established at once one uniform standard of value to which all international transactions are related and can be referred. That standard may, of course, vary in itself from time to time, but the position of all the countries related to it will vary together, like ships in a harbour whose gangways are joined and who rise and fall together with the tide. I believe that the establishment of this great area of common arrangement will facilitate the revival of international trade and of inter-Imperial trade. Such a revival and such a foundation is important to all countries and to no country is it more important than to this island, whose population is larger than its agriculture or its industry can sustain, which is the centre of a wide Empire, and which, in spite of all its burdens, has still retained, if not the primacy, at any rate the central position, in the financial systems of the world. ■

6.14 John Maynard Keynes, *The Economic Consequences of Mr. Churchill*, 1925
(London, Hogarth Press, pp. 6, 10).

■ The policy of improving the foreign-exchange value of sterling up to its pre-war value in gold from being about 10 per cent. below it, means that, whenever we sell anything abroad, either the foreign buyer has to pay 10 per cent. *more in his money* or we have to accept 10 per cent. *less in our money.* That is to say, we have to reduce our sterling prices, for coal or iron or shipping freights or whatever it may be, by 10 per cent. in order to be on a competitive level, unless prices rise elsewhere. Thus the policy of improving the exchange by 10 per cent. involves a reduction of 10 per cent. in the sterling receipts of our export industries …

[These arguments] are not arguments against the Gold Standard as such … They are arguments against having restored gold in conditions which required a substantial readjustment of all our money values. If Mr. Churchill had restored gold by fixing the parity lower than the pre-war figure, or if he had waited until our money values were adjusted to the pre-war parity, then these particular arguments would have no force. But in doing what he did in the actual circumstances of last spring, he was just asking for trouble. For he was committing himself to force down money-wages and all money values, without any idea how it was to be done. ■

The General Strike

One of the most important examples of the disappointing performance of the British economy in the 1920s was in the coal industry. From 1920 the industry was characterised by the loss of export markets, falling world commodity prices and excess capacity. This was exacerbated by continuing poor industrial relations and by the return to the gold standard, which contributed to the declining competitiveness of British coal in the international market.

As the following chart illustrates, all of the major importers of British coal were buying less of it in 1925 than before the war, with the exception of Belgium.

6.15 British coal exports, 1909–25 (derived from *Report of the Royal Commission on the Coal Industry (1925)*, Cmd. 2600, PP XIV, 1926).

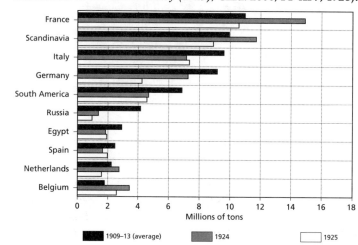

Miners' frustration over, first, the failure of the government to act on the recommendations of the Sankey Commission in 1919 and, second, reductions in wages following the end of the boom led to a series of heated and embittered strikes in the early 1920s. In the summer of 1925, when strike action again loomed in the face of the prospect of sharply reduced wages, the Baldwin government reluctantly intervened the day before a threatened lock-out, offering to subsidise existing wages and profits while a new Royal Commission, chaired by Sir Herbert Samuel, deliberated on how best to raise productivity in the industry. The Samuel Commission's report rejected nationalisation but made a number of wide-ranging suggestions for rationalisation and increasing profitability in the industry. But it was the commission's short-term proposals which proved most controversial.

In the Punch cartoon, 'Master Baldwin' persuades a reluctant 'Uncle John Bull' to fork out the £10 million needed to make the coal mine model work.

6.16   Cartoon by Bernard Partridge, 'A pretty penny in the slot', *Punch*, 12 August 1925.

6.17 **Report of the** *Royal Commission on the Coal Industry,* **1925 (Cmd. 2600, PP XIV, 1926, pp. 235–6).**

■ *The Immediate Problem*

… The dominant fact is that, in the last quarter of 1925, if the subsidy be excluded, 73 per cent of the coal was produced at a loss.

We express no opinion whether the grant of a subsidy last July was unavoidable or not, but we think its continuance indefensible. The subsidy should stop at the end of its authorised term, and should never be repeated.

If the present hours are to be retained, we think a revision of the 'minimum percentage addition to standard rates of wages', fixed in 1924 at a time of temporary prosperity, is indispensable. A disaster is impending over the industry, and the immediate reduction of working costs that can be effected in this way, and in this way alone, is essential to save it. The minimum percentage is not a 'minimum wage' in the usual sense of that term. The wages of the lowest paid men will be safeguarded by the continuance of the system of subsistence allowances. The reductions that we contemplate will still leave the mine-owners without adequate profits in any of the wage-agreement districts and without any profits in most districts. If trade improves and prices rise, a profit will be earned. If prices do not rise, an adequate profit must be sought in the improved methods which should in any case be adopted.

Should the miners freely prefer some extension of hours with a less reduction of wages, Parliament would no doubt be prepared to authorise it. We trust, however, that this will not occur.

We consider that it is essential that there should be, as there always has been hitherto, considerable variation in the rates of wages in the several districts. But we are strongly of opinion that national wage agreements should continue. Such agreements are entered into in all the other British industries of importance.

We recommend that the representatives of the employers and employed should meet together, first nationally and then in the districts, in order to arrive at a settlement by the procedure that we have previously suggested.

By a revision of the minimum percentage coal mining would be saved from an immediate collapse, but it seems inevitable that a number of collieries would still have to be closed. This may give rise to the necessity for a transfer of labour on a considerable scale. We recommend that the Government should be prepared in advance with such plans to assist it as are practicable, and should provide funds for the purpose. … ■

The government accepted the Samuel Report in March 1926, but only provided it was also accepted by both sides in the dispute, which was not a realistic possibility. As it became clear that a new miners' strike was becoming inevitable, attention focused on the extent to which the Trades Union Congress and the labour movement would be prepared to assist the miners' action through a national strike. Government preparations for a general strike were well advanced by this time. Baldwin's attempts to mediate between the mine owners and the unions in April, documented here in the diaries of the Deputy Secretary to the Cabinet, Tom Jones, failed.

6.18   **Report to Cabinet on arrangements for dealing with industrial emergencies, 6 August 1925 (PRO CAB 27/261, CP 390(25)).**

■ <u>ARRANGEMENTS FOR DEALING WITH INDUSTRIAL EMERGENCIES</u>

<u>DRAFT REPORT TO THE CABINET</u>

(A) GENERAL OUTLINE OF MACHINERY.

(1) Supply and Transport Committee of the Cabinet.

The general direction of Government arrangements for dealing with emergencies is entrusted to the Supply and Transport Committee of the Cabinet, to which all questions of policy are submitted for decision. The underlying principle is that each of the Government Departments must be responsible within the limits of its available resources for seeing that such arrangements as are possible are made for dealing with the emergency situation so far as it may be affected by matters within the sphere of that Department.

(2) Supply and Transport Standing Sub-Committee.

This consists of representatives of all the Departments oncerned under the Chairmanship of the Chief Civil Commissioner, and is entrusted with the duty of co-ordinating Departmental arrangements in normal times. On the outbreak of an emergency the Committee splits up as the need arises into the following bodies, the Chairmen of which constitute a co-ordinating Committee under the Chief Civil Commissioner:–

   (*a*) Food, Fuel and Transport Sub-Committee. …
   (*b*) Protection Sub-Committee. …
   (*c*) Communications Sub-Committee. …
   (*d*) Finance Sub-Committee. …
   (*e*) Publicity Organisation. …

(3) Civil Commissioner's Organisation.

For the co-ordination of local services and the local operation of the national services and to stimulate necessary local activity, particularly recruiting, the country is divided into ten districts, each under a Civil Commissioner, who, in the event of a complete rupture of communications would assume the role of the Central Government in his own district …

(4) Volunteer Service Committees.

For the purposes of recruiting labour for services of a national character the country is divided into 88 areas for each of which a Volunteer Service Committee exists. The Chairman of each Committee is a gentleman of local influence ... ∎

6.19 **Thomas Jones, diary, 1–2 May 1926 [in Keith Middlemas, ed.,** *Thomas Jones: Whitehall Diary, Vol. 1: 1916–25,* **London, Oxford University Press, 1969, pp. 25–33).**

∎ *1 May Note of meeting held at 10, Downing Street, 11 p.m.*

The Prime Minister, the Secretary of State for India [Birkenhead], the Minister of Labour [Steel-Maitland], Sir Horace Wilson.

Mr. A. Pugh, Mr. J.H. Thomas, Mr. Swales, Mr. W.M. Citrine.

... They told me that at the Trade Union Congress on Saturday Mr. Herbert Smith had stated that he was prepared to reach a settlement on the lines of the Report. I said I had not understood this, nor had they told the Prime Minister and his colleagues so. What assurances could they give? Repeating emphatically that under no circumstances would the Trade Union Congress authorise them (nor would they be prepared themselves to ask for authority) to continue negotiations unless the [lock-out] notices were withdrawn, they said that their position would be correctly indicated by a statement on the following lines:

The Prime Minister has satisfied himself, as a result of the conversations he has had with the representatives of the Trade Union Congress, that if negotiations are continued (it being understood that the notices cease to be operative) the representatives of the Trade Union Congress are confident that a settlement can be reached on the lines of the Report within a fortnight ...

I reported the gist of my conversation to the Prime Minister and his two colleagues and reduced to writing the statement I had sketched out to the Trade Union Congress representatives ... Mr Pugh and his colleagues were then called in. The Prime Minister read the statement and gave them a copy to read. When the Prime Minister gave them a copy of the statement, Mr Thomas said that he and his colleagues would not give the Prime Minister and his colleagues a reply until they had consulted with the Trade Union Congress full Committee and with the Miners and if they came back accepting the statement they would become authorised by the Miners to say on their behalf that the Miners accepted the Report, recognising that this meant accepting a reduction of wages ...

2 May It was 20 minutes to 2.00 before we heard from the T.U.C. that the Miners had vanished into the country and could not be consulted, but they had been telegraphed for. This failure to tell us earlier thickened the plot. Meanwhile the Cabinet had been told by the Postmaster-General that telegrams calling for the cessation of work had been sent to the railway men, the transport workers, the railway clerks, and the iron and steel workers. This order for a General Strike of course made a deep impression on the Cabinet and Ministers more than ever felt that the P.M. was a helpless innocent moving about amid dangers unrealised ...

3.25. Hankey sent for me. Said he never saw a scene quite like that in this morning's Cabinet (noon) when the formula agreed with the T.U.C. was put before them. All who were not present when it was agreed, reacted in the same way against it, and felt that it would be read by the whole country as a capitulation on the part of the Government to the threat of a general strike. There was nothing on the face of the formula to indicate acceptance of the Report ...

11.30. Herbert Smith and Cook arrived with the recalled Miners' Executive, and I showed them into a waiting room at the Treasury where a fire had been kindled for them. Cook asked me, could he have a wash as he was very tired. I took him to the Treasury lavatory and plunged at once into a discussion of how far he was prepared to go in the matter of wages. He said the word revision would ease matters if he used it instead of reduction. Next, he did not want to depart from the 33⅓%, the present national minimum, but we could get the reduction in another way by knocking off the 14.2 compensation for the loss of an hour to the hewers. This would only hit the better-paid piece workers. We could also use some formula about the revision of wages above a specified figure, e.g. 8/- a day ...

Twice during the evening Ramsay MacDonald rang up Arthur Henderson to enquire how matters were going ... It was about midnight, I think, when messages came through to say that the 'Daily Mail' staff had refused to print an editorial 'for King and Country' and that the paper would not appear next day. ■

The General Strike, which began on 3 May 1926, was never the prelude to a revolution. The union response was well planned and executed; government preparations also worked smoothly, with the assistance of volunteer labour. The TUC General Council called it off on the 12th, after agreeing a general and non-binding solution for the miners' problems with Sir Herbert Samuel. His proposals were based on a National Wages Board for the coal industry to determine a reduced level of wages, to be instituted only when the owners accepted his commission's recommendations for rationalisation in the industry. The miners themselves refused to accept this solution, and struggled on in isolation for a further six months before gradually being forced back to work through hardship and general exhaustion.

The Miners' Federation's final statement on the General Strike, drawn up by its Secretary, A.J. Cook, underlined the miners' feelings of betrayal. The strike had served only to damage further the position of both miners and the industry itself. Widespread wage cuts, a return to the eight-hour day, district agreements and token attempts at some rationalisation in the industry in the years which followed did not prevent the further decline of Britain's share in the world market for coal.

6.20 Miners' Federation of Great Britain, Statement on the General Strike of May 1926, 12 January 1927.

■ The population of these islands had never previously experienced anything resembling the situation created by the General Strike of May 4th to May 12th. Limited though it was both in number of workers affected, in the objectives aimed at and in the time it lasted, the General Strike showed the working class to be possessed of qualities of courage, comradeship, and disciplined resource that had not hitherto been called forth and that gave a good omen for future solidarity.

If we were deserted and forced to fight a lone fight, it was not by the workers that we were abandoned. Their hearts beat true to the end ...

After the decisions of May 1st, we consider that the General Council [of the TUC] had no right whatever to negotiate in our absence, or to modify the decision of the miners and the Trade Union Movement. On Saturday and Sunday, May 8th and 9th, it came to the knowledge of the miners' representatives that discussions had been opened between individuals of the General Council and some person or persons unknown, who upon investigation we found to be Sir Herbert Samuel. On Monday, the 10th May, the officials of the Miners' Federation were invited to meet Sir Herbert, by, and in company with, the officials of the General Council. Sir Herbert then made certain proposals which were not committed to paper, but which represented a departure from the settled policy of the Movement. The Miners' officials re-affirmed the position of their own constituents, and made it perfectly clear to Sir Herbert that they could not accept proposals which involved reductions in wages. Nevertheless, on Tuesday evening, the 11th of May, the Miners' Executive were sent for by the General Council, and were informed that they (the Council) had agreed upon and accepted proposals as the outcome of conversations between their officials and Sir Herbert Samuel that day ...

The action of the General Council in accepting the proposals in advance of any decision by the miners was, in fact, an ultimatum by the Council to the miners; they were obviously determined to compel us to a decision which would mean a breaking of pledges to our own constituents.

... from first to last there was never any possibility of forces arrayed against the miners accepting anything but lower wages, longer hours and district agreements – *unless compelled to do so by the united strength of the working class.* This from the spring right on throughout the struggle the General Council failed to see ...

The fight is not over. The conditions of the employers are imposed conditions and bring with them no goodwill or spirit of conciliation. Longer hours and lower wages cannot bring peace in the coalfields; nor will we allow district agreements to shatter our strength and unity. Our organisation is still intact, and we are determined to recover the ground that has been lost. ■

The General Strike was followed by a downturn in labour unrest, and the labour move-
ment was further weakened by the onset of the Great Depression. The Baldwin
government passed an amendment to the Trade Disputes Act 1906 in the aftermath of
the dispute, under pressure from right-wing Conservatives. The Trade Disputes and
Trade Union Act 1927 was resented greatly within the labour movement as unneces-
sarily vindictive and was eventually repealed by the Attlee government in 1946.

6.21   Trades Disputes and Trade Union Act 1927 (*Public General Acts,* 1927, ch. 22).

■ ...

1.   It is hereby declared –

(*a*) that any strike is illegal if it –

>   (i)   has any object other than or in addition to the furtherance of a
>   trade dispute within the trade or industry in which the strikers are
>   engaged; and

>   (ii) is a strike designed or calculated to coerce the Government either
>   directly or by inflicting hardship upon the community; and

(*b*) that any lock-out is illegal if it –

>   (i)   has any object other than or in addition to the furtherance of a trade
>   dispute within the trade or industry in which the employers locking-
>   out are engaged; and

>   (ii) is a lock-out designed or calculated to coerce the Government either
>   directly or by inflicting hardship upon the community:

and it is further declared that it is illegal to commence, or continue, or apply
any sums in furtherance or support of, any such illegal strike or lock-out ...

2.   (1) No person refusing to take part or to continue to take part in any
strike or lock-out which is by this Act declared to be illegal, shall be, by
reason of such refusal or by reason of any action taken by him under this
section, subject to expulsion from any trade union or society, or to any fine
or penalty, or to deprivation of any right or benefit to which he or his legal
personal representatives would otherwise be entitled ...

3.   (1) It is hereby declared that it is unlawful for one or more persons ...
to attend at or near a house or place where a person resides or works or
carries on business or happens to be, for the purpose of obtaining or
communicating information or of persuading or inducing any person to
work or to abstain from working, if they so attend in such numbers or
otherwise in such manner as to be calculated to intimidate any person in
that house or place, or to obstruct the approach thereto or the egress
therefrom, or to lead to a breach of the peace; ...

4.   (1) It shall not be lawful to require any members of a trade union to
make any contribution to the political fund of a trade union unless he has at

some time after the commencement of this Act and before he is first after the thirty-first day of December, nineteen hundred and twenty-seven, required to make such a contribution delivered at the head office or some branch office of the trade union, notice in writing...of his willingness to contribute to that fund and has not withdrawn the notice in manner hereinafter provided; and every member of a trade union who has not delivered such a notice as aforementioned, or who, having delivered such a notice, has withdrawn it in manner hereinafter provided, shall be deemed for the purposes of the Trade Union Act 1913, to be a member who is exempt from the obligation to contribute to the political fund of the union ...

(2) All contributions to the political fund of a trade union from members of the trade union who are liable to contribute to that fund shall be levied and made separately from any contributions to the other funds of the trade union ... ■

In spite of the 1927 industrial relations legislation, the general effect of the events of 1926 was to strengthen moderate voices within both the labour movement and employers' groups, as the TUC General Secretary in this period, Walter Citrine, remembers in his memoirs. Talks between prominent employers and the TUC, beginning in 1928, may not have achieved any concrete results, but they did indicate a new willingness to consider joint measures to improve productivity.

6.22 Walter Citrine, *Men and Work*, 1964 (London, Hutchinson, pp. 241–5).

■ Shortly after the General Strike I called an informal meeting of our principal officials ... What was to be the policy of the trade union movement? Were we to try to organize the movement so that if the necessity arose we could engage in still bigger and better organized strikes? Where would this lead us to? ... I did not believe that any government would wish to see a recurrence, nor did I believe that any really effective legislation could be devised which would prevent such serious conflicts. I felt we had to rely upon the common sense of all the parties – Government, employers, and trade unionists – and their sense of right and wrong. When I came to look back and recall what Keynes had prophesied I could see that little reason as the miners had to love the coal-owners, the employers had little choice. If they were to remain in business they must get costs down. It was easy to look to wages as the first step in lowering costs ...

It all boiled down to a matter of power. If the trade unionists were more effectively organized and stronger in every respect they could use their power industrially and politically to influence the development of events. I feel almost ashamed to describe this state of reasoning that I passed through. It all seems so elementary in 1964. It was less so in 1926. So it was that I did my best to convince working people that they, too, had great power and that this power was not limited to causing industrial dislocation …

Slender as the prospects seemed of achieving any material progress by discussion with the central employers' organizations I felt convinced that an attempt must somehow be made … I had several approaches from people of influence in the industrial world strongly supporting the idea, and I was not surprised when I received a letter on November 23rd [1927], signed by Alfred Mond and twenty other influential industrialists – four names were later added on – inviting the General Council to a conference to discuss questions related to the entire field of industrial reorganization and industrial relations. I knew most of these people either by direct contact or by repute.

A copy of the letter was circulated to every member of the General Council, and it was decided to accept the invitation. ■

6.23   **Cartoon by David Low, 'The mechanical master',** *Evening Standard,* **22 October 1927.**

The Persistence of Unemployment

The new realism in industrial relations in Britain after 1926 partly reflected an increasing acceptance that wages and employment levels would not improve until the economy as a whole showed firmer signs of recovery. While there were some signs of recovery after 1926, on the whole the performance of the economy remained disappointing.

On one level, the British economy after 1926 showed signs of prosperity, particularly in many new industries, where the value of exports grew in spite of falling prices.

6.24 Change in the value of UK exports (selected industries), 1920–9 (derived from Board of Trade, *Statistical Abstract for the United Kingdom*, 76, Cmd 4233, PP XXV, 1932–3, pp. 374–81).

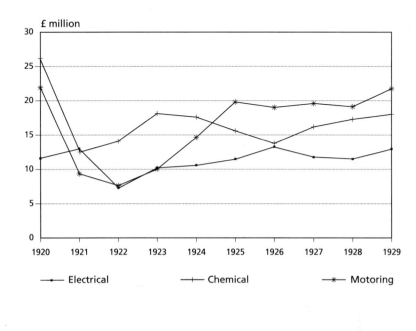

Although living standards and real incomes were rising generally in the later 1920s, and many new industries were performing well, pockets of mass unemployment continued, associated with the staple industries in decline. This problem was acknowledged in the 'Yellow Book', the report of the Liberal Summer School of 1928, which met to consider Britain's industrial future.

6.25 The Liberal Party, Britain's Industrial Future: *Being the Report of the Liberal Industrial Inquiry*, 1928 (London, Ernest Benn, pp. 39–46).

■ Certain industries in particular are proving unable to provide the established standard of life for their workers, with results reflected either in low wages, in unemployment, or in both. Yet these industries occupy a position of exceptional importance in our national life. They are the chief contributors to our export trade; and their expansion in the last century was the basis of our national development as a foreign-trading, foreign-investing country ... It would be impossible to view their decline with the same comparative equanimity with which we have been able in the past to view the decline of other industries against which the tide of fashion or economic opportunity has turned. The coach-building industry might go down before the advent of the motor-car; the saddlery and harness trades might suffer from the same cause. Such changes might involve minor hardship, but they did not spell dislocation on a big scale, or a change in the fundamental nature of our economic equilibrium. The same concern which found its market falling for horse-drawn vehicles might set itself to the production of bodies for motor-cars ... But it is only necessary to ask to what alternative purposes a coal-mine or blast furnace could be converted in order to realise that the decline of our basic industries would confront us with an altogether more formidable problem. We have only to reflect how the economic life of the Clyde, the Tyne, South Wales, East Lancashire, and the mining areas centres around these industries in order to realise the magnitude of the social issues which are involved.

We feel no assurance that a restoration of our old export industries to the same position of relative importance in the economic life of the nation which they held before the war is possible without a reduction of wages or a lengthening or hours or a lowering of the standard of life in some other way. The hope for our export trade generally must lie rather in the development of the newer trades. It seems to us, therefore, that the time is now ripe for a bolder programme of home development which will absorb and employ the national resources of capital and labour in new ways. ■

The Liberal Party, under the leadership of Lloyd George, was anxious to effect a political comeback in the forthcoming general election. It followed up its 1928 report on Britain's Industrial Future with Lloyd George's employment policy proposals, launched with a great fanfare in 1929. Taken together, these two Liberal pamphlets represent the first popular political exposition of Keynesian economic solutions to the problems of industrial decline and mass unemployment.

6.26   Liberal Summer School, *We Can Conquer Unemployment: Mr. Lloyd George's Pledge*, 1929 (London, Cassell, pp. 5–7).

■ ... [T]he problem should be faced in the same spirit as the emergencies of the War. The suffering and waste caused by unemployment are as important as was the provision of munitions during the war. South Wales and the Industrial North are our Devastated Areas ...

For the permanent cure of this situation along normal lines certain long-distance remedies are necessary ... They fall into two groups, the first representing action in the international field, and the second action at home.

The first consists of –

(1) the *faithful and enthusiastic pursuit of a policy of International appeasement and goodwill*; the creation of conditions in which the possibility of war will cease to restrict the full development of international business relations;

(2) the following up of the resolutions of the Economic conference at Geneva in such a way as to secure *ever-increasing freedom of trade* amongst the nations of the world; and

(3) the pursuit of the policy laid down in the Genoa Conference of 1922...designed to *secure stability in the world's level of gold prices* ...

The long-distance policy at home calls for:

(1) the adoption of a currency and banking policy which, consistently with the maintenance of the gold standard, will secure *a greater measure of stability in British prices and easier money conditions for British industry*;

(2) *the raising of the level of the efficiency of British industries* to such a point that, in spite of the special post-war difficulties they may regain, and improve upon, their pre-war prosperity ...

(3) *the development of new industries and the redistribution of workers,* necessitated by permanent changes in other industries ...

But are we to be content with that? *Are we prepared to tolerate the thought of more years of unemployment on something like the scale to which we have recently been accustomed?*

Surely the waste and the folly of such a course are self-evident? Side by side, we have a great army of workers longing for employment and a multitude of tasks waiting to be done. Is statesmanship so barren that by appropriate organisation the two cannot be brought together? Cannot we use this great labour force to improve our roads, house or re-house our workers, develop our power resources, drain our lands? It is not merely a question of finding employment for those who must in any event be maintained. *It is that we should seize this great opportunity to raise the whole level of efficiency and amenity of our national life.* ∎

Despite the arguments of Keynes and the Liberals, public expenditure solutions to the unemployment problem were soundly rejected at the official level. The Treasury's contribution to the White Paper published by Baldwin's government which considered Keynes's proposals has come to be considered the most important public statement of the 'Treasury view' on the cause and treatment of unemployment in the inter-war period.

6.27   *Memoranda on Certain Proposals Relating to Unemployment,* 1929 (Cmd 3331 PP XVI, 1928–9, pp. 45–52).

■ The case in the pamphlet is substantially that though our national savings are generally adequate, sufficient outlet is not provided for them in the form of capital investment at home. It is claimed that by increasing Government borrowing for capital expenditure in each of the next two years employment would be improved, without set-off in the form of diminished employment elsewhere in the country due to the diversion of savings from other home enterprises to these particular plans. It is argued that the additional capital required, which ... is roughly £125 millions in each of the next two years, can be raised out of savings which are not now actively employed, or by withdrawing money from foreign investment, and in either case without depriving British industry of its present resources ...

There is usually some tendency, when business is slack, for money to hang in the banks, particularly on time deposit ... A great part of this money is the loose cash of manufacturing concerns which in a depression they do not employ for the moment, but which they wish to keep liquid and could not in any circumstances put in long-term investments. A further large part is constituted by balances belonging to foreign Banks and institutions, which are believed to have exceptionally large claims on this country at present and probably keep a proportion on time deposit ...

The bulk of the funds in question can, owing to the requirements of the holders, not be employed in long-term investments, and to the extent that they accumulate, they do represent a slackening in the circulation of money and in employment. But while held by the Banks, they are, of course, by no means idle ... The money may be used in commercial advances or credits and in taking up bills or acceptances for traders as well as in loans to the short-term money market ...

The contention of the pamphlet is that the additional £125 millions a year required for new State or local authority borrowing can be found without impinging on the supply of capital for other home requirements.

This, on the face of it, appears to be highly improbable. There is not the least reason to suppose that works under Government auspices would be more remunerative or have more success in attracting capital than any other works. They have the special drawback that the money would have to be attracted by the issue of Government stock, of which there is already a plethora in the market. If large new loans are floated on 'gilt-edged' terms, the higher rates of interest paid by foreign countries and the Dominions, both for short-term and for long-term money, would remain just as attractive to the investor as at present. There can be no presumption that, given a free market, the volume of British money going abroad would be substantially reduced ... Thus the prospect before the British citizen is a marked increase in the rate of interest on Government borrowings, not only on these new borrowings, but on the £30 or £40 millions per annum normal borrowings for Local Loans and Telephone capital expenditure, on the £700 millions of Treasury Bills outstanding and on the other borrowings required to deal with war debt maturities amounting to £322 millions in the next four years. And the prospect of reducing the interest on the 5 per cent. War Loan would be indefinitely postponed. There would clearly also be very serious reaction on the rate at which local authorities and British industry could raise money and a consequent disturbance of trade and employment. We can, in fact, only prevent funds going abroad by offering the inducement of higher rates at home, and the harm that such higher rates would inflict on trade and employment would certainly counterbalance any benefit they got from diverting funds from foreign to home investment ...

It seems clear that in these circumstances a very large proportion of any additional Government borrowings can only be procured, without inflation, by diverting money which otherwise would be taken soon by home industry. That being so, the prospects of adding largely by the means suggested to the existing volume of employment practically disappear. Assuming, however, *that it were possible*, under the plan to secure for home development funds at present going abroad, what would be the result on the different classes of British industry? It would stimulate internal consumption and tend to raise the level of wages and prices; and it would encourage imports and make things more difficult for the export trades which are most susceptible to the competition of foreign goods.

The fact is that from whatever angle one looks at the unemployment problem, one is always forced to the conclusion that the principal (though not, of course, the only) cause of our difficulties is to be found in the fact that in many branches particularly of our heavy industries our costs of production (turning upon organisation and efficiency both of capital and labour) still tend to be excessive, and that these difficulties cannot be solved till these costs have been placed on a competitive level. If Mr. McKenna is right that true deposits are growing excessively, the main reason is probably that our costs of production keep orders away, and in default of orders our manufacturers are either unable or unwilling to replace their plant or build up for fresh developments. But if this is the main source of our difficulties, the loan programme of the pamphlet would do nothing to remove it and if it led to a rise in our internal price level it might in the long run make matters worse. At the very highest, any scheme of this kind is but a palliative, which would produce only a temporary improvement. The ultimate remedy for unemployment is not to be found in such measures. It must be solved by reducing the costs of production and the cost of living. ■

Local Government and Structure of the Social Services

State responsibility for the social welfare of the individual continued to increase in the first post-war decade. Particularly under the sponsorship of Neville Chamberlain (the son of Joseph and brother of Austen Chamberlain), who served as Minister of Health between 1924 and 1929, a number of important new measures were introduced, including the Old Age Pensions Act of 1925 and the National Health Insurance Act of 1928. But as the social services expanded, the structure of responsibility and finance for them became increasingly complex and unsatisfactory.

Local authorities were obliged to pay for social services by raising the rates, which were supplemented by grants from central government. The concentration of poverty and unemployment in particular counties or boroughs made it impossible for the rates burden to be shared equitably, and differing attitudes towards pauperism on the part of Poor Law guardians in different regions underscored this problem. In Poplar, East London, these issues were confronted by a Labour council at the beginning of the 1920s. The Poor Law guardian, borough leader and future leader of the Labour Party George Lansbury recalled several years later the origins of 'Poplarism' in 1921.

6.28   George Lansbury, *My Life*, 1928 (London, Constable, pp. 155–61).

■ All the work in Poplar is hindered because of high rates: high rates are caused by low rateable value and a poverty-stricken population ... The local Labour Party always had on its programme the equalization of rates – that is, we contend that the poor rate, instead of being levied on each borough, should be levied over the whole twenty-eight boroughs [in London], so that those who were financially strong should help bear the burdens of those who were financially weak.

When the local Labour Party came to power in 1919 we were faced with the problem of how to carry out this policy. We found our rates going up by leaps and bounds ... I believed the suggestion came from me in a tentative sort of way that we should refuse to pay the London County Council or the Metropolitan Asylums Board, or the Police precepts. This meant several hundreds of thousands of pounds per year ...

There were some months of negotiation with the central authorities who, in the end, threatened to take proceedings and did so, and we were summoned to the High Court. We went up escorted by our ratepayers with banners flying, headed by a band, with the Mayor, Sam March, marching at the head with his chain of office and the mace bearer ...

We stood firm and after an appeal to the High Court were sent to prison. Our stay lasted six weeks....Lawyers came in and told us that until we purged our offence we would never be let out. There were about twenty-four of us at Brixton and half a dozen women at Holloway ...

All through our imprisonment the unemployed and others came and sang outside the wall of the prison. We could hear the singing quite well and joined in the chorus of the Red Flag. Occasionally I made a speech from the window of my cell. It was impossible to stop us because what could the authorities do? ...

The result of our six weeks' imprisonment was that after a conference at Whitehall, over which Sir Alfred Mond presided, it was decided that the cost of outdoor relief and the major part of indoor relief of the poor should be levied over the whole of London ... This immediately relieved the rates of Poplar to the extent of 6s.6d. in the £ and put 1s. in the £ on the rates of Westminster and the City of London. ■

Poplarism forced short-term concessions on the equalisation of rates, but after 1925 Neville Chamberlain envisaged a far more sweeping 'rationalisation' of the finance and provision of social services. This eventually became embodied in the most important piece of domestic legislation of the period, the Local Government Act of 1929. Under the terms of the Act the boards of guardians were abolished and their duties transferred to the county councils and county borough councils. The Act also replaced the old system of percentage grants from central government to the local authorities with a new system of block grants, which took into account the varying circumstances of the different authorities. This was accompanied by the derating of industry to 25 per cent of its net annual value and of agriculture entirely – which the Chancellor, Churchill, hoped would stimulate the economy by relieving local businesses of much of the burden of local taxes. Chamberlain explained the significance of the Bill to the House of Commons in the second reading debate.

6.29 Neville Chamberlain, speech for the second reading of the Local Government Bill, 26 November 1928 (Hansard, 5th ser., 223: 71–93).

■ ... The trouble with the Poor Law is the same to-day as it was in 1834 in respect of the fact that the charges for Poor Law, which fluctuate violently from time to time, and which are largely beyond the control of the authorities who have to meet them, fall upon areas so small that the burden is apt to become suddenly and completely crushing ... Of course, it will be obvious to the House that those inequalities are not going to be diminished but increased by the proposals of the Government for derating, which will abstract from those authorities a large part of their rateable value and leave only a diminishing portion of it to bear any fluctuating charges which remain ...

Therefore, the House will see that the Government have behind them an overwhelming weight of authority in making this proposal to-day [to abolish the boards of guardians] ... When this Bill becomes law, we shall have a position in which there will be one single health authority in each area, whose duty and function it will be to survey the whole institutional needs of that area. They will have at their disposal all the institutions which are now in the hands of the guardians; in many the accommodation is not fully occupied. They will have an opportunity of reclassifying their institutions, of closing such as are no longer suitable for modern requirements at all, or altering and adapting others, and using one for one purpose and another for another purpose …

I have now traversed half the Bill, and before I ask the House to plunge into the thickets of the financial provisions we may perhaps take breath for a moment and contemplate the smiling landscape provided by the section headed 'Relief from Rates'. Some critics have spoken of rating relief as though it were merely a subsidy to industry and one which therefore ought to be confined to those who can prove that they cannot do without it. I think those critics overlooked the fact that you cannot benefit industry without increasing employment, that what the country wants more than anything else to-day is increased employment, and that if any increase in employment were general throughout the country inevitably the benefit of it must be felt by every member of the community …

At a stroke £24,000,000 a year is going to be lifted from the back of industry. It is safe to say that not less than three-quarters of that huge sum will go to those industries which are most depressed, which used to give the greatest employment, and which to-day are lying derelict and almost helpless … I am fully convinced that this relief is twice blessed. It blesses not only him that takes but also him that gives, because not only is it going by increasing employment to increase the earnings of the workers, but it is bound also to have the most profound effect upon the fortunes of all ratepayers by reducing the burden which now presses so heavily upon them of supporting their unfortunate fellows who cannot support themselves …

There remains only the plan upon which we stand, the Government plan that national contributions to local services shall be distributed, not in accordance with what the local authorities spend, but with what are their needs. The needs, of course, must include their relative ability to pay, and I submit to the House that that is not merely the only equitable solution, but that it is the only one which is going to find a practical remedy for the ills from which local government is suffering to-day …

To start with this rating reform. We sweep away a large source of revenue of the local authorities which exists to-day, and we replace it with a larger sum, but that sum is to be based, instead of on a percentage grant … on needs which are to be reviewed from time to time. While the block grant is to be recalculated every five years, the amount of it is to be fixed for each year in any period of five years. The distribution among the counties and the county boroughs first of all is to be partly, and ultimately entirely, made according to a formula. The result, I anticipate, will be that each local authority will be secured resources which will be adequate, not merely to carry on the services as they are to-day, but to allow for a reasonable expansion during the five-year period for which they will last in accordance with the public conscience and the demands which the increasing revenues of the country will permit. ■

CHAPTER SEVEN

Democracy in Transition: The Politics of Realignment, 1919–1929

THE politics of the 1920s were dominated by the search for national cohesion and social order in the wake of the Great War. Europe at this time was plunged into an era of revolution and counter-revolution. British politics, by contrast, remained relatively stable. The peaceful accommodation of the Labour Party as the principal party of opposition was completed in 1924, when Ramsay MacDonald became the first Labour Prime Minister. Liberal fortunes continued to ebb in the period following the break-up of the Coalition government in 1922; Lloyd George's attempt to reinvigorate his party at the end of the decade was unsuccessful. Throughout these years it was the Conservative Party, led from 1923 by Stanley Baldwin, which dominated British politics.

While many of the issues which had dogged the Asquith government before 1914 were no longer in the public eye in the 1920s – the suffrage movement, constitutional reform and Irish Home Rule after 1922 – labour unrest and mass unemployment were cause enough for concern. The Conservatives under Baldwin met these issues by asserting an image of 'one nation' Disraelian Conservatism. But Baldwin failed to maintain the loyalty of the electorate in the 1929 election. The persistent problems of mass unemployment and poor economic performance contributed to the Conservative defeat in that year. Three-party rivalry between Conservatives, Labour and Liberals was finally killed in that election, and the reassessment which followed formed a critical stage in the development of the modern, predominantly two-party political system.

The Peacetime Coalition

The general election of 1918 inaugurated a period of shifting political behaviour in Britain, which shook the country out of its pre-war pattern. In this new era, political allegiance was formed much more commonly along the lines of class interest, or into a socialist/anti-socialist framework. The context of this, of course, had been the events in Russia in 1917. Initial expectations of reform and reconstruction, as we have seen in Chapter 6, were associated with short-lived confidence within the labour movement, as well as with expectations of reparations payments from Germany.

Faith in the Coalition government led by Lloyd George but dominated by its Conservative and Unionist majority began to break down soon after the war. The most powerful early condemnation of the Coalition came from the Liberal economist John Maynard Keynes.

7.1   John Maynard Keynes, *The Economic Consequences of the Peace*, 1919 (London, Macmillan, pp. 132–3).

■ The Prime Minister never said that he himself believed that Germany could pay the whole cost of the war. But the programme became in the mouths of his supporters on the hustings a great deal more concrete. The ordinary voter was led to believe that Germany could certainly be made to pay the greater part, if not the whole cost, of the war. Those whose practical and selfish fears for the future the expenses of the war had aroused, and those whose emotions its horrors had disordered, were both provided for. A vote for a coalition candidate meant the Crucifixion of Anti-Christ and the assumption by Germany of the British National Debt.

It proved an irresistible combination, and once more Mr. George's political instinct was not at fault. No candidate could safely denounce this programme, and none did so. The old Liberal Party, having nothing comparable to offer to the electorate, was swept out of existence. A new House of Commons came into being, a majority of whose members had pledged themselves to a great deal more than the Prime Minister's guarded promises. Shortly after their arrival at Westminster I asked a Conservative friend, who had known previous Houses, what he thought of them. 'They are a lot of hard-faced men', he said, 'who look as if they had done very well out of the war.' ■

The Coalition government lasted until October 1922. It was never an easy partnership, dominated by the brilliant but erratic figure of Lloyd George. His popular standing was at first ensured by the patriotism and high expectations of the immediate postwar period.

Within months the Coalition was faced with a series of problems which would have stretched the political abilities of any Prime Minister. Lloyd George relied for support upon his Unionist colleagues, who grew increasingly restive over his domestic and foreign policies. Middle-class frustration grew as high taxes continued and the boom faded in 1920.

In January 1921 the Anti-Waste League was formed under the auspices of the newspaper proprietor Lord Rothermere to protest at the continued level of public spending. The chord it struck with disenchanted voters was rapidly evident in two by-election victories for 'anti-waste' candidates in the next six months. The 'Geddes axe', discussed in Chapter 6, was the ultimate result of this pressure, and much of the future bitterness within Liberal and Labour circles which would be directed at Lloyd George was based on the perception that he had given in to the 'anti-waste' wolves among the Unionist backbenchers, sacrificing the social reconstruction.programme in an attempt to maintain his parliamentary majority.

7.2   The formation of the Anti-Waste League, *Sunday Pictorial,* 23 January 1921.

The Communist Party and the 'Red scare'

The political atmosphere of the early post-war years was heavily tainted by anti-Bolshevism and the fear that continental political extremism would spill over into British politics. But the British Communist Party, founded in 1920, remained a relatively small group which failed to make significant gains. The Labour Party retained the loyalty of the working-class vote, and was from the beginning hostile to cooperation with the revolutionary left.

The Communist Party relied on funding from the Comintern (the Communist International) for its survival. This enabled the party to publish a newspaper and propaganda out of proportion to its real domestic support.

7.3   Unsigned article, *The Communist*, 27 January 1921.

■ WORKERS AND THE WORKLESS! Read the handwriting on the wall. It spells your doom or the doom of capitalism.

… The capitalist class … promised the workers a time of luxuriating in the captured trade of Germany. The markets of the world were to be open to Allied trade and closed to the Germans. And they have produced an incredible chaos, so that the pit-heads and sidings of Wales are blocked with coal, which none can use, while the miners work short time. The warehouses of Yorkshire are blocked with raw wool and with woollen goods, which the world needs but cannot have. And hundreds of thousands of wool workers are short of work. It is the old phenomenon, familiar to Marxists, of over-production and under-consumption. The system of high prices and high profits has worked itself to a deadlock … The seeds of decay may be sprouting fast, but their very growth spurs capitalism on to efforts to preserve its power. Unemployment aids those efforts. It provides the opportunity for a general attack on the worker's standard of living. Wages having been cut, the markets open again, the system gets a new lease of life, and the capitalists are happy until the next deadlock arises. And then they are buoyed up by the hope that once more unemployment will solve their problem …

The problem is, therefore, not one of merely finding remedies for unemployment, as the Labour Party imagines … *It is the problem of resisting an attack, and of devising such a method of counter-attack as will unite the workers as a class in opposition to the class which is uniting and oppressing them …*

Faced with the prospect of the reduction of their wages to starvation level, their despair will drive them to the only logical solution of unemployment – the Social Revolution. Wanting this revolution, they will seek for leaders and directing forces … Whence, then, is to come the directing force?

It can be secured by

> *The uniting of the working class in a revolutionary party.*
> *The organisation of the workers as a class on the industrial field.*
> *The control of production by the workers.*
> *By organising the strike for a definite end – the Social Revolution.*

The fight must become the fight of a united class for its own emancipation.

> *Away with the sectionalism of the trade union!*
> *Away with compromises negotiated by officials!*
> *To work in your councils for the control of*
> *production by the workers!*

Work for the organisation of your class in the United Communist Party! ■

7.4   Cartoon by 'Espoir' (Will Hope), 'Homes for heroes', *The Communist,*
8 October 1921.

The sale-of-honours scandal

Throughout 1922 discontent with Lloyd George's leadership of the Coalition grew within the Unionist Party. The party's leader at this time, Austen Chamberlain, remained convinced that the Coalition was necessary to ensure the political defeat of socialism, and the continued allegiance to Lloyd George should be understood in the context of the fear of a Labour government. But an increasing number of Unionists were beginning to doubt the wisdom of this logic.

Unease over the future of party politics was compounded among Unionists by growing concern over the moral atmosphere surrounding the Prime Minister's leadership, which seemed to revolve around his own hunger for continued power.

The publication of the Birthday Honours List in June 1922 brought this to the surface in a debate over the propriety of the government's overt sale of titles to wealthy businessmen.

7.5   The Duke of Northumberland, speech on the sale of honours, 29
June 1922 (*Hansard* [*Lords*], 5th ser., 51: 128–30).

■ …There are two letters to which I should like to draw your Lordships' attention this afternoon. They are both letters from men who purport to be intermediaries between Downing Street and these people who receive honours. In one case this intermediary writes to a gentleman living in the North of England, a gentleman of considerable means, to say that he would like to have a confidential interview with him on a very private matter of a complimentary nature, and would he come to see him about it. He adds: 'If you want to know what the nature of the business is, will you go and see' – and he mentions the name of a recently created baronet – 'and he will tell you all about the matter, and what the business is.' My friend goes to the recently created baronet, and says 'Who is this, and what is the nature of the business?' The other says: 'Oh, I was up on Downing Street the other day, and I mentioned your name, together with others, as well worthy of receiving an honour.' My friend says: 'Indeed! that is very good of you. And how much do you have to pay for a baronetcy?' The other replies: 'Oh, about £40,000.' My friend did not have anything more to do with that little transaction. The next case was that of a gentleman living in London ... A letter was sent to this gentleman, also purporting to come from an intermediary of Downing Street, saying that he wanted an interview ... at the interview he was informed that he was considered a person who was eminently worthy of receiving an honour, but he could not expect to receive it unless he contributed a certain amount of money to the Party Funds ... I would venture to make one suggestion to the Government. At the present moment, whether these people to whom I have referred are authorised or not, they are creating a very bad impression in this country, bringing great discrimination upon the Government, and doing serious injury to the honour of the Government ... ■

The fall of the Coalition

Personal scandal, coming on top of controversial policies on Ireland and, later in the summer, the report of the Geddes Committee, spelled the end of Unionist patience with Lloyd George. Backbenchers and junior ministers were increasingly vocal in their criticism of continued co-operation, and the party leadership was not powerful enough to contain such overwhelming dissent.

By the autumn of 1922 concern over the future viability of the Coalition government had spread to members of the Cabinet, many of whom were finally disillusioned by Lloyd George's apparent willingness to risk war with Turkey to achieve a triumph on which to base an election victory. But there remained widespread concern among Conservatives that only a Liberal/Unionist coalition, or even some sort of merged anti-socialist party, could prevent the continued advance of the Labour Party. The confidence of the Unionist critics of the Coalition was therefore given an important boost when an independent Unionist candidate won a three-way party fight in the Newport by-election on 18 October.

This development certainly influenced the atmosphere on the following day at the Carlton Club meeting called by the party leader Austen Chamberlain, a strong

Coalitionist, to discuss the issue of election tactics. Under pressure from his political allies, the former leader, Bonar Law, agreed at the last minute to take over should the vote go against Chamberlain. But it was Stanley Baldwin's speech, in support of the minority in Cabinet who favoured fighting the election on a straight party ticket, which made the most lasting impression at the Carlton Club. The atmosphere in the meeting was described in the diary of the anti-Coalitionist MP Leo Amery.

7.6 Stanley Baldwin, speech at the Carlton Club, 19 October 1922 (reported in *The Times*, 20 October 1922).

■ The Prime Minister was described this morning in *The Times*, in the words of a distinguished aristocrat, as a live wire. He was described to me, and to others, in more stately language, by the Lord Chancellor, as a dynamic force, and I accept those words. He is a dynamic force, and it is from that very fact that our troubles, in our opinion, arise. A dynamic force is a very terrible thing; it may crush you but it is not necessarily right.

It is owing to that dynamic force, and that remarkable personality, that the Liberal Party, to which he formerly belonged, has been smashed to pieces; and it is my firm conviction that, in time, the same thing will happen to our party. I do not propose to elaborate, in an assembly like this, the dangers and the perils of that happening. We have already seen, during our association with him in the last four years, a section of our party hopelessly alienated. I think that if the present association is continued, and if this meeting agrees that it should be continued, you will see some more breaking up, and I believe the process must go on inevitably until the old Conservative Party is smashed to atoms and lost in ruins.

I would like to give you just one illustration to show what I mean by the disintegrating influence of a dynamic force. Take Mr Chamberlain and myself. Mr Chamberlain's services to the State are infinitely greater than any that I have been able to render, but we are both men who are giving all we can give to the service of the State; we are both men who are, or who try to be, actuated by principle in our conduct; we are men who, I think, have exactly the same views on the political problems of the day; we are men who I believe – certainly on my side – have esteem and perhaps I may add affection for each other; but the result of this dynamic force is that we stand here to-day, he prepared to go into the wilderness if he should be compelled to forsake the Prime Minister, and I prepared to go into the wilderness if I should be compelled to stay with him. If that is the effect of that tremendous personality on two men occupying the position that we do, and related to each other politically in the way the Mr Chamberlain and I are, that process must go on throughout the party. It was for that reason that I took the stand I did, and put forward the views that I did. I do not know what the majority here or in the country may think about it. I said at the time what I thought was right, and I stick all through to what I believe to be right. ■

7.7   Leo Amery, diary, 19 October 1922 [in John Barnes and David Nicholson, eds, *The Leo Amery Diaries, Vol. I: 1896–1929*, London, Hutchinson, 1980, pp. 299–300).

■ *19 October 1922*: The meeting opened at 11 and the much greater volume of cheering for Bonar than for Austen was an indication which way the wind was blowing. Austen opened with a very set speech … the idea underlying his remarks being apparently that it was not for Unionists alone to decide the question of Prime Ministership after an election in which they had enjoyed Liberal support. The speech received rather a cold welcome, and Baldwin who followed with a short speech to the effect that he did not want the PM's dynamic force to break up the Unionist Party as it had broken up the Liberal, got a much greater reception. Pretyman then introduced his resolution in favour of the independence of the Party in a reasonable speech, followed by quite a good one from Lane Fox, Mildmay and Craik whom nobody wanted to hear. There were continuous shouts for Bonar and he pulled himself up and after one of his characteristic soliloquizing speeches made it quite clear that the Party ought to come out of the Coalition and go to the election with a mind to winning on its own. This evoked tremendous enthusiasm and settled the business … ■

Conservative Government, 1922–3

The Unionists' meeting at the Carlton Club on 19 October 1922 voted against continued participation in the Coalition government by a majority of around 100 votes. Lloyd George resigned that afternoon, and the reins of power passed to the Unionist Party, from this period known as the Conservative Party, for the first time since the 1906 election.

Bonar Law, the new Conservative Party leader, proceeded to form a Cabinet in the days which followed the Carlton Club coup. His short stewardship of the first postwar Conservative government was largely uneventful. The party's manifesto for the election which quickly followed the Carlton Club meeting has been remembered as a plea for a return to normality in politics, under the slogan of 'Tranquillity'.

7.8   *Mr. Bonar Law's Election Address*, 1922 (Conservative Party Archives).

■ His Majesty has been graciously pleased to appoint me First Minister of the Crown. I appeal to you to renew your confidence in myself as your representative, and to give your support to the new Government of which I am the head. The crisis which has arisen so suddenly had made it absolutely necessary that an immediate appeal should be made to the people, and in consequence it has been impossible to have an examination with my colleagues into the many questions with which we have to deal. Of necessity, therefore, the outlines of policy which I now submit to you cannot be as definite and precise as in other circumstances would have been possible.

The crying need of the nation at this moment – a need which in my judgement far exceeds any other – is that we should have tranquillity and stability both at home and abroad so that free scope should be given to the initiative and enterprise of our citizens, for it is in that way far more than by any action of the government that we can hope to recover from the economic and social results of the war.

With this in view I think it is of the utmost importance that we should return as quickly as possible, and as completely as possible, to the normal procedure which existed before the war. In pursuance of this aim I am satisfied that the time has now come when a change should be made in the machinery of the central Government. Some of the work which has hitherto been done by the Cabinet Secretariat is essential and must be continued, but we intend to bring that body in its present form to an end, and I am certain that the necessary work can be continued, and the invaluable services of the present Secretary retained, in connection with the Treasury, which in the past has always been the central department of Government …

At home our chief preoccupation at this time is the state of trade and employment. The immediate problem of unemployment this winter will call for emergency measures. Plans for dealing with the situation have already been considered by the late Government. They will be examined afresh by us with a view of seeing whether any improvements are possible, and the necessary steps will then be taken with the least avoidable delay. Such remedies, however, can only be palliatives, and the real recovery will not come except from the revival of trade and industry. To secure this result, the first essential is to reduce expenditure to the lowest attainable level in the hope that the tax-payer may find some relief from the burden of taxation which not only presses so heavily upon individuals, but is the greatest clog upon the wheels of national industry …

There are many measures of legislative and administrative importance which, in themselves, would be desirable, and which, in other circumstances, I should have recommended to the immediate attention of the electorate. But I do not feel that they can, at this moment, claim precedence over the nation's first need, which is, in every walk of life, to get on with its own work with the minimum of interference at home and of disturbance abroad. ■

The Conservatives won the October 1922 election with an overall majority of more than eighty seats, a safe margin. But Law's government was widely thought to have left aside the ablest leaders of the time; Austen Chamberlain, Lord Birkenhead and Sir Robert Horne were among those whose loyalty to the Coalition kept them out of office in 1922–3.

In May 1923 Bonar Law was forced to retire suddenly through ill health. Passing over the Foreign Secretary, Lord Curzon, the King selected Stanley Baldwin to serve as Prime Minister. While he had been serving as Chancellor of the Exchequer under Law, Baldwin was still a relatively unknown figure, and the choice came as a surprise to many. But for the next fifteen years Baldwin would dominate British political life.

The first spell of Baldwin's leadership was dramatically enlivened in the autumn of 1923, when he announced a return to a policy of protectionism, twenty years after the issue first came to divide Conservative politics. The decision meant calling an election, for a change in fiscal policy went against Bonar Law's pledge during the 1922 campaign not to initiate any radical policy changes. This episode, which resulted in defeat for Baldwin and the formation of the first Labour government in 1923, seemed to throw away a comfortable majority. Baldwin explained the decision to the Home Secretary, his close friend William Bridgeman.

7.9   **William Bridgeman, diary, October–December 1923 (in P. Williamson, ed., *The Modernisation of Conservative Politics: The Diaries and Letters of William Bridgeman 1904–1935*, London, The Historian's Press, 1988, pp. 168–9).**

■   *October–December 1923.*

Baldwin had to speak at the National Union Conference at Plymouth shortly before the Autumn Session was to begin. A week or so before he went to Plymouth he asked me to dine alone with him & told me he had come to the conclusion that our remedies for unemployment were merely temporary and in his opinion the only cure was to protect our home markets by a tariff. He took the view that as Europe recovered, our position must get worse in competition with European cheap labour & low exchange, and that we could not face the winter of 1924–5 without a change in our fiscal system. This change he felt could not be brought about in this Parliament owing to Bonar Law's pledge given at the 1922 election not to change our fiscal system without another appeal to the Country. Baldwin's intention was to intimate in his Plymouth speech that he regarded our present steps to deal with unemployment as merely palliatives, and that in his opinion the only real cure was to have a free hand to meet unfair competition with a tariff. I could see that he had practically made up his mind, but I said I thought that if he made such a speech, an election campaign would begin the next day, and that it would be better to postpone any such declaration until we were prepared ... The matter was shortly after discussed at the Cabinet, and much the same advice was offered by others. However, he made his Plymouth speech & as we thought the protection v. free-trade campaign began the next day ... And so the campaign began, and for the first fortnight it looked as if we should win, but in the last 3 or 4 days the election leaflets produced by the Liberals which were most mendacious & said we were going to tax food, and lower pensions etc., began to tell, & it ended in our losing about 100 seats, & coming in with about 256, Labour being second with nearly 200 & Liberals last with some 150 – a stalemate. ■

7.10　Labour Party poster, 1923
general election (National
Museum of Labour History).

GREET THE DAWN: GIVE LABOUR IT'S CHANCE

The First Labour Government

The Conservatives lost eighty-six seats in the December 1923 election. Although they remained the largest single party in the House of Commons, there was no overall Conservative majority and, in the circumstances, certainly no mandate. The Liberals held the balance of power, and there were several uncertain weeks before a new government was formed.

While many people were frightened of a Labour government, others, including the MP Leo Amery, saw opportunity in this unprecedented situation.

7.11　**Leo Amery, diary, 8 December 1923 (in John Barnes and David Nicholson, eds,** *The Leo Amery Diaries, Vol. I: 1896–1929***, London, Hutchinson, 1980, p. 361).**

■ *8 December 1923*: ... dashed off a strong appeal to Stanley urging him to realise that he stood head and shoulders above any man in the country and that if he threw up the sponge he would cart all of us who had pinned our faith to him and would smash the Party. I also pressed him to stay on and meet the House so as to state the issue his own way and force the Liberals to face the necessity of supporting Labour which is bound to mean their eventual break-up and disappearance as a Party. My whole object in this and subsequent talks and letters has been to convince him that our main object in the immediate future is the destruction of the Liberal Party and the absorption of as much of the carcass as we can secure – this in opposition to all the born idiots, from Austen and F.E. downwards, who are clamouring for us to support an Asquith Government which would mean the final break-up of our Party. One of the three parties has to disappear and the one that is spiritually dead and has been so for thirty years or more is the natural victim. ■

The 1923 election results showed the British electoral system in transition. The revival of the protectionist issue had raised the pre-war political allegiances around Conservative protectionism and Liberal free trade. Both parties rid themselves of any lingering coalitionist tendencies as an unintended, if not unwelcomed, result of Baldwin's October decision. But the Labour Party's parliamentary representation also increased by 50 MPs to 192. While the Conservatives remained the largest party in the House, there was no question of a new Conservative/Liberal coalition when the wounds from the previous one had yet to heal and when the election had raised the bogy of protection once more. In these circumstances the King asked Ramsay MacDonald to form the first Labour administration in January 1924.

The Daily Herald *cartoonist 'A.G.' portrayed a succession of establishment figures deriding Labour's so-called inexperience – including, in the final frame, inexperience of that scourge of working people, unemployment.*

7.12 **Cartoon by 'A.G.', 'The latest cry is that Labour ministers will 'lack experience'',** *Daily Herald,* **4 January 1924.**

Fears in establishment circles over the handing of power to the Labour Party in 1924, which in any case was circumscribed by its minority in the Commons, proved ground-less. The social reformer and writer Beatrice Webb, whose husband Sidney served as Secretary to the Board of Trade in the new Cabinet, captured the irony of the situation in her diary.

7.13 Beatrice Webb, diary, 19 January 1924 (in Margaret Cole, ed., *Beatrice Webb's Diaries, 1924–1932*, London, Longmans, 1956, pp. 1–3)

■ On Wednesday the twenty Ministers designate, in their best suits ... went to Buckingham Palace to be sworn in; having been previously drilled by [Cabinet Secretary] Hankey. Four of them came back to our weekly MPs lunch ... they were all laughing over Wheatley – the revolutionary – going down on both knees and actually kissing the King's hand; and CP Trevelyan was remarking that the King seemed quite incapable of saying two words to his new Ministers: 'he went through the ceremony like an automaton!'

Meanwhile I am living a distracted life which does not please me. I have taken over S.'s unofficial correspondence and dictated forty letters in twice as many minutes. What is far more troublesome is acting as the 'Doyenne' among Ministers' wives, in the organisation of their social intercourse within the Party and with outsiders like the Court. Just at present there are two questions – clothes and curtseys. A sort of underground communication is going on between Grosvenor Road and Buckingham Palace which is at once comic and tiresome. ■

The MacDonald government was hampered, on the one hand, by the increasing restive-ness of the left, which with the exception of John Wheatley was not represented on the front bench; and, on the other hand, it was hindered by its dependence upon the Liberal vote for survival. The latter ruled out any radical domestic legislation which could have pacified the former. On the whole, Whitehall tamed the Labour beast with no difficulty at all, as the Deputy Cabinet Secretary recorded in his diary.

7.14 Thomas Jones, diary, 1 February 1924 [in Keith Middlemas, ed., *Thomas Jones: Whitehall Diary, Vol.I: 1916–25*, London, Oxford University Press, 1969, pp. 269–71].

■ *1 February 1924* ... At 11.30 I saw Sidney Webb in his room at the Board of Trade ... We ... talked of unemployment, and it was rather disappointing to find Sidney Webb, the author of pamphlets innumerable on the cure of unemployment regardless of cost, now, as Chairman of the Unemployment Committee, reduced to prescribing a revival of trade as the one remedy left to us.

Wheatley, the Minister of Health, is Chairman of the Cabinet Committee. He is from the Clyde, but 'Pale Pink' rather than 'Turkey Red'. He harangued the Standing Committee a couple of days ago, advocating a ten years' programme of 200,000 houses per annum, each to cost exactly £500 and to be let at exactly 7s. per week. How this stupendous sum is to be raised, and how prices and rents are to be kept static regardless of all market changes, he had no idea, and it had to be pointed out to him that his scheme implied the stabilisation of wages for ten years. The officials, with the aid of Arthur Greenwood, are busily engaged in watering down this scheme also ...

At 1 o'clock, to the Grill Room of the Grand to lunch with Buxton, the Minister for Agriculture ... We went across together to No. 10 at 2.30 where the PM was to receive the Agricultural Advisory Committee ... The PM wears his grey hair almost as long as L.G. His speech, too, had a strong likeness to the sort of speech that L.G. would deliver in similar circumstances. He speaks with greater fluency and greater emphasis, but, closely examined, you had the same assurance of a fervent desire to help the great national industry of Agriculture, to reconcile all conflicting interests, etc., etc., and when at the end George Edwards, the veteran leader of the farm servants, voiced his deep disappointment, the PM pointed out that you could not subsidise the wages of farm labourers without at once being assailed with demands from the miners, the textile workers – all of which was true to precedent. I whispered to Sir Daniel Hall, at my elbow, that we were not going to see just yet the New Jerusalem set up in England's green and pleasant land! ... ■

The experiment with Labour government ended in the early autumn of 1924 when MacDonald lost a vote of confidence, and a general election was held in October. The Conservatives' victory in that campaign was in part due to their skilful manipulation of public fears of Labour's relationship to Soviet Communism. The Zinoviev letter, now known to have been a forgery, was published by the Daily Mail *only days before polling, and the treatment it received at the hands of the anti-socialist press was widely thought to have influenced the results.*

7.15   The Zinoviev letter, 15 September 1924 (reproduced in the *Daily Mail*, 25 October 1924).

■ Executive Committee   VERY SECRET
  Third Communist International Presidium

Sept. 15th 1924
MOSCOW

To the Central Committee, British Communist Party

Dear Comrades,

The time is approaching for the Parliament of England to consider the Treaty concluded between the Governments of Great Britain and the SSSR for the purpose of ratification. The fierce campaign raised by the British bourgeoisie around the question shows that the majority of the same, together with reactionary circles, are against the Treaty for the purpose of breaking off an agreement consolidating the ties between the proletariats of the two countries leading to the restoration of normal relations between England and the SSSR.

The proletariat of Great Britain, which pronounced its weighty word when danger threatened of a break-off of the past negotiations, and compelled the Government of MacDonald to conclude the Treaty, must show the greatest possible energy in the further struggle for ratification and against the endeavours of British capitalists to compel Parliament to annul it.

It is indispensable to stir up the masses of the British proletariat to bring into movement the army of unemployed proletarians whose position can be improved only after a loan has been granted to the SSSR for the restoration of her economics and when business collaboration between the British and Russian proletariats has been put in order. It is imperative that the group in the Labour Party sympathising with the Treaty should bring increased pressure to bear upon the Government and Parliamentary circles in favour of the ratification of the Treaty.

... the establishment of close contact between the British and Russian proletariat, the exchange of delegations and workers, etc., will make it possible for us to extend and develop the propaganda of ideas of Leninism in England and the Colonies. Armed warfare must be preceded by a struggle against the inclinations to compromise which are embedded among the majority of British workmen, against the ideas of evolution and peaceful extermination of capitalism ...

But even in England, as other countries, where the workers are politically developed, events themselves may more rapidly revolutionise the working masses than propaganda. For instance, a strike movement, repressions by the Government etc.

From your last report it is evident that agitation-propaganda work in the army is weak, in the navy a very little better. Your explanation that the quality of the members attracted justifies the quantity is right in principle, nevertheless it would be desirable to have cells in all the units of the troops....

With Communist Greetings,

President of the Presidium of the I.K.K.I.

ZINOVIEV ■

7.16 **Report on the Zinoviev letter,** *Daily Mail,* **27 October 1924.**

■ BRITAIN ROUSED AGAINST REDS.

SHOCKED BY PLOT OF CABINET'S MASTERS.

PREMIER SAYS NOTHING

'FORGERY' SMOKE SCREEN.

MOSCOW SECRETS FORCED OUT BY 'DAILY MAIL'.

The only thing left to do is to vote Conservative.

Polling Day: the day after to-morrow.

The publication of the 'Very Secret' Moscow letter of instruction to Communists in Britain (who are the Socialist Government's masters) to take steps to paralyse our Army and Navy and to plunge England into civil war has profoundly shocked the whole country ...

Throughout the week-end a storm of criticism has been directed against Mr MacDonald and his Ministers, because it was they who signed the treaty to 'lend' British money to these Moscow murderers. These criminals sent their civil war orders over here, despite their solemn undertaking in the treaty to cease all such poison plots ...

There is one thing left to be done. The general election takes place on Wednesday. Vote Conservative and rid the country of the Government that is controlled by the Communists who take their orders from Moscow, the home of wholesale murder and starvation. ■

In part because of the Zinoviev letter, Labour's first experience of government ended in October 1924 on a bitter note. This taste of power served in subsequent years to harden the tactical divisions in the party. John Paton, the left-wing Organising Secretary of the Independent Labour Party, recorded his own views on the election in his memoirs.

7.17   John Paton, *Left Turn!*, 1936 (London, Secker & Warburg, p. 223).

■ One of the consequences of its election defeat was that the Labour Party began a well-marked swing to the 'Right'. Its reading of events was that the 'Zinovieff Letter' dodge was successful only because it was possible, through foolishly militant utterances by some of its spokesmen, to link the Labour Party in the public mind with the fear-inspiring policies of the Communist Party. It had also made the discovery that large numbers of people actually expected that a Labour Government should make some definite attempt to give effect to the pledges so light-heartedly given in the glorious irresponsibility of what had seemed permanent opposition. Therefore it was urged, let us show by our moderation of policy that Communism is as hateful to us as to any Tory, and let us be so careful of pledges as never to promise what cannot be performed.

At the same time the ILP was reading events in a completely opposite sense. For it, the defeat was the outcome of timidity and lack of vision: the result of planlessness and feeble fumbling, where the needs of the time demanded bold, imaginative plans and determined and courageous effort to give them effect. It began to swing farther 'Left' and the tension between the two parties steadily increased. ■

The Decline of the Liberal Party

The biggest losers of the 1924 election were the Liberals, whose share of the vote declined from 29.6 per cent in 1923 to only 17.6 per cent. In the Commons, the Liberal parliamentary party now consisted of only forty-two MPs, and Asquith himself lost his seat. Undoubtedly many Liberal electors had voted Conservative for the first time in 1924, and the Conservatives gained around 100 seats at the Liberals' expense. The performance was all the more disappointing because Liberal hopes had been raised by the 1923 election, in which the newly reunified party had gained forty-two seats.

Although their parliamentary party had still trailed in third place in 1923, the Liberals had seemed set for a recovery from the bitter disputes of the previous seven years. Liberal optimism at that time is evident in the pages of the Liberal Magazine, *which was controlled by the Asquithian wing of the party.*

7.18   Editorial commentary, *Liberal Magazine*, December 1923 (vol. 31, no. 363, pp. 705–6).

■ … Mr. Baldwin's appeal to the country on a Protectionist programme has robbed his party of nearly a hundred seats. These seats have been divided between the Liberal and Labour Parties in a proportion which bears a rough resemblance to the proportionate strength of each party at the dissolution

... The Liberal Party gained many more seats than the Labour Party, but it also lost more. These losses were expected, for in the last Parliament a considerable number of seats were held by Liberals on a temporary and insecure basis, having been won in circumstances which have now passed away. Although the Liberal Members do not constitute much more than one quarter of the House of Commons, they are a solid and united party, and their present strength may be regarded as the rock-bottom upon which united Liberalism may now build with.confidence ... Now that the Liberal Party has got itself once more upon a secure footing, we shall be able to make headway against these temporary and accidental electioneering advantages which the Labour Party has enjoyed during the past two or three years, and if we plainly put forward the whole policy of reform for which Liberalism stands we shall not fail to win the confidence and support of the country. ■

That the Liberals' hopes of 1923 failed to materialise was partly due to the moderation of both the Conservative and the Labour leadership, which left no room in the middle ground in British politics. But it was also the result of continued bitter feuding between the supporters of Asquith and those of Lloyd George. The 'reunion' had been a cosmetic exercise. The 'Asquithians' had the national organisation but lacked money and charismatic leadership. Lloyd George remained a central character in inter-war politics, and through the Lloyd George fund he had amassed through the sale of honours as Prime Minister and successfully invested, he had no financial worries. But he had no formal political organisation to lead. Reunion in that sense was logical, but it came painfully.

The failure to resolve these problems before the 1924 election contributed to the Liberals' heavy defeat. Within the party itself there was mutual and bitter recrimination. Herbert Gladstone, who as the principal organiser of the national campaign was the target of much criticism, put the blame squarely on the shoulders of the Welsh 'Goat' in a memorandum written after the election.

7.19   Herbert Gladstone, 'Narrative of the general election 1924', 1925 (BL Add. MS 46480).

■ ... There were loud shouts after the cataclysm against the Liberal organisation. It was 'antiquated, undemocratic, supported by rich men's money, run by well-meaning but super-annuated persons who should be replaced by vigorous young experts familiar with modern problems and developments. Then only could unity and efficiency be restored.' ...

Was the debacle due to faulty organisation? If so, in what way? ...

Throughout 1924 it appeared that Ll.G. was in a state of constant suspicion and dissatisfaction with regard to our attitude to him and his office. It was our duty to work for unity. Our desire and our efforts were all in that direction. It is true that all four of us had been more or less persistently in opposition to Ll.G. and his post-war Coalition. Undeniably we all saw and felt certain difficulties in co-operation so long as Ll.G. maintained independence of the Party in organisation, in the Press, in a separate office, and with separate funds. Had we not ourselves been conscious of these difficulties, they rained in on us from our best men in all parts of the country. Indeed it may be truly said that unity could not have been maintained had we not been in control. We stuck to it that Mr. Asquith was Leader of the Party, that we were loyally serving him, and in this way we gained the support of numberless persons who would otherwise have joined the Labour party or retired from political life. ...

As soon as we had taken stock of the position after the General Election of 1923, we faced the new situation. Vigorous organisation was obviously necessary. Even greater was the necessity for speeding up at once the fixing of Liberal Candidates in full numbers. We wanted money at H.Q.... . on this hung the fate of the Party ... Ll.G. we knew had large resources at his disposal ... The only possible course was to approach Ll.G. whether or no we liked it ...

[After several meetings] there was nothing for it but to maintain amicable relations and keep on endeavouring to bring him over to our views. Yet all this meant delay. As regards the organisation which we considered essential for the coming General Election, we were absolutely crippled. Exhausted by the strain of two Elections, the local Associations were inert and without money ...

Ll.G.'s remarks on July 23rd, and on other occasions, showed that so far from thinking a large number of candidates was necessary, he held that it would be sufficient to fight with about 300 and concentrate on them. The Liberal chance would come at a subsequent election. It was a fatal view. Unless the electorate saw in the Liberal forces a sure possibility of a Liberal Government, the General Election was certain to be a disastrous swing to the reaction against Labour, and against the Liberals as responsible for putting a Labour Government into office. ■

Many traditional supporters of the Liberal Party became disillusioned in the wake of the 1924 defeat. The radical Liberal philosopher and journalist L.T. Hobhouse was one example. That November he wrote to his close friend, the Manchester Guardian *editor C.P. Scott, of his despair for traditional Liberalism. Their correspondence illustrates well the concerns of Liberal intellectuals in these years.*

7.20   **Correspondence between L.T. Hobhouse and C.P. Scott, November 1924 (in Trevor Wilson, ed.,** *The Political Diaries of C.P. Scott, 1911–28,* **London, Collins, 1970, p. 468).**

■   *L.T. Hobhouse to C.P Scott, 7 November 1924 (extract).*

My difficulty about the Liberal Party lies further back than yours. I doubt if it any longer stands for anything distinctive. My reasons are on the one side that moderate Labour – Labour in office – has on the whole represented essential liberalism, not without mistakes and defects, but *better* than the organised party since Campbell-Bannerman's death. On the other side the Liberal party, however you divide it up, never seems any better agreed within on essentials. Of the present fragment part leans to the Tories, part to Labour, part has nothing distinctive, but is a kind of Free Trade Unionist group. The deduction I draw is that the distinction between that kind of Labour man who does not go whole hog for nationalisation on the one side and the Liberal who wants social progress on the other is obsolete. I myself have always felt it was unreal and than if we divided parties by true principles, the division would be like this

| Communist | ordinary Labour | Bad Liberal Diehards |
| Theoretical Socialists | Good Liberal | ordinary Tory |

But tradition and class distinctions kept many good Liberals outside Labour. Now Labour has grown so much that it tends to absorb them and to leave only the 'bad' Liberals who incline to the Tories and a mass of traditional Liberals who can't desert a party of that name. ■

After 1925 Lloyd George was the inevitable heir apparent to the Liberal Party's leadership. He proceeded in 1925 to begin to put together a platform of dynamic new policies, including the 'Yellow Book' of 1928 discussed in Chapter 6. There were persistent rumours in these years of his defection from the party to lead a new alliance with either progressive Conservatives or right-wing Labourites, lampooned in the cartoon below by Strube. But Lloyd George's intention to rebuild British Liberalism was always clear, as shown in a widely reported speech to Welsh Liberals in 1926.

7.21   Cartoon by Sidney 'George' Strube, 'The rich widow: "Oh! Mr. Rudolph Ramsaytino, wouldn't it be romantic if you *did* elope with me?"', *Daily Express*, 8 December 1925.

7.22   **Lloyd George, speech to Caernarvon Boroughs Liberal Association, 20 January 1926 (reported in the *Manchester Guardian*, 21 January 1926).**

■ … In my judgement it is not the wisdom of Liberalism at this moment to negotiate alliances with another party. Prudence dictates that it should make a powerful position for itself in the country with a view to securing a large representation in the next Parliament. This, I feel assured, it can do by sustained and united effort on the right lines. When that is achieved, then it can decide to co-operate with any body of men who will undertake to carry through the programme it approves. Co-operation does not imply amalgamation; least of all does it presuppose absorption. It may not involve co-operation in forming a Government but merely in constituting a Parliamentary majority that will govern this country on lines which must be agreed upon as a condition of support … It is our duty as Liberals to go on winning support for Liberal principles and Liberal ideals, and Liberal methods of applying those principles and ideals. We have three or four years in which to reach and to teach the nation. The more support we shall have won at the end of that time the greater influence shall we possess in decided action. Our support might then be the determining factor in the situation and may mould the course of events.

The foolish calculation made on the expected disappearance of Liberalism will then have been demonstrably falsified. It will become increasingly apparent to the most demented of the critics of Liberalism that the party is not going to perish and that on the contrary it will count more at the coming election than at any time since 1910. I would only like to add one word of caution, that as long as men and women whose main purpose is the amelioration of the conditions of the people spend their energies in making war on each other so long will those conditions endure.

There are millions of men and women in this country for whom Liberalism supplies the best answer to the questions that perplex them about the social and economic problems of the nation. Let us rally them to our standard. That seems to me to be our immediate task … ■

From October 1926, when Asquith resigned, Lloyd George functioned as the de facto leader of the Liberal Party, in spite of the continued opposition of many of his colleagues. His attempts to resuscitate party fortunes through an injection of money from the Lloyd George Fund, and through the high-profile promotion of a series of radical policies on land, industry and unemployment, failed to halt the progressive erosion of the Liberals' electoral base. The transformation of the party into a small, third force in British politics was virtually completed by the end of the decade.

7.23   Shifts in voting behaviour, 1900–29 (derived from David Butler and Gareth Butler, eds, *British Political Facts, 1900–1985*, London, Macmillan, 6th edn, 1986, pp. 224–5).

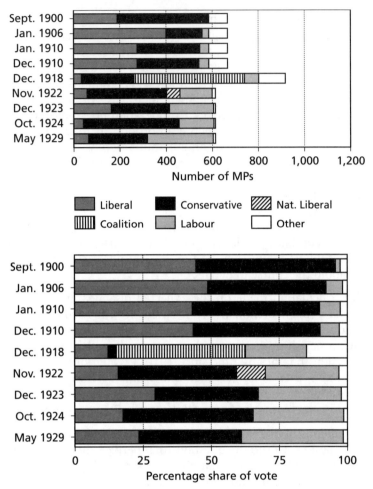

Baldwin and the New Conservatism

A significant factor in the continued decline of the Liberal Party in the 1920s was the style of Stanley Baldwin's leadership of the Conservative and Unionist Party. His moderate approach captured the middle ground of British politics, traditionally occupied by the Liberals. After the political tumult of the previous years, Baldwin's great achievement in 1924 was in winning a solid majority for the Conservative Party. As party leader and Prime Minister, Baldwin unified the party, successfully isolated Lloyd George and defined the role of Conservatism in this period as one of the reconciliation of the class war. The neutralising of socialism and the taming of the Labour Party became his twin objectives.

Political 'Baldwinism' became identified with the management of domestic harmony. In the debate in Parliament over the future of the political levy on the trade unions – a favourite issue of die-hard Conservatives during the 1920s – Baldwin gave one of the most memorable speeches of the inter-war years.

7.24 Stanley Baldwin, House of Commons address, 6 March 1925 (*Hansard*, 5th ser., 181: 834-41).

■ I often wonder if all the people in this country realise the inevitable changes that are coming over the industrial system in England. People are apt either to get their knowledge of the industrial system from textbooks, which must inevitably be half a generation behind, or from some circumstances familiar to them at a fixed and static point in their lives, whereas, as a matter of fact, ever since the industrial system began in this country, it has been not only in a state of evolution, but in a state of evolution which, I think, historians in the centuries to come, when they write its history, will acknowledge to be an evolution that has developed at a far more rapid rate than was visible to the people who lived in these times.

... I worked for many years in an industrial business, and had under me a large number, or what was then a large number, of men ... It was a place where I knew, and had known from childhood, every man on the ground, a place where I was able to talk with the men not only about the troubles in the works, but troubles at home where strikes and lock-outs were unknown. It was a place where the fathers and grandfathers of the men then working there had worked, and where their sons went automatically into the business. It was also a place where nobody ever 'got the sack', and where we had a natural sympathy for those who were less concerned with efficiency than is this generation, and where a number of old gentlemen used to spend their days sitting on the handle of a wheelbarrow, smoking their pipes ...

But ... we were gradually passing into a new state of industry, when the small firms and the small industries were being squeezed out. Business was all tending towards great amalgamations on the one side of employers and on the other side of the men, and when we came in any form between these two forces, God help those who stood outside! ...

Those two forces with which we have to reckon are enormously strong, and they are the two forces in this country to which now, to a great extent, and it will be a greater extent in the future, we are committed. We have to see what wise statesmanship can do to steer the country through this time of evolution, until we can get to the next stage of our industrial civilisation ...

In this great problem which is facing the country in years to come, it may be from one side or the other that disaster may come, but surely it shows that the only progress that can be obtained in this country is by those two bodies of men – so similar in their strength and so similar in their weaknesses – learning to understand each other, and not to fight each other …

… For two years past in the face of great difficulties, perhaps greater than any were aware of, I have striven to consolidate, and to breathe a living force into, my great party … We find ourselves, after these two years in power, in possession of perhaps the greatest majority our party has ever had, and with the general assent of the country. Now how did we get there?...it was because, rightly or wrongly, we succeeded in creating an impression throughout the country that we stood for stable Government and for peace in the country between all classes of the community …

… We, at any rate, are not going to fire the first shot. We stand for peace. We stand for the removal of suspicion in the country. We want to create an atmosphere, a new atmosphere in a new Parliament for a new age, in which the people can come together …

… I have equal confidence in my fellow countrymen throughout the whole of Great Britain. Although I know that there are those who work for different ends from most of us in this House, yet there are many in all ranks and all parties who will re-echo my prayer:

'Give peace in our time, O Lord.' ■

The 1920s were crucial in the development of Conservative strategies for opposing socialism at home and for finding a formula for domestic industrial peace. The young group of backbenchers who came to be known as the YMCA began to develop ideas which would underpin the Conservative approach to domestic policy-making for the rest of the century.

7.25   Noel Skelton, 'Private property: a Unionist ideal', *Spectator*, 3 May 1924.

■ No one would deny that amongst Conservatives there tends to be a section which dislikes change for its own sake – as well as a large non-party body of similar opinion. But that body of opinion is alive now to the impracticability and folly of standing still, and when it moves – as move it is now prepared to – it will prefer to move with progressive Conservatism towards a property-owning democracy rather than towards the *Sturm und Drang* of Socialism or the manoeuvres of a suspect Liberalism. And it is not the safeguarding of industries, or perhaps even a 'general' Tariff, which will alter their new determination.

The real danger to Unionist prospects comes not from fear of Protection, but from the doubt lest the party should not be in earnest about social reforms … The future depends upon Unionism as a whole being able to show a line of advance to the great body of wage-earners. Britain, unlike France, passed from political aristocracy to political democracy without the disaster of a revolution. Can we make a similar advance in the economic sphere? It depends entirely upon Conservatism.

For in its principles, Conservatism holds the key of the situation. It was not for nothing that the Conservative Party used to be called the 'Party of Property'. Private property is, so far as history gives us a clue, the foundation and sine qua non of all progressive civilizations. It follows that the extent of the distribution of private property is the measure, on its economic side, of a civilization's stability and success. Similarly, character and a sense of responsibility are rooted in a man's possession of 'something of his own'. A democracy without scope for the development of economic character and responsibility, cut off from private ownership, cannot be expected to understand the material foundations of civilization. Moreover, it cannot stand. Unless, then, by such means as profit-sharing and industrial co-partnership and the wider distribution of the small ownership of land the Unionist Party can make property-owners of the present wage-earning classes, no hope can be given to the mass of the people that their economic status can be brought abreast of their political and their educational status. It will perhaps be a slow process; but great parties must take a long view, and if an objective is sufficiently important must not fear the toils of the march ...

The hour indeed is struck for the advance of a democratic constructive progressive Conservatism. 1922 preserved Conservatism, 1923 opened its eyes, 1924 will give it at once the desire and the opportunity to do its much-needed work. ■

The General Election of 1929

The 'flapper vote'

In 1928 the government proceeded with the Representation of the People Bill. The major change it provided for was the enfranchisement of women between the ages of 21 and 30, on equal terms with men. There was a good deal of speculation over the effect of the 'flapper vote' on the conduct of politics; and considerable concern was expressed over the impact of an Act which would result in some 2,200,000 more women than men voters.

The Representation of the People Act was passed without serious dissent, and the arguments of die-hards who opposed the Bill were easily countered in the parliamentary debate. Satirical commentary in the press addressed the question of how the parties would compete to attract the new women voters.

7.26   **Debate on the second reading of the Representation of the People Bill, 29 March 1928 (*Hansard*, 5th ser., 216: 1392–3).**

■ Colonel APPLIN: ... There are at least 75 per cent of the people of this country who do not want this thing rushed through now. I feel certain that I am right. It is not an equal franchise; it is an unequal franchise. It will give the women the power over the finances of the country. It will give them greater voting power than men ... I do not believe the women want it. I do not believe that there is any demand whatever. I am certain that the women of the country realise, as many of the older women do, that a franchise on equal terms with men carries with it equal duties. Hitherto, men have done all the heavy work in this country.

Miss WILKINSON: Oh, really! Good gracious!

Colonel APPLIN: You find no women in the stokehold of a ship or in the Navy; you find no women down the coal mines to-day, and I thank God for it; you find no women in blast furnaces. Women cannot physically perform these duties. Therefore, it is a very dangerous thing for women to demand the vote on equal terms with men, without realising what that may involve. Whatever happens, it must involve going into the rough and tumble of life. It must mean taking on grave responsibilities, which would perhaps be too great a burden for women.

Miss WILKINSON *indicated dissent.*

Colonel APPLIN: The hon. Lady shakes her head. Let her reflect. Suppose a woman sat on that Bench as Chancellor of the Exchequer.

Miss WILKINSON: Why not?

Colonel APPLIN: Imagine her introducing her Budget, and in the middle of her speech a message coming in, 'Your child is dangerously ill, come at once.' I should like to know how much of that Budget the House would get, and what the figures would be like. It is obvious that, with a thousand cases like that, the whole system must break down, and the women know it ... ■

The cartoonist Low depicted Baldwin, MacDonald and Lloyd George as elector Joan Bull's choice of 1928 valentines.

7.27   **Cartoon by David Low, 'Joan Bull's valentines', Evening Standard, 13 February 1928.**

Conservative despondency

Baldwin has been criticised for allowing his government to drift after 1926, without any clearly defined set of objectives. He failed to adopt any positive or dynamic policy to grapple with unemployment, fiscal policy or constitutional reform. Although Neville Chamberlain's 'rationalising' social legislation kept Parliament occupied, it was a complex and rather dull subject which failed to inspire either the party or the electorate. Industrial derating was widely unpopular by the spring of 1929, as it became clear that central grants to local government were often inadequate to make up the loss in income from business rates.

The Conservative rank and file became increasingly frustrated during the later 1920s with the leadership's moderation, and with its failure to act on the reduction of government expenditure and taxation, on imperial preference or even on the extension of the 'safeguarding' of domestic industries, on the restoration of the powers of the House of Lords or on aid to agriculture. The mood in the party as the 1929 election approached was recorded by the backbench Conservative MP Cuthbert Headlam.

7.28   **Cuthbert Headlam, diary, March 1929 (in Stuart Ball, ed., *Parliament and Politics in the Age of Baldwin and MacDonald: The Headlam Diaries 1923–1935*, London, The Historian's Press, 1992, pp. 166–8).**

■   *Tuesday 5 March 1929*

The gloom in our Party is odd: one does not understand it – but if we are really at such a low ebb, I cannot for the life of me understand why we should have the election in May – surely if trade is really improving and things are going better, it would be wiser to postpone going to the country until October? My own impression is that such a policy would dish the Labour Party and might very likely help us materially. If trade goes on improving, it is likely that unemployment in the heavy industries will be considerably diminished by the month of October – nothing could help us more than that – and if between now and then Mr. B. would remodel his Cabinet, he could give the Party an assurance – that I gather would be welcome – that our beautiful and generous-minded young men would be given their chance if he is returned to power – altogether it seems to me that we have nothing to lose and much to gain by postponing the election …

Thursday 21 March

I still think that we are quite mad to have the election in May. We have struck a bad patch for the time being and there is no need for us to play the game of L.G. and the Labour people. However – presumably – Mr. B., advised by J.C.C. Davidson, thinks differently – and so there it is. We may quite likely go out with as big a thud as we did in 1906 and become as futile and feeble a party in the H of C as the Liberals are today. Politics are a curious up and down business, and so long as the feeling exists in the minds of the stupid crowd that Governments can give prosperity, it is inevitable that there should be complete upheavals in elections … ■

Baldwin led the Conservative Party into the 1929 general election with the slogan 'Safety First', which was intended to attract voters frightened by Labour socialism and Lloyd Georgian flamboyance. But 'Safety First' seemed a dull and negative basis on which to base a political campaign in. The contrast between the Conservative and Labour Party manifestos gave the voters a clear choice between alternative strategies for dealing with the problems of the economy.

7.29 Conservative and Labour Party posters, 1929 general election campaign (Conservative Party Archives; Geoffrey Ford, private collection).

7.30 *Mr. Stanley Baldwin's Election Address*, 1929 (Conservative Party Archives).

■ Four and a half years ago, you returned me to Parliament and to Office as the leader of a great majority. To-day it is my duty to lay before you the record of the Conservative and Unionist Government and its policy for the future; and to ask at your hands a renewal of your confidence. The Conservative Government has had to face difficulties and dangers at home and abroad which could not have been foreseen at the last Election. In spite of all obstacles, we have fulfilled the pledges given in 1924, to an extent which no Government has equalled, and as a result of our administration the Empire is more firmly united, the prestige of the country stands higher, the prosperity and welfare of our people is greater than ever before in our history. In submitting myself to the electorate, I make no spectacular promises for a sudden transformation of our social or industrial conditions, but I am resolved to maintain and consolidate the advance already made, to bring to fruition the schemes on which we are engaged, and to carry still further the solid work of reconstruction on which depend the unity of the Empire and the peace and well-being of its people …

It is the steady improvement in the resources and spending power of the individual home which should form the main object of our national financial policy. Our opponents in all their schemes to gain votes never count the cost in cash or credit. Yet money is the measure of all that can be done. We are told that immense new burdens are to be placed upon the direct tax-payer by the Socialist Party, and formidable drains upon our credit will be made by the Liberals. All this will simply be taken from the common stock, and the saving power and economic energy of the country will be reduced accordingly ... Instead of placing heavy new burdens upon the tax-payer, the process of strict and steady economies in every branch of the public service must continue to be pursued with the aim of lightening the public burdens and leaving larger sums of money to fructify in the pockets of the people ...

It is for the electors to judge, in the light of our past record, whether we have not faithfully redeemed the promises which we made four and a half years ago. We have striven consistently to build up industrial prosperity on sound and permanent foundations, and to improve the social conditions of our people. The results can be seen in the steady revival of trade, especially in the great basic industries, and in the reduction in the cost of living. The future destinies of the country rest in the hands of the electorate. I am confident that, with the growth of the new spirit of co-operation in industry, the present trade revival will make steady and even rapid progress, provided that British industry is guaranteed a period of stable government and can thus enjoy that confidence in the future without which trade recovery is impossible....I ask the electorate once again to place their confidence in our Party as the only one which can secure stable conditions and ordered progress along sound and practical lines. ∎

7.31 *Labour's Appeal to the Nation*, 1929 (London, Labour Party, pp. 1–3).

∎ The long-awaited opportunity has now come for the Nation to give its verdict on the present Government.

By its inaction during four critical years it has multiplied our difficulties and increased our dangers. Unemployment is more acute than when Labour left office. International relations are worse. Vast areas of the country are derelict ...

In the face of such a state of things this Tory Government has sat supinely with folded arms without a policy, without a vision, waiting for Providence or charity to do its work.

For nine months the Government watched the paralysing struggle in the Coal Industry. It aided and abetted the mine owners when they locked out the men, and provoked the industrial unrest that led to the General Strike, for which the Government was mainly responsible.

The Government's further record is that it has helped its friends by remissions of taxation, whilst it has robbed the funds of the workers' National Health Insurance Societies, reduced Unemployment Benefits, and thrown thousands of workless men and women on to the Poor Law ...

Our schemes for dealing with Unemployment ... are three-fold in character.

1. National Development and Trade Prosperity

Labour will undertake –

– Housing and Slum Clearance
– Land Drainage and Reclamation
– Electrification
– The Re-organisation of Railways and Transport
– New Roads and Road and Bridge Improvements
– Afforestation associated with Small Holdings
– Training and assistance by agreements with the Dominions for those
   who wish to try their fortunes in new lands ...

A Labour Government will set to work at once by using Export Credits and Trade Facilities Guarantees, to stimulate the depressed export trades ... the improved employment in these industries will be a great addition to the purchasing power in the home market.

2. Maintenance

The Labour Party's plan for dealing with Unemployment is to provide work; but pending the absorption of the unemployed in regular occupations it will take steps to relieve the present distress. It will also amend the Unemployment Insurance Act so as to afford more generous maintenance for the unemployed, and will remove those qualifications which deprive them of payments to which they are entitled.

3. The Young and the Old

A Labour Government would also relieve the congestion in the labour market ... The Party would extend the school age to fifteen with the necessary Maintenance Grants and provide Adequate Pensions for Aged Workers ...

LABOUR'S TAXATION POLICY

The Party stands for a system of Taxation which will distribute the burden fairly according to 'ability to pay'.

It will abolish Taxes on Food and other necessaries, and provide what revenue is needed by Death Duties on large estates and by graduating the Income Tax and Sur-Tax with a view to relieving the smaller, while increasing the contribution from the larger, incomes. The Labour Party will carry still further the differentiation between 'earned' and 'unearned' incomes ... ■

The 1929 election returned a Labour government for the second time in a decade, this time as the largest single party in the House, but still without an overall majority. In spite of Lloyd George's tremendous effort, both financial and in terms of policy, the Liberal Party had failed to make a significant come-back. The events of the following two years would come to represent a seismic shift in the shape of the modern British political system.

CHAPTER EIGHT

Responsibility and Illusion: Foreign and Imperial Policy, 1920–1929

A S one of the victors of the First World War, Britain appeared superficially to enjoy a secure world position in the 1920s. With the German fleet dismantled, Britain's naval pre-eminence among the European powers was safe. Equally, with the acquisition of colonial territories formerly belonging to Germany and Turkey, the British Empire was to reach its greatest size. Yet there were underlying strains in the country's position which emerged very soon after the war. Above all, there was the question of maintaining the peace, work in which Britain had to take a share. Although a popular body, the new League of Nations proved an ineffective peacekeeper, especially given the United States' reluctance to participate in it.

Overshadowing Britain's capacity to manoeuvre freely in diplomatic and strategic terms were the country's economic problems, which dictated retrenchment and cuts in defence spending. The war had wreaked havoc with the British economy, enabling the USA to emerge undisputedly as the world's greatest economic power. The financial cost of the war dogged Britain in the inter-war years, as governments struggled to meet their debt obligations to the United States. Facing financial constraints, British governments were reluctant to commit themselves to military guarantees of the peace settlement in Europe. This created tensions with France over policy towards Germany and the reparations question. Very slowly, the international climate improved, and through the Treaty of Locarno of 1925 Britain, France and Germany agreed to guarantee one another's security, paving the way for an easing of tensions in Europe in the later 1920s.

However, threats to British interests were emerging in the wider world. In the Far East, Britain began the decade still allied to Japan, but it proved impossible to maintain close relations simultaneously with Japan and with the rising world power, the United States, whose ascendancy was itself a potential source of concern to Britain. With Japan coming to be seen as a potential threat, Britain was nevertheless obliged to pursue naval limitations, and to abdicate the customary supremacy of the Royal Navy.

The British Empire, though larger than ever before, began to show signs of strain, undermining the strength which the country could expect to derive from its global possessions. After the war, the Dominions refused to accept an inferior status or to be involved automatically in the defence of British interests. During the 1920s the idea of a 'Commonwealth' relationship evolved to give legal definition to the Dominions' effective self-government. Elsewhere in the Empire, the first waves of nationalist discontent were experienced, most importantly in India, where Britain sought to maintain stability through a combination of concession and force.

A factor which Britain's policy-makers had increasingly to take into account was domestic public opinion, even more important since franchise reform in 1918 and 1928. Real doubts were expressed about the public's willingness to subsidise expensive adventures overseas, when so much needed to be done at home in the face of British economic decline. It was not surprising, then, that governments came to prefer modest foreign commitments. There seemed to be too many simultaneous calls on the country's slender resources: problems of domestic post-war readjustment, troubles in Ireland, the possible threat from Bolshevism and the need to consolidate new Middle Eastern gains. Yet it can be argued that Britain's economic problems were not sufficient to wreck its international status, provided that no additional strains arose.

Popular views on Britain's place in the world in the 1920s were characterised by post-war exhaustion and a rejection of the traditional, pre-1914 diplomacy, widely held to be responsible for the outbreak of the First World War. Progress towards a new framework of international relations could seem frustratingly slow, however, a sentiment captured later in the decade by the cartoonist David Low, as well as in election propaganda featured in the general election of 1929.

8.1   **Representations of anti-war sentiment: (*below*) cartoon by David Low, 'Slow progress', *Evening Standard*, 12 November 1927; (*overleaf*) Labour Party poster, 1929 general election (University of Kent Cartoon Archive, National Museum of Labour History).**

Desire to avoid another war explains the widespread enthusiasm for the new League of Nations (established in 1920), which was seen as a means of containing conflict – a view reinforced by the mood of internationalism resurgent by the later 1920s. Although British civil servants had initially voiced reservations about the League and its proposed role, they came to see it as a potentially economical vehicle for preserving peace. Provided the League reduced Britain's burdens, and did not add to them, British governments were prepared to endorse it. At a time of retrenchment, it was attractive to have the option of shedding costly responsibilities, and even those unconvinced by the loftier aims of the League tended to accept that the likely consequences of another major war for Britain and its empire were too terrible to consider.

Early in 1920 the Foreign Secretary, Arthur Balfour, discussed the probable limitations of the League in a detailed memorandum focusing on the particular problems of achieving a peace settlement with Turkey.

8.2   Arthur Balfour, memorandum on the League of Nations, 15 March 1920 (PRO CAB 24/100, CP 898).

■ **1.** ... The two telegraphic messages from the Supreme Council about the Turkish Peace only reached the meeting of the League of Nations at the end of its sittings, and it was impossible to discuss them with any completeness, still less to pass a final judgement upon them.

2. It was however agreed informally by M. Bourgeois and the rest of my colleagues, that I should attempt to give a general impression of the difficulties, which at least a majority of them feel, with regard to the policy sketched out in the two telegrams.

3. The first of these deals with Armenia, and the proposal it contains amounts to this: That the League of Nations should accept a position equivalent to that of a Mandatory Power. That an (as yet undefined) Armenia should be placed under its 'protection', and that it should thus provide an 'effective guarantee for the future security of the proposed state'.

4. The second proposal deals with minorities in Turkey, and suggests that the League of Nations should be saddled with the same responsibilities as regards the Clauses for protecting minorities in Turkey as it has accepted with regard to the corresponding Clauses in some of the European Treaties.

5. As regards the suggestion that the League of Nations should become in fact the mandatory for Armenia it is evident that as yet, and probably for a long time to come, the League of Nations is not and cannot be adequately equipped to carry out duties which may well prove to be of the most onerous kind. It is understood that France is to be the mandatory in Syria; Great Britain in Mesopotamia. But these two Nations possess the resources of Great Powers, and are well aware that these resources may be seriously called upon if they are adequately to fulfil their mandatory functions. The League of Nations have no resources, nor have they at present the machinery for creating them. And there is a serious danger that if they were to undertake a responsibility, which powerful and well organised nations apparently shrink from accepting, they will break down under the strain.

6. The League is of course perfectly ready to act as the supervising authority under the mandatory system. It is to it presumably that the mandatories now being called into being in various parts of the world, will be called upon to report, and we have every hope and expectation that it will exercise, where necessary, a salutary influence in the development of the mandated territories. It is more than doubtful however whether it should itself directly undertake large responsibilities of a mandatory character; especially in remote and half civilised regions where civilised opinion, the chief weapon of the League, carries but little weight ...

7. Somewhat similar considerations must be borne in mind when dealing with the protection of minorities in Asia Minor. We may well hope that the League may perform most valuable functions in securing the observance of the minority clauses in European Treaties. It will strengthen the hands of the Governments, for example at Bucharest or Warsaw, in the suppression of local abuses. It will give the minorities themselves the consciousness that there is an organised public opinion outside their own State prepared to support them. And if unhappily abuses should arise, the machinery of the League may be quite adequate to secure their suppression.

8. The position is very different in Asia Minor. Civilised public opinion has no influence whatever in that country; indeed since civilised public opinion is for the most part Christian opinion, it is a danger rather than a strength to

Christian minorities. Outrages against these minorities are usually inflicted by irregular bands whom the Turkish Government would immediately disavow and over whom, as they would protest, (it may be with truth), they had no power of control.

9. The League of Nations with no force at its immediate disposal, would have no weapon except remonstrance; and remonstrance has been tried in Turkey for 100 years with singularly little effect ...

11. Speaking generally it must be remembered that the chief instruments at the disposal of the League are Public Discussion; Judicial Investigation; Arbitration; and in the last resort, but only in the last resort; some form of Compulsion. These are powerful weapons, but the places where they seem least applicable are those remote and half barbarous regions, where nothing but force is understood, and where force is useless to preserve order unless it can be rapidly applied. It would seem that in those parts of the world to which this description applies the League of Nations can only play an effective part if there be a mandatory through whom it can act. If no such mandatory can be found, it cannot, as at present constituted, play the effectual part of a substitute. ■

At a practical level, the need for financial retrenchment in the 1920s led to massive reductions in Britain's defence expenditure, justified by the so-called Ten-Year Rule. In 1919 Lloyd George told the service chiefs that they need not prepare to fight another major war for another ten years. This assumption, which received general political support, underlay all Britain's overseas policies in the 1920s, and the Ten-Year Rule was renewed each year.

By 1930 Britain was spending much less in real terms on defence than it had in 1910. Hardest hit was the army, whose role was largely that of a colonial police force, and which was given no opportunity to develop the experience of mechanised warfare gained in the war.

8.3   **Defence expenditure, 1921–9 (derived from G.C. Peden, *British Economic and Social Policy: Lloyd George to Margaret Thatcher*, Oxford, Philip Allan, 2nd edn, 1991, p. 72).**

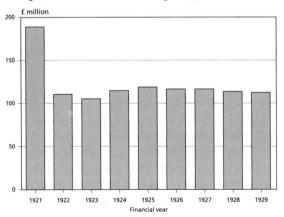

The alarm which this situation created among Britain's military planners is captured in the following memorandum by the Chief of the Imperial General Staff, dated 1927, which described the size and distribution of the British army in relation to its commitments.

8.4   Chief of the Imperial General Staff, memorandum on Britain's defence commitments, November 1927 (PRO CAB 4/17, CID 847B).

■ ... Though the danger of another European war, in which we should be called upon to participate, is remote, we have accepted certain definite military liabilities under the Pact of Locarno which demand the maintenance by us of military forces adequate to meet this obligation. In addition, not only have we accepted mandates for large territories, such as Palestine and Iraq, for the defence of which we are pledged, but, in the general upheaval of the world which has resulted from the war, our military liabilities in the East have been considerably increased by such disturbing factors as the Russian revolution, the chaotic condition of China, the growth of the Swaraj movement in India, and the political ambitions of an independent anti-British Egypt. Added to all this we have the problem of maintaining the internal security of our own country against subversive activities which are largely prompted and financed by Russia, and which have shown, in the General Strike of 1926, what proportions such a danger can very rapidly assume.

If the various problems outlined in the preceding paragraph were viewed from the military standpoint alone, the first step towards their solution would obviously be the strengthening of our foreign garrisons, and the provision of adequate local reserves in the Near, Middle and Far East which could cope, temporarily at any rate, with such dangers as might arise, until the Expeditionary Force, or part of it, from England could arrive on the scene. Unfortunately, the necessity for cutting down our national expenditure, coupled with the disbandment of the Southern Irish regiments in 1922 and the reduction of the British units of the Army in India, has precluded the possibility of taking such an obvious precaution. On the contrary, a comparison of our foreign garrisons to-day with the strengths at which they stood in 1914, shows that in nearly every case they have been reduced ... At the same time it is unfortunate that we have been compelled, from one cause or another, to lower our standard of security in the Mediterranean, in India, and in the Far East.

... I would now turn to the consideration of the adequacy of our general reserve, i.e., the Expeditionary Force, to meet our more extended liabilities. Apart from the somewhat indefinite liability which we have assumed under the Locarno Pact, the chief military liability of the British Empire appears to be the defence of India against Russian aggression. A recent study of this question by a Sub-Committee has enabled us to arrive at the strength of the force which we, so far as can be calculated beforehand, shall have to send out to India during the first twelve months of such a war. This force would amount to the equivalent of 11 divisions, which is more than twice the strength of the force which can to-day be organized out of the regular units in England ... ■

The Far East

Although the Anglo-Japanese alliance remained intact immediately after the First World War, Japan had emerged from the conflict in a much strengthened position. It was apparently secure in its domination of Northern China, and hence a potential threat to Britain's interests in the rest of the country. Most worrying, however, was the extent of Japanese naval power. Very quickly, Japan came to represent a threat to Britain's Far Eastern position. Under United States pressure, and afraid of an expensive naval arms race, Britain took part in the Washington Conference in November 1921; here the British agreed to limit their fleet to the size of the US navy, thus ending their traditional maritime supremacy. An important consequence of the agreement was that, again under pressure from the United States, which now saw Japan as a major threat, Britain ended its alliance with Japan, leaving its interests in the Far East precariously exposed. Britain had been forced to choose between the United States and Japan, since growing rivalry between them in the Pacific made it impossible to have close relations with both. Arguably, the choice was a mistake: in exchange for a definite alliance, which at least in theory made unnecessary a large British naval presence in the Far East, Britain gained only the hope of American friendship.

In May 1921 the Foreign Secretary, Lord Curzon, had set before the Cabinet the arguments for and against renewing the alliance with Japan.

8.5   Cabinet discussion on the Anglo-Japanese alliance, 30 May 1921 (PRO CAB 23/25/43).

■ ... Lord Curzon then said that he proposed to summarise the arguments which had been advanced for and against the renewal of the Alliance. Against the renewal of the Alliance it was said, in the first place, that the reasons which had led originally to His Majesty's Government entering into the Alliance had now ceased to exist. It had been first formed as a counterpoise to an aggressive Russia in the Far East, and the identity of our own and Japanese interests had brought us together against that Power. It was true that Russia was now disintegrated and that Germany, who had later in the day appeared as a dangerous rival in the Far East, had ceased to exist as a Great Power. There was, consequently, force in the argument brought forward to the 'effect that the main reasons for the Alliance had ceased to exist. He would, however, later on, when he came to give the arguments on the other side, call the attention of the Cabinet to how the political situation might again change in the future. The second argument used against the renewal of the Alliance was that its existence was not only a source of suspicion and irritation but of actual embarrassment in the United States ... it could not be denied that there was considerable suspicion of the Alliance in America, and it might almost be said that the United States authorities were tempted to make it an excuse for adding to their naval armaments. The third argument ... was that it was alienating us from the sympathy of China and rendering our tasks there more difficult. Our policy in China had always been that of the 'open door'. Lord Curzon then proceeded to explain what an unwieldy and helpless country China had become, and pointed out how it must naturally be the desire of His Majesty's Government to see China built up again and some sort of cohesion arrived at in that country. Almost at the door of this great, helpless body there existed Japan, whose national temperament was fiercely imperialistic, and where the German spirit of disciplined aggression had been imbibed to a great extent. Japan herself was incapable of maintaining more than her present population, and it was natural that she should look to China ... It would naturally be said by the opponents of the Alliance that its renewal would give strength to this aggressive Power, and that Great Britain was encouraging Japan's policy, which she really ought to resist. Those were the arguments which had been used against a continuance of the Alliance, and he would now explain what, in his opinion, were the reasons that might be advanced in favour of its renewal, and which, he thought, on the whole made out the stronger case.

Firstly, he did not think that anyone could doubt that the Alliance had proved a great and substantial success. It had, at different times during its existence, helped both the contracting parties. It had undoubtedly been of assistance to Japan in her war with Russia, and, similarly, no one could deny that it had benefited us considerably in the late War. People at home, indeed, hardly realised what the Alliance had meant to Great Britain in the Pacific, to say nothing of what the Japanese had done in the Indian Ocean and the Mediterranean ...

The Secretary of State for Foreign Affairs, continuing, said there could be no question that the Alliance had been a success, and that this must be regarded as one argument in favour of its renewal. The second argument in favour of its renewal was that, although Russia and Germany had for the moment ceased to be Great Powers which had to be taken into account, there was no certainty that in a few years' time we should not have a regenerated Russia; and, whatever the form of the Russian Government might then be, the dangers of the past would again be revived. Moreover, with a resuscitated Russia and a revived Germany, it might well be that in ten years' time we might be faced with a combination of these Powers in the Far East, and to meet such a situation an Alliance with Japan would be the natural guarantee. Again, granting the aggressive character of Japan, should it not be remembered that the Alliance had given us the means of putting a check on Japan's ambitions: for example, the Japanese Government had been negotiating railway agreements with China, which had aroused suspicion on all sides; but since he (Lord Curzon) had entered the Foreign Office in succession to Mr. Balfour, the 'consortium' of Powers had been arranged, which Japan, sooner than be left in isolation, had been compelled to join. This included China, Great Britain, the United States, and France, and Belgium as a prospective member. Once such agreement was arrived at it was possible to tell Japan that she must fall into line with these arrangements or else the Powers concerned would fight her commercially. The result was that Japan had agreed to co-operate, and we were now in a position to exert pressure on her. There was another point, from the naval and military point of view, and that was that so long as the Alliance remained in force we were absolved from maintaining large naval and military forces in the Far East. There was yet another argument in favour of a continuance of the Alliance, and that was that it was looked on with considerable favour by our Allies. He ventured to think that France, on account of her Possessions in the Far East, would regard with dismay any proposal on our part not to renew the Alliance. Holland would unquestionably take the same view, on account of her Possessions in the East Indies, since it would be a great temptation to an unfriendly Japan to pounce on and seize these possessions. Lastly, the feeling in Japan itself had to be considered, and there was no question that the Japanese as a whole were in favour of a renewal of the Alliance … ■

The British Empire

The Middle East and India

It was in the Middle East that Britain's impaired capacity to uphold the post-war peace settlement first became obvious. The rejection of the Treaty of Sèvres by Turkey under Mustapha Kemal Atatürk led to war between Turkey and Greece and to a direct confrontation between Turkey and Britain in 1922, because the British government feared that Turkey might attack the Allied army of occupation in the Straits (the Dardanelles). Although Britain and Turkey came close to war, the crisis was eased by negotiation between the two countries' local representatives.

During the 1922 Chanak crisis – named after the location of British troops on the shore of the Dardanelles – Lloyd George and Churchill took a belligerent line.

After difficult negotiations, the Treaty of Lausanne was concluded with Turkey in 1923. The belligerence of Lloyd George's Coalition not only contributed to the downfall of the 'Welsh Wizard', however, but encouraged his successor, Bonar Law, to reflect on the wider significance of the Chanak crisis, and to declare limits to Britain's world role.

8.6   Bonar Law on Britain's world role, letter to the editor, *The Times*, 7 October 1922.

■ I have followed with the greatest anxiety recent events in the Near East, and the position at this moment seems to me very alarming ...

When the Greek forces were annihilated in Asia Minor and driven into the sea at Smyrna, it seems to me certain that, unless a decisive warning had at once been issued, the Turkish forces,- flushed with victory, would have attempted to enter Constantinople and cross into Thrace. If they had been allowed to do so, what would have been the result?

In the first place, our withdrawal in such circumstances would have been regarded throughout the whole Musulman world as the defeat of the British Empire, and, although it may be true that the supposed pro-Greek sympathies of the British Government have alienated Musulman feeling in India, the danger of trouble in India from that cause would be as nothing in comparison with the danger which would arise as a consequence of what would have been regarded as British impotence in the face of a victorious Turkish army.

Further, such an advance of the Turkish forces would probably have meant a repetition in Constantinople of the recent events in Smyrna ... and the probability – indeed, I think it a certainty – of the renewal of war throughout the Balkans.

It was, therefore, undoubtedly right that the British Government should endeavour to prevent these misfortunes. It is not, however, right that the burden of taking necessary action should fall on the British Empire alone. The prevention of war and massacre in Constantinople and the Balkans is not specially a British interest; it is the interest of humanity. The retention also of the freedom of the Straits is not specially a British interest; it is the interest of the world. We are at the Straits and in Constantinople not by our own actions alone, but by the will of the Allied Powers which won the war, and America as one of these Powers.

What, then, in such circumstances ought we to do? Clearly the British Empire, which includes the largest body of Mahomedans in any State, ought not to show any hostility or unfairness to the Turks. In the agreement arranged with the Allies in Paris by Lord Curzon, proposals were made to the Turks which are certainly fair to them, and beyond these terms, in my opinion, the Allies ought not to go.

I see rumours in different newspapers, which I do not credit, that the French representative with the Kemalist forces has encouraged them to make impossible demands. The course of action for our Government seems to me clear. We cannot alone act as the policeman of the world. The financial and social condition of this country makes that impossible. It seems to me, therefore, that our duty is to say plainly to our French Allies that the position in Constantinople and the Straits is as essential a part of the Peace settlement as the arrangement with Germany, and that if they are not prepared to support us there, we shall not be able to bear the burden alone, but shall have no alternative except to imitate the Government of the United States and to restrict our attention to the safeguarding of the more immediate interests of the British Empire. ■

One of Britain's key interests during the 1920s was the maintenance of imperial rule in India. Although India had undeniably contributed magnificently to the war effort, there had at the same time been a growing political restlessness in the country, giving rise to demands for self-government. In the inter-war period, the characteristic pattern of Britain's presence was a mixture of concessions to Indian demands and the use of coercion to uphold British authority. Thus in 1919 the Montagu–Chelmsford reforms were implemented under the Government of India Act, under which Indians were promised a share in provincial government and a role in a new central legislature.

8.7   The Government of India Act 1919 (*Public General Acts*, 1919, ch. 101).

■ Whereas it is the declared policy of Parliament to provide for the increasing association of Indians in every branch of Indian administration, and for the gradual development of self-governing institutions, with a view to the progressive realisation of responsible government in British India as an integral part of the empire:

And whereas progress in giving effect to this policy can only be achieved by successive stages, and it is expedient that substantial steps in this direction should now be taken:

And whereas the time and manner of each advance can be determined only by Parliament, upon whom responsibility lies for the welfare and advancement of the Indian peoples:

And whereas the action of Parliament in such matters must be guided by the co-operation received from those on whom new opportunities of service will be conferred, and by the extent to which it is found that confidence can be reposed in their sense of responsibility:

And whereas concurrently with the gradual development of self-governing institutions in the Provinces of India it is expedient to give to those Provinces in provincial matters the largest measure of independence of the Government of India, which is compatible with the due discharge by the latter of its own responsibilities:

Be it therefore enacted by the King's most Excellent Majesty, by and with the advice and consent of the Lords Spiritual and Temporal, and Commons, in this present Parliament assembled, and by the authority of the same, as follows:

PART I

LOCAL GOVERNMENTS

1. (1) Provision may be made ...

(*a*) for the classification of subjects, in relation to the functions of government, as central and provincial subjects, for the purpose of distinguishing the functions of local governments and local legislatures from the functions of the Governor-General in Council and the Indian legislature;

(*b*) for the devolution of authority in respect of provincial subjects to local governments, and for the allocation of revenues or other moneys to those governments;

(*c*) for the use under the authority of the Governor-General in Council of the agency of local governments in relation to central subjects, in so far as such agency may be found convenient, and for determining the financial conditions of such agency; and

(*d*) for the transfer from among the provincial subjects of subjects... to the administration of the governor acting with ministers appointed under this Act, and for the allocation of revenues or moneys for the purpose of such administration ... ■

The constitutional reforms entailed in the 1919 Act were overshadowed in India by a growing willingness on the part of Britain to resort to coercion. This culminated in the massacre of unarmed Indian demonstrators at the Jallianwala Bagh, an enclosed area of wasteland in the Punjab city of Amritsar, in April 1919 – an incident which became powerfully symbolic to the nationalist movement and embittered British–Indian relations between the wars. Brigadier-General Reginald Dyer, the British army officer responsible for opening fire on the demonstrators was required to explain his actions to a government commission of inquiry. He was subsequently forced to resign his commission.

8.8 **Brigadier-General Dyer's evidence before the Hunter Committee, 19 November 1919 (India Office Records, L/P & J/6/1669).**

■ *Q.* When you got into the Jallianwala Bagh what did you do?

A. I opened fire.

Q. At once?

A. Immediately I had thought about the matter, and it did not take me more than 30 seconds to make up my mind as to what my duty was.

Q. As regards the crowd, what was it doing at the time?

A. Holding a meeting. There was a man in the centre of the place standing on something raised. You could see him above the crowd. His arms were moving about; he was evidently addressing a meeting.

Q. How far was the nearest man in the crowd from you?

A. When I entered first, about 8 or 9 yards off the wall; he ran away to the right, and there were a good many others who ran away and climbed over the wall there.

Q. As I understand the Jallianwala Bagh, at a distance of something like 100 yards from the raised ground? Do I understand where you stationed armed soldiers there is a small ridge? Where was the man who was addressing the crowd standing?

A. He was absolutely in the centre of the section, as far as one could judge; may be within 50 or 60 yards from me. He seemed to be surrounded by them; but most of them were on the further side.

Q. So far as you know, was there any crying except this man's addressing the crowd?

A. No; I cannot say there was anything beyond that he was addressing the crowd.

Q. How many people were there in the crowd?

A. I then estimated it at 5,000. I heard there were many more.

Q. On the assumption that there was a crowd of something like 5,000 and more, have you any doubt that many of these people must have been unaware of your Proclamation?

A. It was being well issued and news spread very rapidly in places like that under prevailing conditions. At the same time, there may have been a good many who had not heard the Proclamation.

Q. On the assumption that there was that risk of people being in the crowd who were not aware of the Proclamation, did it not occur to you that it was a proper measure to ask the crowd to disperse before you took to actually firing upon them?

A. No, at the time it did not occur to me. I merely felt that my orders had not been obeyed, that martial law was flouted, and that it was my duty to immediately disperse it by rifle fire.

Q. Before you dispersed the crowd, had the crowd taken any action at all?

A. No, Sir. They ran away, a few of them. When I began to fire in the centre they began to run to the road.

Q. Martial law had not been proclaimed before you took that step, which was a serious step. Did you consider about the propriety of consulting the Deputy Commissioner who was the civil authority responsible for law and order?

A. There was no Deputy Commissioner there to consult at the time. I did not think it wise to ask anybody further. I had to make up my mind immediately as to what my action should be. I considered it from a military view that I should fire immediately, that if I did not do so, I should fail in my duty...

Q. In firing was your object to disperse the crowd?

A. Yes.

Q. Any other object?

A. No, Sir. I was going to fire until they dispersed.

Q. Did the crowd at once start to disperse as soon as you fired?

A. Immediately.

Q. Did you continue firing?

A. Yes.

Q. If the crowd was going to disperse, why did you not stop firing?

A. I thought it my duty to go on firing until it dispersed. If I had fired a little, the effect would not be sufficient. If I had fired a little I should be wrong in firing at all.

Q. How long did the firing go on?

A. It may be 10 minutes; it may be less, calculating from the number of rounds that we fired.

Q. Could you say whether there were any sticks with the people?

A. I cannot say that. I assume numbers had sticks. I knew they were going to be armed with sticks.

Q. Have you ever, in your military experience, used a similar method of dispersing an assembly?

A. Never, Sir. It was an exceptional case ... ■

In the 1920s a major factor in Indian politics was the success of 'Mahatma' Gandhi in achieving mass support for his nationalist resistance campaign, which employed tactics that the British found difficult to confront effectively. By the end of the decade the British Viceroy of India had secured broad political support in Britain for a speeding up of the devolution process, although 'die-hard' opposition, centred on Churchill, persisted well into the 1930s. Meanwhile, the day-to-day task of governing India had to continue. In July 1930 the Viceroy held a conference at Simla, attended by the governors of all the Indian provinces, at which the problem of dealing with Gandhi's civil disobedience protest campaign were discussed.

8.9 Report of Indian provincial governors' discussion on the civil disobedience campaign, 23 July 1930 (PRO CAB 24/214, CP 289(30)).

■ ... His Excellency the Governor of Bengal said that in his province there is good reason to believe that the movement is definitely on the decline. Picketing is giving a certain amount of trouble, but there is not much force behind it, and although the return of students from their vacations might give an impetus to picketing by providing more volunteers, he is not greatly concerned on this account. Funds appear to be decreasing, and there are signs of lassitude. The position in the rural areas is on the whole not unsatisfactory. If they are left alone, dangerous developments are likely to occur in some districts; but as soon as they are vigorously tackled conditions are soon restored to normal. They have not sufficient police, however, to permit of vigorous action simultaneously in all districts ... He himself considers that the time is now opportune for vigorous propaganda, and that once the movement begins to go it will go quickly. It is, however, generally recognised that the failure of the civil disobedience movement will be followed by an increase in terrorist activities ...

His Excellency the Governor of Bombay said that Sind has so far been very little affected, except in Karachi. The South of the Presidency has also given very little trouble. The Deccan is watching Bombay, and the movement is getting some hold there. In Bombay City and in Gujerat the situation is very bad ... The measures so far taken by His Government have had the effect of keeping down the level of enthusiasm, but on the other hand have increased the size of the movement so far as the number of adherents and sympathisers is concerned ...

He is anxious regarding the future attitude of the rural population. Price of cotton has seriously fallen, and he is afraid that the cultivators will have great difficulty in selling their present crop when it matures ...Economic conditions in the villages are, therefore, likely to be very unfavourable and in consequence one has to expect great discontent and consequent opportunities to Congress to create feelings hostile to Government. He is not very hopeful that the financial losses which the movement is causing, and will continue to cause, to Bombay City will produce serious reactions against the Congress. Many of the industrialists and business men who are supporting the movement do not mind if they are broken, provided that Government is broken also ...

He considered it most desirable that an Ordinance should be prepared with as little delay as possible on the lines of [the] Defence of [the] Realm Act. The chief object to be aimed at would be to give wide powers to local executive officers in those areas where an emergency existed, and, in particular, to invest District Magistrates with the power to make regulations ...

His Excellency the Governor of the Central Provinces said that the movement is gaining force in his province. It is sweeping up from Bombay into Berar and Mahratta country. The popular attitude towards it is semi-religious, and to a considerable extent ignores considerations of personal loss. Women and children are taking an enthusiastic part in it, and owing to the terror of social boycott few non-official leaders have the courage to come forward on the side of Government. It is spreading into the villages, and he also is greatly concerned regarding the future economic prospects … ∎

The Dominions

To many complacent onlookers in Britain, the First World War had amply demonstrated the bonds of loyalty within the British Empire, and underlined the Empire's importance to Britain's strength. Ironically, although the Empire was now larger than ever, this in itself entailed expanded commitments and obligations, which conflicted with the growing mood of retrenchment at home. Furthermore, the war had revealed cracks within the apparently united imperial community. Its older members, the Dominions, had shown an alarming desire to defend their own interests, for example by insisting on having their own representation at the Paris Peace Conference. This prefigured an increasing tendency for British and Dominion interests to diverge between the wars.

In 1921 Canada had urged Britain not to jeopardise relations with the United States by renewing the alliance with Japan. An even more sobering warning for Britain came during the Chanak crisis of 1922, when the Dominions failed to respond unquestioningly to Britain's demands for assistance against Turkey. The Dominions proved equally reluctant to become embroiled in European entanglements, shunning the provisions of the Locarno Treaty of 1925, and thereby casting doubts on the cohesion of imperial foreign policy.

Strube in the Daily Express *showed John Bull being called to the Empire telephone while holding the Locarno baby.*

8.10 **Cartoon by Sidney 'George' Strube, Britain torn between the Empire and Europe,** *Daily Express,* **1 December 1925.**

As the divergence of interests between Britain and the Dominions gathered pace in the 1920s, a new concept of 'Commonwealth' was developed to encompass the changing relationship between Britain and countries like Canada and Australia. At the 1926 Imperial Conference, the 'Balfour definition' emerged to clarify this relationship.

8.11   The 'Balfour definition' of the Commonwealth, 1926 *(Imperial Conference, 1926: Summary of Proceedings,* **Cmd 2768, PP XI, 1926, p. 14).**

■ The Committee are of the opinion that nothing would be gained by attempting to lay down a Constitution for the British Empire. Its widely scattered parts have very different characteristics, very different histories, and are at very different stages of evolution; while, considered as a whole, it defies classification, and bears no real resemblance to any other political organization which now exists or has ever yet been tried.

There is, however, one most important element in it which, from a strictly constitutional point of view, has now, as regards all vital matters, reached its full development – we refer to the group of self-governing communities composed of Great Britain and the Dominions. Their position and mutual relation may be readily defined. *They are autonomous Communities within the British Empire, equal in status, in no way subordinate one to another in any aspect of their domestic or external affairs, though united by a common allegiance to the Crown, and freely associated as members of the British Commonwealth of Nations.*

A foreigner endeavouring to understand the true character of the British Empire by the aid of this formula alone would be tempted to think that it was devised rather to make mutual interference impossible than to make mutual co-operation easy.

Such a criticism, however, completely ignores the historic situation. The rapid evolution of the Oversea Dominions during the last fifty years has involved many complicated adjustments of old political machinery to changing conditions. The tendency towards equality of status was both right and inevitable. Geographical and other conditions made this impossible of attainment by the way of federation. The only alternative was by the way of autonomy; and along this road it has been steadily sought. Every self-governing member of the Empire is now the master of its destiny. In fact, if not always in form, it is subject to no compulsion whatever. ■

Developments such as the emergence of the 'Balfour definition' led ultimately to the 1931 Statute of Westminster, which introduced a legal framework for the emerging self-governing Commonwealth. The loosening of imperial ties which these steps embodied was in marked contrast to the talk of imperial unity so common before 1914. Yet such ideas did not die; throughout the inter-war period, enthusiasts for closer imperial integration were once again able to propose their ambitious, if optimistic, schemes. In reality, nevertheless, the disengagement of the Dominions, however gradual, and however portrayed as a triumph of the diffusion of British democracy throughout the world, undermined Britain's pretensions to be a world power.

8.12   The Statute of Westminster 1931 (*Public General Acts*, 1931, ch. 4).

◼ ... In this Act the expression 'Dominion' means any of the following Dominions, that is to say, the Dominion of Canada, the Commonwealth of Australia, the Dominion of New Zealand, the Union of South Africa, the Irish Free State and Newfoundland.

... No law and no provision of any law made after the commencement of this Act by the Parliament of a Dominion shall be void or inoperative on the ground that it is repugnant to the law of England, or to the provisions of any existing or future Act of Parliament of the United Kingdom, or to any order, rule or regulation made under any such Act, and the powers of the Parliament of a Dominion shall include the power to repeal or amend any such Act, rule or regulation in so far as the same is part of the law of the Dominion.

It is hereby declared and enacted that the Parliament of a Dominion has full power to make laws having extra-territorial operation.

No Act of Parliament of the United Kingdom passed after the commencement of this Act shall extend, or be deemed to extend, to a Dominion as part of the law of that Dominion, unless it is expressly declared in that Act that that Dominion has requested, and consented to, the enactment thereof ... ◼

Europe

Even before the signature of the peace settlement, astute British observers recognised the scope for future European problems. These centred on the threat apparently posed to the West by the new Bolshevik regime in Russia, the question of Germany's future relationship with its neighbours, German reparations to the victors of the war, and the problem of safeguarding French security.

Russia

In the early 1920s Russia, so troublesome to Britain throughout the nineteenth century, was effectively preoccupied with internal problems of civil war and reconstruction. It was difficult to calculate how great a threat Russia might be to Britain's Indian and Middle Eastern interests. Partly because of its need to re-establish export markets, Britain was keenly interested in developments in Bolshevik Russia in the 1920s. Like Germany, Russia emerged from the war as a pariah, and was given no role at the Peace Conference. Moreover, attempts by the West to intervene during the civil war on the side of counter-revolution left a legacy of deep mutual suspicion, reinforced in the West by the new regime's repudiation of all (tsarist) war debts and its policy of nationalising foreign assets without compensation.

The British government had initially been divided in its response to the new regime in Russia. Churchill strongly advocated military force to bring down the Bolsheviks. However, Lloyd George believed that such action would be counter-productive, and sought instead to rebuild the West's economic links with Russia, in much the same way as he sought to revive Germany. Of inescapable concern, however, was the Bolsheviks' apparent commitment to the promotion of 'world revolution'.

Against a background of profound industrial unrest in Britain, the creation of the Communist Party of Great Britain and of the Communist International (Comintern) in 1920 reinforced fears in official circles of Soviet subversion.

8.13 **Cartoon by Westral, 'Watch me stop it', *The Communist*, 30 April 1921**

Lloyd George's ambitions to reintegrate both Russia and Germany within the European 'mainstream' at the Genoa Conference on European economic reconstruction in 1922 proved a failure: Germany and Russia instead drew closer together through the secret Treaty of Rapallo.

8.14 **Cabinet discussion on objects of Genoa Conference and recognition of Russia, 28 March 1922 (PRO CAB 23/29/21).**

■ ... The Prime Minister said that perhaps it would assist his colleagues in their consideration of the Genoa Conference if he were to state the case in the form of two propositions:

(*a*) The economic proposition, namely, the economic conditions under which our traders can be induced to undertake trade in Russia.

(*b*) The larger question at the base of our economic troubles, namely, the position of unrest in the East, which disturbs the trader and makes him suspicious.

With regard to the second point, there was a state of something like menace along the Russian frontier. Russia was full of suspicion of the intentions of Roumania, Poland, Finland, and other neighbouring countries, who were equally suspicious of Russia. One half of Europe was living under a condition of menace of war, and it was absolutely necessary to restore the sense of peace in Europe. The first object of the Genoa Conference should therefore be to establish a pact among all the nations of Europe against aggression. Russia must undertake not to attack Roumania, Latvia, Lithuania, Poland and Finland, and vice versa. Until some such condition of peace was established there would not be an effective revival of trade. The President of the Board of Trade had prepared a valuable document, after consultation with leading business representatives, which indicated serious industrial and commercial prospects for at least two years to come ... Mr. Baldwin's Memorandum showed that very little diminution of unemployment was to be expected in the near future, owing in part to the international situation. The problem of unemployment would need to be considered also apart from the discussion which would take place in Genoa.

With regard to Russia, we had made efforts to restore trading relations with that country which had been only partially successful, because the Soviet Government had failed to carry out the conditions as strictly as we had a right to expect: but the fact remained that Russia was still outside the comity of nations, and until that fact was changed the full restoration of trade would be difficult. Our first object should be to establish peace, and our second object to establish complete commercial relations with Russia. This raised the question of the extent to which those objects involved the recognition of Russia. He did not believe it was possible to get trade going until there was some degree of recognition. Access to Courts of Law was essential to the carrying on of trade. Therefore some measure of recognition was absolutely essential ...

Next, as to the question of a probationary period during which it would be possible to test the bona fides of the Soviet Government, the Home Secretary had circulated a Paper recording an interview with a Russian trader, who represented a very important Corporation. According to this trader, Lenin was personally largely responsible for the promulgation of the recent economic laws, which amount to an abandonment of Communism. If the Russian Delegation came to Genoa having practically surrendered their Communistic principles and willing to enter into negotiation with Capitalistic communities, we ought to give all necessary support to the anti-Communistic elements in Russia, and declare that if Communistic principles are abandoned we are ready to assist in the economic development of Russia ... ■

British hostility towards Moscow thawed when the Labour government recognised the Soviet Union in 1924. But this positive move, reinforced by attempts to establish good commercial relations, served only to discredit Labour and contribute to its fall, helped by the scare fomented by the 'Zinoviev letter' incident. Insecurity during the General Strike in 1926 was compounded by concern about Soviet intentions towards India, and in May 1927 diplomatic relations with the Soviet Union were severed. After an inconclusive secret service raid on the Soviet trade mission in London (Arcos), the Soviet Ambassador was expelled. This diplomatic nadir was, however, relatively short-lived. By 1928 the British government was willing to reassess the position, especially after the General Staff concluded that the Soviet Union need not be seen as a military threat, because its arms industry was in no state to supply a major war. This thaw made it possible for the returning Labour government to re-establish diplomatic ties in October 1929.

Western Europe

Germany's defeat and the humiliation of the Peace of Versailles were unlikely to disable German power permanently, and threatened to generate future tensions. Many British diplomats agreed that the settlement in eastern Europe was unsatisfactory. Not only did many in Britain come to see the treatment of Germany as excessively harsh, but some, including Lloyd George, saw German economic recovery as essential to Britain's own post-war revival. It was not surprising, then, that Anglo-French relations should so quickly have become strained, in some respects being worse than Anglo-German relations. Yet the Anglo-French relationship was critical to European security during the 1920s, especially because both the United States and the Soviet Union had effectively withdrawn from the international sphere.

For much of the 1920s France's overriding concern with obtaining guarantees of its security from German aggression undermined harmonious relations with Britain, where few commentators accurately grasped the depth of French fears. The situation was aggravated by Britain's failure to adopt a clear stance, giving neither an unequivocal commitment to French security, nor the kind of modest concessions to Germany which might have blunted the appeal of extreme nationalism. Churchill summarised this problem during the Imperial Conference of 1921.

**8.15   Winston Churchill on policy towards Germany, 7 July 1921
(Churchill Papers 22/6, in Martin Gilbert, *Winston S. Churchill Vol. IV: 1916–1922*, London, Heinemann, 1975, pp 608–9).**

■ ... The aim is to get an appeasement of the fearful hatreds and antagonisms which exist in Europe and to enable the world to settle down. I have no other object in view. I feel that a greater assurance to France would be a foundation for that. First of all, our duty towards France in this matter is rather an obvious one because she gave up her claims – very illegitimate claims as we thought them, but she waived them – to take a strong strategic position along the Rhine which her Marshals advised her to do, and this Anglo-American guarantee was intended to be a substitute to France. We said to her, if you give up the strategical position, England and America will be with you in the hour of need. Well, America did not make good, and one would have thought France all the more would have needed the British Empire, but it is a fact that the Treaty is naturally invalidated by America not having made good and France got neither Britain nor America, nor did she get her strategic frontier on the Rhine. The result of that is undoubtedly to have created a deep fear in the heart of France, and a fear which anyone can understand who looks at the population of the two countries, one declining and already under forty millions – 38 millions – and the other bounding up, in spite of all that has happened, with great masses of military youths reaching manhood, and in seven or eight years replacing the losses of the war.

No one can doubt the deep rooted nature of the fear which this poor mutilated, impoverished France has of this mighty Germany which is growing up on the other side of the Rhine. It is this fear ... which is the explanation and to a certain extent the excuse for the intolerant and violent action which France is taking. If at any time the means arises of reducing that fear, of giving such an assurance, I think we ought to consider it very carefully indeed ...

There is one more argument which has always moved me very much indeed; that is our relations with Germany. I am anxious to see friendship grow up and the hatred of the war die between Britain and Germany. I am anxious to see trade relations develop with Germany naturally and harmoniously. I am anxious to see Britain getting all the help and use she can out of Germany in the difficult years that lie before us.

I am very much afraid that any friendly relations which grow up in time between Britain and Germany will be terribly suspect to France. France will say 'You are changing sides; you are going over to the other side. We are to be left to ourselves, and England is more the friend of Germany than of France.' But I think if a Treaty were in existence which in the ultimate issue, in the extreme issue, bound the British Empire to protect France, against unprovoked aggression, we could always point to that and say, 'No, if you are attacked, there is our scrap of paper; we shall be as good as our word next time as we were last time.' That will give you greater freedom, in my humble opinion, to establish new relations, new co-operation with Germany in the further reconstruction and rebuilding of Europe, and it might well be that being at once the Ally of France and the friend of Germany, we might be in a position to mitigate the frightful rancour and fear and hatred which exist between France and Germany at the present time and which, if left unchecked, will most certainly in a generation or so bring about a renewal of the struggle of which we have just witnessed the conclusion ... ■

The overriding problem in the eyes of the Foreign Office throughout the 1920s was Germany and its reintegration into Europe. As has been seen, there were strong economic incentives for Britain to promote the revival of Germany. Like Germany, Britain was not committed to the permanence of the eastern settlement, and from an early stage British politicians recognised that concessions to Germany were both desirable and necessary. In this sense, Britain's 'appeasement' of Germany began not with Neville Chamberlain in the 1930s, but with Lloyd George in 1919, and was continued by all succeeding governments.

The immediate issue, and the thorniest, in the early 1920s was the quagmire of reparations. In 1921 Germany had at last been presented with a reparations bill of 50 billion gold marks. The former allies quickly became divided on this problem. Whereas the French were resolved to extract the maximum payment from Germany, Britain found it difficult to challenge Germany's delaying tactics, but was itself constrained by the United States' insistence on the prompt repayment of loans to its former allies.

8.16   International war debts, 1918 (derived from G. Hardach, *The First World War 1914–1918*, London, Penguin, 1987, p. 148).

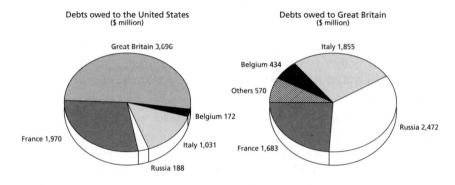

8.17   Cabinet discussion on reparations, 22 December 1921 (PRO CAB 23/27/93).

■ … The Cabinet were informed by the Chancellor of the Exchequer that when arrangements had been made for the forthcoming Conference with M. Briand, it had been contemplated as possible that the representatives of the United States of America, France and Great Britain would have entered upon a general discussion of the various large outstanding economic questions, including the question of inter-allied debts. At such a discussion it would have been possible for Great Britain, in the event of the United States of America agreeing to a cancellation of her European indebtedness, to have similarly cancelled the debts owed to her by the Allies, and also possibly to have forgone any claim to further reparation from Germany, except claims in respect of actual damage sustained. A policy of this character would have left France in a position to obtain from Germany reparation for her devastated regions. M. Loucheur had been willing to entertain proposals of this character, and it was not out of the question that he might have been willing, as part of a general settlement, to forgo the French pension claim against Germany.

As a result of tentative enquiries made in responsible quarters, it was, however, certain that any suggestion to the United States Government to enter upon discussions of this character would meet with a very hostile reception. While certain of the mercantile and trading classes in the Eastern States might be favourable to some general arrangement, the view of the great majority of Americans was that the debts should be paid, and that the failure to pay them was the primary cause of the present distress in the United States. The attitude of the Finance Committee of the Senate was of a similar character, and in a recent discussion on the subject of the funding of Allied Debts, that Committee had laid down that such funding should be subject to the condition that there should be no cancellation, either of interest or principal, and that there should be no acceptance by the United States Treasury of the Bonds of one country in satisfaction of the American debt of another. In these circumstances, American participation in any general discussion must be ruled out and the Allies must turn to the smaller problem of German reparation.

The position as regards German reparation was that on the 15th January and 15th February next, Germany would have to find two instalments amounting to a sum of 30 to 35 millions sterling, and it was pretty clear that the utmost that in the present circumstances the German Government could produce would be £10 to £12 millions. In the main the money would have to go to Belgium by reason of her priority. It must be borne in mind that France was at present receiving reparation Coal on very lucrative terms, and in fact she was only being debited in the accounts of the Reparation Commission for coal at a price of 8/4 per ton. Notwithstanding the great size and extravagant cost of her Army of Occupation, the amount received by her in respect of German coal was more than sufficient to pay for the cost of the Army of Occupation.

If Germany defaulted on the instalments, the question arose whether she should be granted a moratorium. Undoubtedly her inability to pay was due to a very large extent to her own action. As a result of the generous subsidies given by the German Government, the State Budget showed a deficit, while the German manufacturers were in receipt of enhanced profits, some of which they were converting into foreign credits. Herr Rathenau was of opinion that these credits were not more than enough to finance German industry, but while doubts might be felt on this point, it was quite clear that it would be most difficult for the German Government to lay their hands upon the actual money. The real fact was that the German Government was a very weak Government, in fear of Bolshevism on the one hand, and a revival of Prussianism on the other. Any moratorium granted to Germany should be upon conditions, such as the cessation of all subsidies, the balancing of the State Budget, the stoppage of note printing, the calculation in gold of customs duties, the re-constitution on more independent lines of the Reichsbank, and the raising of the internal price of coal in Germany.

The experts were unanimously of opinion that if the Allies were to insist on Germany making considerably heavier payments than she could at present afford to make, she would before the winter collapse into a hopeless state of chaos … ■

By the end of 1922 British and French attitudes towards German reparations were widely divergent. Whereas Britain was willing to agree to a suspension of payments, France insisted on full payment on schedule. In January 1923, contrary to British advice, France occupied the Ruhr with the intention of forcing Germany to meet its obligations, and inducing Britain and the United States to guarantee a new reparations scheme. Under the Dawes plan of 1924 a restructuring of Germany's finances was negotiated, together with a large US loan to Germany. The British government took a major role at the London Conference in July 1924 and succeeded in obtaining French and German acceptance of the plan. Under these arrangements, France agreed to withdraw from the Ruhr, and Germany promised to resume reparations payments. However, the episode had demonstrated clearly the weakness of the system of controls designed to uphold the peace settlement, and implied that future enforcement would be difficult. When Baldwin met the French Premier, Poincaré, in September 1923, the threat which France's conduct in the Ruhr posed to Anglo-French relations emerged as a major topic.

8.18 Record of discussions between Baldwin and Poincaré, September 1923 (*Documents on British Foreign Policy*, 1, XXI, no. 367).

■ After the preliminaries were over I expressed the hope that although M. Poincaré was a lawyer and I was not, we might none the less converse with perfect frankness and without prejudice, to which he entirely agreed. I then explained that amongst my early impressions on assuming Office I was struck by the absence of harmony and close confidence so necessary between the two countries if the Entente were to be preserved …

I dealt with the temperamental difference between the two nations showing how this had been greatly discounted before the war by the common fear inspired by Germany's attitude; how that fear had been largely removed together with the natural necessity of self-preservation; and how English people were puzzled by the impression that France apparently no longer wanted England to be with her – that the two national temperaments were therefore gradually causing a divergence of view and that if he and I failed to agree, bad results would assuredly follow …

M. Poincaré replied at some length and in terms no less sincere, for all of which I thanked him and then passed to The present state of public feeling in England, which counted for a great deal. Despite a commonly expressed view I assured him that it was not possible to manufacture English opinion by means of newspapers, as was said to be the case to a great extent in France ... I emphasised the wide-spread fear that every day's delay in effecting a settlement of the reparation question made a final settlement more difficult and precarious; that, although the general feeling was directly opposed to discounting German liability, yet, contrary to the belief prevalent in France, many people in England thought that the events of the last few months had postponed the possibility of a settlement and had indeed tended to dissipate existing German assets ... English temperament was peculiar in certain respects and was doubtless difficult to French understanding; but the average Englishman pre-eminently disliked the military occupation of a civilian district; it antagonised and roused him. This might appear difficult to understand but was none the less a fact which had to be reckoned with, and no British Government would be able to make the Entente what it ought to be as long as the military character of the occupation of the Ruhr remained unchanged.

M. Poincaré ... emphatically agreed that the two countries must not be allowed to drift apart, and that the causes of misunderstanding must be examined and removed. ■

An important source of friction between Britain and France during the 1920s was the latter's continuing search for a military alliance to guarantee its frontiers, as outlined at Versailles. Britain, which did not believe the peace settlement to be irrevocable, refused to offer such an alliance. A major reason for British reluctance to underwrite French security was that its co-guarantor, the United States, had already disengaged from its wartime promises of continuing commitment to European security. More generally, Britain's priorities in this period remained definitely imperial, not European.

Dealing with the question of French security and promoting disarmament proved to be even more difficult than settling the reparations issue. France welcomed a draft treaty of mutual assistance, put to the League of Nations in 1923. Britain, however, already had extensive imperial commitments, and, under pressure from the Dominions, vetoed the plan. Instead, Ramsay MacDonald backed the 'Geneva protocol', which provided for compulsory arbitration between nations in dispute, and for disarmament. This idea was quietly dropped by the new Conservative government, whose Foreign Secretary, Austen Chamberlain, preferred conventional great power diplomacy. However, Chamberlain understood that unless France received reassurance, there was little prospect of long-term stability in Europe. Germany's Foreign Minister, Gustav Stresemann, was compliant, not only because he wanted to speed up the withdrawal of Allied troops from Germany, but also because he was keen to forestall a full Anglo-French alliance. This eased the passage of the Locarno Treaty of December 1925, which Chamberlain regarded as his greatest achievement. In a letter to Lord Crewe, written earlier in the year, Chamberlain set out his ideas on the pact.

8.19   Austen Chamberlain on Locarno, letter to Lord Crewe, 16 February 1925 (in Sir Charles Petrie, *The Life and Letters of the Right Hon. Sir Austin Chamberlain, Vol. II*, London, Cassell, 1940, pp. 258–9)).

■ My dear Crewe,

The pressure of work here has again been very severe during the last few days, and though I have worked very long hours I have not had time for as close a correspondence with you as I should have liked ...

As to the [German] memorandum itself and the spirit which it discloses, I think that they are the most helpful signs that I have yet seen. I am absolutely precluded from saying a word to any Ambassador which would indicate what the ultimate attitude of the British Government to the question of French security will be. Public opinion in this country is intensely suspicious of any particular undertaking, and both the Liberal and Labour Parties in their present mood are ready to start on the warpath at the first indication that I could be contemplating a regional pact. The League of Nations Union is equally on the alert and equally predisposed against partial and particular arrangements.

Yet I am firmly convinced that the true line of progress is to proceed from the particular to the general, and not, as has hitherto been embodied in Covenant and Protocol, to reverse the process and attempt to eliminate the particular by the general. A form of guarantee which is so general that we undertake exactly the same obligations in defence, shall I say of the Polish Corridor (for which no British Government ever will or ever can risk the bones of a British grenadier) as we extend to those international arrangements or conditions on which, as our history shows, our national existence depends, is a guarantee so wide and general that it carries no conviction whatever and gives no sense of security to those who are concerned in our action.

If, then, we are to relieve the tension of Europe in the only way in which it can be done, namely, by relieving French fear, a more particular and specific guarantee is in my opinion necessary. I am not sure that in 1919, or even a little later, public opinion would have been prepared to admit the signature of Germany, so lately and flagrantly dishonoured, to any pact of that character, but I am disposed to think that in the circumstances of to-day a guarantee of the Eastern frontiers of France and Belgium by Great Britain would be rendered a much more practical policy if Germany was associated with it ... ■

Effectively a recognition that the League of Nations could not guarantee peace, the Locarno Treaty provided for French, German and Belgian pledges to respect one another's frontiers, with guarantees supplied by Britain and Italy, although this ignored the fact that the British army was in no position to underwrite the treaty.

Superficially, the Locarno Treaty encouraged easier international relations in the later 1920s, and a generally more optimistic mood. On the other hand, it has been seen by some as prompting Germany to take an even more 'revisionist' line in the future. Furthermore, the treaty's provisions applied only to western Europe, and Germany's eastern neighbours noted with concern that no guarantees of their frontiers with Germany emerged. Britain had made it plain that it did not intend to guarantee the French alliance system in eastern Europe. In this respect, Chamberlain, though sympathetic to France, made his famous remark that the Polish Corridor was territory 'for which no British Government ever will or ever can risk the bones of a British grenadier'.

In 1926 Germany finally reclaimed its great power status and became a member of the League of Nations. In the following year, Allied military controls in Germany were lifted, removing the only effective means of verifying German disarmament. Stresemann's successful process of treaty revision continued. In 1929 the Young plan reduced Germany's reparations burden to one-third of the original sum demanded, and in the same year the former Allies agreed to evacuate all their troops from Germany by mid-1930, five years ahead of schedule. Such diplomatic successes in the later 1920s seemed to justify the British government's stance on European affairs, and encouraged optimism among many about the prospects for general disarmament. The Foreign Office, as shown by the following memorandum extract, was more circumspect.

8.20 Foreign Office memorandum, 31 January 1928 (*Documents on British Foreign Policy*, 1a, IV, no.267).

■ Since the last meeting of the Cabinet Committee on Reduction and Limitation of Armaments, there have been some developments which it may well to summarize, in order to be able to survey the position in which we find ourselves on the eve of the resumption of serious discussion at Geneva.

In the first place, it will be remembered that the Cabinet Committee held its former sittings in November, before the meetings of the Preparatory and Security Committees at Geneva in December. It was then (in November) hoped that these meetings would be of a purely formal character, and that the actual problems of security and disarmament would not be tackled. This hope proved to be justified and we were not involved in discussion of the Disarmament issues on which we had already found ourselves at variance with other governments. But against the possibility of such discussion, instructions were given to the British delegate, which were summarized thus: 'To state once more, though without controversy, our naval proposals, putting in the forefront the proposed reduction in the size and power of capital ships; to use our influence with the French Government to make military disarmament practicable; and to confirm the international agreement, so far as it has been reached, upon the Air Forces, with a view to establishing a basis of equality between the principal Air Powers of Europe.' Little difficulty was anticipated in regard to the Air. The two formidable issues were (1) limitation of warships and (2) limitation of trained reserves. In relation to these two points the conclusion really was that on the former we could make no concession and that in regard to the latter we must, partly for tactical reasons, maintain our view that in the absence of any limitation of trained reserves there could be no effective disarmament calculated to affect the general sense of security and so reduce the chance of hostilities.

It was hoped that an adjournment of the discussion for some months – an adjournment which was happily secured – would give time for reflection and for discussion between the governments, and it is time now, on the eve of the resumption of the sessions at Geneva, to review the result of such discussion as has taken place.

On the naval question, there are the discussions which Admiral Kelly had with the French naval authorities in Paris in November last ... These show that, although the French are prepared to make a slight advance, this does not, in the view of the Admiralty, alter the situation materially, and the Admiralty memorandum on those discussions concludes: 'It does not appear that there is any reason to modify our attitude on the question of disarmament. The above should show that it is only her present feeling of insecurity that prevents France from agreeing to the British method of limitation, and that as regards sound principles we are on firmer ground than she is.'

Further in regard to the naval question, there is the interview between Lord Cushendun and the French Ambassador on 19 January, at which the latter was unable to indicate any further concession on the part of his Government, though he promised to discuss the matter with them during his impending visit to Paris. We have not heard that he has brought anything back with him.

From the above it seems that, on the naval question, the French may make a small advance towards our position, but the Admiralty are clear that this is not sufficient, and are also insistent on maintaining our point of view. The situation therefore is not materially different from what it was in November.

As regards the military question, the situation has undergone, if possible, even less change. Colonel Temperley's conversation with Colonel R_quin... shows that, although the French views on limitation of expenditure, and on control, may be modified, their attitude in regard to the main issue – trained reserves – remains immovable. This is only confirmed by Lord Cushendun's interview with M. de Fleuriau ...

The above has been written on the assumption that we are committed to work on disarmament on the present lines, whether we really think this is the best method or not. It is true that we are pledged several times over to disarm: it is not so clear that we are pledged anywhere to sign a general disarmament convention. It is true that under the Covenant the Council is to 'formulate plans' for reduction, but these are for 'consideration and action of the several Governments'. What we told the Germans in 1919 was that the first step towards general disarmament must be a disarmament of Germany. Germany accepted the military, naval and air clauses of the Treaty of Versailles (and may have carried them out). Without that, evidently, no one could disarm. Once that was done, other nations were free to reduce their armaments to the 'lowest point consistent with national safety'. At any rate we have done so. After the Armistice we scrapped a large proportion of our fleet – a process which was carried still further by the Washington Treaty. We very soon reduced our army to proportions even more 'contemptible' than those of 1914. Other nations have done something of the same – how much, is a matter between them and their consciences. But it does not seem quite certain that 'plans for the consideration and action of the several governments' necessarily involves a general convention for all-round proportional reduction of armaments. Certainly we are nowhere pledged to reduction to the German level. And if German disarmament, carried to the point to which we believe it has been carried, does not produce sufficient sense of security to enable other nations to spare themselves expense which they must grudge, that is no argument in favour of freeing the Germans from restrictions which do not appear to have been severe enough.

But the League has chosen to act as if it were bound to produce a general disarmament convention. The Germans have seized on this and sought to connect general disarmament with their own disarmament in such a way that they can claim to be freed from their part of the bargain if the Allied Governments do not perform theirs. This course has been adopted with our consent, however reluctant, and we are therefore presumably committed to it ... ∎

CHAPTER NINE

Britain and the Depression: Slump and Recovery, 1929–1939

URING 1929 it was widely assumed that the economic improvements of the later 1920s would continue. However, 1929 saw the onset of the Great Depression worldwide. Following the Wall Street Crash in October 1929, business confidence fell sharply and international trade declined, encouraging some observers to believe that the capitalist system as a whole was doomed. Between 1929 and 1931 the volume of Britain's exports fell by a half, the consequence of the United States depression and the difficulties of the non-industrial countries, many of which were important markets for Britain. Not only did this create problems for Britain's balance of trade, since imports declined less sharply than exports, but the slump in the export industries gradually spread to those sectors of the economy supplying domestic demand.

The most visible result of this situation was the rapid growth of unemployment. By the middle of 1930 Britain had over 2 million unemployed workers. Aggravating the problems of the export industries was the drop in demand affecting the service sector, an important source of 'invisible' exports, such as shipping and insurance. By 1931 Britain faced a trade deficit of some £114 million, whereas in 1928 there had been a surplus of around £104 million.

However, while some parts of the country remained in the grip of recession throughout the 1930s, elsewhere there were signs of healthy economic growth, amounting to conditions of virtual 'boom'. This was associated with the development of relatively new industries, especially those producing for a mass consumer market, and with a huge expansion in the construction industry. Observers of the period commented upon the wide disparity between economic and social conditions in, for example, the depressed North-East of England, and those in prosperous areas such as the Home Counties.

The Impact of the Depression

Britain's problems in the 1930s prompted wide-ranging debates on the government's responsibilities in the economic and social spheres. While many continued to argue along traditional lines of economic thinking, minimising the state's role, others were beginning to suggest that government could do much to counteract the effects of the Depression and to promote recovery and growth. Although these debates were not fully resolved by the end of the decade, new possibilities had been revealed which would be explored more fully after the Second World War.

One measure which might have helped Britain's export trade to recover from the slump was a deliberate devaluation of the pound, designed to make British exports more competitive. However, this was shunned by most contemporary observers. In the summer of 1931 the report of the Macmillan Committee on Finance and Industry endorsed the view that such a move would shake the confidence of the financial world, and do more harm than good. Ironically, the pound was subsequently devalued with Britain's departure from the gold standard.

9.1   *Report of the Committee on Finance and Industry,* **June 1931 (Cmd 3897, PP XIII, 1930–1, pp. 110–11).**

■   3. DEVALUATION

255. It has been represented to us that, without in any way departing from the principle or the practice of adherence to an international standard, it is desirable for us in the national interest to do now what might have been accomplished with much less difficulty in 1925, namely, to revise the gold-parity of sterling. Such a step is urged on the ground that, if we diminished the gold equivalent of the £ sterling by 10 per cent. thereby reducing our gold-costs automatically by the same percentage, this would restore to our export industries and to the industries which compete with imported goods what they lost by the return to gold at a figure which was inappropriate to the then existing facts, and that it would also have the great advantage of affecting all sterling costs equally, whether or not they were protected by contract.

256. We have no hesitation in rejecting this course. It is no doubt true that an essential attribute of a sovereign state is a power at any time to alter the value of its currency for any reasons deemed to be in the national interest, and that legally, therefore, there is nothing to prevent the British Government and Parliament from taking such a step. The same may be said of a measure writing down all debts, including those owing by the State itself, by a prescribed percentage – an expedient which would in fact over a considerable field have precisely the same effect. But, while all things may be lawful, all things are not expedient, and in our opinion the devaluation by any Government of a currency standing at its par value suddenly and without notice (as must be the case to prevent foreign creditors removing their property) is emphatically one of those things which are not expedient. International trade, commerce and finance are based on confidence. One of the foundation stones on which that confidence reposes is the general belief that all countries will seek to

maintain so far as lies in their power the value of their national currency as it has been fixed by law, and will only give legal recognition to its depreciation when that depreciation has already come about *de facto*. It has frequently been the case – we have numerous examples of recent years – that either through the misfortunes of war, or mistakes of policy, or the collapse of prices, currencies have fallen so far below par that their restoration would involve either great social injustices or national efforts and sacrifices for which no adequate compensation can be expected. The view may be held that our own case in 1925 was of this character. The British currency had been depreciated for some years. It was obvious to the whole world that it was an open question whether its restoration to par was in the national interest and there is no doubt in our minds as to our absolute freedom at that time to fix it, if it suited us, at a lower par value corresponding to the then existing exchange. But it would be to adopt an entirely new principle, and one which would undoubtedly be an immense shock to the international financial world, if the Government of the greatest creditor nation were deliberately and by an act of positive policy to announce one morning that it had reduced by law the value of its currency from the par at which it was standing to some lower value.

257. Moreover, considering the matter from another point of view, in the environment of the present world slump the relief to be obtained from a 10 per cent. devaluation might prove to be disappointing. It is not certain that, with world demand at its present low ebb, such a measure would serve by itself to restore our export trades to their former position or to effect a radical cure of unemployment. On the contrary, in the atmosphere of crisis and distress which would inevitably surround such an extreme and sensational measure as the devaluation of sterling, we might well find that the state of affairs immediately ensuing on such an event would be worse than that which had preceded it. ■

The British government's difficulties in balancing its budget were aggravated by the rise of unemployment, and a looming financial crisis compounded the collapse of international trade. While the government was committed to maintaining the gold standard as the cornerstone of international finance, during the summer of 1931 confidence in the stability of the pound began to evaporate, partly because of Britain's balance of payments problems. Coinciding with an international banking crisis originating in Austria, this prompted a massive drain of gold abroad and, increasingly, panic among foreign bankers and speculators as it appeared that the British government would be unable to balance its budget. The likelihood of a budget deficit was itself strengthened by the fall of exports and the consequent rise in unemployment, since added strains were put on the unemployment benefits system at a time when tax revenue was shrinking.

In July 1931 the May Committee, chaired by Sir George May, a former Secretary of the Prudential Assurance Company, was appointed by the government to suggest how adequate cuts in public spending could be achieved. The committee predicted a budget deficit of some £120 million, undermining foreign confidence still further, and recommended a 20 per cent cut in unemployment benefits and reductions in public employees' pay. The report went on to condemn what it saw as the politically motivated abandonment of strict financial orthodoxy since 1918.

9.2 *Report of the Committee on National Expenditure,* July 1931 (Cmd 3920, PP XVI, 1930–1, pp. 222–3).

■ 571. Our chief concern however is for the future. If action is limited to these adjustments of expenditure or income, experience since the War does not allow us to hope for that sustained effort for national economy which we regard as essential to the restoration of prosperity. Some further action is needed if retrenchment is not soon to give way once more to expansion as has happened twice in the short period since the War ...

573. ...The root cause of our financial difficulties since the war is that the machinery has been largely nullified in its operation. It has secured the utmost regularity in Government accounting and high standards of administration and organisation, but as regards major items of policy – where the real expense of Government lies – the machinery of control has again and again been put out of action before it has had any chance of functioning.

574. We referred in our opening chapter to the political developments since the war which have resulted in Members of Parliament and Governments being returned to Westminster pledged in advance to vast and expensive schemes. The electoral programme of each successive Party in power, particularly where it was formerly in opposition, has usually been prepared with more regard to attracting electoral support than to a careful balancing of national interests. When the time comes to put that programme into force, matters which had formerly appeared easy and attractive are found to involve such grave questions as whether the proposals are administratively possible, whether they will have the desired results, whether the country can bear the cost; whether, in short, they are really in the national interest. It is almost inevitable that a new Cabinet should find itself driven to the conclusion that many of its promised reforms ought not to proceed, but it has a difficult course to steer before it can persuade its supporters in the House to recognise this in view of their pledges so freely given to the electorate. The problem is a serious one and it is hardly for us to suggest a solution: yet a solution has to be found if democracy is not to suffer shipwreck on the hard rock of finance. ■

The National government

The prevailing financial orthodoxy of the inter-war years demanded that the government take steps to balance the budget, proving itself credit-worthy, in order to restore confidence in sterling. This could only be achieved by making large savings in public expenditure. Moreover, foreign banks refused to

9.3   (*right*) **Britain's trade with the Empire, (excluding trade with the Irish Free State), 1929–38 (derived from C.L. Mowat,** *Britain between the Wars 1918–1940,* **London, Methuen, 1955, p. 437).**

consider lending the British government the money it needed to cover its shortfall unless major spending cuts were made. The Cabinet considered reducing public servants' pay and making a 10 per cent cut in unemployment benefits, but on this point ministers could not agree. This brought about the collapse of the Labour government in August 1931 and its replacement by a new 'National government' coalition under the Labour leader Ramsay MacDonald.

The National government quickly demonstrated its orthodox financial beliefs, seeing its most important function as being to defend the pound and the gold standard. In order to secure the foreign credits these goals required, the government set about implementing the cuts which its predecessor had balked at. A 10 per cent cut was imposed on unemployment benefits and public sector pay, and taxes were increased. Thereafter, until public spending rose once again with the onset of rearmament, the government managed to achieve modest budget surpluses. Ironically, even after these measures had been implemented, the drain on Britain's gold reserves had become so great that the government was obliged to abandon the gold standard in September 1931.

The financial crisis forced the government to embrace monetary management. In April 1932 the Exchange Equalisation Account was established, which traded in the foreign exchange market, enabling the government to support the pound at the stable level which exports needed. In addition, it effectively protected domestic finance from disturbances caused by the free movement of capital in and out of the country. This in turn made it possible to keep interest rates at the relatively low level of 2 per cent, since it was no longer necessary to keep the rate high in order to attract overseas funds and so prop up the value of sterling.

One of the most important policy shifts resulting from the Depression was the abandonment of free trade in 1932 and the introduction of protection under the Import Duties Act. This involved the grant of preferred status to the British Empire, negotiated at the Imperial Conference in Ottawa, which encouraged a growth in the volume of trade conducted between Britain and the Empire (although no overall increase in Britain's total trade). Nevertheless, successive governments did not see the Empire as a solution to Britain's trading difficulties; on the contrary, they continued to hope for a revival of international trade, and negotiated a series of bilateral trade agreements to promote this, the most important being with the United States in 1938.

9.4   (*right*) **Britain's external visible trade, 1928–39 (derived from B.R. Mitchell,** *British Historical Statistics,* **Cambridge, Cambridge University Press, 1988, p. 479).**

The devaluation of sterling, which accompanied the abandonment of the gold standard in 1931, helped to make British exports more competitive in terms of price. The formation of the National government also perhaps helped to restore business confidence. At any rate, by late 1932 there were already indications of economic revival, suggesting that the Depression proper was fairly brief. By 1935, although the overall level of unemployment was still high, revival was clearly in sight, helped by the gradual revival of the international economy. There were even some signs of an economic boom in some sectors, notably a shortage of skilled labour and an increase in the volume of imports. By 1937, however, there were worrying indications of another imminent recession, stemming in part from economic problems in the United States. Although this downturn was forestalled by an increase of expenditure on rearmament, it can be argued that this episode calls into question the strength of the recovery achieved up to 1937.

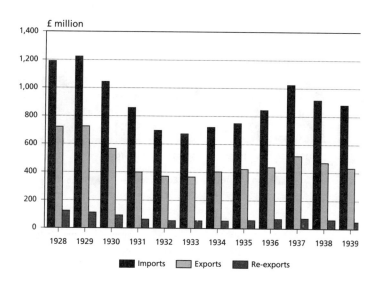

The Depression and the Staple Industries

The image of the 1930s as a period of stagnation, poverty and wasted human resources is inextricably linked to the fate of Britain's traditional or 'staple' export trades. These older sectors of the economy, already facing problems in the 1920s, were where the worst effects of the depression were felt; and the plight of industries such as coal, shipbuilding and cotton textiles lowered the overall performance of the British economy in the 1930s.

The fundamental problem facing Britain's staple industries was a fall in demand for their products, caused by the growth of foreign competition and protectionism. Their failure to keep abreast of technological developments, new processes and new methods of organisation reduced their strength as exporters. Exports of cotton, for example, declined from 7,000 million square yards in 1913 to just 2,000 million square yards in 1937. Even hitherto 'safe' home markets became vulnerable to foreign competition – Lancashire, for example, having to contend with cheaper Indian cotton imports. These developments pointed to deep-seated structural problems within the British economy.

9.5   **Britain's exports from the staple industries, 1921–37 (derived from S. Glynn and J. Oxborrow, *Interwar Britain: A Social and Economic History*, London, Allen & Unwin, 1976, p. 77).**

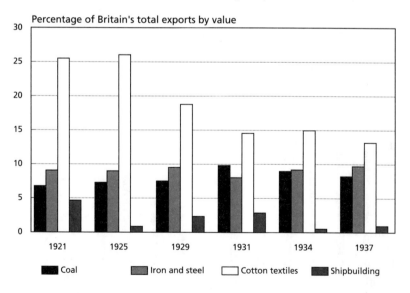

'Rationalisation', or the reduction of excess productive capacity in order to reduce competition within an industry, sometimes with government encouragement, was much in vogue in official circles in the 1930s. For example, in 1930 the Bank of England created the Bankers' Industrial Development Corporation, which raised the funds needed by National Shipbuilders' Security, which bought and closed down shipyards for which orders could not be found. The painful effects of rationalisation were captured by Ellen Wilkinson, Labour MP for Jarrow, who described the consequences for that community of the closure of Palmer's Shipyard in 1934.

9.6   Ellen Wilkinson, *The Town That Was Murdered,* 1939 (London, Victor Gollancz, p. 149).

■ On February 28, 1930, the first public statement was made regarding National Shipbuilders' Security Ltd. Its purpose was defined as being to assist the shipbuilding industry by the purchase of redundant or obsolete yards. To ensure that the productive capacity of the industry was definitely reduced the shipbuilding equipment was to be scrapped and the site of the yard was to be restricted against further use for shipbuilding. Furthermore, the company was empowered to make payments to other firms to contract not to build ships. By concentrating production in this way the promoters felt that they would be able to effect substantial reductions in overhead charges.

… Anxious about the future of their members the trade unions approached the Shipbuilding Employers' Federation and National Shipbuilders' Security Ltd., for an opportunity to discuss the activities of the latter company. With the scrapping of the shipyards the trade unions were anxious to secure for their unemployed members either some compensation or alternative employment without loss of status or income. Will Sherwood, then President of the Federation of Shipbuilding Trade Unions, led the Union delegates. In reply to their request … Sir James Lithgow [Chairman of NSS] produced as soothing syrup the optimistic claim that no men would be displaced. For, argued Sir James, the improved efficiency of the industry resulting from concentration would enable more work to be obtained when trade improved, since the work available would have to bear the charges of smaller capacity and would thus be produced at more economical prices …

On the point of attracting new industries to the cleared sites Sir James Lithgow assured the union leaders that the N.S.S. directors were of course anxious to do this. Empty shipyards meant heavy maintenance charges. Therefore they were trying to attract industrialists to take over the shipyard sites for other purposes …

… In the early summer of 1934 it was announced that Palmer's had been sold to N.S.S. The death warrant of Palmer's was signed. The reason for Jarrow's existence had vanished overnight.

Why was Palmer's Yard sold? It certainly was not an obsolete yard. One of the biggest firms in the industry and one which had invariably secured a fair share on competitive tenders cannot be classed as obsolete ... Financial weakness, and not technical inefficiency, decided the fate of the company. The rationalization of the shipbuilding industry has been carried through in that way – with an eye on the balance sheet rather than on the efficiency of the particular companies ... Palmer's was scrapped to safeguard the profits of some of the firms remaining in the industry ...

Sold by National Shipbuilding Security to a demolition firm, work was commenced to clear the site. Oxy-acetylene burners made short work of steel girders. Cranes crashed to the ground, the machine shops were emptied, the blast furnaces and their numerous chimneys were demolished. The familiar overhead cranes vanished ...

... Of the total unemployed in Jarrow 73 per cent. have been out of work for such long periods as not to be able to qualify for Unemployment Insurance benefit ...

43.3 per cent. of the men have been continuously without work for over a year ... Indeed, in Jarrow there are 251 who have never had a week's work in five years. ■

Besides 'rationalization' another course of action was to form price-fixing cartels among companies in the same industry, perhaps the most important example being that created within the steel industry. Here, too, the government provided encouragement. Under the Finance Act 1935, industries which undertook to reorganise, and so cut surplus capacity, received tax relief. Rationalisation and cartelisation had only limited success, however: as late as 1937 the old staples still produced one quarter of Britain's total output. Moreover, the immediate effect of these changes was generally to increase unemployment in the traditional industries, already those worst affected by long-term joblessness.

The Problem of Unemployment

One enduring image of the 1930s is that of mass unemployment – the dole queue and the locked factory gate. Certainly, unemployment was one of Britain's major social and economic problems of this period.

Unemployment in Britain reached its peak in August 1932, when there were some 3,750,000 jobless workers, about 23 per cent of the insured working population. If their dependants are included, then a total emerges of about 6.7 million people subsisting on the 'dole'. The official figures for unemployment, shown in the following chart, record only those people who registered at employment exchanges, and therefore disguise the true figure.

9.7   **Registered unemployment, 1929–40 (derived from A. Thorpe,**
Britain in the 1930s, **Oxford, Blackwell, 1992, p. 128).**

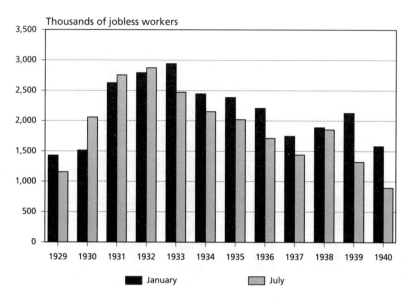

The Daily Express *cartoonist Strube, captured the frustration which accompanied*
unemployment.

9.8   **Cartoon by Sidney 'George' Strube, 'Thinking aloud',** *Daily Express,*
11 November 1932.

It became clear during the 1930s that long-term unemployment – unemployment for twelve months or longer – demonstrated a marked regional pattern. It was especially pronounced in those parts of Britain most dependent on the staple industries.

9.9   Unemployment in the staple industries, 1932 and 1937 (derived from S. Constantine, *Unemployment in Britain between the Wars*, Harlow, Longman, 1980, pp. 8–9).

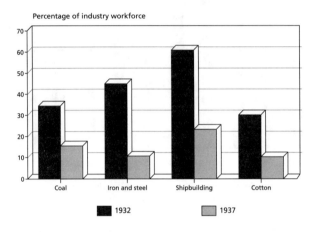

By 1937 nearly one British worker in ten was still jobless, but this was due largely to entrenched structural economic problems, rather than to the relatively short-term, 'cyclical' impact of the slump. Although unemployment was hardly a new phenomenon, its extent and persistence in the 1930s were both new and troubling. Even when recovery had begun, large numbers of long-term unemployed remained. Many of these workers had little hope of finding work again.

One of the most vivid contemporary accounts of the effects of unemployment was written by the novelist and journalist George Orwell. In 1936 Orwell was commissioned by Victor Gollancz, publisher and founder of the Left Book Club, to visit areas of mass unemployment and describe what he saw. The result was a powerful and polemical indictment of poverty.

9.10   George Orwell, *The Road to Wigan Pier*, 1937 (London, Penguin, 1989 edn, pp. 69–74).

■ When you see the unemployment figures quoted at two millions, it is fatally easy to take this as meaning that two million people are out of work and the rest of the population is comparatively comfortable. I admit that till recently I was in the habit of doing so myself. I used to calculate that if you put the registered unemployed at round about two millions and threw in the destitute and those who for one reason and another were not registered, you might take the number of underfed people in England (for everyone on the dole or thereabouts is underfed) as being, at the very most, five millions.

This is an enormous under-estimate, because, in the first place, the only people shown on unemployment figures are those actually drawing the dole – that is, in general, heads of families. An unemployed man's dependants do not figure on the list unless they too are drawing a separate allowance. A Labour Exchange officer told me that to get at the real number of people living on (not drawing) the dole, you have got to multiply the official figures by something over three. This alone brings the number of unemployed to round about six millions ...

It will be seen that the income of a family on the dole normally averages round about thirty shillings a week. One can write at least a quarter of this off as rent, which is to say that the average person, child or adult, has got to be fed, clothed, warmed, and otherwise cared-for for six or seven shillings a week. Enormous groups of people, probably at least a third of the whole population of the industrial areas, are living at this level. The Means Test is very strictly enforced, and you are liable to be refused relief at the slightest hint that you are getting money from another source ...

Nevertheless, in spite of the frightful extent of unemployment, it is a fact that poverty – extreme poverty – is less in evidence in the industrial North than it is in London. Everything is poorer and shabbier, there are fewer motor-cars and fewer well-dressed people; but also there are fewer people who are obviously destitute. Even in a town the size of Liverpool or Manchester you are struck by the fewness of the beggars. London is a sort of whirlpool which draws derelict people towards it, and it is so vast that life there is solitary and anonymous ... But in the industrial towns the old communal way of life has not yet broken up, tradition is still strong and almost everyone has a family – potentially, therefore, a home. Moreover, there is just this to be said for the unemployment regulations, that they do not discourage people from marrying. A man and wife on twenty-three shillings a week are not far from the starvation line, but they can make a home of sorts; they are vastly better off than a single man on fifteen shillings. The life for a single unemployed man is dreadful. He lives sometimes in a common lodging-house, more often in a 'furnished' room for which he usually pays six shillings a week, finding for himself as best he can on the other nine (say six shillings a week for food and three for clothes, tobacco and amusements). Of course he cannot feed or look after himself properly, and a man who pays six shillings a week for his room is not encouraged to be indoors more than is necessary. So he spends his days loafing in the public library or any other place where he can keep warm. That – keeping warm – is almost the sole preoccupation of a single unemployed man in winter. In Wigan a favourite refuge was the pictures, which are fantastically cheap there. You can always get a seat for fourpence, and at the matinée at some houses you can even get a seat for twopence. Even people on the verge of starvation will readily pay twopence to get out of the ghastly cold of a winter afternoon. In Sheffield I was taken to a public hall to listen to a lecture by a clergyman, and it was by a long way the silliest and worst-delivered lecture I have ever heard or ever expect to hear. I found it physically impossible to sit it out, indeed my feet carried me out, seemingly of their own accord, before it was half-way through. Yet the hall was thronged with unemployed men; they would have sat through far worse drivel for the sake of a warm place to shelter in. ■

In a similar vein to Orwell, Hilda Jennings, in her study of a stricken South Wales mining village, described the numbing routine of the long-term unemployed.

9.11   H. Jennings, *Brynmawr*, 1934 (London, Allenson, pp. 138-42).

■ While some effects of unemployment are general, individual men and their families of course react in different ways, and out of some six hundred families normally dependent upon unemployment benefit probably no two have precisely the same attitude to life and circumstances. The unemployed man must register twice a week at the Exchange; he must draw his pay there on Fridays. If he has been out for some time, each Friday he will have a short period of sickening anxiety lest the clerk should single him out and tell him that he is to be sent to the 'Court of Referees', then will follow a few days consequent dread lest his benefits should be stopped and he be cast on to the Poor Law, have to do 'task work' for his maintenance, and to take home less to his family in return for it. Having received his 'pay', duly contributed his 'Penny' to the Unemployed Lodge of the Miners' Federation, and conversed with his fellow unemployed, he returns home. The wife awaits his return in order that she may do the weekly shopping, and in many cases almost all of his unemployment pay, with the exception of a little pocket-money for 'fags', goes straight to her.

So far, there is similarity of practice, but beneath the surface this similarity does not reign. One man will approach the Exchange with impatience and bitterness at his dependence and impotency to help himself; one in a mood to find causes of complaint and irritation with the officials; one with growing apathy, and no conscious feeling except when his pay is threatened; one again with each visit feels the need for a change in the economic and social system; his political consciousness is inflamed, and he will fumble in his mind for an alternative, or shout the current formulae at the next 'unemployed' or 'party' meeting according to his mental outlook and capacity.

Visits to the Exchange at most take up part of two half-days in the week. For the rest, some men stand aimlessly on the Market Square or at the street corners, content apparently with a passive animal existence, or with the hour-long observation of passers-by, varied by an occasional whiff at a cigarette. Others work on allotment or garden, tend fowl or pigs, or do carpentry in their backyard or kitchen, making sideboards out of orange boxes stained brown with permanganate of potash, while their wives cook and tend the children in a restricted space around the fireplace, uncomplaining because they realise the necessity of providing some occupation for their husbands in order to keep them even moderately content. ■

The issue of unemployment prompted a number of investigations during the 1930s. Early in the Depression, most parts of Britain were affected by abnormally high levels of unemployment. Increasingly, however, major·regional variations became apparent, the highest rates being recorded in the North-East, the North-West, Scotland and Wales, with rates below the national average in the Midlands, the South-West, the South-East and London. There seemed, in effect, to be a growing divide between the hardest-hit old industrial regions and those regions, especially in the Midlands and South-East, which were generating new industries and enjoying relative prosperity.

9.12 **Regional variations in unemployment, 1929 and 1937 (derived from S. Constantine, *Unemployment in Britain between the Wars*, Harlow, Longman, 1980, p. 18).**

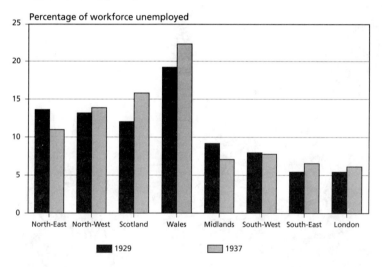

The Government and Unemployment

The scale and nature of unemployment posed serious problems which governments were increasingly expected to address. The impact of the Depression and the revelation of long-term unemployment forced politicians and officials to reconsider conventional ideas about their responsibilities towards the unemployed, and about oversight of the economy in general. Although governments were unwilling to spend large sums to create work for the unemployed, they remained committed to providing unemployment insurance. By the onset of the slump, the majority of industrial workers were included in state unemployment insurance schemes. Moreover, those workers who had exhausted their entitlement to unemployment insurance benefit were eligible for 'transitional' benefits, provided they could demonstrate that they were 'genuinely seeking work'. When this condition was abolished in 1930, the number of claimants increased.

As unemployment grew, and especially as the problem of long-term unemployment deepened, more and more British workers had to be provided with transitional benefits, not only adding to public spending, but placing the country's entire benefit system under intolerable strain. By 1931 the unemployment insurance fund was bankrupt. Low in the Evening Standard *portrayed MacDonald, Baldwin and Lloyd George 'squaring up' ineffectually to the looming crisis.*

9.13   **Cartoon by David Low, 'Fright-wait championship' (the unemployment insurance crisis),** *Evening Standard,* **8 June 1931.**

Late in 1930 MacDonald set up a Royal Commission on Unemployment Insurance. The commission produced its first report in 1931, demonstrating how government borrowing for unemployment benefits was making it impossible to balance the budget

9.14   *Royal Commission on Unemployment Insurance, First Report,* **June 1931 (Cmd 3872, PP XVII, 1930–1, pp. 6-7).**

■ 12. The average percentage of the insured population recorded as unemployed at the end of each month since December 1920, when the Unemployment Insurance Scheme was extended to its present limits, is

12.2; representing nearly one and a half million persons. The contributions and benefits provided by the Unemployment Insurance Act, 1922, and continuing to the second Act of 1924, balanced at about this percentage, and the Scheme may be taken to have been at this stage solvent and self-supporting. No other Act since 1920 has satisfied this condition. The Acts now in operation fall far short of it …

20. It is clear … that the most serious element in the situation is the average level of unemployment of 12.2 per cent. This represents a persistent and obdurate problem, and in our view it would be unwise to treat this experience of the last ten years as transitory or to assume that it over-values the risk that has to be provided for in the next few years. Moreover, for the purpose of immediate measures, it must be noted that the percentage of unemployment today is, in fact, far higher than 12.2 per cent; since December 1930 it has been 20 per cent or over. This excess over average is due to … the world wide depression of the last eighteen months. The indications are that unemployment will not fall appreciably in the next few months below the present level. What is necessary now is to adjust the finances of the Fund to present circumstances, and for the purposes of this Report we do not feel justified in anticipating an average Live Register (of unemployed persons) of less than 2,500,000 …

65. Under present conditions the income and expenditure of the Unemployment Fund balance when 900,000 persons are qualified for Insurance benefit. The decrease in contribution income is about £350,000 per annum for each 100,000 persons added to the Live Register while the increase in benefit paid is about £4,500,000. Assuming that the average Live Register is 2,500,000 the annual income of the Fund by contributions in respect of employed persons is as follows:

From employers	£15,650,000
From employed persons	13,650,000
From the Exchequer	14,850,000
Other receipts	400,000
	£44,550,000

66. The corresponding payments for Insurance benefit are estimated to amount to:

To the claimant	£61,250,000
Additional payment for dependants	13,250,000
Cost of administration	5,000,000
Interest on debt	4,500,000
	£84,000,000

67. … At this rate of unemployment, the beneficiaries are drawing out of the Unemployment Fund more than two and a half times the amount paid in contributions by employers and workers … ∎

The National government imposed the cuts in benefit demanded by orthodox financial thinking, and these remained in force until 1934. Henceforward, benefits were payable for a maximum of twenty-six weeks, after which transitional payments were made subject to a means test on claimants. Initially, the means test was operated by the Public Assistance Committees, the same local authorities which had been responsible for administering the Poor Law since 1930.

The government's policy in the 1930s was shaped above all by a continuing desire to keep public spending down. But policy towards the unemployed also enshrined the traditional principle of 'less eligibility' – the idea that benefits should always be lower in value than wages, so that unemployment could never be seen as being more attractive than work, and so that wage levels would not be pushed up. Balancing these ideas was the government's recognition that the entire benefits system was an important buttress of social stability. For this reason, it was thought necessary to safeguard the 'respectable' unemployed from utter destitution, not least because this was a means of elevating unemployment above party politics.

Neville Chamberlain, as Chancellor of the Exchequer in 1932, was anxious to introduce a clear administrative distinction between provision for the short- and the long-term unemployed. Armed with the final report of the Royal Commission on Unemployment Insurance, he drew up the Unemployment Act, which became law in 1934. Part I of the Act concerned benefits for the short-term unemployed, restoring a balance to the insurance budget. Part II concerned the long-term unemployed. A new Unemployment Assistance Board was to pay means-tested benefits through its local staff, taking this responsibility out of the hands of the Poor Law authorities. Although this was a welcome reform, an outcry greeted the publication of the UAB's proposed scale of payments, often lower than those provided by the local authorities. The Labour MP for the Gorbals Division of Glasgow, George Buchanan, addressed the problems associated with the new regulations early in 1935.

9.15 House of Commons debate on unemployment, 4 March 1935 (*Hansard*, 5th ser., 298: 1686, 1691–2).

■ Mr. BUCHANAN: ... I return, therefore, to the theme of the maintenance of the unemployed ... I should like to refer to the new regulations and the relationship of the board to those regulations. It is commonly stated that it is not the board that is to blame, but the Government. I take the view that the Government and the board and the House of Commons are to blame. All those who voted for the regulations are also to blame. The regulations were approved by the board. In a Glasgow newspaper on the 16th of last month a town councillor was reported to have said quite definitely that he had been in conversation with a member of the Board and that member had informed him that he had fought night and day with the Treasury to try and get them to increase the amount of the benefit. From the Treasury Box we had the statement that far from the Government having interfered with the scales they had actually increased them. That is the important fact in this consideration. A member of the Board, who is chief of the Glasgow Public Assistance Committee, tells one of his committee that he has had to fight the Treasury; and we get a different statement from the Government. We have the convener of the Public Assistance Committee making a definite statement in the "Daily Herald" that a member of the Board had informed him that the Treasury and the Government were behind the reduction of the amount to the unemployed ... ■

In its handling of the crisis surrounding unemployment payments, and by delaying introduction of the new scheme until 1937, the government showed that it was willing to modify the details of its policy so as to protect its broad character. Arguably, for all its inadequacies, the National government's unemployment policy blunted demands for a more radical approach to economic management.

Apart from the Unemployment Act of 1934, the government's other major response to unemployment was its regional policy. The relative prosperity of some parts of the country threw into relief the problems of those areas most dependent on the staple industries. Growing concern about conditions in these 'depressed areas' was reflected in a series of authoritative articles published in The Times, *authoritative enough to attract the government's attention.*

9.16   Editorial on 'The derelict areas', *The Times*, 22 March 1934.

■ ... The problem of the derelict area is a special problem requiring separate examination and separate treatment. Too often it has been lost sight of in the general problem of unemployment and of unemployment relief. In fact it is fundamentally different ... The derelict areas are as clearly a separate part of the problem of unemployment as slum areas are a separate part of the problem of housing. They can be as easily defined as a slum and are as easily susceptible of separate treatment. Moreover the derelict areas are a non-recurrent problem of an emergency type; and if they call for abnormal action and methods of treatment – as undoubtedly they do – those methods will be self-liquidating. Their success will bring them to an end. In the consideration of remedial measures for a situation of emergency there need therefore be no cautious search for administrative parallels nor fear of establishing precedents. Well-considered but rapid action is required, and comprehensive many-sided measures of help. The life-lines to be passed to the derelict areas will be composed of many strands intertwined; and all the strands will not be equally suitable for all places.

There should be a Director of Operations against the derelict areas. The holder of the office should be untrammelled by departmental limitations and – if not himself a Minister – should be responsible directly to the Cabinet. He should be the channel and instrument of a concerted national effort to rid the land of these terrible pools of idleness in which manhood is slowly and fatally sinking. He would bind together the agencies of relief and amelioration and direct remedial measures with concentrated force. He would supervise administrative action and summon voluntary aid. The agencies of relief exist, and the apparatus of the new Unemployment Bill will soon be available. Some of the remedial measures are known, but others, more effective, have to be discovered. They will vary with the place, and with the character and courage of the people themselves, and with the degree of local initiative and resource where these remain or can be recovered. But in the main the energy and the drive, the reviving impulse will have to be supplied from outside, and not casually, or intermittently, but with steady and sustained direction. Areas of decay must be cleared if they cannot be restored, and the people must be rescued from an encroaching desolation which they and their local authorities have been unable to resist. Men must be set on their feet again and given a purpose in life. The help to be supplied will not be (what is always unsatisfactory) rate relief to the locality – although local burdens will have to be dealt with – nor doles to individuals. The object will certainly not be to give pecuniary advantages to local authorities which can boast of the most distressed areas or to diminish local duties. But an external, and national, administrator, with the authority of Parliament, would go into the desolate areas and take whatever measures are needed to remove the desolation; to restore the communal health; to assist, probably, in the introduction of minor industries as well as in the provision, at least, of useful occupations; and in preparing, physically and morally, those whose only hope of a career depends upon their removal elsewhere. He would be an initiating and directing centre, surveying each area of decay and setting it and its inhabitants into relation with the rest of the country.

... The false hope of industrial revival in the derelict areas is injurious to the welfare of the inhabitants. It discourages movement outwards. Migration must be stimulated, not retarded. The Ministry of Labour's efforts to transport the younger men and women have been kept back by the general depression of industry; but the policy is right and should be furthered by preparatory reconditioning and training. Nevertheless the complete abandonment of the derelict areas will be impossible, and it is not desirable to any greater extent than is necessary because of the ensuing loss of social capital. The possibilities of starting new industries, quite small perhaps, to meet local requirements, and of training in the handicrafts that are generically classified as rural industries, should be fully ascertained ... Things have been allowed far too much to take an unhindered course from bad to worse. Again and again the investigator in the derelict districts is made aware of the lack of initiative and spontaneous effort. There is numbness, and half-despairing, half-hopeful, and frequently resentful misery. The direction which the areas lack must be supplied from outside. The derelict areas must be cleaned up, and the dependent populations which, for a shorter or longer time, remain in them must be given occupations – meeting each other's wants, it may be, in the requirements of the home and of the table. Up to now the task before the nation has not been measured in its exact nature or extent. Let it be measured, without dismay at its apparent difficulties, and a concentrated national effort be directed to its completion. ■

Public concern about the depressed areas prompted the government's Special Areas Act, under which two Commissioners were appointed, one for Central Scotland, and one for North-East England, West Cumberland and South Wales. These Commissioners were responsible for dispensing £2 million a year to promote enterprise. However, the Special Areas, strikingly, excluded blighted regions such as Lancashire, struggling with its over-dependence on cotton textiles. Furthermore, the Act was clearly intended to reinforce, not to supplant, private enterprise, and most of the schemes funded were designed to improve local amenities.

Frustrated by the limitations on his powers, the Commissioner for England and Wales resigned in 1936. Although the Commissioners' powers were subsequently increased to enable them encourage new industries in the depressed areas, and although 'trading estates' were promoted to this end, this strategy had little success, most new industry taking root in the more affluent Midlands and South-East. Ultimately, it was rearmament and then the war which gave the depressed areas a new lease of economic life. In his report for 1936 the Commissioner for England and Wales described some of the difficulties of bringing new business to these areas.

9.17   *Third Report of the Commissioner for the Special Areas (England and Wales), 1936–7 (Cmd. 5303, PP XII, 1936–37, pp. 3–4, 10).*

■ 9. Efforts to administer the Special Areas Act on sound lines were at the outset often looked upon with suspicion and sometimes with hostility. They are now receiving a considerable degree of cordial support. There is evidence that the work done and the measures initiated are proving helpful to the Areas and that their benefits will in many cases be increasingly felt. Nevertheless, it has to be admitted that no appreciable reduction of the number of those unemployed has been effected. This, however, was not to be looked for seeing that the Special Areas Act makes no direct provision for this purpose. Such increased employment as is likely to result from the operation of the many schemes initiated will prove altogether insufficient, in the absence of a spontaneous growth of new industries and expansion of existing industries, to offset the release of labour brought about by increased mechanisation and rationalisation. The position has been further influenced by the addition to the supply of labour due to natural increase of population …

The all-important question that arises from a study of the results obtained from its administration is whether the time is not now ripe for a second experiment which, whilst continuing work already embarked upon, would make an attempt to deal more directly with the problem of unemployment …

… Industry is not seeking the Special Areas; therefore, it must be attracted to those districts of the Areas which are endowed with suitable economic facilities, and many are available. How can this be effected? My recommendation is that by means of *State-provided inducements* a determined attempt should be made to attract industrialists to the Special Areas. The failure of these Areas to attract cannot be simply explained away by lack of opportunity for economic expansion. Fear is the dominant deterrent which holds back industrialists from taking risks in the Areas; fear that their very distress makes them unsuitable for the development of industrial activity; fear of labour unrest and of further increases of already high rates. However well or ill founded these fears may be, they not only prevail but often engender a habit of mind which is wholly prejudicial to any favourable consideration of the Special Areas. This mental attitude can be considerably changed if new conditions which challenge attention are set up in the Areas and make industrialists seeking expansion feel that, unless they study them, opportunity may be lost. It is sought by means of State-provided inducements to supply the required incentive. Unless something is done to banish fear, its influence will continue to rule out consideration of the possibilities of the Special Areas. ■

Recovery and Prosperity

It would be misleading to portray the 1930s in Britain as a period marked only by gloom, depression and decay. Paradoxically, while the depressed areas were stagnating, other parts of the country were enjoying something of a boom. Economic recovery was most pronounced in those sectors of the economy which supplied the domestic market, and which were less dependent than the old staples on export markets.

An important factor promoting recovery was the construction boom of the 1930s. This was assisted by the government's 'cheap money' policy, which kept interest rates at two per cent from 1932 to 1939, making mortgages a realistic proposition for a growing

9.18   Chart: The construction boom, 1923–39 (derived from B.R. Mitchell, *British Historical Statistics*, Cambridge, Cambridge University Press, 1988, p. 392).

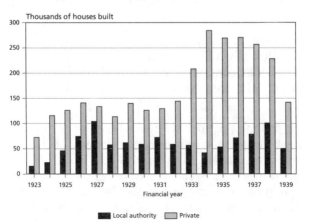

section of society. Because construction was a labour-intensive industry, this boom created many new jobs. Moreover, house-building created demand for the products of numerous other industries, especially those producing consumer goods.

In 1934 the writer J.B. Priestley described the regional differences to which new economic development was giving rise.

9.19   J.B. Priestley, *English Journey*, 1934 (London, Heinemann, pp. 397–412).

■ I had seen England. I had seen a lot of Englands. How many? At once, three disengaged themselves from the shifting mass. There was, first, Old England, the country of the cathedrals and minsters and manor houses and inns, of Parson and Squire; guidebook and quaint highways and byways England... But we all know this England, which at its best cannot be improved upon in this world ...

Then, I decided, there is the nineteenth-century England, the industrial England of coal, iron, steel, cotton, wool, railways; of thousands of rows of little houses all alike, sham Gothic churches, square-faced chapels, Town Halls, Mechanics' Institutes, mills, foundries, warehouses, refined watering-places, Pier Pavilions, Family and Commercial Hotels, Literary and Philosophical Societies, back-to-back houses, detached villas with monkey-trees, Grill Rooms, railway stations, slag-heaps and 'tips', dock roads, Refreshment Rooms, doss-houses, Unionist or Liberal Clubs, cindery waste ground, mill chimneys, fried-fish shops, public-houses ... This England makes up the larger part of the Midlands and the North and exists everywhere; but it is not being added to and has no new life poured into it. To the more fortunate people it was not a bad England at all, very solid and comfortable ... The third England, I concluded, was the new post-war England, belonging far more to the age itself than to this island. America, I supposed, was its real birthplace. This is the England of arterial and by-pass roads, of filling stations and factories that look like exhibiting buildings, of giant cinemas and dance-halls and cafés, bungalows with tiny garages, cocktail bars, Woolworths, motor-coaches, wireless, hiking, factory girls looking like actresses, greyhound racing and dirt tracks, swimming pools and everything given away for cigarette coupons ... Care is necessary too, for you can easily approve or disapprove of it too hastily. It is, of course, essentially democratic ... You need money in this England, but you do not need much money. It is a large-scale, mass-production job, with cut prices. You could almost accept Woolworths as its symbol ... In this England, for the first time in history, Jack and Jill are nearly as good as their master and mistress ... Most of the work ... is rapidly becoming standardised in this new England, and its leisure is being handed over to standardisation too. It is a cleaner, tidier, healthier, saner world than that of nineteenth-century industrialism ...

Here then were the three Englands I had seen, the Old, the Nineteenth-Century and the New; and as I looked back on my journey I saw how these three were variously and most fascinatingly mingled in every part of the country I had visited. ∎

An important factor underlining recovery in the 1930s was the consolidation of new industries, notably motor vehicle manufacturing, the electrical industries and the artificial-fibre and chemicals industries. Because of the fall in prices associated with the Depression, real wages were higher overall in the 1930s and working hours were shorter than in the previous decade. This meant that those in work (always by far the majority) often enjoyed both higher living standards and greater amounts of leisure time. This was reflected in rising levels of domestic consumption and the growth of the entertainment industries.

9.20   'Into the concrete age with Alpha', advertisement, 1936 (*The Builder*, 5 June 1936).

9.21   'Well ahead again', Vauxhall advertisement, 1936 (*The Autocar*, 25 September 1936).

9.22 The spread of radio and television: broadcast receiving licences, 1928–40 (derived from B.R. Mitchell, *British Historical Statistics*, Cambridge, Cambridge University Press, 1988, p. 569).

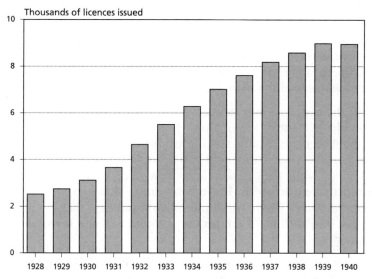

Thousands of licences issued

Economic Management: the Developing Debate

During the Depression, government economic policies were described as unimaginative and uncaring – as they have been almost ever since. Budget-balancing remained a priority, and there was no concerted attempt to revive the economy through deficit financing. Cheap money, devaluation, protectionism and rationalisation were the hallmarks of government policy throughout the 1930s. Private investment, not public spending, was judged to be the surest basis for recovery, hence the importance attached to stimulating business confidence.

An early, and bitter, critic of the conventional economic wisdom was Sir Oswald Mosley, later leader of the British Union of Fascists. In 1930, while still a junior minister in the Labour government, he proposed an ambitious scheme of state-financed public works to alleviate unemployment. The Treasury dismissed such ideas as threatening to financial confidence. A senior Treasury official, Sir Richard Hopkins, summarised his colleagues' views.

9.23 Sir Richard Hopkins, 'Notes on Sir Oswald Mosley's speech in the House of Commons', 16 June 1930 (PRO T 175/42, p. 28).

■ … The programme he [Mosley] has borrowed first saw the light in a political brochure, but it was hatched in the study of an economist – a political economist. Its object must surely be a rise in the price level to be secured by the outpouring of a flood of money. That is commonly called inflation. Vast Government loans are to be raised – at what rate of interest you will – and the proceeds are to be poured with breakneck speed into the hands of quarry owners, of road contractors and of the proprietors of businesses, limited in range, which supply the goods the Government will need in unexampled quantities. And thence the gain is to spread to the shopkeepers along the routes of the roads and to those other trades who supply the needs of the working population.

What is the use of it? Our stricken trades are the export trades, Coal, Steel, Shipbuilding, Cotton, Wool. How is any one of these to be benefited if other sheltered trades are making profits far beyond their high level of recent years? How will it benefit any depressed export trade if prices rise in this country while they remain low elsewhere? There is no doubt that the plan can make prices rise. There is no doubt that it would in the process reduce real wages. There is not the smallest prospect that it will restore the industrial equilibrium. There is every ground to think it will disturb it still more.

The activity of the Government in promoting capital development can only be an amelioration of our industrial difficulties. It is a delusion to suppose it can be a cure.

The cure must be found elsewhere. In the first place great and sudden world depressions are not a new phenomenon: they have occurred before: and experience shows that they carry with them the seeds of recovery. Already we have cheap money ... Cheap money with its revivifying influence is perhaps the most hopeful sign of better times to come ... In addition cheap money should encourage the return of confidence, a growing volume of business and the restoration of the ordinary rhythm of currency and trade. ∎

In 1933, following a press campaign calling for state-financed public works to promote recovery, the Chancellor of the Exchequer used his Budget speech to defend orthodox finance.

9.24 Neville Chamberlain's Budget speech, 25 April 1933 (*Hansard*, 5th ser., 277: 60–1).

∎ Look around the world today and you see that badly unbalanced Budgets are the rule rather than the exception. Everywhere there appear Budget deficits piling up, yet they do not produce those favourable results which it is claimed would happen to us. On the contrary, I find that Budget deficits repeated year after year may be accompanied by deepening recession and by a constantly falling price level. Before we embark upon so dangerous a course as that, let us reflect upon this indisputable fact. Of all the countries passing through these difficult times the one that has stood the test with the greatest measure of success is the United Kingdom. Without under-estimating the hardships of our situation – the long tragedy of the unemployed, the grievous burden of taxation, the arduous and painful struggle of those engaged in trade and industry – at any rate we are free from that fear, which besets so many less fortunately placed, the fear that things are going to get worse. We owe our freedom from that fear largely to the fact that we have balanced our Budget. By following a sound financial policy we have been enabled to secure low interest rates for industry and it would be the height of folly to throw away that advantage. If we were to reverse our policy, just at the very moment when other Governments are striving to follow our example and to balance their Budgets, after experience of the policy which we are now asked to adopt, we would stultify ourselves in the eyes of the world and forfeit in a moment the respect with which we are regarded to-day. ■

Enthusiasts for US President Roosevelt's 'New Deal' found little positive response from Whitehall. When in 1935 Lloyd George called for a British 'New Deal', one official was prompted to make the following response.

9.25 Sir Frederick Leith-Ross, memorandum on a British 'New Deal', 1935 (PRO T 188/117).

■ It is becoming the fashion to call for a 'New Deal'. The fashion started in the United States ... where gambling holds much the same place in national life as cricket does in ours. Nothing, therefore, is more natural than that the American government should indulge in a gamble while a British government has to keep a straight bat and sometimes to stone wall. Such tactics may not appeal to those spectators who have more enthusiasm than knowledge of the pitch, but it is to be hoped that the barracking will not affect the batsmen. For the state of England is not such that they can afford to take great risks.

... By whatever standard we judge them, the resources of the United States are overwhelmingly superior to those of this country. She is in a position of independence and invulnerability and can afford experiments which no other country – least of all this country – could afford. But have these experiments in the United States been successful? On the contrary, the continuous outpouring of public money by the present Administration has reduced confidence and stopped investment ... The United States have not found unbalanced budgets and profligate public expenditure any remedy for unemployment: indeed, they are looking with growing envy at the results achieved here by less spectacular methods. ■

Despite British disparagement of 'New Deal'-style approaches, radical ideas were emerging in the 1930s, especially associated with the economist John Maynard Keynes. Keynes argued that the state could intervene to correct malfunctions in the economy, managing demand in order to secure full employment. He produced a full exposition of this thinking in his General Theory of Employment, Interest and Money *of 1936; and early in 1937 he produced a series of articles in* The Times, *aimed at a wider audience.*

9.26   John Maynard Keynes, 'How to avoid a slump I: the problem of the steady level', 1937 (*The Times*, 12 January 1937).

■ It is clear that by painful degrees we have climbed out of the Slump. It is also clear that we are well advanced on the upward slopes of prosperity – I will not say 'of the boom' ... and what we are enjoying is desirable. But many are already preoccupied with what is to come. It is widely agreed that it is more important to avoid a descent into another slump than to stimulate ... a still greater activity than we have. This means that all of us – politicians, bankers, industrialists, and economists – are faced with a scientific problem which we have never tried to solve before.

I emphasized that point. Not only have we never solved it; we have never tried to. Not once. The booms and slumps of the past have been neither courted nor contrived against. The action of Central Banks has been hitherto an almost automatic response to the unforeseen and undesigned impact of outside events. But this time it is different. We have already freed ourselves – this applies to every party and every quarter – from the philosophy of the *laissez-faire* state. We have new means at our disposal which we intend to use. Perhaps we know more. But chiefly it is a general conviction that the stability of our institutions absolutely requires a resolute attempt to apply what perhaps we know to preventing the recurrence of another steep descent. I should like to try, therefore, to render a complicated problem to its essential elements.

THE DISTRESSED AREAS

It is natural to interject that it is premature to abate our efforts to increase employment so long as the figures of unemployment remain so large. In a sense this must be true. But I believe that we are approaching, or have reached, the point where there is not much advantage in applying a further general stimulus at the centre. So long as surplus resources were widely diffused between industries and localities it was no great matter at what point in the economic structure the impulse of an increased demand was applied. But the evidence grows that – for several reasons ... the economic structure is unfortunately rigid, and that (for example) building activity in the home counties is less effective than one might have hoped in decreasing unemployment in the distressed areas. It follows that the later stages of recovery require a different technique. To remedy the condition of the distressed areas, *ad hoc* measures are necessary. The Jarrow marchers were, so to speak, theoretically correct. The Government have been wrong in their reluctance to accept the strenuous *ad hoc* measures recommended by those in close touch with the problem. Nevertheless a change of policy in the right direction seems to be imminent. We are in more need to-day of a rightly distributed demand than of a greater aggregate demand; and the Treasury would be entitled to economize elsewhere to compensate for the cost of special assistance to the distressed areas ...

Why is it that good times have been so intermittent? The explanation is not difficult. The public, especially when they are prosperous, do not spend the whole of their incomes on current consumption. It follows that the productive activities, from which their incomes are derived, must not be devoted to preparing for consumption in any greater proportion than that in which the corresponding incomes will be spent on consumption; since, if they are, the resulting goods cannot be sold at a profit and production will have to be curtailed. If when incomes are at a given level the public consume, let us say, nine-tenths of their incomes, the productive efforts devoted to consumption goods cannot be more than nine times the efforts devoted to investment, if the results are to be sold without loss. Thus it is an indispensable condition of a stable increase in incomes that the production of investment goods (which must be interpreted in a wide sense so as to include working capital; and also relief works and armaments if they are paid for by borrowing) should advance *pari passu* and in the right proportion. Otherwise the proportion of income spent on consumption will be less than the proportion of income earned by producing consumption goods, which means that the receipts of the producers of consumption goods will be less than their costs, so that business losses and a curtailment of output will ensue. ■

CHAPTER TEN

The Search for a Middle Way: From Crisis to National Government, 1929–1939

THE 1930s were years of political controversy in Britain and have produced a mythology of their own. When the decade opened, a minority Labour government was in office. When it closed, Britain was at war, and a new coalition government soon became necessary. The entire fabric of politics was tested by the impact of economic recession after 1929. This impact, and the measures thought necessary to deal with it, divided Ramsay MacDonald's Cabinet and brought down the Labour government. In consultation with senior Conservatives and Liberals, MacDonald formed a 'National government' which remained in office until May 1940. MacDonald was never forgiven by the left for his 'betrayal' of the labour movement.

The general election of 1931 confirmed the National government in office with a landslide victory. The Labour Party's representation, in contrast, shrank dramatically. The picture was only modified at the next election in 1935. In effect, the National government was dominated by the Conservative Party, and its broad character was less convincing once most Liberals departed in 1933. Yet the government achieved striking success in uniting the anti-Labour vote. The political extremes of left and right both grew as a direct consequence of the Depression, but neither Communism nor Fascism attracted mass support during this period. Unlike other major democracies, Britain managed to contain the bulk of political debate within the parliamentary system.

Conservatives and Labour 1929–31

Conservatives in opposition

The election of October 1929 was the last truly three-cornered contest of the inter-war years. The Conservatives, fighting on a 'safety first' platform, won more votes than Labour but fewer seats. Stanley Baldwin was unwilling to do a deal with the Liberals, and so MacDonald was enabled to form a minority Labour government.

Soon after the 1929 election defeat a movement developed within the Conservative Party to remove Baldwin, helped by the rightwards shift of much of the party. This was seen particularly in the campaign, led by the press lords Rothermere and Beaverbrook, to commit the Conservatives to full trade protectionism. Although this was achieved by October 1930, there remained divisions within the party. The recently ennobled former Conservative MP William Bridgeman took stock of the party's situation in his diary.

10.1　William Bridgeman on the Conservatives in opposition, 1929–30 (in P. Williamson, ed., *The Modernisation of Conservative Politics: The Diaries and Letters of William Bridgeman 1904–1935*, London, The Historians' Press, 1988, pp. 223–6).

■ July [1929] The election is over, the Socialists in office, the Liberals if they are united could just turn them out by voting with us. I am a peer, facing a Govt. front bench with about seven men on it, and no followers at all behind, and I have time to take a survey of the last six months, and make some comments on the Govt. of 1924–29.

The last few months before the election were spent mainly in preparing our case for the electors, & devising a few attractions for the voters to induce them to return us again …

The election was lost, not I think from any wave of resentment against the Govt. & certainly not against Baldwin, nor on any one particular piece of policy or legislation. Of the items which together produced our defeat I put the love of change common to all democracies or the swing of the pendulum as some call it, as the first; after that the coincidence of reassessment with the derating bill which greatly prejudiced the latter, the cry of 'Safety First', the rather lukewarm action of past years in Safeguarding, the failure of most candidates to explain the Derating Bill, and put it forward as it ought to have been, as a winning card, and the wild promises of Liberals & Labour. Of course the money of L. George & his insistence on fighting every seat gave Socialism a victory which they could not have won, if arrangements had been made to avoid three-cornered fights where it was sure to lose the seat to a Socialist …

On the whole the Govt. of 1924–29 can well be proud of its achievement, & Baldwin of the way he kept us together. At first he was disinclined to give a lead firm enough to be useful in Cabinet, and though he got much better in throwing in his weight at the right moment, I think his fault is to be too sanguine that things will come right without his having to take a strong line … ■

A year later, Bridgeman reflected on the fate of the Conservatives since the 1929 election.

■ July [1930] After the Election of 1929 we had a display of the worst qualities of the Conservative Party under the effects of defeat. Everyone, and especially those who had done least to help, sought to find some reason for the failure, too often unfortunately in personal fault-finding against Baldwin's leadership, or the conduct of Davidson [Chairman of the Conservative Party, who was obliged to resign in 1930] at the Central Office – in both cases very unfair. Baldwin was very much in the same position as Balfour had been during his last term of office 1900–5 in having to try & reconcile two sections of his party – the advanced protectionists & the timid semi-free-traders. Both had to suffer the accusation of want of boldness in leadership. The election was really lost by the failure of candidates to take advantage of our great derating measure, which they funked on the platform, because of the difficulty of disentangling the assessment from the Relief of Rates. If the assessment could have been a year sooner, it would have been an easier task. The swing of the pendulum too was a tremendous force against us. But we might have borne the defeat with more dignity & less internecine recriminations. ■

The Second Labour government

Labour emerged in 1929 as the largest party in Parliament, with 287 seats compared to the Conservatives' 260. The Liberals, holding the balance of power, had 59. There was a brief period of exhilaration as MacDonald formed his second minority Labour government. As Britain's economic position worsened, however, this mood quickly changed. Fundamentally, Labour's problem was that it had produced a great deal of rhetoric but few practical ideas on how to tackle mounting unemployment. Another difficulty was the government's dependence on the tacit consent of the Liberals, the party which MacDonald had sought to eliminate in the 1920s, and on the Liberals' enthusiasm for electoral reform.

Early in 1930 Lloyd George pressed for a deal with the government whereby continued Liberal support for Labour would be rewarded by the introduction of proportional representation. MacDonald's uneasiness was captured in his record of a meeting with Lloyd George on 3 February.

10.2   Ramsay MacDonald, note, 4 February 1930 (PRO 30/69/1305).

■ ... I am a little disturbed about the possible development of the conversation we had with Mr Lloyd George yesterday. In general terms, I am in favour of some agreement, but I am not in favour of making it definite in details or committing it to writing. We should apply the conditions which, without hampering either Party, were observed after the second election of 1910, when we held a balance and kept the Liberals in.

If we go further than that, we shall have to face the following difficulties: –

1. Neither an agreement nor an understanding can be kept private, and

will have reactions on the spirit of the Party, both inside and outside the House of Commons.

2. Its details will be almost impossible to fix, and once we admit that we are definitely in the hands of the Liberals and cannot in any way appeal for consideration at the hands of the Conservatives, the attempt to fix details from week to week will put us more and more in a position subordinate to the Liberals.

3. It will strengthen Mr Lloyd George's grip upon his own Party and will increase his authority in the country.

4. It will hamper us at bye-elections and generally in carrying on in the country an offensive against the Liberals.

5. It will commit us to a Government Electoral Reform measure, and in the present temper of our Party no such measure could be introduced in an agreed form. It would lead us to an abandonment of any expectation we may have [of] returning to a two-Party system.

6. Up to the present we have kept the initiative in our hands, however troublesome some of the situations which have arisen and will arise, may be. If, as I see it, we will have to face a conflict with the House of Lords sooner or later, that will put the Liberals very much in our hands and we should lose whatever advantage that will give us.

7. We should, therefore, delay the conversations and endeavour to go on week by week negotiating on troubles as they arise. That undoubtedly leaves our tenure of office somewhat uncertain, but the price we shall pay for a two years' security will be so high that we cannot pay it. ■

Political Crisis and Formation of the National Government

Faced with deepening economic problems at the start of the 1930s, some members of the Labour government, notably the junior minister Sir Oswald Mosley, called for radical policy initiatives. The Chancellor of the Exchequer, Philip Snowden, warned that experiments in economic policy would undermine international financial confidence and make matters worse. Like MacDonald, he was convinced that socialism could only be achieved on the basis of thriving capitalist foundations. The leadership's response to the looming crisis was therefore highly conventional, involving cuts in taxation and public spending.

As the budget went into deficit, Snowden attempted to force his Cabinet colleagues to appreciate the nature of the crisis by publishing the report of the May Committee in

July 1931. This called for sweeping cuts in public spending, but, coming at the same time as a financial crisis in Europe, it served only to encourage panic and a flight from the pound. Equally, opposition to the proposed cuts from the labour movement was firm, as MacDonald recalled when describing his meeting with a Trades Union Congress delegation on 20 August at the height of the crisis.

10.3   Ramsay MacDonald, diary, 21 August 1931 (PRO 30/69/1753).

■ ... [The delegation] included Citrine, Bevin ... Their statement was that they were not to support the policy indicated by us in the afternoon, that we could balance the Budget by taxing the rentier, suspending the Sinking Fund and such like, but no economies. Chancellor replied and I observed that all I had to say was that their observations did not touch our problems arising out of immediate financial necessity. They withdrew. It was practically a declaration of war. I was very tired and snatched a few minutes rest whilst Henderson once more told us what he had proposed two days ago and how everything had been initiated by him – except the things opposed by the T.U.C. people. He surrendered. He proposed to balance the Budget with insignificant economies, keep the Unemployed assistance what it is now ... suspending Sinking Funds (which he stated many times was his proposal) made days ago ... and putting on a revenue tariff. How tired of it all one feels. We had a rather pointless discussion without concentrating on the one point of any importance: 'Are we to go on?' Henderson never showed his vanity and ignorance more painfully. I told them to go to bed and we rose at 11 p.m. I was depressed and saw nothing but great humiliation for us all. The T.U.C. undoubtedly voice the feeling of the mass of workers. They do not know and their minds are rigid and think of superficial appearances and so grasping at the shadow lose the bone. ■

On 21 August 1931 the Cabinet reluctantly agreed to cuts in government spending, but on nothing like the scale sought by the May Committee. On 23 August, eleven out of twenty Cabinet ministers voted for a 10 per cent cut in unemployment benefit, which the Bank of England had deemed essential if Britain were to obtain foreign credits. As the opponents in Cabinet included the Foreign Secretary, Arthur Henderson, MacDonald saw no alternative to offering the government's resignation. The following extract records the Cabinet's discussions.

10.4 Cabinet meeting minutes, 23 August 1931 (PRO CAB 23/67).

■ ... The Prime Minister informed the Cabinet that a situation had now to be faced of a peculiarly difficult character because, if the Labour Party was not prepared to join with the Conservative and Liberal Parties in accepting the proposals as a whole, the condition mentioned in Mr. Harrison's message regarding a national agreement would not be fulfilled.

So far as he was concerned, he was strongly in favour of such acceptance while at the same time making it clear that the scheme represented the extreme limit to which he was prepared to go.

The Country was suffering from lack of confidence abroad. There was, as yet, no panic at home but the Prime Minister warned the Cabinet of the calamitous nature of the consequences which would immediately and inevitably follow from a financial panic and a flight from the pound. No one could be blind to the very great political difficulties in which the giving effect to the proposals as a whole would involve the Government.

But when the immediate crisis was over and before Parliament met, it would be possible to give the Labour Party that full explanation of the circumstances which had rendered it necessary for the Government to formulate such a drastic scheme, which could not be given at the moment. The only alternative was a reduction of not 10 per cent, but of at least 20 per cent, and he could not believe that the Labour Party would reject the proposals when they knew the true facts of the position: he was confident, indeed, that a majority of the Party would accept them. A scheme which inflicted reductions and burdens in almost every other direction, but made no appreciable cut in Unemployment Insurance benefit, would alienate much support and lose the Party their moral prestige which was one of their greatest assets. In conclusion, the Prime Minister said that it must be admitted that the proposals as a whole represented the negation of every-thing that the Labour Party stood for, and yet he was absolutely satisfied that it was in the national interest to implement them if the country was to be secured. He then pointed out that, if on this question there were any important resignations, the Government as a whole must resign.

Each member of the Cabinet then expressed his views on the question of the inclusion, or otherwise, in the proposals of the 10 per cent reduction in Unemployment Insurance benefit. In the course of these expressions of view, indications were given that, while a majority of the Cabinet favoured the inclusion in the economy proposals of the 10 per cent reduction in Unemployment Insurance benefit, the adoption of this as part and parcel of the scheme would involve the resignation of certain Ministers from the Government. ■

Encouraged by King George V, on 24 August 1931 Macdonald formed a 'National government', composed of Conservatives and Liberals, plus three of MacDonald's former Labour colleagues, to deal with the immediate crisis. The bulk of the Labour Party was left behind in opposition. For the Conservatives, Baldwin welcomed the coalition as a means of taming his own party's right wing, while Sir Herbert Samuel, the Liberal leader, saw an opportunity to return his party to the centre of political activity. J.C.C. Davidson, then Chancellor of the Duchy of Lancaster and until 1930 Chairman of the Conservative Party, provided the following account of the National government's formation in his draft memoirs.

10.5   **J.C.C. Davidson, diary, 23/24 August 1931 (in R.R. James, ed.,**
      Memoirs of a Conservative: J.C.C. Davidson's Memoirs and Papers 1910–37,
      London, Weidenfeld & Nicolson, 1969, pp. 370–1).

■ Shortly after the Cabinet dispersed, S[tanley] B[aldwin] went to Downing Street in response to a request from MacDonald. Samuel had already arrived and within a few minutes they were joined by Neville Chamberlain and Josiah Stamp. MacDonald told them of the situation in the Cabinet, and of his advice to the King. It was quite clear that he intended to resign and that he had no intention of joining in a Coalition, even though the King had urged him to head one. Neville, however, pressed on him the support in the country that he would bring to such an administration and the effect it would have in restoring confidence. His arguments seemed to have no effect. To every one else at the meeting it seemed quite certain that MacDonald intended to resign, and SB returned from it convinced that he would have to form a Government. Nor did he think this a bad thing since, as I had emphasized before, he had little love for Coalitions.

The next morning [Monday, 24 August] all was dramatically changed. The Party leaders were to meet with the King at 10 a.m. and I walked with SB to the Palace. Their discussions lasted for two hours and ended in complete agreement. The King had urged that MacDonald should not resign, and both Baldwin and Samuel had agreed to serve under him. By noon, they had decided on the terms of their relationship. There was to be no Coalition, but a co-operation of individuals to cope with the emergency. Once the required measures had been passed, Parliament would be dissolved and the Parties could go to the country independently. The King was then told of their decision and MacDonald set out for Downing Street to tell the Cabinet what had been decided.

SB walked back from the Palace with me and told me everything that had happened. He immediately consulted with his colleagues and told them that he had agreed in their name to join the Administration, and they completely supported his action. MacDonald resigned at four o'clock that afternoon and was immediately commissioned to form a National Government. The remainder of that evening and the next day were taken up with prolonged and sometimes acrimonious discussion about the membership of the new Cabinet. In the end, despite Neville Chamberlain's claims for Hailsham, it was agreed that SB should be joined by Neville, Hoare and Cunliffe-Lister. MacDonald, Snowden, Thomas and Lord Sankey were to remain in the Labour Cabinet, and the membership was completed by Samuel and Reading. The new Cabinet was sworn in on 26 August. ■

The National government quickly implemented the government spending cuts proposed in August 1931, but ironically proved unable to defend the gold standard, which had been its prime purpose. Bewildered and angry at recent developments, the Labour Party, having expelled MacDonald and his three Labour colleagues in the National gov-

*ernment, and backed by the TUC, distanced itself from the government in a manifesto
issued soon after the crisis.*

10.6   *Labour's Joint Manifesto*, 1931 (reported in *The Times*, 28 August 1931).

■ The following manifesto was yesterday approved and issued by the joint
meeting of the Trades Union Congress General Council, the National
Executive Committee of the Labour Party, and the Consultative Committee
of the Parliamentary Labour Party:

A financial crisis, the true causes of which have not been publicly
explained, has brought about the sudden resignation of the Labour
Government.

Forces in finance and politics made demands which no Labour
Government could accept. A new Coalition Government, for which the
Labour Movement repudiates all responsibility, has been formed. It is a
Government of persons acting without authority from the people.

It is determined to attack the standard of living of the workers in order to
meet a situation caused by a policy pursued by private banking interests in
the control of which the public has no part.

It seeks to enforce a complete change in national policy: not because the
nation's resources have suddenly diminished, not because the nation
cannot afford to provide for its unemployed, not because the Budget
cannot be balanced, but primarily financial interests have decided that this
country is setting a bad example to other countries in taxing the rich to
provide for the necessities of the poor.

Fundamentally, it is an attempt to reverse the social policy which in this
country has within limits provided for the unemployed, the aged and the
sick, the disabled, the orphaned, and the widowed. Unemployment benefit
is attacked on the ground that it strengthens resistance to wage reductions.

The new government's policy has yet to be fully disclosed, but the
knowledge that it is irrevocably committed to serious cuts ... has roused
the entire Labour movement to determined opposition.

The justification offered for these methods is the existence of a financial
crisis which has been aggravated beyond measure by deliberately alarmist
statements in sections of the Press and by a protracted campaign that has
created the impression abroad that Great Britain is on the verge of
bankruptcy. Nothing could be farther from the truth ...

If the will were present we could overcome the immediate difficulty by
mobilising the country's foreign investment, by a temporary suspension of
the Sinking Fund, by taxing fixed interest securities and other unearned
income, which had benefited by the fall in prices, and by measures to
reduce the burden of War debts.

The phrase 'equality of sacrifice' has been invoked as a justification for cuts in social expenditure, but no comparable sacrifice has so far been demanded from the wealthier sections of the community ...

The present crisis is essentially part of a bigger one. The policy of the Labour Movement for national reconstruction and international co-operation, including a reconsideration of the problem of debts and reparations, provides the only basis for the restoration of credit and the re-establishment of world prosperity.

The forces of Labour are vitally concerned with the national interest, but we emphatically reject the view that this can only be secured by the impoverishment of the workers. We therefore call upon the masses of the people and all men and women of good will to stand firmly against the new Government and to rally to the aid of the Labour Movement in its defence of true national interests and its constructive efforts towards the new social order. ■

When the immediate financial crisis of 1931 had been dealt with, MacDonald, with strong Conservative encouragement, decided that a general election was necessary to restore the country's unity and confidence. During the bitter campaign which followed, MacDonald asked the electorate for a 'doctor's mandate' to use whatever methods seemed appropriate to achieve recovery. The National government's appeal was broad. Above all, it alone appeared to have, in protectionism, a policy designed to address the country's economic ills. Its manifesto stressed the 'non-party' character of the government, an apparently persuasive factor.

10.7   **Ramsay MacDonald's** *National Labour Manifesto,* **1931 (F.W.S. Craig,** *British General Election Manifestos 1900–1974,* **London, Macmillan, 1975, pp. 91–9).**

■ The Present National Government was formed in haste to meet a swiftly approaching crisis. It stopped borrowing, imposed economy, and balanced the Budget.

World conditions and internal financial weakness, however, made it impossible for the Government to achieve its immediate object. Sterling came off gold and the country must now go through a period of recovery and readjustment during which steps of the utmost importance, nationally and internationally, must be taken to secure stability and avoid a recurrence of recent troubles.

A monetary policy which will establish sterling in confidence and authority, international agreements which will remove some of the most fruitful causes of the economic misfortunes – like War Debts and Reparations – from which the whole world now suffers so grievously, plans to change any adverse into a favourable balance of trade, will have to be set going without delay.

In the background of this work, and studied at every point in connection with it, must be the question of unemployment, especially in its most important aspect of finding work by the expansion of markets, both at home and abroad.

WE MUST ALL PULL TOGETHER

The Government will have to come to grips with a great variety of problems, and apply, confident of general national support, its decisions regarding them.

These are times of exceptional national urgency and exceptional conditions, which demand exceptional treatment. As it is impossible to foresee in the changing conditions of to-day what may arise, no one can set out a programme of detail on which specific pledges can be given.

The Government must therefore be free to consider every proposal likely to help, such as tariffs, expansion of exports, and contraction of imports, commercial treaties, and mutual economic arrangements with the Dominions. It must watch how the devaluation of money and the economies which had to be made to balance the Budget affect the lives of our people, and take every step which can be made effective to protect them against exploitation.

It must be made plain, however, that whilst everything possible will be done to meet hardship, the Budget must not be allowed to slip into deficits. The possibility of home and Imperial development in all its aspects must be studied.

The Government is to be comprehensively national, and not sectional, in the obligations which it is to keep before it. In these days of transition and uncertainty we must all pull together, and by our co-operation now, strive to put a new spirit of energy and hope into our people.

NATIONAL UNITY ESSENTIAL

Whilst our present conditions last, these things cannot be done by political parties fighting partisan battles on platforms and in Parliament. But they must not involve a loss of political identity, because the immediate tasks are temporary, and, when finished, will be followed by normal political activities.

They do mean, however, a willing co-operation between all political parties, acting through their representatives and shouldering joint responsibility for discussion, examination, and action. National unity through the co-operation of parties – all the parties by preference, if that were possible – is as essential now as it was in August ... ◼

10.8 Conservative and Labour Party posters, 1931 general election (Conservative Party Archives; British Library).

The general election held in October 1931 gave the National government an overwhelming victory, with a total of 554 MPs elected, of whom 473 were Conservatives. The Liberals, partners in the government, fared badly, returning 72 MPs. For Labour, however, the result was a disaster. The party's parliamentary representation was slashed to 52 seats, though its vote had fallen by only a quarter. Moreover, most of the party's leadership lost their seats.

Beatrice Webb, the Fabian socialist and a leading intellectual within the labour movement, offered the following reflections on the electoral humiliation of October 1931, and on its implications for the future.

10.9 Beatrice Webb, diary, October 1931 (N. and J. Mackenzie, eds, *The Diary of Beatrice Webb, Vol. IV: 1924–43*, London, Virago, 1985, pp. 263–4).

■ The Parliamentary Labour Party has been not defeated but annihilated, largely, we think, by the women's vote. On the Front Opposition Bench there will be only one ex-Cabinet Minister – George Lansbury; only two ex-Ministers of rank – Stafford Cripps and Attlee; with one or two ex-Under Secretaries and Household Officers. This Parliament will last four or five years; and the Labour Party will be out of office for at least ten years. The capitalists will remain, for this fourth decade of the twentieth century, in complete and unchallenged control of Great Britain, as they are of the U.S.A., France and Italy. Meanwhile the Labour Movement may discover a philosophy, a policy and a code of personal conduct all of which we lack today. The desertion of the three leaders was not the cause of our defeat; it was the final and most violent symptom of the disease from which the Party was suffering ...

The Great War and the world upheaval brought the Labour Party on to the Front Opposition Bench and transformed it into a definitely Socialist party. Two spells of office and the embraces of the old governing class converted the more prominent leaders into upholders of the existing order. Gradually becoming conscious of their leaders' lack of faith, the P.L.P. rapidly disintegrated. The dramatic desertion of the three leaders on the eve of the battle turned a certain defeat into a rout. But it revealed a solid core of seven million stalwart Labour supporters, mostly convinced Socialists. Whether new leaders will spring up with sufficient faith, will-power and knowledge to break through the tough and massive defences of British profit-making capitalism with its press and its pulpits, its Royalties and House of Lords, its elaborate financial entanglements of credit and currency all designed to maintain intact ancient loyalties, and when necessary, promote panics in favour of the status quo, I cannot foresee. Have we the material in the British Labour Movement from which can be evolved something of the nature of a religious order – a congregation of the faithful who will also be skilful technicians in social reconstruction? What undid the two Labour Governments was not merely their lack of knowledge and the will to apply what knowledge they had, but also their acceptance, as individuals, of the way of life of men of property and men of rank ... The Labour Party leaders have shown that they have neither the faith, the code of conduct, nor the knowledge needed for the equalitarian state. ■

The National Government after 1931

After the 1931 election, the National government enjoyed a commanding lead in Parliament. In the new Cabinet formed by MacDonald, Conservatives and Liberals were dominant. Of its 20 members, 11 were Conservatives, 5 were Liberals, and 4 'National Labour' – that is, the four defectors from the second Labour government. Although some Conservatives grumbled at this over-representation of their junior partners, the key economic posts went to Conservatives. Furthermore, Baldwin worked closely with MacDonald, who was now in a difficult and isolated position. When Baldwin replaced the ailing MacDonald as Prime Minister in 1935, the Conservative character of the National government became even more apparent.

By 1935 economic recovery was becoming apparent. Unemployment was declining, the cuts of 1931 had been restored, and taxes had been reduced. The National government, having relented over the Unemployment Assistance Board crisis early in 1935 (see Chapter 9), appeared competent. The Conservative Party was no longer deeply divided over the future of India and in foreign affairs the government had committed itself to collective action, through sanctions, against the aggression of Mussolini's Italy – thereby robbing Labour of one of its main platforms. Baldwin, as Prime Minister, appeared therefore to be in a strong position when he led the National government into the general election of November 1935. In its campaign, the government stressed the need to continue the stability achieved since 1931, especially in the face of uncertainty in international affairs.

10.10 A Call to the Nation: The Joint Manifesto of the Leaders of the National Government, 1935 (F.W.S. *Craig, British General Election Manifestos 1900–1974*, Macmillan, London, 1975, pp. 102–7).

■ The decision of the Nation four years ago to put its trust in a National Government, formed from various Parties in the State, was a turning point in the history of Britain and has exercised a profound influence upon the course of international events. Under this leadership we have emerged from the depths of depression to a condition of steadily returning prosperity, and the name of Britain stands high in the councils of the world. There now falls upon the people of this country the grave responsibility of exercising a choice which may well prove equally momentous for the future.

The broad issue is whether the stability and confidence which the National Government have built up are to be preserved in a period of special difficulty and anxiety. But we have considered it right, for the information of the Electors, to set forth on behalf of a united Government their general aims and policy on various aspects of home and foreign affairs ...

The advent to power of the Labour Opposition, pledged to a number of revolutionary measures of which the ultimate results could not be clearly foreseen, would inevitably be followed by a collapse of confidence. The measures we have outlined above can only be carried through if the resources of the country are such as to enable it to support the necessary cost. Those resources must be derived from the income of the country, and that income can only increase if the country can rely on a period in which stability will be assured and confidence remain undisturbed.

The international situation reinforced the same lesson. The influence of Britain among other nations, now so conspicuous, could never be maintained under an Administration drawn from a Party whose leaders of experience in foreign affairs no longer co-operate with it, and which is hopelessly divided on the most important points in foreign policy.

In present circumstances it is more than ever necessary that the British Government should not only be united among themselves, but that they should represent that spirit of national co-operation which will best secure the confidence and respect of the world. ■

The result of the 1935 election was another victory for the National government, which won 432 seats compared to Labour's 154. Labour, with an inexperienced leadership and policies still being developed, failed to attract the all-important 'middle ground' of former Liberal voters.

Despite, or perhaps because of, its electoral strength, the National government faced growing internal challenges in the later 1930s. The most vocal criticism came from those, like Churchill, Anthony Eden and Duff Cooper, who opposed the 'appeasement' of Hitler and Mussolini. Arguably more significant in the long term, however, were calls from a younger generation of Conservative MPs for more progressive social and economic policies. Among these a leading figure was Harold Macmillan, MP for Stockton and a future Conservative Prime Minister. Macmillan's book, The Middle Way, published in 1938, advocated increased government intervention in the economy, planning and public works, thus preparing the ground for shifts in Conservative policies after 1945.

10.11 Harold Macmillan, *The Middle Way: A Study of the Problem of Economic and Social Progress in a Free and Democratic Society,* **1938 (London, Macmillan, pp. 93–7).**

■ I do not intend to discuss the relative merits or demerits of the different dictatorships – Fascist, Nazi or Communist. They have each sprung from different economic, social, and psychological circumstances and they have been dominated by totally different ideologies aiming at different objectives. I am merely concerned with pointing the lesson. In the long run no class, no social group, no nation can benefit from the adoption of those methods which run contrary to the best impulses in mankind. Certainly no man is qualified to withstand the influence of such unrelieved power; and the whole future progress of humanity will depend upon our ability to resist the spread of this tyranny and find along the paths of human freedom a solution to our problems which will be based upon consent and not upon coercion.

Even if it could be shown that these methods were desirable, they are, as far as this country is concerned, still happily impossible. Neither the Fascist nor the Communist revolutionary technique holds out the slightest hope of success with us within any period of time it is possible to foresee. Nor will that time ever come, if we make an intelligent effort to deal with our social problems now. The policy of the official Labour movement, which renounces the methods of violence, is a very different matter, but it seems to me to be making a similar error. In alluding to the apparent contradictions between man's desire for economic advancement depending upon the discipline of co-operation, and his desire for personal liberation which frees him from disciplines and restraints, I suggested that it was the task of statesmanship to reconcile these opposites in a policy which produced greater compensations and lesser sacrifices. What has been said regarding the totalitarian States comes into my argument as a warning as to the kind of error into which we are prone to fall ...

My contention is that the way in which these opposite desires of men are to be reconciled is by a clear differentiation as between the proper sphere of State, social, or co-operative activity, and the proper sphere to be deliberately reserved for private enterprise.

The Socialist relies upon the argument of poverty and insecurity as evidence of the failure of Capitalist society, and proposes, not a direct attack on the immediate causes of poverty, but a complete reconstruction of society on Socialist lines. He argues from the particular to the general, and he is led into an acceptance of what might be called 'economic totalitarianism'. Along this route he might achievé a considerable elimination of poverty, but the further he goes the greater will become the danger of a surrender of individual liberty. By applying his theory to the whole of economic activity he will produce a state of affairs in which human life will be compressed within a common pattern; and in which the individual will be forced to conform to the kind of life which others think he ought to lead...

Instead of liberating the individual – even assuming that poverty is abolished – such a society will enslave him by the subordination of his personal desires and tastes into conformity with a national policy. It makes little difference to the individual even if the democratice forms are preserved and the infringements of his leisure and cultural opportunity are the result of majority decisions. It may be argued that he will be receiving a greater return in terms of economic wealth for the labour he is expending. He may be given motor cars, dress clothes, and circuses, but this will be no compensation to an individual who desires leisure for the expression of his individuality in quite uneconomic ways. For he will be asking to be allowed to contract out of a social obligation to produce more and more of the things that the State power, or the majority of the citizens, desire to have. This is precisely what the ruling group in such a community cannot permit.

The purpose of these arguments has been to show why I reject the approach to our problem adopted by the different schools of political thought. I reject the old method of humanitarian social reform on the basis of a transference of wealth through taxation, because it has reached almost the limits of what it can achieve. It is an obsolete and inadequate policy in the circumstances of today. I reject the Fascist and the Communist theories of violent change because (a) they are politically impossible, and (b) the revolutionary seizure of power would be, and must be, followed by a political tyranny in which man's cultural freedom (which is the prerequisite of human progress) would be sacrificed. I reject the constitutional Socialist approach because, even if their 'economic totalitarianism' would work without political tyranny, it would sacrifice the beneficial dynamic element that private enterprise can give to society when exercised in its proper sphere, and because it would not provide the scope for human diversity which is essential if men are really to be free. But the most important reason for the rejection of these theories is that they are remote from what is immediately practicable in the circumstances of our time. ■

In 1936 King George V died and was succeeded by Edward VIII, a popular Prince of Wales, but one whose public statements on government policies had sometimes caused embarrassment in official circles. The immediate cause of the abdication crisis of 1936 was Edward's wish to marry an American divorcee, Wallis Simpson. Though there was some sympathy for the King, the Church of England, the Dominions and the bulk of public opinion seemed to oppose the marriage. Baldwin played a central role in the delicate discussions with Edward which led ultimately to his abdication. Having successfully dealt with the crisis, Baldwin was able to resign and hand over power to Neville Chamberlain following the coronation of Edward's brother, George VI, in May 1937. Speaking to the House of Commons in December 1936, immediately after Edward's abdication speech, Baldwin described the issues which had been at stake.

10.12 Stanley Baldwin on the abdication crisis, 10 December 1936 (*Hansard*, 5th ser., 318: 2176–87).

■ I told His Majesty that I had two great anxieties – one the effect of a continuance of the kind of criticism that at that time was proceeding in the American Press, the effect it would have in the Dominions and particularly in Canada, where it was widespread, the effect it would have in this country.

That was the first anxiety. And then I reminded him of what I had often told him and his brothers in years past. The British Monarchy is a unique institution. The Crown in this country through the centuries has been deprived of many of its prerogatives, but to-day, while that is true, it stands for far more than it ever has done in its history. The importance of its integrity is, beyond all question, far greater than it has ever been, being as it is not only the last link of Empire that is left, but the guarantee in this country so long as it exists in that integrity, against many evils that have affected and afflicted other countries. There is no man in this country, to whatever party he may belong, who would not subscribe to that. But while this feeling largely depends on the respect that has grown up in the last three generations for the Monarchy, it might not take so long, in face of the kind of criticisms to which it was being exposed, to lose that power far more rapidly than it was built up, and once lost I doubt if anything could restore it ...

I then pointed out the danger of the divorce proceedings, that if a verdict was given in that case that left the matter in suspense for some time, that period of suspense might be dangerous, because then everyone would be talking, and when once the Press began, as it must begin some time in this country, a most difficult situation would arise for me, for him, and there might well be a danger which both he and I had seen all through this ... that there might be sides taken and factions grow up in this country in a matter where no faction ought ever to exist ...

He [the King] sent for me again Wednesday, 25th November. In the meantime a suggestion had been made to me that a possible compromise might be arranged ... The compromise was that the King should marry, that Parliament should pass an Act enabling the lady to be the Queen's wife without the position of Queen; and when I saw His Majesty on 25th November he asked me whether that proposition had been put to me, and I said yes. He asked me what I thought of it. I told him that I had not considered it ... I said that if he desired it I would examine it formally. He said he did so desire. Then I said, 'It will mean my putting that formally before the whole Cabinet and communicating with the Prime Ministers of all the Dominions.' ...

On 2nd December the King asked me to go and see him. Again I had intended asking for an audience later that week, because such inquiries as I thought proper to make I had not completed. The inquiries had gone far enough to show that neither in the Dominions nor here would there be any prospect of such legislation being accepted ...

The House must remember – it is difficult to realise – that His Majesty is not a boy, although he looks so young. We have all thought of him as our Prince, but he is a mature man, with wide and great experience of life and the world, and he always had before him three, nay, four, things, which in these conversations at all hours, he repeated again and again – That if he went he would go with dignity. He would not allow a situation to arise in which he could not do that. He wanted to go with as little disturbance of his Ministers and his people as possible. He wished to go in circumstances that would make the succession of his brother as little difficult for his brother as possible; and I may say that any idea to him of what might be called a King's party, was abhorrent ...

This House to-day is a theatre which is being watched by the whole world. Let us conduct ourselves with that dignity which His Majesty is showing in this hour of his trial ... We have, after all, as the guardians of democracy in this little island to see that we do our work to maintain the integrity of that democracy and of the monarchy, which ... is now the sole link of our whole Empire and the guardian of our freedom ... ■

Labour in the 1930s

Throughout the 1930s the Labour Party was preoccupied with digesting the lessons, and repairing the damage, of 1931. The most immediate effect of the election disaster had been the removal of much of the party's leadership from Parliament. MacDonald was expelled from the Labour Party soon after he formed the National government. The only former Cabinet minister who retained his seat was the ageing pacifist George Lansbury, veteran champion of municipal socialism in the East End of London in the 1920s. In the wake of the crisis, the party shifted to the left. Theories that the disaster was the unavoidable consequence of trying to work within a capitalist framework became temporarily popular, paving the way for radical policy statements, such as the 1933 party conference decision to prevent a future war by calling a general strike.

One of Labour's greatest problems in the 1930s was maintaining party unity. Soon after 1931 relations between the Labour Party and its affiliate, the Independent Labour

Party, deteriorated. Unimpressed by Labour's record in government, and arguing that the Labour Party clung to a 'reformist' outlook, the ILP formally disaffiliated in 1932. Some former ILP members combined with sections of the Labour left to form a new Socialist League, in which the dominant voice was that of Stafford Cripps. Initially successful, the League became marginalised within the party, in part because it advocated closer ties with other parties on the left, such as the Communist Party, regarding which Labour's leadership remained suspicious and hostile. By 1937 the League was obliged to disband.

10.13 Stafford Cripps, 'Can socialism come by Constitutional means?', London, Socialist League, 1933, pp. 37–8, 42–3).

■ Those who have held radical and humanitarian views have counted upon the pressure of the ever-widening democratic basis of the electoral franchise to compel capitalism to yield better and better terms to the workers. In the pre-war period this theory of gradual advance seemed plausible enough. With a growing national prosperity, the national standard of living showed a steady rise. Capitalism was ready to pay a price for its continued control in the form of higher wages and fuller and better social services of all kinds. During and immediately after the war this tendency became more developed. The workers demonstrated their strength and their power to protect capitalism with their lives and their labour; their demands were satisfied so far as the capitalists considered it economically possible, but always with the reservation that nothing must be done to deprive capitalism of its effective power of control, whether in the financial, economic or political sphere.

As soon as it became apparent that the limit of concession was being reached and that, with a growing slump in world trade, capitalism would break down under the burden it had taken upon itself in more prosperous times, an immediate halt was called; the National Government was formed to protect capitalism and to bring about a rapid reversal of the progress by the withdrawal of the concessions which had been made to the workers. It was essential that the Government should be called National, as otherwise it might have occurred to the great mass of the electorate that it was merely a device to stabilise capitalism and not, as was claimed for it, a means to save the country ...

From the moment when the Government takes control rapid and effective action must be possible in every sphere of the national life. It will not be easy to detect the machinations of the capitalists, and, when discovered, there must be means ready to hand by which they can be dealt with promptly. The greatest danger point will be the financial and credit structure of the country and the Foreign Exchange position. We may liken the position that will arise somewhat to that which arose in August 1914, but with this difference, that at the beginning of the war the capitalists, though very nervous and excited, were behind the Government to a man, whereas when the Socialist Government takes office they will not only be nervous and excited but against the Government to a man. The Government's first step will be to call Parliament together at the earliest possible opportunity and place before it an Emergency Powers Bill to be passed through all its stages in one day. This Bill would be wide enough in its terms to allow all that will be immediately necessary to be done by ministerial orders. These orders must be incapable of challenge in the Courts or in any way except in the House of Commons.

This Bill must be ready in draft beforehand, together with the main orders that will be made immediately upon its becoming law.

It is probable that the passage of this Bill will raise in its most acute form the constitutional crisis. ■

The General Council of the TUC began gradually to reclaim its influence over Labour, urging that the party should aim for the step-by-step introduction of socialist measures. An important lesson of Labour's first two periods of office, however, was that its future policies needed to be carefully formulated and organised according to priority.

Although Labour's humiliation in 1931 cast a shadow over the next decade, the party gradually re-established itself in electoral terms, winning some notable by-election victories, such as that at East Fulham in 1933. However, the party's revival in local government was especially striking. In March 1934, under the guidance of Labour's London leader, Herbert Morrison, the party took control for the first time of the London County Council, the largest unit of local government in the country. The Labour press was understandably jubilant at this result, if prone to exaggerate its significance for the future.

10.14 Editorial on LCC elections, *Daily Herald*, 9 March 1934.

■   VICTORY!

Labour has captured London. Seldom in the history of municipal elections has there been a more decisive verdict than that given yesterday.

The 'Municipal Reformers' have paid the penalty for years of misgovernment, and, more particularly, for the pinchbeck policy they have pursued since economania began to hold sway.

Before the impetus of the attack of Labour, its demand for progressive administration, the tackling of the slum problem, for humane administration of public assistance, the champions of the Conservatives have gone down like ninepins.

Ignominious defeat, at North West Camberwell, is the lot of Mr. Webbe, leader of the 'Municipal Reformers', and protégé of Lord Beaverbrook ...

Unequivocally, also, London has expressed its preference for Labour against the Liberals. Their leader, Sir Percy Harris, has been defeated at Bethnal Green ...

What is the meaning of this sensational rejection of the Conservatives, this whole-hearted turning to Labour?

First it is clear that the electors of London are tired of the Conservative drift and apathy in municipal and national affairs. They want vigorous action; they want a progressive policy, and a determined tackling of social justice.

And it is not only in London that this spirit is evinced. In all parts of the country, and notably in areas where the Conservatives have hitherto held sway, Labour has made headway. ■

One of the most important consequences of the setback of 1931 was that it convinced Labour's leadership that the party required realistic policies before it next took office. Soon after the 1931 election, committees were established to produce these, under the growing influence of moderates such as Morrison and Hugh Dalton. In 1934 Labour produced For Socialism and Peace, *its first wide-ranging programme since the appearance of* Labour and the Nation *in 1928. This document clearly committed the party to a policy of nationalisation. It formed the basis of Labour's 1935 election manifesto, which, later modified into* Labour's Immediate Programme *(1937), established definite priorities and set the framework for Labour's post-1945 programme of legislation.*

10.15 *The Labour Party's Call to Power*, **1935 (London, Labour Party).**

■   FOUR BARREN YEARS

At the end of four years the country faces the grim spectacle of two million workless with an army of well over a million and a half people on the Poor Law, and with the deepening tragedy of the distressed areas. Whilst doles of varying kinds have been dispensed on a lavish scale to industry after industry, not a single constructive step has been taken to improve the lot of the people.

The Government has robbed the unemployed of benefit and subjected them to a harsh and cruel household means test.

It withdrew, under a storm of public indignation, its new Unemployment Regulations, and after nine months of reconsideration of this burning question it has ignominiously failed to produce any policy for the proper care of the unemployed ...

THE INTERNATIONAL SITUATION

The Government has a terrible responsibility for the present international situation. It did nothing to check the aggression of Japan in the Far East, and thus seriously discredited the League of Nations and undermined the Collective Peace System.

It has wrecked the Disarmament Conference by resisting all the constructive proposals made by other States. As regards air armaments, in particular, Lord Londonderry has boasted that he succeeded, though with great difficulty, in preventing an agreement for the complete abolition of all national air forces.

The Government has helped to restart the arms race, and it failed to make Signor Mussolini understand that, if he broke the peace in Africa, Britain would join with other nations in upholding the authority of the League ...

LABOUR'S PEACE POLICY

The Labour Party calls for a reversal of this suicidal foreign policy. It seeks whole-hearted co-operation with the League of Nations and with all States outside the League which desire peace. It stands firmly for the Collective Peace System. It demands speedy action, through the League, to bring the war in Africa to an end, to be followed by an immediate resumption of negotiations for all-round disarmament ...

A BOLD POLICY OF SOCIALIST RECONSTRUCTION

At home, the Labour Party will pursue its policy of Socialist Reconstruction. Labour has already put before the country, boldly and clearly, schemes of public ownership for the efficient conduct, in the national interest, of banking, coal and its products, transport, electricity, iron and steel, and cotton ...

Labour in power will attack the problem of the distressed areas by special steps designed to deal with the root causes of their troubles, as part of a vigorous policy of national planning. Labour will sweep away the humiliating means test imposed by the 'National' Government and will provide adequately for the unemployed, but will seek above all to reabsorb idle workers into productive employment by far-reaching schemes of national development. The Labour Party stands for a big move forward in education, including the raising of the school-leaving age with adequate maintenance allowances. It will vigorously develop the health services, and, in particular, will treat as one of its immediate concerns the terrible and neglected problem of maternal mortality. It favours an increase in the amount of old age pensions and a lowering of the qualifying age. It will go ahead with the provision of healthy homes for the people at reasonable rents, until the needs of the nation are fully met ... ■

As Labour gradually arrived at a more moderate position by the mid-1930s, the pacifist Lansbury became an increasingly isolated leader, out of step with his colleagues. Following a withering attack on pacifism by the powerful trade unionist Ernest Bevin at the 1935 party conference, Lansbury resigned and was succeeded on a temporary basis by his deputy, Clement Attlee. Immediately after Labour's defeat in the general election of November 1935, the party had to elect a new leader. Attlee defeated his rivals – Arthur Greenwood, widely distrusted in the party, and Morrison, whose power-base was too concentrated in London. Attlee, in contrast, had the backing of Bevin and the trade unions, and his unassuming personality and moderation made him acceptable to large sections of the party. He survived as leader until 1955, having been Prime Minister from 1945 to 1951.

Labour's left wing, and the Socialist League especially, could focus on several major 'causes' in the 1930s, including the rise of Fascism and the Spanish Civil War. A constant theme was the need for co-operation among the parties of the left against the threat of Fascism. In 1936 the Socialist League, the ILP and the Communist Party launched a 'Unity Campaign' to achieve this, and in their Unity Manifesto *called for vigorous left-wing policies. The Labour Party, anxious to woo moderate opinion, was firmly opposed to collaboration with the Communists, even though the latter had in 1933 stopped dismissing Labour as being 'social fascist'. Although the Unity Campaign was abandoned in 1937, followed soon after by the demise of the Socialist League, Cripps continued to advocate a 'popular front' on the left. In 1939 Cripps and his closest associates, George Strauss and Aneurin Bevan, were expelled from the Labour Party.*

10.16 The Unity Manifesto, 17 January 1937 (reported in *The Times*, 18 January 1937).

■ … Now is the time for the workers, conscious of their power and of the movement's strength of purpose, to wage incessant struggle, political and industrial alike, for simple things the workers need. Let the movement not wait for General Elections but now by active demonstration win and organize support for:–

Abolition of the Means Test.

T.U.C. scales of unemployment benefit.

National work of social value for Distressed Areas.

Forty-hour week in industry and the public service.

Paid holidays for all workers.

High wages, the abolition of tied cottages, for agricultural workers.

Coordinated trade union action for higher wages in industry, especially in mining, cotton, and sweated trades.

Non-contributory pensions of £1 at 60.

Immediate rehousing of the workers in town and countryside in houses that are homes.

Power to get back the land for the people.

Nationalization of the mining industry.

Effective control of the banks, the Stock Exchanges with their gambling and private profiteering – profiteering accentuated by the armament boom.

Making the rich pay for social amelioration.

We stand for action, for attack, for the ending of retreat, for the building of the strength, unity, and power of the working-class movement. ■

The Liberals in Decline

The 1930s witnessed the decline of the Liberal Party as a major influence in British politics. In 1929, though dismayed by the election result, the Liberals had still polled 5 million votes, and attempted to influence MacDonald's minority government. As the recession deepened, the unorthodox Liberal proposals of the late 1920s, such as those in the 'Yellow Book' (see Chapter 6), appeared more risky than ever; and, above all, the continuing Liberal adherence to free trade seemed out of step with the times.

The Liberals, and especially Sir Herbert Samuel, played a major role in the formation of the National government in 1931 and were rewarded with important posts in the new Cabinet. The 1931 election saw the Liberals clearly divided between free-trading 'Samuelites' and the 'Simonites', who were close to the Conservatives on many issues. 33 Samuelites and 35 Simonites were returned. An uncomfortable 'agreement to differ' over trade policy enabled the Samuelites to remain in the National government, but when protection was adopted in 1932 Samuel led his followers into opposition. In the 1935 general election only twenty-one Liberals were elected, Samuel losing his seat. By then the Liberals had ceased to be a major factor in politics. In his memoirs, Samuel reproduced the letter he had sent to King George V, who had been instrumental in forming the National government, explaining why the Liberals had chosen to resign from the government.

10.17 **Sir Herbert Samuel on the Liberals' resignation, 16 September 1932 (letter to Sir Clive Wigram, the King's Private Secretary, 16 September 1932, in Viscount Samuel, *Memoirs*, London, The Cresset Press, 1945, pp. 229–32).**

■ I feel that the King ought now to be informed of the reasons that animate the Liberal members of the Government in the course they are taking at this juncture …

We are very fully conscious that the national interest must suffer from the withdrawal from the Government of one of the sections which compose it, and which help to give it its unique position in the world. But, in our view, there are still graver disadvantages to the national interest in our remaining, if the announced policy of the Government is carried into effect. They are these.

1. The chief task which the Government set before itself at the time of its formation and at the General Election was to lift the country out of the terrible economic depression which has been prevailing, and to relieve it of the enormous burden of unemployment. The first condition of this was to balance the Budget, to stop borrowing for unemployment, to re-establish the national credit, and to save the £ sterling from collapse. We all united in that effort, and these objects were achieved. The means which should

next have been adopted to accomplish our purpose should have been for this country to play an active part in helping the world to rid itself of the restrictions on trade by tariffs, quotas and barriers of all kinds. These, in our view, are now the main cause of the economic disaster which continues to afflict the world, and our own country with the rest. Instead of doing this, the Government has itself built up an immense structure of similar restrictions. It is stated that this is in order to compel other countries to lessen their restrictions, but it has not had that effect.

2. Now come the Ottawa agreements, which pledge us to maintain many of those barriers to our foreign trade for a period of years, no matter what offers other countries might possibly make to us. The World Economic Conference offers an opportunity for trying to secure general reductions in tariffs. We ought to take the lead there. We shall be disqualified from doing so because at the very moment of its meeting we shall have been passing through Parliament yet another statute establishing a fresh series of permanent tariffs and quotas. The whole of the Government is united in declaring that such restrictions are mischievous. No one has been more emphatic in expressing this view than Mr. Baldwin. The actions of the Government are diametrically opposed to its declarations ...

If the leaders of the Liberal Party continue to be participants in a Government responsible for this policy, they will necessarily, and deservedly, forfeit the confidence of their followers. The Party will lose any possibility of offering to the electorate an alternative both to Protectionist Conservatism and to Socialism. The only real peril to national stability at the present time is the establishment in power of a Socialist Government with a policy such as that now advocated by the leaders of the Socialist Party. If the Liberal Party disappears from the political scene, that must some day come about. To expect otherwise would be to anticipate that Conservative Governments would continue in perpetuity, which would not be good for the country, and in any case is most improbable. We consider therefore that we have a definite obligation to the State to maintain the Liberal Party in being, and are convinced that the effect of our longer association in the present Government, with its present programme, would be to abandon that duty. Further, we should lose the representative authority we now possess, and would become of little value either to this Government now or to the country in the future ... ■

Communism

The Communist Party entered the period of depression hostile to the Labour Party and claiming to be the only authentic voice of the working class. Its relatively weak position at the start of the 1930s had changed significantly by the end of the decade.

In 1930 membership of the Communist Party in Britain was only half that in 1920, the year of its foundation, though when the Depression was at its trough, between late 1930 and early 1932, the party's size trebled. By 1939 membership had risen to 18,000, thanks largely to the recruitment of young middle-class intellectuals, and to the party's prominence in campaigning for the unemployed and organising resistance to Fascism – not only in Britain, but also during the Spanish Civil War, in which more than half the British volunteers who died were Communist Party members. Interest in the Communist Party also grew after 1933, when the party abandoned its 'class against class' line and sought closer links with the rest of the Labour movement.

10.18 **Membership of the Communist Party of Great Britain, 1929–39 (derived from J. Stevenson and C. Cook, *The Slump: Society and Politics during the Depression*, London, Quartet, 1979, p. 290).**

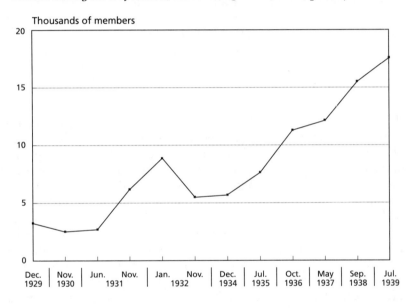

Probably the Communist Party's single most successful strategy during the 1930s was its campaigning on behalf of the unemployed through the National Unemployed Workers' Movement, founded in 1921. At a time when the trade unions and the Labour Party were often preoccupied with organisational or policy problems, the NUWM proved often to be the only effective representative of the interests of the unemployed, especially at a local level. As many as half a million people were members of the NUWM at some point in this period, although their involvement was usually transitory. The numerous 'hunger marches' organised by the NUWM were generally met with official suspicion, and sometimes dispersed by the police, in contrast to widespread approval for 'non-political' demonstrations such as the 'Jarrow Crusade' of 1936. Wal Hannington, National Organiser of the NUWM, later described his organisation's work and some of the problems it encountered.

10.19 Wal Hannington, *Unemployed Struggles*, 1936 (London, Lawrence & Wishart, pp. 219–20).

■ The new drastic threat to the standards of the unemployed in the form of the economy measures led the N.U.W.M. to organise a hunger march of Welsh miners to the Bristol Trades Union Congress at the beginning of September 1931, to call upon the congress to resist the attack. All over the country trade union branches were protesting against the new onslaught, but the T.U.C. ... was giving no lead for action.

The Welsh hunger marchers arrived in Bristol on the evening of Monday, 7th September. Mr. Walter Citrine, general secretary of the T.U.C., had announced that the marchers would not be permitted to state their case to the congress – an attitude which no doubt encouraged police hostility against the marchers. Following a demonstration in the Horsefair that evening, as the marchers were about to proceed peacefully to their sleeping quarters, the police tried to ban the march and launched a fierce baton charge; six workers were arrested.

The following day, 8th September, when Parliament re-opened under the provisional National government, a big demonstration of London unemployed mobilised in British Museum Square and marched to Parliament. Severe fighting took place in the vicinity of Whitehall and eighteen workers were arrested.

Two days later the Welsh unemployed marchers marched to the Trades Union Congress hall to press for the deputation to be heard. A powerful police cordon was drawn up to prevent them from reaching their objective, but a small deputation of six under my leadership were permitted to go through the cordon. When we reached the entrance to the congress hall we found our way barred by another force of police and hefty stewards. An altercation arose, and although there were only six of us we attempted to force an entry; a fierce fight took place at the top of the high steps, whilst the main body of marchers, 300 yards away, were being held back and threatened by the main police cordon. Our small deputation were finally overpowered by police and stewards and in the melée I received a blow which cut open my head and necessitated its being stitched at the hospital. ■

Fascism and Public Order

Sir Oswald Mosley, the ex-Conservative and junior minister in the second Labour government, had responded to the Depression by proposing radical policies to tackle unemployment. When these were rebuffed by the weight of orthodox opinion, Mosley became disillusioned, resigned from the Labour Party and in 1931 formed the New Party. Mosley's Fascist sympathies soon surfaced, causing many of the New Party's other leading members to leave.

Having met Mussolini early in 1932, Mosley wrote The Greater Britain, *his Fascist manifesto. This focused on the decline of Britain and the steps needed to reverse that decline and safeguard the British Empire, involving corporatism, state controls, economic autarky within the Empire and high wage levels to boost demand and cut unemployment. At the same time, parliamentary and trade union powers were to be reduced. In October 1932 Mosley formed the British Union of Fascists, which enjoyed a rapid expansion, having 50,000 members by spring 1934.*

10.20 Oswald Mosley, *The Greater Britain*, 1932 (London, BUF, pp. 11–16, 24–6, 150–1).

■ In Great Britain during the past ten years there have never been less than a million unemployed, and at present unemployment approaches the three million figure ... We have tragic proof that economic life has outgrown our political institutions. Britain has failed to recover from the War period; and this result, however complicated by special causes, is largely due to a system of Government designed by, and for, the nineteenth century ... I believe that, under the existing system, Government cannot be efficiently conducted ...

Hence the need for a New Movement, not only in politics, but in the whole of our national life. The movement is Fascist, (i) because it is based on a high conception of citizenship – ideals as lofty as those which inspired the reformers of a hundred years ago; (ii) because it recognises the necessity for an authoritative state, above party and sectional interests ... We seek to organise the Modern Movement in this country by British methods in a form which is suitable to and characteristic of Great Britain. We are essentially a national movement, and if our policy could be summarised in two words, they would be 'Britain First' ...

Fascism is the greatest constructive and revolutionary creed in the world. It seeks to achieve its aim legally and constitutionally, by methods of law and order, but in objective it is revolutionary or it is nothing. It challenges the existing order and advances the constructive alternative of the Corporate State. To many of us this creed represents the thing which we have sought throughout our political lives. It combines the dynamic urge to change and progress with the authority, the discipline and the order without which nothing great can be achieved ... The essence of Fascism is the power of adaptation to fresh facts. Above all, it is a realist creed. It has no use for immortal principles in relation to the facts of bread-and-butter; and it despises the windy rhetoric which ascribes importance to mere formulae. The steel creed of an iron age, it cuts through the verbiage of illusion to the achievement of a new reality ... We have seen the political parties of the old democracy collapse into futility through the sterility of committee government and the cowardice and irresponsibility of their leadership ... the only effective instrument of revolutionary change is absolute authority. We are organised, therefore, as a disciplined army, not as a bewildered mob with every member bellowing orders. Fascist leadership must lead, and its discipline must be respected. ■

One factor assisting the rapid growth of the BUF was the favourable publicity the movement received from the Rothermere newspapers. Initially, Mosley attracted little coverage, but soon the Daily Mail *began to describe the BUF in enthusiastic terms, with Lord Rothermere himself contributing articles extolling the virtues of Fascism. This mood was changed by the violence employed against hecklers by 'Blackshirt' stewards at the BUF's Olympia rally in June 1934, and by horrified reactions to Hitler's treatment of his Nazi rivals during the 'Night of the Long Knives'. Shortly afterwards, Rothermere, at heart a conventional reactionary rather than a Fascist sympathiser, stopped endorsing Mosley, and membership of the BUF began to decline.*

10.21 Viscount Rothermere, 'Hurrah for the Blackshirts', *Daily Mail*, 15 January 1934.

■ Because Fascism comes from Italy, shortsighted people in this country think they show a sturdy national spirit by deriding it.

If their ancestors had been equally stupid, Britain would have had no banking system, no Roman law, nor even any football, since all of these are of Italian invention.

The Socialists, especially, who jeer at the principles and uniform of the Blackshirts as being of foreign origin, forget that the founder and High Priest of their own creed was the German Jew Karl Marx.

Though the name and form of Fascism originated in Italy, that movement is not now peculiar to any nation. *It stands in every country for the Party of Youth.* It represents the effort of the young generation to put new life into out-of-date political systems.

That alone is enough to make it a factor of immense value in our national affairs.

Youth is a force that for generations has been allowed to run to waste in Britain. This country has been governed since far back in Victorian times by men in the middle sixties. When prosperity was general and the international horizon calm, that mattered little, but to cope with the grim problems of the present day the energy and vigour of younger men are needed. Being myself in my middle sixties, I know how stealthily and steadily that seventh decade saps one's powers and stiffens one's prejudices.

Under the inert and irresolute control of these elderly statesmen, the British Government is equally without real popularity at home and prestige abroad. In the vital matter of air-defence this country has been allowed to sink from the foremost to the lowest position among the Great Powers. While the leaders of other States are reorganising their national resources to break the crushing grip of the world crisis, our own are content to drift and dawdle ...

The Blackshirt movement is the organised effort of the younger generation to break this stranglehold which senile politicians have so long maintained on our public affairs ...

Such an effort was long overdue. The nation's realisation of the need for it is shown by the astonishing progress the Blackshirts are making, especially in the big industrial areas ... *A crusading spirit has come back to British politics* ...

What are these Blackshirts who hold 500 meetings a week throughout the country and whose uniform has become so familiar a feature of our political life?...

Blackshirts proclaim a fact which politicians dating from pre-war days will never face – that the new age requires new methods and new men. They base their contention on the simple truth that parliamentary government is conducted on the same lines as it was in the eighteenth century, though the conditions with which it deals have altered beyong recognition. They want to bring our national administration up to date.

This purpose does not rest on theory alone. It can be justified by the gigantic revival of national strength and spirit which a similar process of modernisation has brought about in Italy and Germany. ■

The most active of the BUF's local campaigns was that directed against the large Jewish community in the East End of London. Mosley, whose speeches acquired an increasingly anti-Semitic tone after 1934, successfully tapped the vein of anti-Jewish feeling in the area, which was the BUF's stronghold. The campaign in the East End provoked violence, most notoriously at the 'battle of Cable Street' in October 1936, when around 100,000 anti-Fascist protesters prevented a BUF march. This incident briefly revived recruitment into the BUF, but anti-Semitism's geographical appeal was severely circumscribed, and offered little prospect for continued BUF expansion. More importantly, 'Cable Street' convinced the government that steps should be taken to limit the BUF's activities. This resulted in the Public Order Act of 1936, which banned the wearing of political uniforms and gave the police authority either to prohibit or to redirect demonstration marches.

Fifty-five years after Cable Street, the Institute of Contemporary British History in London arranged a seminar at which participants in the incident, both Fascist and anti-Fascist, were invited to share their recollections.

10.22 Institute of Contemporary British History, witness seminar on the 1936 battle of Cable Street, 1 May 1991 (Institute of Historical Research, University of London).

■ ... *RONALD F. WEBB:* ... I was an ordinary member of the British Union, and I have never beat up anybody in my life, and I hope I never will. But the point is, I went to this national rally, which was the annual national rally, which was quite legal and organised ... Going down to Tower Hill station there was a mob outside screaming their heads off, and I had butterflies in my stomach, I don't mind admitting. And I arrived down at Royal Mint Street where we lined up, and the rumours were going round somebody was killed and all this sort of thing, but there was a number of our members there when we arrived who had got bandages round their heads – they had been beaten up. Because they had got there early and the mob set on them ... And while I was there the point came that the Home Secretary had banned it OK, so we marched back to Westminster where we dispersed on the Embankment, back to our headquarters after that, no disorder, nothing at all. Mosley spoke and said that the Home Secretary had bowed down to mob rule, which I thought he had anyway, and then we dispersed home ...

JOYCE GOODMAN: On October 4th 1936, I was 12 years old. Now if you were a youngster brought up in the East End in the 1930s you were no stranger to politics because there were political meetings on every corner. And as a kid you stood there and listened to the Communist Party, the Labour Party, and you took it all in, and the fascists had their regular meetings too. If you were a Jewish kid and you stood there listening to them belting out their message of hate, you learned to hate back, because you heard of all the attacks in the East End ...

It has been described as non-violent but I didn't find it so. The violence wasn't coming from us, it's true we went there as peaceful demonstrators, but for two young girls it was absolute terror. The police first tried just to clear the roadway so that the traffic could get through. They were pushing us onto Gardiner's windows, there were people going straight through the plate glass windows. There were horses coming straight into the crowd and the police were just hitting anyone indiscriminately. We never saw a fascist all that day, we never fought with the fascists. You were fighting the police. They were just hitting everyone, there were women going down under the horses' hooves, absolute terror ... ∎

CHAPTER ELEVEN

Facing the Dictators:
Foreign Policy and Appeasement,
1930–1939

THE 1930s saw growing threats to Britain's world position. At a time when economic recession dictated cuts in government spending and precluded expensive foreign policy commitments, Britain faced Japanese expansionism in the Far East, insecurity in the Mediterranean and Africa as a result of Italian ambitions and, perhaps most worrying, the prospect of German military resurgence, directed towards the eradication of the 1919 peace settlement. A major preoccupation of British policy-makers was the need to avoid a situation in which the country had to confront two or, worse still, all three of these potential adversaries simultaneously. This concern explains in part London's willingness to reach accommodation with these aggressive regimes, to appease them by making concessions designed to alleviate grievances and so ensure continuing peace. Reinforcing this outlook was Britain's demonstrable lack of preparedness for military conflict, and what was understood to be popular aversion to another war, a war which informed commentators accurately predicted would call into question Britain's claims to be a world power. Even the British Empire appeared to be as much a source of strain as a bolster to Britain's status, as scarce resources were stretched to defend the country's global interests.

An important consideration facing all makers of British foreign policy between the wars was, paradoxically, domestic policy. In an age of mass democracy, increasing importance had to be attached by governments to social and other forms of domestic expenditure. To some contemporaries, the process had gone so far that foreign policy interests had been repeatedly sacrificed in order to safeguard domestic spending, leading to retreat in the face of overseas threats and a consequent decline in Britain's prestige. This attitude was reflected privately by Sir Maurice Hankey, Secretary to the Cabinet, early in the 1930s.

11.1 **Sir Maurice Hankey, diary, 6 September 1931 (in S. Roskill, *Hankey: Man of Secrets, Vol. II: 1919–1931*, London, Collins, 1972, pp. 544–5).**

■ We are living just now through the most serious crisis since the war and future outlook is black. After the war we failed to adopt the measures of economy necessary to a nation that had dissipated a large part of its wealth in smoke and explosions. The beginning of it all was Ll.G.'s election speech in 1919 about 'a home fit for heroes to live in' – as I have more than once noted in this journal. Thereafter it has been a 'rake's progress' for which each successive Government has its share of responsibility. As I once told Ll. G., many years ago, when he was Prime Minister, and as I have told his successors, the only real cure is to preach to the people that they must pull in their belts and economise, and that the standard of living must be lowered so as to enable us – a nation dependent on oversea trade – to compete effectively with our rivals. Nevertheless, the exigencies of party politics have compelled each party leader to declare repeatedly, and right up to the present time, that the standard of living must be maintained. While our fighting strength has been reduced by repeated 'cuts' – relatively to foreign nations – there has been an orgy of extravagance on social reform ... Our policy in India, Egypt and China has been weak and reacts on our prestige in all Eastern countries. The result has been a great fall in our prestige throughout the world. Broadly speaking, foreigners, and especially the French, who have a great following in Central Europe, and the Italians, who are still Fascists, have lost confidence in us. They don't believe in our policy on disarmament – especially the reduction of the fleet and the insufficiency of our air force to defend London; they disagree with our policy in India, China, Egypt, and our general pacifism and idealism. Some understand, and in theory approve it. But many – as I know from conversations at the Hague Conferences and the London Naval Conference – think that it is really due less to idealism than to our realisation of our exhaustion and economic weakness ... ■

The Far East

One of the first intimations of the challenges Britain would face in the 1930s came in September 1931, when Japanese forces seized Manchuria from China. It has sometimes been suggested that the failure of the other powers to confront Japan's actions effectively encouraged the European dictators to press their expansionist claims later in the decade. The episode damaged the League of Nations and the notion of 'collective security', and the measures taken by the League, including sanctions and the dispatch of a commission of inquiry, caused Japan little concern. Yet even if the Western powers had seen Japan's actions as threatening to their interests, they were hardly in a position to respond with force, given their own domestic problems arising from the economic depression.

The Manchurian crisis was far from a local incident, as the following Foreign Office memorandum, written as the crisis deepened, made clear. At issue was not merely

Britain's relationship with Japan, but its continued presence in the Far East as a major imperial power, a presence which the Foreign Office reluctantly conceded could not be defended with force.

11.2   Sir John Pratt (Foreign Office), memorandum on the situation in Shanghai, 1 February 1932 (*Documents on British Foreign Policy*, 2nd series, IX, no. 238).

■ 1. There are two significant items of news to-day (a) Mr Yoshizawa's [Japan's delegate to the League] statement reported in to-day's 'Times' foreshadowing the sending of military (as distinct from naval) reinforcements to Shanghai, (b) the naval demonstration at Nanking.

2. We must expect that hostilities will continue in Shanghai as long as the Japanese forces remain there, that they will become more and more serious, and that more and more Japanese troops will be poured into Shanghai.

3. This situation may (and indeed is likely to) end in the Japanese forces destroying a large part of the native city and suburbs of Shanghai (which have a Chinese population of approximately two million) and ousting the authority of the Shanghai Municipal Council from the whole area of the International Settlement. I gather from a recent telegram of Mr Brenan's that once this has happened the former status of the Settlement will never be restored: it will become a Japanese concession.

4. If Japan continues unchecked the British will have to retire altogether from the Far East. If it is decided that we must check Japan certain preliminary measures could be adopted – such as rupture of diplomatic and economic relations – but in the end Japan can only be checked by force. Ultimately we will be faced with the alternatives of going to war with Japan or retiring from the Far East. A retirement from the Far East might be the prelude to a retirement from India ... ■

Germany, Italy and the Spanish Civil War

In January 1933 Adolf Hitler became Chancellor of Germany, brought to power by the devastating effects of the Depression on the Weimar Republic. Hitler quickly mobilised the resentments of Germany at the provisions of the Treaty of Versailles. In Britain there was a good deal of sympathy for German grievances, a tendency to overlook the realities of life in the Third Reich and to underestimate Hitler, and, in some circles, approval for strident Nazi anti-Communism. Given the British government's inclination to see European Fascism as less threatening than Communism, the important consequence was a protracted commitment to achieving negotiated agreement with Hitler as the basis of a lasting peace.

In October 1933 Germany left the League of Nations and withdrew from the Geneva Disarmament Conference. In future, Hitler would seek equal status for Germany in the strength of its armed forces. Rumbold's successor as British Ambassador in Berlin, Sir Eric Phipps, commented on these developments with a sense of foreboding.

11.3   Sir Eric Phipps, letter to Sir John Simon, 25 October 1933 (*Documents on British Foreign Policy*, 2nd series, V, no. 492).

■ As I reported in my telegram ... of the 23rd October, it appears that the decision to leave Geneva is viewed with some misgiving by the more reasonable members of the Government, a feeling which is shared by certain sections of the public. In fact, the attitude of Germany may be likened to that of a small boy who has thrown a stone at an adult. It was great fun at the time, but how will the gentleman take it? The Germans are deeply conscious of their defenceless position, and their vulnerability to air attack has been brought home to them, perhaps unwisely, for political purposes by the Government. Hence it is only natural that the German Government should, particularly at this moment, be anxious to emphasise their peaceful intentions. The ordinary German in conversation is at pains to impress one with the fact that it would be madness for Germany to embark on a warlike adventure, that the Nazis are only concerned with building up the internal structure of Germany, that they have no real interest in foreign politics, and that Herr Hitler may be relied upon to keep the peace ... As I listened to the Chancellor's wireless speech on the 14th October I was struck by the sincerity of his tone, and I can well believe my German friends when they tell me that the present German Government is not planning a war. The future is, however, quite another matter. The Italians are not a warlike people; they are indolent and peaceful in charac-ter. The action of fascism may be described as the action of massage on an atrophied limb, whereas in Germany it is a case of massage applied to a fevered, but otherwise muscular, limb. In my despatch ... of the 10th October, I drew your attention to the declaration in which the Nazi Chief of Staff endeavoured to demonstrate the wholly peaceful character of the Nazi movement. His arguments, which are those in general use in Germany today, arouse misgivings which no peaceful assurances, however sincere, can allay so long as the Government persist in giving the country spectac-ular military displays and bringing up the younger generation on garbled versions of Germany's history since 1914. ■

Early in 1934 the British government concluded that Germany was a potential enemy. However, it seemed clear to many officials, including Sir Warren Fisher of the Treasury, that Britain was in no position to confront Germany and its other potential enemy, Japan, simultaneously, and that an understanding between Britain and Japan should be sought. The idea was taken up by Neville Chamberlain, then Chancellor of the Exchequer and acting Prime Minister, who wrote to the Foreign Secretary, Sir John Simon, encouraging him to pursue it. However, the proposal foundered because of

United States resistance, when Washington threatened to encourage the Dominions to look to the USA to protect their interests.

11.4   Neville Chamberlain's proposal for an Anglo-Japanese alliance, letter to Sir John Simon, 1 September 1934 (*Documents on British Foreign Policy*, 2nd series, XIII, no. 14).

■ My dear John,

While I have been here I have been thinking a great deal about the European situation, the coming Naval Conference and the position of the Government. It seems to me that some immensely important question, affecting the whole future of G[reat] B[ritain] and the Empire, may turn upon the actions we take this autumn, and the more I have turned it over the more convinced I have become that this is one of those crucial points in history which test the statesman's capacity and foresight.

The result of my cogitations has led me to certain conclusions which as they would require Cabinet authority to carry out, I have embodied in a memorandum to the Cabinet. I propose to circulate this memorandum very soon, as time presses, but I am sending you this letter and an advance copy in the hope that you may have time to consider it before you go to Geneva.

I am sending it to you, not only because you are the Minister most directly concerned, but because I attach particular weight to your cool and analytical judgement. Moreover, I can't help reflecting that if you could bring off an agreement with Japan such as I have suggested it would stamp your tenure of office with the special distinction that is attached to memorable historical events, and, incidentally would add greatly to the prestige of the National Government in the most difficult of all fields.

I have been immensely impressed and confirmed in my views by two things since I wrote this paper. One is the report from Sir R. Clive referred to in the PS which relates how he was actually offered a Pact of Non-aggression by Japan and how Hirota [Japan's Foreign Minister] impressed upon him the friendliness of the Emperor. The second is more recent, namely the semi-official statement of Japanese ideas about the Naval Conference in which suggestions were made very closely approximating to those I have sketched in my paper. (See The Times, 30 August)

Surely with these two confirmatory bits of evidence I must be on the right tack. But if we neglected even to enquire what were Japan's ideas about a Pact, what might not be said of us by future historians if we drifted into unfriendly relations with Japan, lost our Far Eastern trade to them, had to look on helplessly while she marched from one aggression to another.

As for USA don't let us be browbeaten by her. She will never repay us for sacrificing our interests in order to conciliate her and if we maintain at once a bold and a frank attitude towards her I am not afraid of the result.

Although Van [Vansittart] has not seen my paper he knows it is on the stocks, and as a result of some remarks I made when he sent me Clive's report, he has written to me that he was having the whole question of the Pact very carefully examined.He has therefore begun the good work; I hope you may think sufficiently well of the idea to pursue it and that you will some day be remembered (inter alia!) as the author of the 'Simon-Hirota Pact'. ■

In 1935 the threatening nature of Hitler's ambitions became clearer. In March he reintroduced conscription and announced a target for the German army of thirty-six divisions. As Germany revived, both Britain and France looked to Italy as the key to peace in Europe. However, in October 1935 Mussolini invaded Abyssinia as part of his scheme to 'reconstruct the Roman Empire'. The League of Nations condemned the Italian invasion, but, as over Manchuria, proved helpless. Britain and France, still keen to appease Mussolini, considered means of satisfying Italy's African ambitions while preserving something of Abyssinia. Sir Samuel Hoare, the British Foreign Secretary, met Pierre Laval, his French counterpart, late in 1935 and produced a plan which would have surrendered two-thirds of Abyssinia to Italy.

11.5 **The Hoare–Laval talks on Abyssinia, 7 December 1935 (*Documents on British Foreign Policy*, 2nd series, XV, no. 338).**

■ … Turning to the question of the peace conversations he enquired what M. Laval would consider the best procedure to be adopted at Geneva on the supposition that the conversations with Italy had begun satisfactorily. It was essential to avoid any impression that the League of Nations was weakening.

M. Laval agreed. But he emphasized that Geneva would accept whatever France and Great Britain approved. If there were to be an exception it would no doubt be Moscow.

As regards peace conditions the Italian pretensions were excessive, but the British reservations were too severe. Mussolini must have at least part of the territory he had conquered. Nor could he be expected to surrender to the vengeance of the Negus that part of the population which had yielded to him. Tigré must be ceded in part. In addition Italy wanted regions in which to settle her colonists south of the 8th parallel and excluding Ogaden which was of no value for the purpose; on the other hand he was fully prepared to see the Negus afforded access to the sea. Great Britain's ideas had hitherto been unduly restricted: he appealed to her to be more generous. It was the substance that mattered and the question of procedure was really of small importance.

Sir Samuel Hoare emphasized that it was essential not to offer the appearance of rewarding aggression. As he saw it the main principles to be kept in view were the following:

1 The proposals must be kept within the framework of the report of the Committee of Five. Abyssinia must have a definite outlet to the sea.

2 Any question of mandate must be excluded.

3 The arrangement must be a judicious mixture of an exchange of territory and the conferring of economic concessions. The cession of territory by Ethiopia in the north must depend for its extent upon what was done in the south and southwest. As to Tigré he was prepared to agree that Italy must retain Adowa and Adigrat. But to go too far would lead to the Emperor's overthrow and provoke the accusation that all the League had managed to do was to ruin Abyssinia.

In the south there must be an exchange of territory against the port which Abyssinia was to receive: in the southwest the best way to deal with the question seemed to him to be an economic monopoly for Italy.

Sir Robert Vansittart said that above everything there must be joint Franco-British proposals. There must be no question of mediation in the sense that France put up British proposals to Italy and Italian proposals to Great Britain. And it was essential to remember that there must be some limit set to what Abyssinia could be expected to cede even in return for a port: to extend this limit would be to expose the League itself to the gravest danger.   ■

When the British press revealed the Hoare–Laval plan, there was an outraged public response, and Hoare was forced to resign.

While Britain and France were still preoccupied with the Abyssinian crisis in March 1936, Hitler took his first major step to reverse the territorial provisions of Versailles by marching troops into the Rhineland, assuming correctly that Britain and France would not try to stop him. Duff Cooper was one of a minority of Conservative MPs, including Winston Churchill, who recognised the dangers posed by Hitler and who opposed the government's attempts to appease him. In his memoirs, Cooper, who resigned from ministerial office at the time of Munich, gave his assessment of the significance of the remilitarisation of the Rhineland.

11.6 Duff Cooper on the German threat, *Old Men Forget: The Autobiography of Duff Cooper (Viscount Norwich)*, (London, Hart-Davis, 1954, pp. 190, 195–6).

■ In the early summer of this same year [1935] those of us who were already aware of the ever-growing German menace were deeply concerned lest disagreement with Italy over Abyssinia might weaken or destroy what was then termed 'the Stresa Front', meaning the solidarity of Great Britain, France and Italy ...

Hitler was not slow to act upon the evidence which Great Britain's handling of the Abyssinian question seemed to have betrayed. In March 1936 he marched German troops into the Rhineland. Hitherto, in the rantings with which he delighted the German people, he had referred only to the hardships inflicted on Germany by what he described as the 'dictated' Treaty of Versailles, a treaty that had been so much criticised both in Great Britain and America that to this day there are many people in both countries who are unaware that the terms of it were generous to Germany, that no effort was ever made to enforce the harsher financial clauses, that it sought to carry out President Wilson's idealistic theories of self-determination, and that it had already permitted defeated Germany in the course of sixteen years to become the most powerful nation on the continent of Europe. It was true to say that it was a treaty agreed to by a conquered country, but it was signed by the accredited representatives of that country, and if it was to be considered invalid because one party to it was weaker than the other, few if any treaties would ever be valid again.

But the occupation of the Rhineland went further than the already familiar denunciations of the Treaty of Versailles. It was a flagrant, unprovoked and indefensible violation of the Treaty of Locarno, which was supposed to take the place of the former peace treaty, and which had been freely negotiated and agreed upon with the full and openly expressed approval of the German people.

In the light of after-events, a light that is always denied to us, this was undoubtedly the moment when Great Britain and France should have taken a firm line and insisted upon the withdrawal of the German troops as a preliminary to any discussion. Germany was not ready for war and had no allies. Hitler would have been forced to capitulate and the corner-stone of the great prestige that he built up in the minds of his fellow-countrymen would not have been laid. But even if we had been more determined, and even if we had received greater encouragement from a stronger French Government, there would have been one almost insuperable obstacle to firm action. It was not the strength of our armed forces but the mind of the British people that was unprepared for war.

… The average Englishman was quite unable to appreciate the significance of Hitler's military occupation of the Rhineland. 'Why shouldn't the Germans move soldiers about in their own country?' was the not unnatural reaction of the ignorant. They could not understand that by this act a ruthless dictator had torn into shreds a treaty upon which the peace of Europe depended. ∎

In July 1936 the Spanish Civil War began. The tense situation in Europe ensured that the war quickly acquired international significance. While the legitimate Republican government sought French assistance, the Nationalist rebels turned for help to Germany and Italy. The war came to be portrayed in ideological terms, with Hitler and Mussolini backing Franco, and only the Soviet Union offering effective aid to the Republicans. Fearing that the war would escalate into a general conflict, Britain and France suggested an agreement by the powers guaranteeing non-intervention in Spain. Though Germany, Italy, the Soviet Union and France signed the agreement, Britain claimed to be the only power respecting its provisions. Non-intervention in Spain arguably gave a fresh signal to Europe's dictators that the Western democracies preferred conciliation to confrontation.

11.7 Cabinet Foreign Policy Committee discussion on non-intervention in Spain, 25 August 1936 (PRO CAB 27/622)

■ ... MR. EDEN reminded the Committee that earlier in the month M. Blum had taken the initiative in an effort to secure the general agreement of the Powers against any intervention in Spanish affairs. We had strongly supported M. Blum throughout and the efforts made by our representatives in Berlin, Rome and Lisbon had largely contributed to the success which had been obtained in securing general international agreement on this subject. In pursuing this policy, M. Blum had exposed himself to very serious trouble from his own extremists in France and the unexpected action of Signor Mussolini and Herr Hitler in agreeing in principle to the French proposals had enabled M. Blum to avoid a very grave general crisis.

MR. EDEN added that some days ago he had seen a deputation of the Labour Party headed by Mr. Arthur Greenwood and Sir Walter Citrine. The general complaint of the deputation had been that they did not know what the Government's policy was, but that our action seemed likely to help the insurgents and not the legally constituted Spanish Government. In reply, he (Mr. Eden) had been able to point out that in this matter the Government was giving whole-hearted support to the policy initiated by M. Blum ...

On the previous day, the French Ambassador had raised the question of the implementing of our non-intervention agreement. The French Government did not wish that Paris should be the clearing house for any further action and favoured London as the clearing house with an International Committee to supervise the arrangements. He (Mr. Eden) had agreed in principle ... to the French Ambassador's proposals, as he was satisfied that they would find favour with our own public opinion. The work of the International Committee would be concerned with reaching agreement on such questions as the categories of arms to be included in the prohibition of exports to Spain, transit prohibitions, etc...

MR. EDEN observed that Mr. Arthur Greenwood had informed him that the Labour Party were sending a Red Cross Unit to Spain and that he made it quite clear that the personnel of this Unit went to Spain at their own peril and the Government could assume no responsibility of any kind for them ...

The Committee agreed:

(1) To approve the action taken by Mr. Eden in agreeing to the French suggestion that London should be the clearing house for further non-intervention action and the setting up of an International Supervisory Committee.

(2) That a Technical Committee presided over by the Financial Secretary to

the Treasury and composed of representatives of the Treasury, Foreign Office, the Board of Trade and other Departments should be set up to assist in implementing the agreement respecting the non-intervention in Spain.

... MR. EDEN informed the Committee that in the opinion of those best competent to judge, the situation in Spain would almost certainly result in a stalemate, provided that there was no foreign intervention on one side or the other. ■

Appeasement

In May 1937 Neville Chamberlain became Prime Minister, taking a particular interest in foreign affairs. Above all, Chamberlain's name is associated with the policy of 'appeasement', involving concessions to Hitler in the belief that a general settlement of all outstanding grievances was possible, and should be pursued before the European situation deteriorated further.

In November 1937 Lord Halifax, the Lord President of the Council, visited Germany as part of Chamberlain's new strategy of securing détente. During his meeting with the German leaders, many of whom Halifax warmed to, a new British bargaining ploy was discussed, whereby some of the colonies Germany had lost under Versailles would be restored to it. On Halifax's return, Chamberlain approvingly took stock.

11.8 **Neville Chamberlain, memorandum, 26 November 1937 (in K. Feiling,** *The Life of Neville Chamberlain***, London, Macmillan, 1946 pp. 332–3).**

■ ... the German visit was from my point of view a great success, because it achieved its object, that of creating an atmosphere in which it is possible to discuss with Germany the practical questions involved in a European settlement... Both Hitler and Goering said separately, and emphatically, that they had no desire or intention of making war, and I think we may take this as correct, at any rate for the present. Of course they want to dominate Eastern Europe; they want as close a union with Austria as they can get without incorporating her in the Reich, and they want much the same things for the Sudetendeutsche as we did for the Uitlanders in the Transvaal.

They want Togoland and Kameruns. I am not quite sure where they stand about S.W. Africa; but they do not insist on Tanganyika, if they can be given some reasonably equivalent territory on the West Coast, possibly to be carved out of Belgian Congo and Angola. I think they would be prepared to come back to the League, if it were shorn of its compulsory powers, now clearly shown to be ineffective, and though Hitler was rather non-committal about disarmament, he did declare himself in favour of the abolition of bombing aeroplanes.

Now here, it seems to me, is a fair basis of discussion, though no doubt all these points bristle with difficulties. But I don't see why we shouldn't say to Germany, 'give us satisfactory assurances that you won't use force to deal with the Austrians and Czechoslovakians, and we will give you similar assurances that we won't use force to prevent the changes you want, if you can get them by peaceful means'. ■

Rearmament and the Road to Munich

Central to an understanding of the background of appeasement is the fact that rearmament, under way in Britain since 1934, was still subject to strict Treasury scrutiny, and was proceeding at a pace which left the country militarily vulnerable. The government received repeated warnings that Britain could not successfully fight a war in the near future. Negotiation therefore appeared to be the only available option.

The bias in British rearmament after 1934 was towards increasing the Royal Air Force's bomber forces, not the size of the army. While rearmament had important side-effects in stimulating economic recovery, it remained a controversial issue in domestic politics. In the following cartoon, Low allowed one of his most celebrated characters, Colonel Blimp, to rehearse official justifications of defence policy skilfully merging the image of the aeroplane with that of the mass grave, the expected outcome of air raids.

11.9   **Cartoon by David Low, 'Gad, sir, at any rate we are restoring prosperity', *Evening Standard*, 8 July 1935.**

Although, as Mr Baldwin says, air-planes offer no real protection from air attack, undoubtedly the construction of air forces stimulates industry and relieves unemployment —— *Colonel Blimp.*

For commentators alert to the growing German threat, the limits imposed by Treasury control on government expenditure, and hence on rearmament, were frustrating. Duff Cooper later provided the following observations on Chamberlain and his reservations about rearmament.

11.10 **Duff Cooper on Chamberlain and rearmament,** *Old Men Forget: The Autobiography of Duff Cooper (Viscount Norwich),* **(London, Hart-Davis, 1954, p. 200).**

■ I had sympathy with Chamberlain's attitude. He had become Chancellor of the Exchequer in 1931 when the country, we were told, was on the verge of bankruptcy. He had brought about a great financial recovery. He was about to welcome the return of prosperity and he hoped to use the money in beneficial measures of social reform. Suddenly he saw his dream dissolving. The plenty that he had laboured so hard to collect was going to be thrown away upon rearmament, the least remunerative form of expenditure. But all was not yet lost. There was no certainty of war. He himself hated the idea of it. So, he believed, did all sensible men. Mussolini and Hitler must surely be sensible men too or they would never have risen to the great positions they occupied. Therefore they could not want war. There were certain things they did want, and there were certain things that we could give them. If he were in control of foreign policy he could meet these men round a table and come to terms with them. The danger of war would be removed and we could all get on with social reform.

Chamberlain had many good qualities but he lacked experience of the world, and he lacked also the imagination which can fill the gaps of inexperience. He had never moved in the great world of politics or of finance, and the continent of Europe was for him a closed book. He had been a successful Lord Mayor of Birmingham, and for him the Dictators of Germany and of Italy were like the Lord Mayors of Liverpool and Manchester, who might belong to different political parties and have different interests, but who must desire the welfare of humanity, and be fundamentally reasonable, decent men like himself. This profound misconception lay at the root of his policy and explains his mistakes. ■

The practical limitations imposed on diplomacy by defence considerations were illustrated at the end of 1937 when the Cabinet discussed a major review of defence policy conducted by Sir Thomas Inskip, Minister for the Co-ordination of Defence. This produced pessimism from the country's military chiefs, and gave priority to the defence of Britain, especially through fighter aircraft and naval strength to deter an aggressor. The possibility of preparing a continental fighting force was discarded. Given Britain's wide-ranging commitments, and the special problems posed to British Far Eastern interests by Japan, there seemed no alternative to limiting as far as possible the number of potential enemies the country might have to face at any one time.

11.11 Cabinet discussion on defence policy, 8 December 1937 (PRO CAB 23/90A).

■ He [The Prime Minister] then summarized the main considerations that had been brought to the notice of the Committee. It was true, as the Chiefs of Staff had pointed out, that we could not hope to confront satisfactorily Germany, Italy and Japan simultaneously and, when we looked round as to what help we could get from other nations, the results were not very encouraging. France was our most important friend. Though she was strongly defensive and possessed a powerful army, the French Air Force was far from satisfactory. During the Anglo-French visit, M. Chautemps had admitted to an output of aircraft that was only about one-fifth (60–300) of our own. A long time must elapse before France would be able to give us much help in the air. The Power that had the greatest strength was the United States of America, but he would be a rash man who based his calculations on help from that quarter. Our position in relation to the smaller Powers was much better than formerly, but he did not think that they would add much to our offensive or defensive strength. In time of peace their support was useful, but in war less so. The Chiefs of Staff, as he had mentioned, said they could not foresee the time when our defence forces would be strong enough to safeguard our territory, trade and vital interests against Germany, Italy and Japan simultaneously. They had urged that our foreign policy must be governed by this consideration, and they had made rather a strong appeal to this effect. Of course, it would be possible to make an effort to detach one of the three Powers from the other two and it might even succeed. This, however, could only be done at the cost of concessions which would involve humiliations and disadvantages to this country by destroying the confidence of other nations. No one would suppose, therefore, that we should try and bribe one of the three nations to leave the other two. What the Foreign Secretary was doing was to try and prevent a situation arising in which the three Powers mentioned would ever be at war with us. He recalled that before the trouble had arisen in the Far East, we had been making great efforts to improve our relations with Japan and that considerable progress had been made. Owing to recent events, we had been compelled to break off these negotiations, but we had tried to keep open the position of resuming them later on. We had avoided threats ourselves and had restrained others from making them. The improvement in relations with Italy was not easy, but we had made some efforts to get on better terms, in spite of the difficult attitude of Mussolini and we were about to make a further effort at that end of the Berlin–Rome Axis. As he himself had pointed out before, however, Germany was the real key to the question. In view of the recent consideration given by the Cabinet to the question of improving relations with Germany, it was unnecessary to develop that theme any further. He thought, however, that he had said enough to show that the strategic considerations urged by the Chiefs of Staff were fully taken into account in our foreign policy and that was what underlay the taking note by the Committee of Imperial Defence of conclusion (i)(b) quoted above, namely –

'(b) The statement on foreign policy made at this meeting by the Secretary of State for Foreign Affairs, which, it was agreed, takes proper account of the facts of the situation, including those mentioned in the Report by the Chiefs of Staff.'

In the course of a short discussion, attention was drawn to the late Prime Minister's undertaking as to the maintenance of parity between the Air Force of the United Kingdom and that of Germany.

The Minister for Coordination of Defence pointed out that Lord Baldwin's statement required interpretation. He had never taken it to mean that we must have exactly the same number of fighters and bombers as Germany in order to carry out the contemplated equality.

The Prime Minister said that he did not intend to repeat Lord Baldwin's words and if the question were raised, he would make it clear that the Government did not consider it necessary to have precise equality in every class of aircraft. It might be necessary to make a statement on this subject before very long. After some further discussion, the Cabinet agreed:

To take note of the Report contained in C.P.296(37) with the Prime Minister's remarks thereon and summarized above. ■

With Germany's forced anschluss *with Austria in March 1938, London's attention turned to the increasingly dominant German problem. Underpinning Chamberlain's policy was the conviction that Germany need not be Britain's enemy. For him, appeasement entailed restoring Germany to its rightful status in Europe, thus removing a major potential source of tension. After the* anschluss, *a shift in German interest towards Czechoslovakia seemed likely. In the Sudetenland a large German-speaking minority complained of Czech 'discrimination', and found a sympathetic audience in Hitler. The importance of this development was that it drew British attention away from Mussolini's Italy, making Germany the undisputed focus of foreign policy.*

11.12 Neville Chamberlain on British policy towards Europe, 24 March 1938 (*Hansard*, 5th ser., 333: 1399–413).

■ His Majesty's Government have expressed the view that recent events in Austria have created a new situation, and we think it right to state the conclusions to which consideration of these events has led us. We have already placed on record our judgement upon the action taken by the German Government. I have nothing to add to that. But the consequences still remain. There has been a profound disturbance of international confidence. In these circumstances the problem before Europe, to which in the opinion of His Majesty's Government it is their most urgent duty to direct their attention, is how best to restore this shaken confidence, how to maintain the rule of law in international affairs, how to seek peaceful solutions to questions that continue to cause anxiety. Of these the one which is necessarily most present to many minds is that which concerns the relations between the Government of Czechoslovakia and the German minority in that country; and it is probable that a solution of this question, if it could be achieved, would go far to re-establish a sense of stability over an area much wider than that immediately concerned.

Accordingly, the Government have given special attention to this matter, and in particular they have fully considered the question whether the United Kingdom, in addition to those obligations by which she is already bound by the Covenant of the League and the Treaty of Locarno, should, as a further contribution towards preserving peace in Europe, now undertake new and specific commitments in Europe, and in particular such a commitment in relation to Czechoslovakia.

The question now arises, whether we should go further. Should we forthwith give an assurance to France that, in the event of her being called upon by reason of German aggression on Czechoslovakia to implement her obligations under the Franco-Czechoslovak Treaty, we would immediately employ our full military force on her behalf? Or, alternatively, should we at once declare our readiness to take military action in resistance to any forcible interference with the independence and integrity of Czechoslovakia, and invite any other nations, which might so desire, to associate themselves with us in such a declaration?

From a consideration of these two alternatives it clearly emerges that under either of them the decision as to whether or not this country should find itself involved in war would be automatically removed from the discretion of His Majesty's Government, and the suggested guarantee would apply irrespective of the circumstances by which it was brought into operation, and over which His Majesty's Government might not have been able to exercise any control. This position is not one that His Majesty's Government could see their way to accept, in relation to an area where their vital interests are not concerned in the same degree as they are in the case of France and Belgium; it is certainly not the position that results from the Covenant. For these reasons His Majesty's Government feel themselves unable to give the prior guarantee suggested ...

So far as Czechoslovakia is concerned, it seems to His Majesty's Government that now is the time when all the resources of diplomacy should be enlisted in the cause of peace. They have been glad to take note of and in no way underrate the definite assurances given by the German Government as to their attitude. On the other side they have observed with satisfaction that the Government of Czechoslovakia are addressing themselves to the practical steps that can be taken within the framework of the Czechoslovak constitution to meet the reasonable wishes of the German minority. For their part, His Majesty's Government will at all times be ready to render any help in their power, by whatever means might seem most appropriate, towards the solution of questions likely to cause difficulty between the German and Czechoslovak Governments. In the meantime, there is no need to assume the use of force, or, indeed, to talk about it. Such talk is to be strongly deprecated. Not only can it do no good; it is bound to do harm. It must interfere with the progress of diplomacy, and it must increase feelings of insecurity and uncertainty. ■

Chamberlain saw the Sudetenland problem as an opportunity to demonstrate to Hitler that it was possible to negotiate this and other German claims without resorting to force, making possible a stabilisation in central Europe. In August 1938 the Czech government was persuaded to offer the Sudeten Germans a substantial measure of autonomy. Suddenly, on 12 September, Hitler denounced the Czech stance, demanding 'self-determination' for the Sudetens. This encouraged the Sudetens to reject the Czech offer. As the crisis deepened, a German invasion seemed imminent. Chamberlain privately believed that no fundamental British interests were at stake. He responded by seeking personal negotiations with Hitler in order to assure him that Britain would not encourage Czech resistance.

To great acclaim in Britain, Chamberlain flew to Germany on 15 September, where he met Hitler at Berchtesgaden. Chamberlain understood that agreement had been reached on a plebiscite in the Sudetenland to decide frontier revision. In London the Cabinet agreed to this; the French, too, reluctantly concurred. On 19 September the Czechs were informed of these terms, though the precise nature of the guarantee by Britain to Czechoslovakia which would underwrite the agreement remained unclear. The cartoonist Illingworth captured the mood of hope surrounding the Prime Minister's visit.

11.13 **Cartoon by L.G. Illingworth, 'Still hope', *Punch*, 21 September 1938.**

When Chamberlain made his second German trip, to Godesberg on 22 September, Hitler raised his demands, insisting that the Czechs withdraw from the Sudetenland by

28 September and allow immediate occupation of the territory by Germany. Hitler subsequently extended his deadline until 1 October, giving Chamberlain time to secure Franco-Czech approval. War now seemed inevitable, and Britain braced itself. In London trenches were dug in the parks and gas-masks were distributed. The apparent imminence of war enabled the Prime Minister to persuade his colleagues that there was no alternative but to accede to Hitler's demands. Yet Hitler's violent attitude alarmed the British government. The Permanent Under-Secretary at the Foreign Office, Sir Alexander Cadogan, described his reactions.

11.14 **Sir Alexander Cadogan, diary, 24 September 1938 (in D.N. Dilks, ed., *The Diaries of Sir Alexander Cadogan*, London, Cassell, 1971, pp. 103–4).**

■ Hitler's memo. now in. It's awful. A week ago when we moved (or were pushed) from 'autonomy' to cession, many of us found great difficulty in the idea of ceding people to Nazi Germany. We salved our consciences (at least I did) by stipulating it must be an 'orderly' cession – i.e. under international supervision, with safeguards for exchange of populations, compensation, &c. Now Hitler says he must march into the whole area at once (to keep order!) and the safeguards – and plebiscites! can be held after! This is throwing away every last safeguard that we had. P.M. is transmitting this 'proposal' to Prague. Thank God he hasn't yet recommended it for acceptance ...

Meeting of 'Inner Cabinet' at 3.30 and P.M. made his report to us. I was completely horrified – he was quite calmly for total surrender. More horrified still to find that Hitler has evidently hypnotised him to a point ... I know there is a shattering telegram from Phipps about position in France: I know we and they are in no condition to fight: but I'd rather be beat than dishonoured. How can we look any foreigner in the face after this? How can we hold Egypt, India and the rest? ■

However great the sense of shame among British observers in September 1938, the military constraints on policy remained: the government was informed that Britain's chances of success would be greater if war could be postponed by six to twelve months. In March 1938 the Chiefs of Staff had warned that war would be disastrous, though then they had overestimated Germany's true military strength. Although by the time of the Munich crisis the Chiefs recognised that South-East England was unlikely to be obliterated by the Luftwaffe *immediately, they knew that in a land war Britain would depend on support from the French, who seemed neither willing nor ready to fight.*

Chamberlain's aim was not only to avoid war, but also to show that appeasement worked by establishing long-term international arrangements. The British government produced a fresh plan, having promised to assist France if the latter went to war. The Czechs, having already made substantial concessions, refused to consider the new proposals. Britain was now under at least a moral obligation to help Czechoslovakia if a negotiated settlement proved elusive. Under British pressure, the Czech government eventually relented. On 28 September, Chamberlain described the recent unfolding of events to the Commons. His speech was dramatically interrupted by the news that Hitler had invited him to a four-power conference in Munich on 29 September.

In the early hours of 30 September 1938 Hitler, Chamberlain, Daladier and Mussolini achieved the 'Munich agreement'. This set out a timetable for German occupation of the Sudetenland, proposed a future meeting to resolve the outstanding Hungarian and Polish claims on Czech territory and referred, vaguely, to a four-power guarantee of Czechoslovakia's borders. Sir Horace Wilson, the government's Chief Industrial Adviser, who accompanied Chamberlain to Munich, described the meeting.

11.15 Sir Horace Wilson, note on the Munich Conference, 29–30 September 1938 (*Documents on British Foreign Policy*, series 3, II, pp. 631–3).

■ It began by a brief statement by Herr Hitler thanking those present for their acceptances of his invitations and pointing out the need for speedy decisions. Mr Chamberlain replied suitably, as did M. Daladier and Signor Mussolini. Towards the close of his remarks Signor Mussolini said that he thought the best way of making progress was for someone to produce a basis for discussion, and he therefore read his Memorandum. It was evident that this document was a reasonable re-statement of much that had been discussed in the Anglo-French and the Anglo-German conversations, and the Prime Minister was ready to accept it as a basis of discussion by the Conference.

... In the course of this discussion the Prime Minister raised the question of the representation at the Conference of the Czech Government. The conclusion was reached that the heads of the four Powers must accept responsibility for deciding – in the circumstances – how the situation should be dealt with ... The German proposals for evacuation and occupation surprised us by their moderation and by the degree of latitude which they left to the International Commission. They were explained in detail by Herr Hitler by reference to a map, copies of which we were given.

... We inserted in the preamble words to show that the Conference had been working in the light of the fact that it had already been agreed in principle that the Sudeten German areas should be ceded ...

After very long delays due to inefficient organisation and lack of control, the Agreement and supplementaries were signed a little before 2 a.m. on the 30th September, and the proceedings concluded by brief expressions of satisfaction. ■

In addition to the formal agreement at Munich, Chamberlain persuaded Hitler to sign a joint declaration, which Chamberlain had himself drawn up.

11.16 Joint declaration by Hitler and Chamberlain 30 September, 1938 (in N. Chamberlain, *The Struggle for Peace*, London, Hutchinson, 1939, p. 189).

■ We, the German Fuhrer and Chancellor and the British Prime Minister, have had a further meeting today and are agreed in recognizing that the question of Anglo-German relations is of the first importance for the two countries and for Europe.

We regard the agreement signed last night, the Munich Agreement, and the Anglo-German Naval Agreement as symbolic of the desire of our two peoples never to go to war with one another again.

We are resolved that the method of consultation shall be the method adopted to deal with any other questions that may concern our two countries, and we are determined to continue our efforts to remove possible sources of difference and thus to contribute to assure the peace of Europe. ■

Enthusiastic crowds greeted Chamberlain on his return to London from Munich. In its leader of 1 October 1938 The Times *recorded its approval.*

11.17 Report on Chamberlain's return from Germany, *The Times*, 1 October 1938.

■   A NEW DAWN

No conqueror returning from a victory on the battlefield has come home adorned with nobler laurels than Mr Chamberlain from Munich yesterday … He has not only relegated an agonizing episode to the past; he has found for the nations a new hope for the future. The joint declarations made by Herr Hitler and Mr Chamberlain … shall henceforth govern the whole of their relationships. There have been times when such a manifesto could be dismissed as a pious platitude … The present, it is fair to think, is not such a time … By inserting a specific reference to the Anglo-German Naval Agreement, as well as to the negotiations so happily concluded at Munich, the Führer reminds us of an earnest of his good intentions, which the British people, in the new atmosphere, will readily acknowledge. ■

It is difficult with hindsight to assess whether general British reactions to the Munich agreement reflected popular approval for Chamberlain's policy, or merely widespread relief that war had apparently been averted. Halifax, writing to Chamberlain before the Godesberg meeting, had detected a shift in opinion at home.

11.18 Lord Halifax, message to the British delegation at Godesberg, 23 September 1938 (*Documents on British Foreign Policy*, 3rd series, II, p. 490).

■ Following for Prime Minister from Lord Halifax.

It may help you if we give you some indication of what seems predominant public opinion as expressed in press and elsewhere. While mistrustful of our plan but prepared perhaps to accept it with reluctance as alternative to war, great mass of public opinion seems to be hardening in sense of feeling that we have gone to limit of concession and that it is up to the Chancellor to make some contribution. We, of course, can imagine immense difficulties with which you are confronted but from point of view of your own position, that of Government, and of the country, it seems to your colleagues of vital importance that you should not leave without making it plain to Chancellor if possible by special interview that, after great concessions made by Czechoslovakia, for him to reject opportunity of peaceful solution in favour of one that must involve war would be an unpardonable crime against humanity. ■

When the Munich agreement was debated in the Commons, the Prime Minister was unrepentant, but a number of Conservatives, including Eden and Churchill, abstained from voting for the government. On the other hand, some Labour members abstained from their party's vote of censure against the government. Churchill's contribution in the debate was sobering and prophetic.

11.19 Winston Churchill, debate on the Munich agreement, 5 October 1938 (*Hansard*, 5th ser., 339: 364–6).

■ All is over. Silent, mournful, abandoned, broken, Czechoslovakia recedes into the darkness ...

We in this country, as in other liberal and democratic countries, have a perfect right to exalt the principle of self-determination, but it comes ill out of the mouths of those in totalitarian states who deny even the smallest element of toleration to every section and creed within their bounds. But, however, you put it, this particular block of land, this mass of human beings to be handed over, has never expressed the desire to go into the Nazi rule. I do not believe that even now, if their opinion could be asked, they would exercise such an opinion ...

I venture to think that in future the Czechoslovak State cannot be maintained as an independent entity. I think you will find that in a period of time which may be measured by years, but may be measured only by months, Czechoslovakia will be engulfed in the Nazi regime. Perhaps they may join it in despair or in revenge. At any rate, that story is over and told. But we cannot consider the abandonment and ruin of Czechoslovakia in the light only of what happened only last month. It is the most grievous consequence of what we have done and of what we have left undone in the last five years – five years of futile good intentions, five years of eager search for the line of least resistance, five years of uninterrupted retreat of British power, five years of neglect of our air defences. Those are the features which I stand here to expose and which marked an improvident stewardship for which Great Britain and France have dearly to pay. We have been reduced in those years from a position of security so overwhelming and so unchallengeable that we never cared to think about it. We have been reduced from a position where the very word 'war' was considered one which could be used only by persons qualifying for a lunatic asylum. We have been reduced from a position of safety and power – power to do good, power to be generous to a beaten foe, power to make terms with Germany, power to give her proper redress for her grievances, power to stop her arming if we chose, power to take any step in strength or mercy or justice which we thought right – reduced in five years from a position safe and unchallenged to where we stand now. ■

As a result of the Munich agreement, Hitler gained the Sudeten territory. The remainder of Czechoslovakia was left less secure, having lost its protective mountainous frontiers as well as its major arms-producing centre. This prompted the question whether Britain would guarantee the new Czech frontiers, as the government had implied in October 1938. Only one member of the government, Duff Cooper, the First Lord of the Admiralty, resigned following Munich, but several of his Cabinet colleagues had private reservations about Hitler's future reliability. Whatever public relief there had been at the outcome of the crisis, the government was appalled by its demonstration of the country's lack of readiness for war. Very quickly, steps were taken to accelerate the rearmament programme, and a new air programme was approved in November 1938, geared towards strengthening the Royal Air Force's defensive capacity.

Before long, however, the relief generated by the Munich agreement was ebbing. Even during the crisis, Halifax had begun to suspect that Hitler had much wider ambitions, but it was the events in Germany during the 'Kristallnacht', an orgy of anti-Semitic violence on 10 November 1938, that undermined much residual British goodwill towards Hitler's regime. Halifax concluded that 'no useful purpose' could be served by Anglo-German discussions 'in the foreseeable future'. Even Chamberlain appeared to be steeling himself during the winter of 1938–9: 'It would be a tragic blunder [by Germany] to mistake our love of peace and our faculty for compromise, for weakness.' Early in 1939 rumours of impending German aggression swept through London. Although unfounded, they shifted official thinking away from the resignation apparent after Munich. Not long after the September crisis, for example, Sir Alexander Cadogan had been gloomy about the lessons of Munich.

11.20 Sir Alexander Cadogan, diary, 14 October 1938 (in D.N. Dilks, ed., *The Diaries of Sir Alexander Cadogan*, London, Cassell, 1971, p.119).

■ There are many hard facts to be faced, and one is that in present conditions we alone cannot hope to equal Germany's military effort. (It seems doubtful whether we and France by our combined efforts could do more than attain something like equality with Germany.)

It is not a question of this country being unwilling to make the sacrifices required; it is not a question of the difference between a totalitarian and a democratic State. The point is that Germany is far more nearly self-sufficient than these islands can ever hope to be and, with her closed economy, can concentrate the greater part of her industry on the production of engines of war. We have to import the greater part of our food, and consequently to maintain the value of the £ on the foreign exchanges. It is vital to us, therefore, to maintain our ordinary export trade ...

But if we cannot compete with Germany in potentially aggressive armaments, we can and must at least put our defences in order. This again is a matter for experts, but it would seem to the layman that the essentials are the Fleet, the Air Arm and A.A. Defences. There is a great deal to be done, particularly as regards the last two, before our diplomacy can become effective again.

And as regards defence, there is another point. We have inherited responsibilities all over the world, which have become more onerous with the rise to power of other nations such as Japan. In the Far East, we have British interests in China to defend. They are considerable, and are concentrated mainly in the hands of a not very numerous body of British individuals and concerns. It might not be intrinsically vital to protect them, though it might be important from the point of view of our prestige in Asia generally. What involves us vitally in the Far East is the necessity of protecting Australia and New Zealand against possible attack by Japan. These Dominions make some contribution towards their own defence, but it is very much to be hoped that, with the growth of population and of wealth, they may find it possible to take a rather larger share, and to that extent leave us with a freer hand to deal with menace nearer home ...

... In the first place, we must, so long as these conditions last, give up any idea of policing Europe such as has come down to us from Versailles and the Covenant of the League. We simply cannot protect our own interests all over the world and at the same time claim a preponderant voice in the ordering of affairs in continental Europe.

For some time to come, we must be on the defensive. That involves the maintenance of the closest relations with France, dictated by the necessity of denying the channel ports to Germany. If we have need of France's friendship and support, she equally has need of ours, and there is no reason why France (a very uncertain guide) should dictate the foreign policy of the partnership. She has led us down the wrong path before now but perhaps, with the loss of her dominant military position on the continent, she may be expected to be more amenable ...

That is not to say that we are to abdicate from such positions as we have been able to create for ourselves in eastern and south-eastern Europe ... But any deliberate, uneconomic, 'encirclement' of Germany appears to me to be a mistake, and probably a costly one ...

The moral seems to be:-

(1) The League system, and 'collective security', are, if not dead, in a state of suspended animation:

(2) Far from ordering the affairs of Europe, we, and the French, are on the defensive:

(3) Let us make those defences good:

(4) We must try to maintain our influence in Western Europe and the Mediterranean:

(5) We must cut our losses in central and eastern Europe – let Germany, if she can, find there her 'lebensraum', and establish herself, if she can, as a powerful economic unit. ∎

Growing suspicions in British government circles that Hitler's ambitions were not limited to eastern Europe gained substance on 15 March 1939 when Hitler, in flagrant defiance of the Munich agreement, occupied Prague. What remained of Czechoslovakia was absorbed as a German 'protectorate'. At the same time, secret intelligence reports on Germany's fighting capacity were reaching London, contributing to a hardening resolve to set limits to the concessions which could be made to Hitler.

11.21 Memorandum on the German military situation by the British military attaché in Berlin, 28 March 1939 (*Documents on British Foreign Policy*, 3rd series, IV, pp. 623–7).

∎ Let us examine firstly Germany's situation at the moment. From the point of view of the German Army it is extremely unsound. A considerable proportion of the active Army – unmobilised and in many cases under peace strength – is scattered throughout Moravia and Bohemia, with elements in Slovakia. It must be at least several months before the Germans can hope to produce units or formations with the help of arms they have acquired from the Czechs. The process will call for the services of many officers and NCOs who can ill be spared from the active German army ... If we can only convince our potential allies in the east of the patent fact that Germany is in no position to fight a major war now with any hope of evading inevitable and swift strangulation, there seems every reason why we should do our best to produce a situation leading to such a war and definitely welcome it. It is indeed, in my opinion, the only sound solution to the problem with which we are faced ... Nothing but the internal disruption of Germany can save us. Have we any right to consider such disruption more than an outside possibility?

It is true that grave elements of discontent within the country exist. But to produce the organised resistance to the Party or dissension within its ranks which can alone produce disruption, something more than a continuation or even an appreciable increase in the present perfectly bearable 'hardships' and inconveniences under which the German people suffer is required. War, and war now with a 'near' eastern front, would hit them hard and quickly and might well produce the hoped-for results. Without war, and with increasing benefits from Germany's eastern neighbours, these results may never be achieved. ∎

The German occupation of Prague in March 1939 destroyed the basis of Chamberlain's policy of appeasement. Clearly, Hitler's aims were not confined to uniting the German-speaking peoples, nor could his word be trusted any longer. The result was a 'diplomatic revolution': Britain, together with France, issued guarantees to Poland, Greece, Romania and Turkey, even though there was no military basis for these. Tentative, and ultimately unsuccessful, Anglo-French discussions with the Soviet Union also began. In April conscription was introduced. Nevertheless, Chamberlain still clung to the idea of détente, of persuading Germany to reach accommodation, and refused to believe that war was inevitable. Early in April 1939 the guarantees to eastern Europe were debated in the Commons, giving Chamberlain an opportunity to restate his position.

11.22 Neville Chamberlain, statement in the House of Commons, 3 April 1939 (*Hansard*, 5th ser., 345: 2482–5).

■ If ... the result of this Debate is to show that fundamentally and generally this House is unanimous in its approval of the declaration which I made on Friday, and is united and determined to take whatever measures may be necessary to make that declaration effective, the Debate may well serve a very useful purpose. The declaration that I made on Friday has been described ... as a cover note issued in advance of the complete insurance policy. I myself emphasised its transitional or temporary character, and the description of it as a cover note is not at all a bad one so far as it goes; but where I think it is altogether incomplete is that, while, of course, the issue of a cover note does not imply that it is to be followed by something more substantial, it is the nature of the complete insurance policy which is such a tremendous departure from anything which this country has undertaken hitherto. It does really constitute a new point – I would say a new epoch – in the course of our foreign policy ...

Of course, a declaration of that importance is not concerned with some minor little frontier incident; it is concerned with the big things that may lie behind even a frontier incident. If the independence of the State of Poland should be threatened – and if it were threatened I have no doubt that the Polish people would resist any attempt on it – then the declaration which I made means that France and ourselves would immediately come to her assistance ...

It is true we are told now that there are other reasons for recent events in Czecho-Slovakia – historical associations, the fear of attack. Well, there may be excellent reasons, but they do not accord with the assurances which were given before. It is inevitable that they should raise doubts as to whether further reasons may not presently be found for further expansion. I am not asserting that to-day this challenge has been made. No official statement that I know of has ever formulated such ambitions, although there has been plenty of unofficial talk; but the effect of these recent events has penetrated far beyond the limits of the countries concerned, and per-haps far further than was anticipated by those who brought them about. It is no exaggeration to say that public opinion throughout the whole world has been profoundly shocked and alarmed. This country has been united from end to end by the conviction that we must now make our position clear and unmistakable whatever may be the result.

No one can regret more than I do the necessity to have to speak such words as those. I am no more a man of war to-day than I was in September. I have no intention, no desire, to treat the great German people otherwise than as I would have our own people treated. I was looking forward with strong hopes to the result of those trade discussions which had already begun in Germany, and which, I thought, might have benefits for both our countries and many other countries besides, but confidence which has been so grievously shaken is not easily restored. We have been obliged, therefore, to consider the situation afresh.

It is not so long ago that I declared my view that this country ought not to be asked to enter into indefinite, unspecified commitments operating under conditions which could not be foreseen. I still hold that view; but here what we are doing is to enter into a specific engagement directed to a certain eventuality, namely, if such an attempt should be made to dominate the world by force. ■

The strengthening British resolve expressed by Chamberlain was voiced more clearly by Halifax, speaking at the Royal Institute for International Affairs in June 1939. Intimately associated with appeasement before Munich, Halifax had subsequently distanced himself from it. Similar sentiments were expressed even more forcefully by the cartoonist Low, satirising the half-hearted warnings of Chamberlain and Halifax, and calling for clear statements of intent by the British government. How far Low was capturing the popular mood, and how far he sought to influence it, is another question.

11.23 Lord Halifax, speech at Chatham House, 29 June 1939 (*Documents concerning German–Polish Relations and the Outbreak of Hostilities between Britain and Germany*, London, HMSO, 1939, pp. 58–65).

■ A year ago we had undertaken no specific commitments on the Continent of Europe beyond those which had then existed for some considerable time and are familiar to you all. Today we are bound by new agreements for mutual defence with Poland and Turkey: we have guaranteed assistance to Greece and Roumania against aggression, and we are now engaged with the Soviet Government in a negotiation, to which I hope there may very shortly be a successful issue, with a view to associating them with us for the defence of the States of Europe whose independence and neutrality may be threatened. We have assumed obligations, and are preparing to assume more, with full understanding of their consequences. We know that, if the security and independence of other countries are to disappear, our own security and our own independence will be gravely threatened. We know that, if international law and order is to be preserved, we must be prepared to fight in its defence.

In the past we have always stood out against the attempt by any single Power to dominate Europe at the expense of the liberties of other nations, and British policy is, therefore, only following the inevitable line of its own history, if such an attempt were to be made again ... The threat of military force is holding the world to ransom, and our immediate task is to resist aggression. I would emphasise that tonight with all the strength at my command, so that nobody may misunderstand it. ■

11.24 **Cartoon by David Low, 'Just in case there's any mistake',** *Evening Standard,* **3 July 1939.**

The prospects for co-operation between the Western democracies and the Soviet Union were finally dashed when the Nazi–Soviet non-aggression pact was signed on 23 August 1939, freeing Hitler to turn on Poland. On the following day the Anglo-Polish Treaty of April 1939 was ratified. Whereas Hitler assumed he could repeat the success of Munich in 1938, the British and French governments sought agreement but negotiated from a position of strength. Following the German invasion of Poland on 1 September, Britain and France declared war on 3 September. A telegram from Sir Nevile Henderson, the British Ambassador in Berlin, sent five days before the outbreak of war, captures the mood of deadlock between Britain and Germany.

11.25 **Sir Nevile Henderson, telegram to Viscount Halifax, 29 August 1939** **(***Documents on British Foreign Policy,* **3rd series, VII, no. 455).**

■ I saw the Chancellor at 10.30 this evening ...

I told Herr Hitler that he must choose between England and Poland. If he put forward immoderate demands there was no hope of a peaceful solution. Corridor was inhabited almost entirely by (? Poles). Herr Hitler interrupted me here by observing that this was only true because a million Germans had been driven out of that district since the war. I again said the choice lay with him. He had offered a corridor over the Corridor in March and I must honestly tell him that anything more than that, if that, would have no hope of acceptance. I begged him very earnestly to reflect before raising his price. He said his original offer had been contemptuously refused and he would not make it again. I observed that it had been made in the form of a dictate and therein lay the whole difference.

Herr Hitler continued to argue that Poland could never be reasonable: she had England and France behind her and imagined that even if she were beaten she would latterly recover, thanks to their help, more than she might lose. He spoke of annihilating Poland. I said that reminded me of similar talk last year of annihilation of the Czechs. He retorted that we were incapable of inducing Poland to be reasonable. I said that it was just because we remembered the experience of Czecho-Slovakia last year that we hesitated to press Poland too far today. Nevertheless we reserved to ourselves the right to form our own judgement as to what was or what was not reasonable so far as Poland or Germany were concerned. We kept our hands free in that respect.

Generally speaking Herr Hitler kept harping on Poland and I kept on just as consistently telling Herr Hitler that he had to choose between friendship with England which we offered him and excessive demands on Poland which would put an end to all hope of British friendship. If we were to come to an understanding it would entail sacrifices on our part. If he was not prepared to make sacrifices on his part there was nothing to be done. Herr Hitler said that he had to satisfy the demands of his people, his army was ready and eager for battle, his people united behind him and he could not tolerate further ill-treatment of Germans in Poland etc., etc., etc. ... ■

List of Documents

2.17   The National League for Opposing Woman Suffrage, Deputation to Mr. Asquith on Woman's Suffrage, December 1912.
2.18   NUWSS, Election Fighting Fund minutes, 8 November 1912.
2.19   Poster: National League for Opposing Women's Suffrage, 'A Suffragette's Home', ca.1912.
2.20   Propaganda: Women's Freedom League, 'Mrs. How Martyn Makes Jam', ca.1912.
2.21   Press report on the Osborne Judgement, *Reynold's Newspaper*, 26 December 1909.
2.22   Lloyd George, speech proposing the payment of members of parliament, 10 August 1911.
2.23   Chart: Industrial militancy, 1900–1910.
2.24   Press report on rioting in Tonypandy, *Daily Mail*, 10 November 1910.
2.25   The Unofficial Reform Committee, *The Miner's Next Step. Being a Suggested Scheme for the Reorganisation of the Federation*, 1912.
2.26   John Redmond, speech delivered at Mansion House, Dublin, 4 September 1907.
2.27   Bonar Law, speech at Blenheim Palace, 28 July 1912.
2.28   Ulster solemn league and covenant, 19 September 1912.
2.29   Winston Churchill, speech at Bradford, 15 March 1914.
2.30   Army memorandum to the Cabinet on the military situation in Ireland, 4 July 1914.

3.1   Arthur Conan Doyle, *The Great Boer War. A Two Years' Record, 1899-1901*, 1901.
3.2   Emily Hobhouse, *Report of a Visit to the Camps of Women and Children in the Cape and Orange River Colonies*, 1901.
3.3   Cartoon: John Tenniel, 'So Perplexing', 1 August 1900.
3.4   Joseph Chamberlain, speech to the Colonial Conference, 1 July 1902.
3.5   Report of the War Office (Reconstitution) Committee, 1904.
3.6   Lord Selborne, 'The Balance of Naval Power in the Far East', 4 September 1901.
3.7   Despatch to His Majesty's Ambassador at Paris, 8 April 1904.
3.8   Lord Grey, *Twenty-Five Years, 1892-1916*. Vol.I, 1925.
3.9   David Lloyd George, *War Memoirs of David Lloyd George. Vol.I*, 1938.
3.10   Sir Edward Grey, memorandum on Franco-German tension in Morocco, 20 February 1906.
3.11   Foreign Office, *Memorandum respecting the Anglo-Russian Convention*, 29 January 1908.
3.12   Erskine Childers, *The Riddle of the Sands*, 1903.
3.13   Photograph: Launch of HMS *Dreadnought*, 10 February 1906.
3.14   Eyre Crow, *Memorandum on the Present State of British Relations with France and Germany*, 1 January 1907.
3.15   Winston Churchill, speech to miners at Swansea, 15 August 1908.
3.16   Charts: The Anglo-German Naval Race, 1906-14.
3.17   David Lloyd George, speech at the Mansion House, 21 July 1911.
3.18   Sir Edward Grey, letter to Paul Cambon on Anglo-French naval cooperation, 22 November 1912.
3.19   Sir Arthur Nicolson, letter to Sir Edward Goschen, 18 May 1914.
3.20   Sir Edward Grey, telegram to Sir Edward Goschen, 27 July 1914.
3.21   Sir Edward Grey, telegram to Sir Edward Goschen, 29 July 1914.
3.22   Sir Edward Grey, speech to the House of Commons, 3 August 1914.

4.1   Committee of Imperial Defence (Historical Section), 'Report on the opening of the war', 1 November 1914.
4.2   Chart: government expenditure and revenue.
4.3   Lloyd George, memorandum, 'Some further considerations on the conduct of the war', 22 February 1915.
4.4   Major Charles Repington on the 'Shell Scandal', 1915.
4.5   William Bridgeman, diary, May 1915.
4.6   A. MacCallum Scott, diary entry for 19 May 1915.
4.7   Chart: shell production, 1914–18.
4.8   Chart: military enlistment, 1914–15.
4.9   Charles Hobhouse, diary, 14 October 1915.
4.10   Lord Selborne, 'Memorandum on the crisis in Irish affairs which caused my Resignation from the Cabinet June, 1916' , 30 June 1916.
4.11   Lord Lansdowne, memorandum, 13 November 1916.
4.12   Lloyd George's 'Knock-out Blow' speech, 29 September 1916.
4.13   Lloyd George, letter to Asquith, 5 December 1916.

10.5   J.C.C.Davidson, diary, 23/24 August 1931.
10.6   Labour's Joint Manifesto, 27 August 1931.
10.7   Extract from Ramsay MacDonald's 'National Labour Manifesto', 1931.
10.8   Posters: general election, 1931.
10.9   Beatrice Webb, diary, October 1931.
10.10   *A Call to the Nation: The Joint Manifesto of the Leaders of the National Government*, 1935.
10.11   Harold Macmillan, *The Middle Way. A Study of the Problem of Economic and Social Progress in a Free and Democratic Society*, 1938.
10.12   Stanley Baldwin, speech to the House on the Abdication Crisis, 10 December 1936.
10.13   Stafford Cripps, 'Can Socialism come by constitutional means', 1933.
10.14   Press report on LCC elections, *Daily Herald* editorial, 9 March 1934.
10.15   *The Labour Party's Call to Power*, 1935.
10.16   The 'Unity Manifesto', 17 January 1937.
10.17   Sir Herbert Samuel on the Liberals' resignation, 16 September 1932.
10.18   Chart: membership of the Communist Party of Great Britain, 1929–39.
10.19   Wal Hannington, *Unemployed Struggles*, 1936.
10.20   Oswald Mosley, *The Greater Britain*, 1932.
10.21   Viscount Rothermere, 'Hurrah for the Blackshirts', *Daily Mail*, 15 January 1934.
10.22   Witness seminar, 'The Battle of Cable Street, 1936', 1 May 1991.

11.1   Sir Maurice Hankey, diary, 6 September 1931.
11.2   Sir John Pratt (Foreign Office), memorandum on the situation in Shanghai, 1 February 1932.
11.3   Sir E. Phipps, letter to Sir John Simon, 25 October 1933.
11.4   Neville Chamberlain's proposal for an Anglo-Japanese alliance, letter to Sir John Simon, 1 September 1934.
11.5   The Hoare-Laval talks on Abyssinia, 7 December 1935.
11.6   Duff Cooper on the German threat, Old Men Forget. *The Autobiography of Duff Cooper (Viscount Norwich)*, 1954.
11.7   Cabinet Foreign Policy Committee discussion on Non-intervention in Spain, 25 August 1936.
11.8   Chamberlain, memorandum, 26 November 1937.
11.9   Cartoon: David Low, 'Gad, sir, at any rate we are restoring prosperity', *Evening Standard*, 8 July 1935.
11.10   Duff Cooper on Chamberlain and rearmament, *Old Men Forget. The Autobiography of Duff Cooper (Viscount Norwich)*, 1954.
11.11   Cabinet discussion on defence policy, 8 December 1937.
11.12   Neville Chamberlain, speech to the House on British policy towards Europe, 24 March 1938.
11.13   Cartoon: Illingworth, 'Still Hope', *Punch*, 21 September 1938.
11.14   Sir Alexander Cadogan, diary, 24 September 1938.
11.15   Sir Horace Wilson, note on the Munich Conference, 29–30 September 1938.
11.16   Joint declaration by Hitler and Chamberlain, 30 September 1938.
11.17   Press report on Chamberlain's return from Germany, *The Times*, 1 October 1938.
11.18   Halifax's message to the British Delegation at Godesberg, 23 September 1938.
11.19   Churchill on the Munich agreement, 5 October 1938.
11.20   Sir Alexander Cadogan, diary, 14 October 1938.
11.21   Memorandum on the German military situation by the British military attaché in Berlin, 28 March 1939.
11.22   Neville Chamberlain, statement in the House of Commons, 3 April 1939.
11.23   Lord Halifax, speech at Chatham House, 29 June 1939.
11.24   Cartoon: David Low, 'Just in case there's any mistake', *Evening Standard*, 3 July 1939.
11.25   Sir Nicholas Henderson (Berlin), telegram to Viscount Halifax, 29 August 1939.

Index